Examining the Intersection of Circular Economy, Forestry, and International Trade

Badri Narayanan Gopalakrishnan
University of Washington, USA

Taranjeet Duggal
Amity University, India

Tavishi Tewary
Jaipuria Institute of Management Noida, India

IGI Global
PUBLISHER of TIMELY KNOWLEDGE

A volume in the Advances in Finance, Accounting, and Economics (AFAE) Book Series

Published in the United States of America by
IGI Global
Business Science Reference (an imprint of IGI Global)
701 E. Chocolate Avenue
Hershey PA, USA 17033
Tel: 717-533-8845
Fax: 717-533-8661
E-mail: cust@igi-global.com
Web site: http://www.igi-global.com

Library of Congress Cataloging-in-Publication Data

Names: Gopalakrishnan, Badri Narayanan, editor. | Duggal, Taranjeet, 1974- editor. | Tewary, Tavishi, 1984- editor.
Title: Examining the intersection of circular economy, forestry, and international trade / Badri Narayanan Gopalakrishnan, Taranjeet Duggal, and Tavishi Tewary, editors.
Description: Hershey, PA : Business Science Reference, [2021] | Includes bibliographical references and index. | Summary: "This book examines the intersection of circular economy, forestry, and international trade"-- Provided by publisher.
Identifiers: LCCN 2020012007 (print) | LCCN 2020012008 (ebook) | ISBN 9781799849902 (hardcover) | ISBN 9781799856634 (paperback) | ISBN 9781799849919 (ebook)
Subjects: LCSH: Sustainable development. | Industrial ecology. | International trade--Environmental aspects.
Classification: LCC HC79.E5 E973 2021 (print) | LCC HC79.E5 (ebook) | DDC 338.9/27--dc23
LC record available at https://lccn.loc.gov/2020012007
LC ebook record available at https://lccn.loc.gov/2020012008

This book is published in the IGI Global book series Advances in Finance, Accounting, and Economics (AFAE) (ISSN: 2327-5677; eISSN: 2327-5685)

British Cataloguing in Publication Data
A Cataloguing in Publication record for this book is available from the British Library.

All work contributed to this book is new, previously-unpublished material. The views expressed in this book are those of the authors, but not necessarily of the publisher.

For electronic access to this publication, please contact: eresources@igi-global.com.

Advances in Finance, Accounting, and Economics (AFAE) Book Series

Ahmed Driouchi
Al Akhawayn University, Morocco

ISSN:2327-5677
EISSN:2327-5685

MISSION

In our changing economic and business environment, it is important to consider the financial changes occurring internationally as well as within individual organizations and business environments. Understanding these changes as well as the factors that influence them is crucial in preparing for our financial future and ensuring economic sustainability and growth.

The **Advances in Finance, Accounting, and Economics (AFAE)** book series aims to publish comprehensive and informative titles in all areas of economics and economic theory, finance, and accounting to assist in advancing the available knowledge and providing for further research development in these dynamic fields.

COVERAGE

- Borrowing and Lending
- Economic Downturn
- Economics of Agriculture and Biotechnology
- Corporate Finance
- Economics of Innovation and Knowledge
- International Economics
- Evidence-Based Studies
- Finance
- Applied economics
- E-Accounting

IGI Global is currently accepting manuscripts for publication within this series. To submit a proposal for a volume in this series, please contact our Acquisition Editors at Acquisitions@igi-global.com or visit: http://www.igi-global.com/publish/.

The Advances in Finance, Accounting, and Economics (AFAE) Book Series (ISSN 2327-5677) is published by IGI Global, 701 E. Chocolate Avenue, Hershey, PA 17033-1240, USA, www.igi-global.com. This series is composed of titles available for purchase individually; each title is edited to be contextually exclusive from any other title within the series. For pricing and ordering information please visit http://www.igi-global.com/book-series/advances-finance-accounting-economics/73685. Postmaster: Send all address changes to above address.

Titles in this Series

For a list of additional titles in this series, please visit:
http://www.igi-global.com/book-series/advances-finance-accounting-economics/73685

Handbook of Research on Changing World Economic Order in the Post-Pandemic Period
Vishal Sarin (Lovely Professional University, India) Badri Narayanan Gopalakrishnan (Infinite Sum Modelling, USA) Sushanta Kumar Mahapatra (IBS Hyderabad, The ICFAI Foundation for Higher Education, India) and Tanima Dutta (Lovely Professional University, India)
Business Science Reference • © 2021 • 470pp • H/C (ISBN: 9781799868965) • US $295.00

Financial Management and Risk Analysis Strategies for Business Sustainability
Joaquín Enríquez-Díaz (University of A Coruña, Spain) Laura Castro-Santos (University of A Coruña, Spain) and Félix Puime-Guillén (University of A Coruña, Spain)
Business Science Reference • © 2021 • 320pp • H/C (ISBN: 9781799876342) • US $215.00

Theory of Shocks, COVID-19, and Normative Fundamentals for Policy Responses Emerging Research and Opportunities
Olga Ivanovna Pilipenko (The Russian Presidential Academy of National Economy and Public Administration, Russia) Zoya Andreevna Pilipenko (Bank of Russia, Russia) and Andrey Igorevich Pilipenko (The Russian Presidential Academy of National Economy and Public Administration, Russia)
Business Science Reference • © 2021 • 250pp • H/C (ISBN: 9781799843092) • US $165.00

Handbook of Research on Theory and Practice of Financial Crimes
Abdul Rafay (University of Management and Technology, Pakistan)
Business Science Reference • © 2021 • 650pp • H/C (ISBN: 9781799855675) • US $345.00

Comparative Research on Earnings Management, Corporate Governance, and Economic Value
Elisabete S. Vieira (University of Aveiro, Portugal) Mara Madaleno (University of Aveiro, Portugal) and Graça Azevedo (University of Aveiro, Portugal)
Business Science Reference • © 2021 • 433pp • H/C (ISBN: 9781799875963) • US $215.00

Influence of FinTech on Management Transformation
Amira Sghari (Faculty of Economics and Management, University of Sfax, Tunisia) and Karim Mezghani (Al Imam Mohammad Ibn Saud Islamic University, Saudi Arabia & University of Sfax, Tunisia)
Business Science Reference • © 2021 • 273pp • H/C (ISBN: 9781799871101) • US $215.00

Handbook of Research on Institutional, Economic, and Social Impacts of Globalization and Liberalization
Yilmaz Bayar (Bandirma Onyedi Eylul University, Turkey)
Information Science Reference • © 2021 • 699pp • H/C (ISBN: 9781799844594) • US $445.00

IGI Global
PUBLISHER of TIMELY KNOWLEDGE

701 East Chocolate Avenue, Hershey, PA 17033, USA
Tel: 717-533-8845 x100 • Fax: 717-533-8661
E-Mail: cust@igi-global.com • www.igi-global.com

Editorial Advisory Board

Table of Contents

Detailed Table of Contents

review some strategies for the households, based on the literature, to minimize waste.

The world is presently facing a climate catastrophe of its own making through the unabated increase in greenhouse gas emissions. Global consumption patterns are to blame, as presently, the global annual demand for resources outpaces the annual rate of the earth's ability to regenerate those resources. Thus, there is an urgent need to reduce the global demand for resources to a sustainable level, through the adoption of a circular economy. Individual consumption behavior habits form the basis of global consumption patterns, and therefore, adoption of sustainable consumption habits and lifestyles are necessary for addressing the climate crisis. In this chapter, the authors assess the potential for addressing the climate crisis through the adoption of a circular economy and sustainable consumption behavior. The authors also evaluate the extent of adoption of sustainable consumption behavior in India and make recommendations for adopting a circular economy in India.

The ongoing discourse of zero-waste and the circular economy in recent time have been underscored by key players, such as the European Commission, NGOs, INGOs, academia, and multinational companies. The discourse revolves around the fact that capitalist form of development has pushed the environment to the brink of destruction. The need of the hour is sustainable growth through the model of the circular economy. Thus, the idea of growth is being de-politicized by a post-growth narrative. This chapter wants to delve into the critical aspect of circular economy which propounds itself as a solution to capitalism driven growth. The first theme it addresses the actual materialization of circular economy whether it is actually a possible phenomenon or not. The second theme it deals with the concept of social sustainability and fulfillment of human wants. The last theme revolves around ideological dimension of post-growth, how the circular growth in the garb of post-growth ideology propels and legitimizes a more growth -driven society.

This is the dawn of an innovation and knowledge-driven economy, and the volatile business environment is forcing the industries to undergo a paradigm shift. This is causing volatility of business parameters from value creation to value maximization through reduction of value loss., instead of merely focusing on the value creation. This value maximization gels with quality, binding the end outcomes of enterprise, and quality of these end outcomes cumulatively shows the dependability towards the various inputs like

In recent years, the need of every corporation to address the environmental issues has grown multifold. The corporate social responsibility concerns are growing, and it has become an indicator to judge a business performance. In the context of increasing environmental concerns where issues of pollution, generation of wastes, use of toxic substances for packaging, etc. are gaining strong ground, the consumers have also become alarmed and they fully understand the implications of such issues both on nature and earth. The chapter aims to study the behaviour and the change therein of Indian consumers. It is true that all the efforts and policies targeted towards initiative of green marketing cannot be realised if it is not received by the consumers. The chapter proposes to cover the concept of green marketing and its relation to the circular economy, the green marketing practices in Indian context, the attitude and preference of the Indian consumer towards green products, and the switch in the purchase pattern of the Indian consumers with respect to green/recycled products.

Corporate greening practices such as measures to reduce pollution emission, management of waste, use of green technologies, sustainable reporting, consuming removable energy sources, implementation of ISO environment management certification, auditing, etc. are required for sustainability. A lot of studies of stakeholder perceptions of corporate responses towards societal concerns are mostly from the point of view of marketing, existing or prospective customers, and industry at a large, but the employee's aspects is most neglected. This chapter investigates the employee's perception of corporate citizenship (CC) and organisational sustainability and also the interrelationship of these variables.

E-waste is a rising problem given the volumes of e-waste being generated and the content of both toxic and valuable materials in them. This new kind of waste has raised serious concerns regarding their disposition and recycling all over the world. Having hazardous components in television and computer monitors (lead, mercury, and cadmium) and in circuit boards (nickel, beryllium, and zinc), the recycling and discarding of e-waste becomes a key concern. Disposal of e-waste poses serious environmental and health hazards. However, these problems can be tackled with the help of a circular approach. In this backdrop, the chapter discusses the problem of e-waste management in India, the related environmental and health issues in e-waste handling and disposal. It also discusses e-waste recycling practices in India and the current policy level interventions by the government. The chapter also highlights the possible business opportunities offered by the circular approach to e-waste management.

Virtual water flows (VWF) among states or countries have been proposed as a viable solution to mitigate water scarcity. The aim of this study is to assess the virtual water content and flows from India, for six cash crops, coffee, cotton, jute, sugarcane, tea, and tobacco, and their derived products over a period 1980-2013. The virtual water trade (VWT) estimates across three time periods show India to be a net exporter of virtual water for all the cash crops, except jute. The quantity of virtual water traded has increased over the decades with the increase in the quantum of crops traded. With free trade policies and the opening up of the economy, export quantities increased during the 1990s and the period thereafter, leading to larger virtual water exports. Sustainable agricultural practices for all crops, and in all countries, can help in reducing the water flow of these crops and help in controlling the water scarcity solution.

The circular economy is based on three fundamental principles as defined by the Ellen MacArthur Foundation: design out waste and pollution, keep products and materials in use, and regenerate natural systems. This chapter explores the relationship between the circular economy principles and the water management systems to identify the integration points where the water systems can be aligned with the circular economy. The chapter also ascertains the impediments which hinder this transition and identifies the opportunities that will present themselves in this endeavor. This chapter aims to help the readers understand the social, economic, and environmental impacts that will be created when water systems get integrated into the circular economy framework.

The convention concerning the protection of cultural and natural heritage only emphasizes the protection of tangible cultural heritage. However, the present convention completely turned a blind eye and a deaf ear to the intangible cultural heritage. "Cultural heritage" as a term and its content are largely taken from other fields like anthropology and archaeology. The legal aspect of cultural heritage is most complex and difficult to understand. There also exist elements of intangible culture which would include songs or folklore musical traditions, ceremonial or ritual traditions, aspects of the life of ancient societies, and any special relationship between the people and the land that they inhabited. With the term property also comes the idea of assigning the artifact a market value whereas they are historically priceless. Cultural heritage has been made global and a part of universal heritage or "common heritage of mankind."

Foreword

Sustainable development and its impact on the performance of economy is being discussed, researched, and debated with thoughts coming from multiple schools of authors for over 30 years of time. However, with the change in times and development, circular solutions are predominantly vital to balance and mitigate the present and future challenges of depleting resources and impacting the generations.

The transition to circular economy from linear economy will make much relevance to the people at large after been seeing the impacts of pandemic and other such situation world is currently facing.

We are all sitting on the most urgent issues affecting ecological and environment balance hence impacting economies at large. There are sincere efforts taken at the strategic levels of Government stakeholders, Think Tanks, etc. However, it is important to introduce these topics which cover wider perspective and has its outreach to maximum strata of readers, educators and implementors. This book is very helpful to give you an understanding of analyzing intersecting relationship of circular economy with both environment and business.

The authors of the book are coming from diverse fields which presents very practical and research driven view to the concept as well as explains the intersection behavior in a peculiar manner. Book represents the study on intersectionality and impact not just to business and government at large but also to the society.

As a reader and an avid interest holder to understand the intersecting behavior of circular economy and how this shift could affect largely. The authors has presented a remarkable flow of concepts and diverse introduction of topics to show a wiser and wider view to a reader.

Concepts covered in the book are of great relevance for business houses, educators, researchers, implementors, practitioners and students who are exploring the concept of circular economy and how it can affect various functions of business as well as the implementation, usage, and viability of a widespread adoption of a circular economy. The topics covered highlight the transition to the circular economy, its implementation across society, its intersection with forestry and international trade, and the solutions and challenges of the circular economy.

The book focuses on topics as such Anti-Waste Politics, impacts of Artificial Intelligence, implementable Business Models, Circular Economy, Climate Change, Consumer Behaviour, E-Waste Management, Economic Sustainability, Green Human Resources, International Trade, and Sustainable Development.

The detailed focus of the chapters highlights Green and Circular Economy (GCE) model from the point of view of the resources and capacities of the organization and also comparing the business models in global context where the multiple facets of circular economy are examined which are related to public policy, technology availability and public participation. Book further reflects the analysis of circular economy from the perspective of households to examine extent of reduction of GHG emissions by adopting zero waste strategies. The wider view for addressing the climate crisis through the adoption of circular economy and sustainable consumption behaviour is shown with detailed analysis and research. It picks up an interest of the reader to study a detailed impact with practices on circular economy. It draws an attention to study circular growth in the garb of post-growth ideology propels and legitimizes a more growth -driven society as well to study the concepts and models to impel Sustainable Competitive Advantage.

This book is a wholesome read for anyone who is either on an understanding stage of concept or on the advanced and mature stages. It will pick an attention to gather insights on present policies which supports circular economy adaptation as well as present case studies to visualise circular economy prospective and closing economy loops.

The reader would be able to collect a wider understanding of circular economies impacts on international trade as well as Agri business in India. The most vital function for majority of the organisations is to bring a cultural shift through policies and practices which are sustainable in nature, the book does an immense justice to not only present intersectionality in direct economic functions but also to the organisations strategic functions such as Human Resources, where a detail description on explaining of Green Human Resource Management is given along with the examples and cases which organisations can implement to begin with the same and make sustainable contributions.

The impact of sustainable banking sector on organisations commitment present readers with an appreciable view of increasing organisation citizenship of employees. Consumer is a centre for the functioning of any economy and while we encourage readers through the nook to understand the realm of circular economy, book also presents a study of consumer's switching behaviours with introduction of recycled products. E-Waste Management, Water Footprint, Virtual Water Trade increases the outreach of the concepts and offers a diverse perspective to circular economy models.

Protection of intangible Heritage and Artificial Intelligence in circular economy completes the overall coverage book starting from explaining the concepts, their study on intersectionality and implementing strategies of the concept.

The coverage of concepts will drive an encouragement and understanding of radical transformation to circular economy from linear economy models with the representation of well researched models and implementable practices of circular economy. A circular economy aimed at eliminating waste and the continual use of resources. It gained it ground in the era of disruptive technological advancement and a dynamic global value chain. By supporting resource-efficient industrial models, the circular economy preserves and improves natural capital, optimizes the value of resources, and abolishes negative environmental externalities such as pollution.

The authors gave deep diving knowledge with usage of primary and secondary research to build the concepts and present to the readers. Authors are focussed to contribute through the book where a society at large would get deeper understanding of concepts and helping the stakeholders to understand and implement the most sustainable practices.

I was always keen to have such resource which not only introduces the circular economy but present an intersecting impact of it on vital parts contributing to it. The read enough can encourage to adapt the practices which are contributing back to the society's sustainable future.

Gagandeep Singh Bajwa
World Resources Institute, India

Preface

Sustainable development has always been a contested concept and has been extensively debated over the last 30 years with new classifications arising since then. There was a previous push for the radical transformations of the market economy to downscale production and consumption that would increase human well-being and enhance ecological conditions. Because of this conflict, there was a need for a new model that challenges and could be the alternative for the liner economy; this new model is called the circular economy. A circular economy aimed at eliminating waste and the continual use of resources. It gained its ground in the era of disruptive technological advancement and a dynamic global value chain. By supporting resource-efficient industrial models, the circular economy preserves and improves natural capital, optimizes the value of resources, and abolishes negative environmental externalities such as pollution.

The first law of thermodynamics dictates that the number of resources that are used in the process of production and consumption cannot be destroyed and is equal to the waste that eventually winds up in the environmental system. Kenneth Boulding in 1996 described the earth as a closed economic system where the environment and the economy are said to be in a circular relationship.

Rules and policies to reduce the negative impact on the environment caused by economic growth have come into place. Various countries have adopted the concept of the circular economy. Germany was the first to implement a circular economy in 1996. It was accompanied by the Closed Substance Cycle and Waste Management Act. This law provides certain standards that industry must abide by or follow while generating and disposing of waste. In Japan, a legal framework was put in place to move towards a recycling-based society.

Despite the downside of excessive consumption of finite resources (natural resources), many organizations in this day and age, continue to use business models that are heavily reliant on non-renewable resources or give negligible significance to regulations that address the principles of sustainability. However, non-renewable resources are running out at an appalling rate and it is not only the responsibility of the government and households to slow down the rate of consumption but also of organizations that take in major resources from society to sustain themselves.

Even though some organizations undertake the responsibility of recycling and reusing goods, there is still a lack of strong, integrated management concepts which support the process of a circular economy. Organizations across the globe should implement profound changes in their daily practices with regard to their usage of resources and raw materials, and the management of waste they generate. The business model designs have to be tweaked to give weight to the principles of the circular economy. The 5Rs (Reduce, Reuse, Recycle, Repair, and Refurbish) should be actively employed in their policies and growth strategies.

Efficient use of resources can lead to less use of primary resources. This process is aimed towards the concept of cleaner production that focuses on achieving material and energy resources efficiency in processes. It involves careful use of resources and replacement of hazardous resources or resources with short life spans. Cleaner production by way of improvements in industrial production processes and products includes reduction of impacts (environmental, health, and safety) along the whole life chain of a product (from raw material extraction to the final disposal).

Examining the Intersection of Circular Economy, Forestry, and International Trade explores the link between the circular economy and various aspects of the business and environment to understand the usage and viability of adapting the circular economy from a business perspective. This book is a collection of current research on the applicability of the circular economy concept in various domains of business and the linkage between the interlinkages circularity and forestry and International trade. This book is aimed at researchers in the field of business management, economics, and environmental studies along with practitioners, stakeholders, researchers, academicians, and students looking for more information on the various fields impacting the circular economy as well as the implementation, usage, and viability of widespread adoption of a circular economy.

Examining the Intersection of Circular Economy, Forestry, and International Trade is organized into 18 chapters which provide insight on circularity, forestry, and trade as a whole.

Chapter 1 (Circular-Green Economy: Analysis Based on the Theory of Resources and Capabilities) focuses on the concept of green economy and highlights the significance of harnessing resources judicially and developing capabilities to attain it.

Chapter 2 (Analysis of Circular Economy From a Household Perspective in the USA) applies the CGE approach to test the household emissions based on data from various sources in the literature. The study analyzes the extent of reduction of GHG emissions by adopting zero waste strategies by the households voluntarily, incurring no costs, but rather savings in wasteful expenditure. The chapter also reviews strategies for the households to minimize waste.

Chapter 3 (Climate Change and Circular Economy: Analysis of Policy and Individual Behavior in the Indian Ecosystem) talks about the current status of linearity and greenhouse gas emissions. Individual consumption behavior habits form the basis of global consumption patterns and therefore adoption of sustainable consumption habits and lifestyles are necessary for addressing the climate crisis. In this chapter, the authors assess the potential for addressing the climate crisis through the adoption of a circular economy and sustainable consumption behavior. The authors also evaluate the extent of adoption of sustainable consumption behavior in India and make recommendations for adopting a circular economy in India.

Chapter 4 (Circular Economy: A Critical Understanding of Anti-Waste Politics) highlights the role of politics in progressing towards a circular economy. The chapter highlights the role of politics as a facilitator as well as of a restrictor.

Chapter 5 (Innovation With Competitive Risk: A Locus of Sustainable Competitive Advantage in the Circular Economy) emphasizes the importance of innovation and a knowledge-driven economy, to achieve circularity. The chapter is a study of concepts and models to impel the SCA. It will also analyze, the innovation as a measure driver for sustainable competitive advantage (SCA) with various types of risk associated with it, in the context of the circular economy.

Chapter 6 (Policies for Promoting Circular Economy in India) discovers the major challenge for the policymakers in achieving circularity. The framework to achieve efficiency in resource use can be appropriately designed through innovative ways and policies. Indian Economy over the last few years has moved to controlled regulation from command through the practice of economic instruments for regulations. The policy adopted by India to achieve circularity includes the financial support and guidance for research and development, formulation of standards like ECOMARKS, public procurements, and certification and self-regulation which are discussed in the Chapter.

Chapter 7 (Visualising the Circular Economy Perspective: Closing the Economic Loop – The Case of India) describes the principles of Sharing, Leasing, Reuse, Repair, Refurbishment, and Recycling that revolve in a closed-loop. From an Indian perspective, the chapter unearths certain challenges like financing issues, the need for key economic enablers, skill requirements, consumer behaviour, and business models, and the need for multi-level governance.

Chapter 8 (International Trade in the realms of Circular Economy) advocates the use of resources for the longest time and emphasizes that nations introduce superfluous trade restrictions and at times enter into trade disputes with trade partners. it is imperative that circular economy policies and trade policies are reciprocally supportive. International co-operation on circular economy value chains should thus be explored for coordination of quality standards of materials, promoting demand for second-hand goods and secondary raw materials, removing unnecessary regulatory barriers, and to avoid environmentally harmful activities.

Chapter 9 (Sustainable and Circular Mango Farming Through Redesigning Sales Contracts) attempts to appraise the impact of different types of sales contracts on mango yield and farmers' income. The higher sustainability of last quarter's sales contract is attributed to clean landholding of the owners, optimal use of flowering inducers (PBZ), and segregated rights of merchants and owners.

Chapter 10 (Sustainable and Green Human Resource Practices) tries to bring together circular economy and human resource practices on the same platform. The chapter calls for more innovations in better management with various stakeholders and employees to create HR as a more solution-based function.

Chapter 11 (Impact of Sustainable Banking [E-Banking] on the Organisation Commitment Level of Bank Employees in Delhi) proposes organization commitment as a tool among bank employees to achieve sustainable banking. The chapter empirically tests the proposition and provides ways to increase the commitment level among the employees.

Chapter12 (A Study of Consumer Switching Behaviour in the Indian Context With Respect to Recycled Products) aims at highlighting the switching behavior of Indian consumers as a result of increasing environmental concerns where issues of pollution, generation of wastes, use of toxic substances for packaging, etc. are gaining strong ground.

Chapter 13 (An Investigation of the Relationship Between Employee Perception of Corporate Citizenship Behaviour and Orgnisational Sustainability) discusses the role of corporate citizenship in Society and Business Cooperation. Corporate greening practices such as measures to reduce pollution emission, management of waste, use of green technologies, sustainable reporting, consuming removable energy sources, implementation of ISO environment management certification, auditing, etc are required for sustainability. This chapter investigates the employee's perception of corporate citizenship (CC) and organisational sustainability and also the interrelationship of these variables.

Chapter 14 (E-Waste Management in India: Need for a Circular Approach) deliberates on the problem of e-waste disposal. It also discusses the problem of e-waste management in India, the related environmental and health issues in e-waste handling and disposal. The chapter also highlights the possible business opportunities offered by the circular approach to e-waste management.

Chapter 15 (Water Footprint and Virtual Water Trade of Cash Crops) discusses virtual water flows' (VWF) among states or countries as a viable solution to mitigate water scarcity. The aim of this study is to assess the virtual water content and flows from India, for six cash crops- coffee, cotton, jute, sugarcane, tea, and tobacco and their derived products. The Virtual Water Trade (VWT) estimates across three time periods show India to be a net exporter of virtual water for all the cash crops, except jute. The chapter concludes that sustainable agricultural practices for all crops, and in all countries, can help in reducing the water flow of these crops and help in controlling the water scarcity solution.

Chapter 16 (Water Systems in a Circular Economy: Extracting Value Through Integration) begins with mentioning the three fundamental principles as defined by Ellen MacArthur Foundation. This chapter explores the relationship between the circular economy principles and the water management systems to identify the integration points where the water systems can be aligned with the circular economy. The chapter also ascertains the impediments which hinder this transition and identifies the opportunities that will present themselves in this endeavor.

Chapter 17 (Protection of Intangible Heritage: Need to Reassess the Framework) emphasizes the existing elements of intangible culture which would include songs or folklore musical traditions, ceremonial or ritual traditions, aspects of the life of ancient societies, and any special relationship between the people and the land that they inhabited. With the term property also comes the idea of assigning the artifact a market value whereas they are historically priceless Cultural Heritage has been made global and a part of universal heritage or "Common Heritage of Mankind"

Chapter 18 (Prospects of Artificial Intelligence [AI] Towards Circular Economy) stresses the widely growing applications of AI in various fields. The chapter raises serious concern on the effectiveness of currently employed recycling methods to minimize wastage and advocated the need to think about state of art technological support like artificial intelligence.

Acknowledgment

This book has seen the light of the day due to the divine blessings and kind inspiration of Almighty, the highest powers of power, who is beyond space, time and the chain of cause and effect.

Almighty has bestowed on us the opportunity of being a teacher and has thus placed a very big responsibility on our shoulders. The fact that we are in the pursuit of knowledge and truth, is a testimony of a divine plan, which was pre-decided by lord himself.

At this juncture, we would like to talk about some very distinguished and revered people without whom we wouldn't have been in a position, where we are today! We are talking about the presence of our respected teachers, *our gurus*, who have shaped our thinking, lives and character.

As an ode to them, we had been thinking for a while to come up with a book where we wanted to include a contemporary and an interdisciplinary perspective, with a difference. As a result, this book took more than an year to come in its current form, in the area of Circular Economy , an area which is most needed in contemporary times.

We wish to acknowledge and express our deep sense of gratitude towards our authors who have been instrumental in writing the chapters and have put in a lot of effort and research during the preparation of each manuscript.

Towards the end we wish to place on record the unconditional support of our near and dear ones who have helped us with the manuscripts.

Badri Narayan Gopalakrishnan

Taranjeet Duggal

Tavishi Tewary

Chapter 1
Circular-Green Economy:
Analysis Based on the Theory of Resources and Capabilities

José G. Vargas-Hernández
https://orcid.org/0000-0003-0938-4197
University Center for Economic and Managerial Sciences, University of Guadalajara, Mexico

ABSTRACT

The purpose of this chapter is to analyze the green and circular economy (GCE) model from the point of view of the resources and capacities of the organization. How is the application of the circular economy model related to strategic management? At first glance, it seems that the CE is operating within an operational level with a social impact, but it also has implications that allow us to think that it can be used as an internal resource of the company that, if applied in the right way, it can become a competitive advantage; in other words, the application of the CE is related to strategic management through the point of view based on resources and capabilities. Therefore, the present investigation has a descriptive-correlational nature, which was analyzed through Peng's VRIO framework.

INTRODUCTION

In recent decades, the care of the planet has begun to appear on international political agendas as a matter of urgent concern, since we have begun to notice the consequences of the decisions taken by past generations to obtain economic benefits without worrying about the damage to the environment they caused (Brundtland, 1987). As such, it has been decided that it is time to worry and take measures to survive in a planet of limited resources with a population that does not stop growing.

What can be done? Beyond the individual responsibility of each person, those who can make a noticeable change and chain reaction are the companies that, regardless of size or classification, are important actors in the global scope since they have an active role in the degradation or preservation of its environment close to social, economic and environmental level. Then, it can be considered that it

DOI: 10.4018/978-1-7998-4990-2.ch001

is of vital importance that companies begin to have the main goal of achieving sustainability, but how can they achieve it?

One way to achieve this is through the reengineering of existing products or the creation of new products that are generated from the principles of the Circular Economy. According to the Ellen MacArthur Foundation, an organization devoted to the study and dissemination of the circular economy, the beginning of the concept as such has not been registered, but rather is the result of an evolution of several schools of thought such as Regenerative Design, the Economics of Performance, Crandel to Crandel, Industrial Ecology, Biomimicry, Blue Economy, and Natural Capitalism (Ellen MacArthur Foundation, 2019).

Regenerative Design is a school of thought created by John T. Lyle, whose approach is rooted in the theory of systems oriented to design processes. When speaking of regeneration, the theory refers to the fact that existing processes are modified in order to improve, remove or adhere new sources of energy and / or materials. This school has a base derived from the ecology of systems that is in charge of providing a biokinetic in the ecosystems with the objective of achieving a system of ecological economy that is viable and closed for any industry. In addition to the above, it seeks to ensure that the resulting system does not generate waste, that they are fully effective, to achieve this it is necessary to redesign the culture of human habitats (Heaven Grown, s.f.).

The Economics of Performance was born in the 70's when the economist and architect Walter Stahel, in contribution with Genevieve Reday, created The Potential for Substituting Manpower for Energy, a report for the European Commission where they describe the probability of achieving an economy in the existence of processes in a loop (Ecointeligencia, 2017). in addition to the possible impact that these processes would have at the social level with the generation of jobs, in economic competitiveness, in the new distribution in the use of resources and waste. In general aspects, the economy of performance has four main objectives: to extend the useful life of existing products, to generate new products that from their design are thought to be long-lasting, to think ahead about campaigns or activities for the prevention of waste, and reuse of these (Ellen MacArthur Foundation, 2019).

The Cradle to Cradle, also known as cradle to cradle or C2C, is the result of work done by Michael Braungart and Bill McDonough, a chemist and an architect respectively. This research consists of visualizing that from the beginning and during a process it is known if the materials used are technical or biological (Ellen MacArthur Foundation, 2019). McDonough mentions in his work that durability is not applicable to all the materials used, some simply cannot be reused or cannot be recovered easily, for this reason the proposal to design the products is presented so that their components can be reused in completely or completely degrade in the environment (McDonough, Braungart, & Bollinger, 2007). C2C has been one of the models that gave rise to the circular economy as such, highlighted the importance of creating a process in which intelligent design is used to achieve lengthen or improve the life cycle of finished products.

Industrial Ecology or science of sustainability is part of the engineering that aims to support the promotion and dissemination of sustainable development through the efficient use of resources, unleashing improvements in the quality of life. in other words, create sustainable societies. On the other hand, it seeks to reduce the impact that industrial processes have on the environment (Ellen MacArthur Foundation, 2019). Industrial Ecology is composed of several disciplines and not only applies to the products sector but also to the creation of services, seeking to achieve social and industrial well-being (Mejía Dugand, 2010). In itself, this school of thought tries to generate processes in which the raw material is processed, converted into a finished product and when its life cycle ends, it is recycled and, in turn, used by other companies or industries as a supply for production. so a new cycle.

Biomimicry defined for the first time in 2012 by Janine Benyus, as a way to innovate human processes based on the designs of nature. It is based on three principles for its proper functioning (Ellen MacArthur Foundation, 2019):

1) Use nature as a base model for the creation of forms, processes and strategies applicable to the resolution of everyday problems.
2) Use nature as a unit of measurement to have a standard to be able to quantify innovations with respect to their ecological sustainability.
3) Nature as a guide, always looking for ways to imitate for the betterment of life.

The next trend is the Blue Economy, which was promoted by Gunter Pauli, an entrepreneur of Belgian origin who reported an alleged resemblance to Biomimicry, seeking answers to the knowledge that nature has accumulated throughout its history, in order to transfer that efficiency to the way of producing (Alvial Muñoz, 2015). This school aims to use the existing resources in something called "cascade system", that is, the waste or waste of the finished product would be used as raw material or inputs to generate a new flow of movements. The blue economy appeared in a code written by Pauli in which it seeks to generate a hundred innovations that would generate one hundred million jobs in a span of ten years (Ellen MacArthur Foundation, 2019).

Finally, Natural Capitalism was proposed by Paul Hawken, Amory Lovins and Hunter Lovins, an interdisciplinary team made up of an ecologist, a physicist and a sociologist, in his book Natural Capitalism: Creating the Next Industrial Revolution. (Balboa & Domínguez Somonte, 2014). In this book, a criticism against traditional industrial capitalism is shown, it also explains how business and environmental interests are linked, or between production and resources generated by nature - natural capital. This school states that there are four necessary changes to move from industrial capital to natural capitalism (Hawken, Lovins, & Lovins, 2000):

1) Achieve optimizing the productivity of natural resources through changes in designs. As a consequence, the saving of resources was generated, the profits increased, the time was improved, and the initial capital was reduced (optional).
2) Eliminate the concept of waste, through the reduction of waste and the creation of a production model based on biological systems, converting it into an outlet at the entrance.
3) The aim is for business models to stop focusing on achieving sales and begin to focus on the search for solutions, on sustaining a new perception of the satisfaction of quality, functionality and utility of goods and services.
4) Increase in the investment of the natural capital model, in order to expand the new sustainable ecosystems in the world at the same time as the population grows and, consequently, increase the production of biologically responsible products / services.

Having as precedent the schools of thought mentioned above, in the previous century there has been a continuous struggle in search of a balance in business that includes human resources, care for the environment and, obviously, profits. Companies, regardless of size or classification, are important players in the global arena because they have an active role in the. Sometimes, companies that use the word Sustainability in their Corporate Social Responsibility reports do so as a synonym of support for the environment, which is incorrect. Due to this and the ambiguity of some of the related concepts we can reach the conclusion that the true meaning of Sustainability or the way to achieve it is not known (Kavinski, De Souza-Lima, Maciel-Lima, & Floriani, 2010).

GREEN ECONOMY, GREEN GROWTH AND SUSTAINABLE DEVELOPMENT

The green economy concept is called the next oxymoron after sustainable development because they overlap each other (Brand 2012). Conference on Sustainable Development (Rio+20) in 2012 agreed that in the context of sustainable development, the concept of green economy should be promoted. The transition to a green economy has economic and social justifications for public and private actors to contribute offering opportunities for investments and green procurement by providing new market-based incentives and mechanisms.

Environmental sustainability and economic growth are compatible. Green economy prioritizes well-being for the present and for future generations and not necessarily is sufficient the efficiency of improved technology. A green economy is essential to sustainable development, improving social equity, human well-being, reducing ecological scarcities and environmental risks. The Global Green New Deal report based on green economy proposed policy actions to stimulate a sustainable economic development. Identification and eradication of unsustainable activities in different economic sectors to enhance an enabling environment, are necessary actions of the green economy.

Green economy supports sustainable development aimed to replace the social and environmental costs of the current economic model that is reaching limits in terms of greenhouse gas emissions, use of natural resources, water, land, forests, etc. Green economy transformation and inclusive greener growth strategy initiatives are needed to pursue the economic and social benefits of sustainable development while reducing negative environmental, inequality and poverty impacts, sustainable management of natural resources, reduce greenhouse gas emissions, climate change, resilience to natural disasters, improve public services, etc. Green economy and sustainable development strategies strengthen the resilience of communities and regions.

Green growth responds to critical emerging issues by facing the global challenge of environmental sustainability. However, the elements of the green economy concept are already integrated in strategic documents focused on achieving sustainable green growth, rather than merely achieving a green economy. Green growth is based upon the sustainable development strategies used to support the transition to green economy defined as the process of improving the economic, social and cultural and environmental well-being of future generations.

Green growth fosters economic growth and development, ensures natural assets providing the resources and environmental services to the benefit of humanity well-being focusing on the synergies and tradeoffs between the environmental and economic sustainable development. The interactions between society and the environment drive forces for change and transformation for the green economy as an opportunity to achieve sustainable development and human well-being. Green economy is worth to pursuit as an opportunity to prioritize well-being and sustainable development for the present and for future generations.

Green economy is one of tools used to achieve sustainable development goals (SDG) of end poverty, hunger and food security, good health and well-being, education, gender equality and women´s empowerment, water and sanitation, energy, economic growth, infrastructure, industrialization, inequality, cities, sustainable consumption and production, climate change, oceans, biodiversity, partnerships, etc. The socio-ecological and SDGs' indicators of the green economy outlined moves beyond the GDP as the transformational concept to measure the wellbeing (Ferguson 2014; Fioramonti 2014; Stiglitz et al. 2009). Green economy visions are relevant for the legitimacy and global green economy under the SDGs.

The post-2015 development agenda and The Sustainable Development Goals (SDGs) overcome inherent conflicts emerging from the implementation of the green economy concept at different spatial levels. The SDGs created the imperative for the implementation of the green economy beginning to deliver changes. The SDGs is a platform to reintegrate the green economy into the sustainable development agenda. Green economy framework has universal goals flexible to be adapted for different contexts and aligned on monitoring green growth (Kamp-Roelands 2013; OECD 2011; UNEP 2014 2012a 2012b).

Green sectors and industries have the potential to become engines of green growth by reducing the use of fossil fuels as climate climate-resilient development. Some of the most relevant sectors to green economy are agriculture, energy, water management, tourism, waste, etc. Green growth policies promote economic growth and environmental development ensuring that natural resources provide environmental services to human well-being.

Green economy is acritical component of sustainable development which implies a greening change in the social construct of all the economy sectors. Details about the scale of the greening of specific sectors of the green economy development and implementation are required to be explicitly for absolute decoupling. Rural and urban development programs are a vehicle for enabling the transition from traditional rural and urban economy to a rural and urban green economy. Locally led development programs and group actions can often respond more effectively to local needs in the transition to the green economy. Urban green brands are already developing focusing more on green growth and low carbon economy which may be stronger and attract greater interest.

Green economy approaches offer economic opportunities of low carbon transitions under the framework of an agreement of a collective carbon finance goal (United Nations 2015). Resource and energy efficiency supports green products, services and low-carbon green economy as part of the transition to deliver economic, social and environmental benefits. Low carbon actions are part of a transition towards green economies can make the most of the resources available. The transition towards a green economy by investing and preserving the natural capital to generate growth, create jobs and eradicate poverty. A green job is defined as one that works with information, data, technologies, and materials, and requires specialized knowledge, training, skills, and experience for activities that minimize environmental impact.

The green economy concept is mutually complementary between different dimensions of sustainable development and poverty eradication to enhance convergence through different approaches, among which are the internalization of externalities, systemic economic structure, reconciling social goals, policies and objectives and the macroeconomic framework of development strategy (UNDESA 2010).

The design of green economy to contribute to sustainable development is away from the dysfunctionalities of traditional mainstream economy and results in human well-being and equitable access to opportunities safeguarding economic and environmental economic integrity. Green economy contributes to sustainable development with different forms of implementation for different countries. Resource efficiency is a green economy process is supported by environmental awareness and technological green innovation, although the increase in consumption may occur when efficiency gains are lost leading to the so called Jevons paradox, which may be addressed by specific policies on fiscal mechanisms and education.

GREEN ECONOMY PRINCIPLES

Guiding principles of a Green Economy helping practitioners in the application of the green economy concept are sustaining that it is a means for sustainable development, is equitable, just and fair, creating green jobs, protects biodiversity and ecosystem services, provide green resources and efficient green energy within the ecological limits, delivers well-being, access to essential services, poverty reduction, livelihoods, social protection. The principles of a green economy that according to GEC deliver a sustainable, inclusive and participative green economy are: sustainability, justice, dignity, healthy planet, inclusion, good governance and accountability, resilience, efficiency and sufficiency and generations.

The sustainable development and green economy strategies and policies is a model based on the core principles of economic efficiency, equity, social inclusion, environmental sufficiency and accountability which requires dialogue among all the involved stakeholders and participative policy design.

Also, these principles consider the measurement of green economy using appropriate metrics and indicators, internalizes externalities, improves governance and the rule of law being democratic, participatory, inclusive, transparent and accountable and more other principles. A good indicator of the relevance of green growth and economy for a specific society is to identify the number or share of population involved in any form, as employee, consumer, etc.

Equitable green economy is linked to sustainable development supported by principles and informed by policy and market decisions. Green economy principles must be integrated in sustainable development programs and initiatives such as in pollution prevention and sustainable production and consumption. Green economy principles aimed to develop a fair and inclusive economy to provide a better quality of life are the sustainability, justice, dignity, healthy planet, inclusion, good governance and accountability, resilience, efficiency and sufficiency and generations principles (Green Economy Coalition 2012).

Green economy principles can be applied to urban sustainable development by coordinating some deliverables with other organizations and donors relating to methodologies, platforms, best practices and tools that contribute to poverty eradication (UNCSD, 2012).

Green economy principles must be developed after engaging in discussion with the different stakeholders to meet the vision, priorities and needs of each sector. A set of green economy principles emerging from dialogue can serve as guidelines for making decisions which can be applied across sectors and institutions to operationalize a green economy. Social equity, ecological limits and community ownership are core principles for green economy.

TRANSFORMATIONAL TRANSITION OF GREEN ECONOMY

The transition towards green economy can solve the interconnected economic, social, and environmental crises. Green economy and transformation as enabling approaches are related to potentially create dynamic change (Pelling and Manuel Navarrete 2011; Pelling et al. 2014). Green economies integrate economic, social and environmental activities. The concept of green economy represents a transition for more environmentally friendly and resource-efficiency technologies to tackle environmental degradation by reducing carbon emissions and mitigating the effects of climate change (Jänicke 2012).

Transition to green economies require that green activities and investments in the interlinkages between rural-urban areas can contribute to green economic growth. Public and private funding of green economy has to be scaled up at all institutional levels and sectors supporting sustainable and responsible green investments in green business and companies, clean technology, green investments, etc. A green company is defined as a company that produces goods and services designed to reduce their environmental impact.

Green technologies should be developed with government financial support and subject to wider dissemination. Private investment flows in green technology should ensure that achieve full potential in spin-off benefits. Any percentage of global GDP invested to green economy sectors increase the growth, employment and reduce water, energy, etc. Public and private investments in green economy, promote revenue growth and employment from a rational use of natural and financial resources and energy efficiency that reduce carbon emissions and pollution and prevent loss of biodiversity and environmental services.

Development programs structured according priorities supports transition to the green economy in practice although the term may not be explicitly used, planning authorities may use different approaches and measures. Design and implementation of rural and urban and urban development programs support the transition of business activities to the green economy and the environmental performance. Development programs can provide financial support to support the transition towards a green economy with impact in long-term business opportunities. Business can foster practices that contribute to the green economy transition.

Equitable green economy is a transformation process in constant dynamic progression, although it has been questioned if green economy is equitable. One of the four green economy typologies is green transformation of economic growth through political interventions (Death 2015, 2216). Building on Ferguson's typologies based on weak/strong green economy, the UNEP's concept is more transformational providing enabling conditions for green economy transitions (UNEP 2011). Transformational green economy renders strong green economy and growth concepts deployed as organizing principles for climate change (Pelling et al. 2014).

The term green economy comprises the application of some economic instruments which requires social, institutional and political contexts to harness economic activities in support of sustainable development goals. Design of development plans can contribute to the transition to the green economy activities such as mitigation of climate warming, sustainable water and waste management, sustainable infrastructure, ecosystems services and buildings, investment in natural resources and capital, renewable energy feedstocks and energy efficiency, green research, green tourism and eco-innovation, agricultural and forest land management, forestry and fisheries (bio economics) green manufacturing and supply chain green public procurement, etc.

The transition to the green economy makes sure that agriculture and forestry are both economically and environmentally sustainable activities for the long-term. For example, the use of procurement policies for the greening of business. Green agriculture requires natural and physical capital assets, knowledge and financial investments and enhance the capacity building in efficient and sustainable management of soil fertility, water use, farm mechanization, crop and livestock diversification; etc. the analysis of investments measures benefits and costs of green economy and green energy policies taking into account capacity building, management, operation, research and development, expenditures in infrastructure, incentives, etc.

Measures for business and farm diversification can support transition activities to green economy. The sectors considered to have green potential are energy renewable, water, waste/recycling, sustainable farming and forestry, fisheries, public transport, green buildings, tourism, health care, education and training, green finances, etc.

Greening the fishery sector requires strengthening the fisheries management and financing fishing activities to maintain sustainable stocks within biological limits limit the environmental impact. Assessment of the impact on the dynamics of the fishing and marine ecosystem and biodiversity using quantitative indicators for socio-economic factors is required for a more effective exploitation of fisheries.

Greening the sector of forestry must be focused on reducing deforestation and increasing reforestation in accordance with economic and market mechanisms including payments for ecosystem services, certified benefit sharing and other schemes, community-based partnerships, sustainable forest management instruments aimed to carbon reduction, enhance protection of forests against fires and pollution, biodiversity and forest ecosystems, provision of environmental services, etc.

Greening the industry and manufacturing sector implies design to extend the useful life of goods and recycling them to support the use of by-products and alternatives for substitution to achieve a circular economy with a close-loop manufacturing in eco-industrial parks.

Greening the building sector requires a policy framework with instruments for development of sustainable building capacities and standards, cost-efficiency and incentives. Greening building requires investment and incentives for energy supply and renewable performance for sustainability of new and renovated buildings.

Greening transport policies intend to integrate land use and transportation planning for more environmentally efficient modes shifting to non-motorized transport and improving vehicle and fuel technology, avoiding or reducing trips and using water and rail transport for freight. All these policies are aimed to reduce the negative environmental and social effects. A greening transport policy framework to enhance sustainability though greener and efficient roads includes a strategy focused on the cost of transport in terms of environmental damage to society and reducing noise pollution.

Greening the tourism sector can be done by increasing the involvement of the local community in the tourism value chain and the interplay between internal factors and structural conditions.

Greening the waste management sector requires decoupling waste from economic growth and addressing the challenges of increasing the recycle rate of electrical and electronic equipment or e-waste, turning bio mass waste into recovered energy and other valuable resources, reducing food waste in the food chain, etc. The treatment of waste in the whole cycle from waste generation to waste disposal, should emphasize recovery for reuse and recycling of waste materials. Strategy for the prevention of industrial waste are based on industrial symbiosis resulting of collaboration to facilitate the exchange of by-products, water, energy and other materials.

Greening the water sector requires water management based on quality standards, to increase investments with better financial arrangements, to achieve a more efficient water supply, to improve the institutional arrangements and allocation systems, entitlements and use pf payments for ecosystem services.

Green economy transition is relevant to all economic sectors and requires a change in their economic activities perspective. Green economic transformation should be supported by new institutional forms for organization and decision making supported by participation and collaboration structures between public, private and community agents and actors for sharing resources and knowledge in green economic activities. One of these economic transformations into green economy is the circular economy.

CIRCULAR ECONOMY (EC)

Since its creation, the Circular Economy has been defined in different ways, in order to make it more understandable and easy to transmit for its application. Here are three ways to define this concept:

1) Claudia García Caicedo, in her publication Circular economy and its role in sustainable design and innovation, mentions that the Circular Economy aims to achieve product designs that reduce or completely eliminate waste, and also seeks to ensure that products are simple to dismantle-disassemble for reuse in new products. The CB is also responsible for defining business models that are exclusively dedicated to companies that apply the Circular Economy in their processes to achieve sustainable innovation and consequently feel economically motivated to recover their product after fulfilling its main function, use it again in manufacturing and repeating the cycle (Caceido García, 2017).
2) Catalina Balboa and Manuel Domínguez, in their work Circular economy as a framework for ecodesign: the ECO-3 model, define CS as a "philosophy of systems organization inspired by living beings, which pursued the change of an economy linear (produce, use and throw) increasingly difficult to implement due to the depletion of resources towards a circular and regenerative model, as occurs in nature and which also represents a great opportunity in the business world "(Balboa & Domínguez Somonte, 2014). The interesting thing in the definition of Balboa and Dominguez is that they mention it as a way to try to solve the problem of scarcity of resources.
3) The Ellen MacArthur Foundation mentions that the Circular Economy usually has other names related to the schools of thought on which it is based, and that were already mentioned above, for example: economy of the cradle to the cradle or economy of closed loop (Ellen MacArthur Foundation (2), 2019). It is important to mention that this foundation declares that the defenders of the theory do not consider the Circular Economy as part of an ecological movement, but as a form of improvement of the design.

CONCEPTUAL BACKGROUND

Strategy

To define the strategy, the present work was based on the works of Michael Eugene Porter. This author defines the strategy as a differentiator that is created by making choices about several options that in the end would generate a unique value combination. Based on the conclusion by Porter, what really defines a strategy are the activities to which it specializes, that is, decision making is conditioned by the company's interest in differentiating itself from the competition. If the above is not respected, competitive advantage would not work as a differentiator but as an idea of marketing (Porter, 1996).

Porter talks about how a strategy can scale a company in the market, and become a strategic position. This position comes from three sources that sometimes work together:

1) Positioning based on the variety of products or services that exist in the area. The companies that use this positioning are usually those that have a better possibility of producing some good or service due to certain special characteristics that only they handle in the process.

2) Positioning based on needs, is one that is responsible for trying to meet the needs, or most of these, of a certain group of people. In a market there are many types of customers who request special products, which require certain characteristics in the good they want to buy, with different tastes or preferences, so they usually need guidance, support or very specific services.
3) Positioning by customer segmentation according to the way to access them or positioning based on access. Normally, this type of positioning is determined by the position or geographic location in which the client of interest is located. It can also be determined by the dimension or some specific situation that would hinder or hinder easy access to the client.

According to Porter, usually more threats come from sources outside the organization. When a strategy becomes part of a competitive advantage, it is likely to be threatened by changes in areas such as technology or the actions of competitors. It is mentioned that the event that can cause a certain strategy to fail is internal to the firm, and is mainly due to the underestimation of rival companies in the industry, poor planning, lack of information, or great ambition to grow without finalizing details.

Sustainability

The term Sustainability does not have a precise definition by itself, it is a rather ambiguous term that derives from the word sustainable, an adjective that implies "that can be maintained for a long time without exhausting resources or causing serious damage to the environment" (RAE, 2017, page sp). We can also find that Sustainability comes from Latin etymologies such as sustenance, sustenance, sustentare, sustentavi, sustentatum, which mean: sustain, maintain in good condition, care, conserve, support, favor (Ecología UNAM, 2015). In practice, we define Sustainability as a process that aims to ensure the satisfaction of the needs of the current and future generations.

Competitive Advantage

Competitive advantage can be defined as the essential aspect that demonstrates the performance of markets that are competitive, over the years the focus on competitive advantage has been lost to focus on the diversification and growth of organizations (Porter, 2015). Porter declares that the source or origin of the competitive advantage is the value that the firm generates in its products or services to satisfy the clientele, in other words, it is considered as a plus that manages to surpass the competition, even when the rivals try reach the company that has an advantage of this kind. In Porter's book "Competitive Strategy" he describes three general strategies for achieving competitive advantage: cost leadership, differentiation and concentration.

THEORETICAL BACKGROUND

The main objective of any firm is to generate high rates of return, in other words, obtain profits. Because of this, in the research work Sustainable Competitive Advantage: Combining Institutional and Resource-Based Views, Christine Oliver decided to create a hybrid model that would include the Approaches Based on Resources and Institutions, in this way the Model of the Advantage was born. Competitive

Sustainable This author mentions that the reason why the resource-based approach is not only used is due to its limitations (Oliver, 1998):

1) Explain the heterogeneity of companies through the properties of resources and the markets of resources.
2) Does not worry about including the social context, which affects the decision making about the use of resources.
3) It does not talk about how the selection of resources is made.

By including the Institutional Approach, we seek to complete the spaces left, in the social sphere, by the Resource-based Approach, so that the Institutional will contribute (Oliver, 1998):

1) A study on how social influence affects decision making within a company.
2) It will show us the close relationship that exists between the selection of resources and sustainable competitive advantage in relation to decision making.
3) The importance of having an "institutional context" in the three levels of the company:
    a) Individual level, are the normal and individual values.
    b) Company level, are represented by the organizational culture and politics.
    c) Inter-company level, as an example: public relations and its pressure on the market, regulations and standards faced by firms.

Oliver also inspected the general notions of the new hybrid approach of the Sustainable Competitive Advantage, which turned out to be the following:

1) The model divides decision making into three levels, as does the institutional one: Individual or managerial choice, company level, and inter-company.
2) Includes the way in which managers select resources and capacities, that is, the decision of which resources and capacities to implement.
3) Determines that in order to create and apply strategies, resources and institutional regulations must be taken into account.
4) It defines what is a capacity, resources and its idea of sustainability of an advantage that must be competitive.
5) Its analytical model consists of three determinants that assure us a sustainable competitive advantage, if it is integrated in the right way: those based on resources, such as managerial decisions; the selection of resources, the heterogeneity of the company; the institutional determinants: rational / individual regulation, institutional / business factors, and isomorphic pressure / between companies.

In relation to the selection of resources for its application, this new approach mentions that there are three cases in which it is more likely that a company is willing to acquire them or use the ones they have in reserve (Oliver, 1998):

1) When resources are acquired that are not major for the company, in this way we managers do not feel that they are risking their main activity.

2) Companies tend to be traditional, they are affected by their institutional part, so the acquisition of resources must belong to the same item that the company manages.
3) When a resource of the company is no longer considered productive, it is time to acquire new, since the organization does not feel so threatened by the change. The opportunity cost will have less impact.
4) The accumulated resources should be periodically monitored to know what we have and what we can use.
5) The training of the assets of the company helps them to know how to use potential resources.
6) From the moment of hiring, people with attitudes that have a notion of the use of resources for an optimal management should be chosen.

From the point of view of the Institutions approach, there are certain assumptions that would allow achieving a sustainable competitive advantage, in relation to the use of valuable resources (Oliver, 1998):

1) The acquisition of a valuable resource will be accepted by the company when it does not violate the regulations or the corporate culture.
2) The acquisition will be accepted if senior management gives it political support.
3) For reasons of power struggle, certain valuable resources will be acquired if with it the power of a decisive voter increases or strengthens its place in the company.

The creation of a model that unites the two approaches was necessary, since all approaches have deficiencies that tend to focus too much on production, resources or institutions and their regulations at different levels. This theory also shows concern for the factors that affect the individual as such and the impact that this would have on the decision-making process when selecting resources and applying them in the correct manner. The Focus of the Sustainable Competitive Advantage can be considered as an advance in the evolution of the strategies, since not only is oriented to obtain an objective, but also it is in charge of making known how to achieve it.

RESEARCH METHODS

Although the theoretical perspective that will be used in the present work is the theory of resources and capacities slightly influenced by the approach of the institutions, an analysis will be carried out through the VRIO Framework (Value, rarity, inimitability, and organization) to determine if The Circular Economy model could be considered as a viable resource as a competitive advantage that allows the company to achieve its objectives and position itself in the market, which would generate a competitive strategy.

ANALYSIS OF RESULTS

As already mentioned before, the tool that will be used to analyze the situation of the Circular Economy as a competitive resource within an organization, is through an internal analysis called Marco VRIO. First the analysis will be shown in the form of a table and after the explanation will be made by means of the answer to the four questions that this frame generates.

To obtain the results, the research work matrix was used as a base: ICT as a source of competitive advantage in SMEs (Moncada Niño & Oviedo Franco, 2013). The pertinent changes were made to be able to apply it in this specific case, shown below:

VRIO Analysis (By Concept)

Next, the explanation of the previous table, concept by concept, in addition to the specific interpretation to this particular case:

Valuable: answer the following question: is it a valuable resource to gain an advantage? According to Álvaro Fernando Moncada Niño and Martha Lucía Oviedo Franco in their work, valuable resources are considered those that can be used as a response to external threats, and in turn, help take advantage of opportunities. "The definition of the value of the resource or capacity is related to its possibility to exploit an opportunity or mitigate a threat in the market. If one of those two things is done, it can be considered as a strength of the company; otherwise, it is a weakness. When these are properly exploited, they generally lead to an increase in income or a decrease in costs or both "(Moncada Niño & Oviedo Franco, 2013, page 129).

Due to the above, the Circular economy can be considered a valuable asset, by exploiting the opportunity to reduce costs and reduce the waste generated by the company through a reengineering of processes and design.

Rarity: is it being used by a small group of firms? The VRIO framework considers that resources must be rare, limited or unique, that is, very few companies are using it in their activities, otherwise the resource would not serve as a competitive advantage. If the rarity remains, and few companies manage to acquire it this would mean that the resource would remain scarce, which would give it the characteristic of sustainable competitive advantage (Moncada Niño & Oviedo Franco, 2013). The Circular Economy is a scarce resource that has not been applied in a large number of companies due to its complexity, but it is very likely that this rarity is not held too long, because of the changes in the policies related to sustainability and its derivatives, so it is considered as a temporary competitive advantage.

Inimitability: is it expensive to imitate? "... resources are inimitable when the possibility for competitors to analyze and duplicate them makes their acquisition or acquisition costly or takes too long to replicate" (Moncada Niño & Oviedo Franco, 2013, page 129). This characteristic of the VRIO Framework is usually related to the previous two, since the cost of use or application directly affects the rarity and its value. The CE is considered an inimitable resource, because when applied it would be considered quite expensive, since the generation of totally new designs thinking about the reduction of waste is expensive at the beginning, not any company can achieve it.

Organization: Is the organization prepared in its policies and procedures to use this resource? "Relating to the fact that the company has certain organizational aspects, such as the organizational structure, processes and systems, as well as the business culture itself, to exploit the full competitive potential of its resources and capabilities. Therefore, the resources and capacities have to be exploited efficiently by the company "(Moncada Niño & Oviedo Franco, 2013, page 130).

When referring to this characteristic, it is deduced that the companies are not prepared, in their great majority, to install and use the Circular Economy, due to the great complexity changes and improvements necessary for an optimal operation.

CONCLUSIONS AND RECOMMENDATIONS

At the beginning, it was mentioned that this document aims to determine if the Circular Economy is a resource with the aim of becoming a competitive advantage that will impact on the focus of resources and capabilities. In this specific case, it turns out that, if it has the majority of the features of the VRIO Framework that allow it to be a competitive advantage, but of a temporary nature, because in the Rarity it is considered that in the coming years the business political demands will change, forcing companies to look for ways to include this type of model, regardless of the cost.

As a recommendation, it can be highlighted that organizations that wish to implement this model in their activities will need to have a good economic position. The initial costs of application are usually very high as a result of the changes that must be made from the root of the product: the design of this.

In conclusion, it was proved that the Circular Economy can be considered as a competitive advantage, but of a temporary nature according to the characteristics of the VRIO Framework.

REFERENCES

Alvial Muñoz, A. (2015). *Economía Azul: Una revisión en el marco de nuevas tendencias en Economía.* Obtenido de Bioeconomía Argentina: http://www.bioeconomia.mincyt.gob.ar/wp-content/uploads/2014/12/1.-Econom%C3%ADa-azul-A.-Alvial.pdf

Balboa, C. H., & Domínguez Somonte, M. (2014). *Economía circular como marco para el ecodiseño: el modelo ECO-3.* Obtenido de Universidad Nacional de Educación a Distancia: https://www2.uned.es/egi/publicaciones/articulos/Economia_circular_como_marco_para_el_ecodiseno_el_modelo_ECO-3.pdf

Brand, U. (2012). Green economy – the next oxymoron? No lessons learned from failures of implementing sustainable development. *GAIA - Ecological Perspectives for Science and Society, 21*, 28–32.

Brundtland, G. H. (1987). *Our Common Future.* Obtenido de UN: http://www.un-documents.net/our-common-future.pdf

Caceido García, C. L. (2017). *Economía circular y su papel en el diseño e innovación sustentable.* Obtenido de Libros Editorial UNIMAR: http://ojseditorialumariana.com/index.php/libroseditorialunimar/article/view/1154

Ecointeligencia. (2017). *¿En qué consiste la Economía del Rendimiento?* Recuperado el Mayo de 2019, de Ecointeligencia: https://www.ecointeligencia.com/2017/01/economia-rendimiento/

Ecología, U. N. A. M. (2015). *Fundación UNAM.* Obtenido de UNAM: https://www.fundacionunam.org.mx/ecologia/sostenibilidad-vs-sustentabilidad/

Ellen MacArthur Foundation. (2019a). *Economía Circular: Escuelas de pensamiento.* Recuperado el 16 de Mayo de 2019, de Ellen MacArthur Foundation: https://www.ellenmacarthurfoundation.org/es/economia-circular/escuelas-de-pensamiento

Ellen MacArthur Foundation. (2019b). *Economía Circular: Concepto.* Recuperado el 10 de Mayo de 2019, de Ellen MacArthur Foundation: https://www.ellenmacarthurfoundation.org/es/economia-circular/concepto

Ferguson, P. (2014). The green economy agenda: Business as usual or transformational discourse? *Environmental Politics*, *24*(1), 17–37. doi:10.1080/09644016.2014.919748

Fioramonti, L. (2014). The world's most powerful number: An assessment of 80 years of GDP ideology. *Anthropology Today*, *30*(2), 16–19. doi:10.1111/1467-8322.12098

Gro Harlem Brundtland. (1987). *Our Common Future.* Obtenido de UN Documents: http://www.un-documents.net/our-common-future.pdf

Grown, H. (n.d.). *Diseño Regenerativo*. Recuperado el Mayo de 2019, de Heaven Grown: http://heavengrown.com/arquitectura-regenerativa/

Hawken, P., Lovins, A., & Lovins, L. (2000). *Natural Capitalism: Creating the Next Industrial Revolution.* Obtenido de Research Gate: https://www.researchgate.net/publication/265074221_Natural_Capitalism

Jänicke, M. (2012). Green growth: From a growing eco-industry to economic sustainability. *Energy Policy*, *48*, 13–21. doi:10.1016/j.enpol.2012.04.045

Kamp-Roelands, N. (2013). *Private sector initiatives on measuring and reporting on green growth.* OECD Publishing.

Kavinski, H., De Souza-Lima, J. E., Maciel-Lima, S. M., & Floriani, D. (2010). La apropiación del discurso de la sustentabilidad por las organizaciones empresariales brasileñas. *Cultura y Representaciones Sociales*, *4*(8), 34–69.

McDonough, W., Braungart, M., & Bollinger, A. (2007). *Cradle-to-cradle design: creating healthy emissions – a strategy for eco-effective product and system design.* Obtenido de Science Direct: https://www.sciencedirect.com/science/article/pii/S0959652606002587

Mejía Dugand, S. (2010). *La Ecología Industrial.* Obtenido de El Colombiano: https://www.elcolombiano.com/historico/la_ecologia_industrial-HEEC_101107

Missé, A., Moreno, J. A., Vázquez Oteo, O., Escorsa, P., & Casado Cañeque, F. (2015). *Responsabilidad Social de la Empresa: ¿RSE o RIP?* Obtenido de jstor: http://www.jstor.org/stable/26360524

Moncada Niño, Á. F., & Oviedo Franco, M. L. (17 de Junio de 2013). Las TIC como fuente de ventaja competitiva en las PYMES. *Sotavento M.B.A., 21*, 126-134. Recuperado el Mayo de 2019, de Universidad Externado de Colombia: https://revistas.uexternado.edu.co/index.php/sotavento/article/view/3441/3128

OECD. (2011). Towards green growth: monitoring progress: OECD indicators Organisation for Economic Co-operation & Development. OECD Publishing.

Oliver, C. (1998). *Sustainable Competitive Advantage: Combining Institutional and Resource-Based Views.* Recuperado el Mayo de 2019, de Strategic Management Journal: http://www.jstor.org/stable/3088134

Pelling, M., & Manuel-Navarrete, D. (2011). From resilience to transformation: The adaptive cycle in two Mexican urban centers. *Ecology and Society*, *16*(2), 1–11. doi:10.5751/ES-04038-160211

Pelling, M., O'Brien, K., & Matyas, D. (2014). Adaptation and transformation. *Climatic Change*, *133*(1), 113–127. doi:10.100710584-014-1303-0

Porter, M. (1996). *¿Qué es la estrategia?* Recuperado el Mayo de 2019, de Harvard Business Review: https://s3.amazonaws.com/academia.edu.documents/37851742/4_Que_es_Estrategia.pdf?AWSAccessKeyId=AKIAIWOWYYGZ2Y53UL3A&Expires=1558381861&Signature=132Q27yedrcb1MADZWvjsnckcC8%3D&response-content-disposition=inline%3B%20filename%3DQue_es_la_estrategia.pdf

Porter, M. (2015). *Ventaja Competitiva: Creación y sostenimiento de un desempeño superior.* Recuperado el Mayo de 2019, de Grupo Editorial Patria: https://books.google.com.mx/books?hl=es&lr=&id=wV4JDAAAQBAJ&oi=fnd&pg=PT3&dq=que+es+ventaja+competitiva&ots=mwvClbT58A&sig=O2eioD4ADfMxwU5PBfOy20qH-SA#v=onepage&q=que%20es%20ventaja%20competitiva&f=false

Puentes-Poyatos, R., Yebra-Rodríguez, Á., & Guerrero, F. (2016). *Responsabilidad Social Corporativa: El compromiso de la Universidad con los ciudadanos.* Obtenido de Revista de Antropología Experimental: https://revistaselectronicas.ujaen.es/index.php/rae

RAE. (2017). *Real Academia Española.* Obtenido de DLE: http://dle.rae.es/?w=diccionario

Saavedra García, M. L., & Saavedra García, M. E. (2014). La PYME como generadora de empleo en México. *Revista Clío América*, 153-172.

Secretaria Internacional de la Carta de la Tierra. (2019). *La Carta de la Tierra.* Obtenido de https://cartadelatierra.org/descubra/la-carta-de-la-tierra/

Stiglitz, J. E., Sen, A., & Fitoussi, J.-P. (2009). *Report by the Commission on the Measurement of Economic Performance and Social Progress.* Commission on the Measurement of Economic Performance and Social Progress.

UANL. (2013). *El desarrollo sustentable en México.* Obtenido de Sustentabilidad: http://sds.uanl.mx/el-desarrollo-sustentable-en-mexico-3/

UNAM. (2015). *Ecología UNAM.* Obtenido de Fundación UNAM: https://www.fundacionunam.org.mx/ecologia/sostenibilidad-vs-sustentabilidad/

UNCSD. (2012). *The Future we want, outcome of the United Nations Conference on Sustainable Development (Rio+20).* UNCSD.

UNDESA. (2010). Progress to date and remaining gaps in the implementation of the outcoms of the major summits in the area of sustainable development, as well as an analysis of the themes of the Conference. Preparatory Committee for the UNCSD.

UNEP. (2012a). *Indicators: a UNEP green economy briefing paper.* United Nations Environment Programme.

UNEP. (2012b) *Measuring progress towards a green economy: draft working paper.* United Nations Environment Programme.

UNEP. (2014). *Using indicators for green economy policymaking United Nations Environment Programme.*

KEY TERMS AND DEFINITIONS

Circular Economy: The circular economy proposes an economic and productive model characterized by sustainability and saving of resources and energy sources in which goods are produced, consumed, recycled, produced and re-consumed, entering a life cycle.

Green Economy: That which leads to the improvement of human well-being and social equality, while environmental risks and ecological scarcity are significantly reduced.

Green Growth: The one that promote economic growth and development while ensuring that natural assets continue to provide the environmental resources and services on which our well-being depends.

Resources and Capabilities: The theory of resources and capabilities states that organizations are different from each other based on the resources and capabilities they have at a given time, as well as the different characteristics of the same and that these resources and capabilities are not available to all companies in the same.

Strategic Plan: It is a document integrated in the business plan that includes the planning at the economic-financial, strategic and organizational level with which a company or organization has to address its objectives and achieve its future mission.

Sustainable Development: It is development that meets the needs of the present without compromising the ability of future generations to meet their own needs.

Transformation: The result of a process of change of form. It happens when one thing, fact or idea is converted into another.

Transition: A change from one form or type to another, or the process by which this happens.

VRIO Analysis: VRIO analysis is an internal business analysis tool that is included in the theory of resources and responds to the four basic characteristics that a resource must meet to give the company a competitive advantage.

Chapter 2
Analysis of Circular Economy From a Household Perspective in the USA

Badri Narayanan Gopalakrishnan
University of Washington, USA

Anchal Jain
Infinitesum Modeling, India

Nathalie Chalon
Infinitesum Modeling, Canada

ABSTRACT

In this chapter, the authors conduct original research on household emissions based on data from various sources in the literature. They analyze the extent of reduction of GHG emissions by adopting zero waste strategies by the households voluntarily, incurring no costs, but rather savings in wasteful expenditure. They then model this extent of reductions using a global computable general equilibrium (CGE) model to understand what could have been the carbon tax imposed to achieve this extent of GHG reduction. From the analysis, they find about 50% of GHG potential can be reduced from household emissions, as well as the associated life cycle emissions of products consumed. Reduced wasteful expenditure may facilitate both savings-led investments and the purchase of more green products by consumers, thereby boosting the economy. Therefore, they conclude that policies that incentivize zero waste lifestyle may go a long way in reducing the supposed tradeoff between the economy and the environment. They also review some strategies for the households, based on the literature, to minimize waste.

DOI: 10.4018/978-1-7998-4990-2.ch002

INTRODUCTION

In the last decade of the 21st century, World has faced many challenges in the form of natural disasters because of the effects of Climate Change. The year 2017 would become the most expensive hurricane season on record in the US. To count on, damage caused by Hurricane Harvey in the Houston area of southeastern Texas in August 2017 is humungous. Subsequently, Hurricane Irma has affected the mainland of Florida, and Hurricane Maria pummeled Puerto Rico (Ornes, 2018), New Wales and Victoria regions of Australia caught fires and more than 1.2 million hectares of area has been affected. It is also estimated that 25,000 koalas were killed in flames of Kangaroo Island in the state of South Australia (BBC News, 2020).

Behind the widespread bushfires in Australia, one of the reasons attributed is intensifying of wildfires by drying out soil and vegetation which is envisaged to be caused by global warming, creating more fuel to burn farther and faster (BBC News, 2020).

Unprecedented events discussed above are consequences of global warming which is one of the effects of climate change which has happened due mainly to the increasing concentrations of greenhouse gases in the atmosphere (What is the difference between global warming and climate change?,). It has also led to an increase in heat-trapping gases that humans are adding by burning fossil fuels to the upper layer (Kennedy, 2015). It implies the triggering of a basic phenomenon which is the buildup of excess heat energy in the Earth system due to human intervention.

The world is witnessing long term effects of climate change which does not only include increase in heavy precipitation and heat waves, but also increase in frequent coastal flooding and inland flash floods. The incoming effects range from decrease in snowpack in the western mountains in North America to Freshwater availability projected to decrease in Central, South, East and Southeast Asia by the 2050s (What are the long-term effects of climate change?, 2002).

As iterated above, if not taken the measures to contain the Climate change, it can affect the future generations as it has already started altering the present lives on Earth. To combat Climate change, steps can be taken globally, locally or an individual level. The approach to tackle Climate change can be split into three categories based on the levels of handling the issue- Action Driven Approach, Reactive Focussed Approach and Preventive Mind Set Approach.

Action Driven Approach-To address Climate change strategically at global level, The Intergovernmental Panel on Climate Change (IPCC) was set up by the World Meteorological Organization (WMO) and United Nations Environment. IPPC declared in 2013-"Climate change is real and human activities are the main cause" (Climate Change,). Much before conceptualisation of IPPC, Kyoto Protocol was formed which legally binds developed country Parties to emission reduction targets. Following IPCC, Paris Agreement was built in 2015 with an aim to strengthen the global response to the threat of climate change by keeping the global temperature rise this century well below 2 degrees Celsius above pre-industrial levels and to pursue efforts to limit the temperature increase even further to 1.5 degrees Celsius (Climate Change,). The agreement came effective in 2016. This forms an umbrella guidance for all the countries to take adequate measures which can have a prominent effect globally.

Reactive Focussed Approach- This approach is a response based approach which is driven by local prevailing factors in tackling climate change challenges. Local governments can customise the measures required taking international policies as the baseline (Kyoto Protocol is one such example). It can cover transitioning their local energy grid based on renewable energies in one area and convert fuel options in public transportation systems for another area. One of the key focus areas which local governance can contribute is the supply chain aspect of local products. Producing goods and food locally can lower the cost of transportation, reduce waste and help local economies (United Nations,). Local implementation of policies will result in measurable outcomes which will assist in providing Government for visibility and response towards local effects manifested by Climate Change.

Preventive Mind Set Approach- We as individuals can contribute in the measures to be taken against climate change, which will certainly help in the long run. As populations, economies and standards of living grow, so does the cumulative level of greenhouse gas (GHGs) emissions in the atmosphere. One of the key contributions an individual can start with by changing consumption patterns at household level. Its effect on a large scale will be able to influence companies to change their production patterns to more sustainable methods. Individuals at household level can initiate by consuming less products in day to day life. This preventive approach will eventually lead to reduction in waste which in turn lead to less generation of greenhouse gases in the atmosphere. Consumer behaviour is directly proportional to the waste generated and can make progress in disrupting 'Take-Make-Waste Model' (FCC Environment CEE,). In this model, raw materials derived from primary resources are utilised in production of usable products (at household level). After the consumption of the product, when the product is no longer in the cycle of usage, it is thrown away as it is. This model makes individuals as an incharge for generation of more waste, which in turn leads to filling of landfills at a faster rate, increased transportation and emission of GHG gases.

We need to shift our focus in making the life cycle of a product more efficient by bringing back the products after their usability in the cycle of product for another product as a raw material. The loop, wherein more materials can be utilised again in different forms, give rise to the concept of 'Circular Economy'.

Circular Economy is redefining the system so that wastes can be reduced and minimised at the same. It is a concept which revolves around extraction of materials with less application of energy. It applies cradle to cradle framework with an aim to give back to nature in maximum amounts (Circular Economy,).

Figure 1.
Ref: https://www.bitcoininsider.org/article/31401/swachhcoin-and-circular-economy

Circularity applies to the life cycle of a product which starts from Manufacturing, packaging, distribution, transportation, retailer, User and ultimately its disposal as depicted below:

Further, Circular Economy enunciates the reduction of every type of waste being produced by human activities. Waste management at household level offers an opportunity which is overlooked most of the time. Tracking of the generation of waste and consumption patterns provides a key foundation towards implanting the concept of circular economy at an individual level (Circular Economy,).

As per data published by the Environmental Protection Agency, USA, the total generation of municipal solid waste (MSW) in 2017 was 267.8 million tons. Wherein, about 139.6 million tons of MSW were landfilled with 22% of food waste, which was the largest component ending up at the landfill. The generation of MSW has increased from 88.1 million tons in 1960 to 267 millions tons in 2017 (United States Environmental Protection Agency,).

Scenario of a Waste Accumulation Arrangement in a Typical North American Household:

Let's Consider a family of 4 persons on average which includes two (2) Adults and two (2) kids. As per data released by the United States Environmental Protection Agency in 2017, the generation of Municipal Solid Waste is 4.5 pounds/person/day on average from a person living in a house in a whole day (United States Environmental Protection Agency,).

The waste generated from a household typically includes food waste (plant and animal based products), left overs, water bottles, cans, grass cuttings, packaging materials, paper and wood products (tissue papers, boxes for keeping food etc, metal clippings like iron, aluminium wires, glass products.

Due to increase in urbanisation and reach of the products to provide more comfort to the individuals at home, there has been an increase in per capita of MSW generation from year 2015 to year 2017.

Modelling exercise

As per the below table, municipal solid waste generation from an individual is considered as 4.51 pounds/person/day. Generation of municipal waste from a kid is assumed to be 20% more than generation by an individual in a typical household setup. Keeping at the higher end, the total generation of waste is calculated at 20 pounds/person/day as shown in the table below.

Table 1. Calculation of Total Generation of Waste

MSW production from one individual	4.51pounds/person/day
Consider 2 adults	9.02 pounds/person/day
Consider 2 kids (assuming kids produce 20% more waste than an adult)	10.824 pounds/person/day
Total MSW production from an household on daily basis at an higher end	19.844 pounds/person/day
Taking a rough figure (this includes MSW generated in a single day including all items covered in a category of MSW)	20 pounds/person/day

Various categories of waste generation have been considered with their contribution in daily waste accumulation from a household. The main broad categories are:

Food Category: Leftover food products contribute maximum to the waste generated from a household. The various percentages with resources considered are:

-Meat products leftovers, 15% contribution
-Dairy products leftovers, 5% contribution
-Plant products leftover, 5% contribution
-leafy vegetables pilings, 5% contribution

Plastics- This also forms a major part of the waste produced from a household. The various form of plastic generation has been considered as follows:

-Empty bottles (0.5 litres), 10%
-packaging (plastics- Polyethylene), 20%
-disposables (preferred over ceramics), 10%
-small clothings, 1%
-Glass pièces, 1%

Paper products- Paper utilised on a daily basis ends up in the waste generated from the household. 15% of the total waste generated is considered to be paper.

Metals: Metal ends up in waste in the form of cans and small wires of different metals. The percentage considered are:

-aluminium cans, 8%
-Metal wires, 2%

Garden and Wood Chippings: this type of waste is generated during revamping of the backyard and maintaining a small household garden. the percentage of waste generation is considered as 3%.

Greenhouse Gas potential for various categories has been collected from various resources and total potential of CO2 emission has been calculated as 55.6 kg on a daily basis from a household of 4 people. The table below depicts the flow of calculation done:

Practices which can reduce the generation of waste for various categories and eventually the total GHG potential on a daily basis. The table below showcases the assumptions made and the eventually reduction in GHG potential.

The reduced GHG potential is 23.21 Kg of CO2e which is almost half of the original GHG Potential as calculated above.

Measures to Initiate for implementation of Circular Economy

Measures which can be taken at household level to implement the concept of circular economy seek mindful efforts which will create the whole difference. Individuals can start inculcating small habits in day to day life at household levels which will not cost as well as will decrease the amount of waste generated to the environment substantially. The action can be taken by following of the strategies:

Make Your Kitchen Sustainable: Most of the products or consumables in our day to day life are utilised in daily consumption.

Table 2. Calculations for Green House Potential

Catégories	% contribution	Generation in Pounds/day	Greenhouse potential / carbon footprint(kg of CO2e)	Total potential in kg of CO2e
Food				
meat products	0.15	3	1.35	36.45
Dairy products	0.05	1	0.45	6.075
Plant products	0.05	1	0.45	0.9
leafy vegetables	0.05	1	0.45	0.9
Plastics				
empty bottles(0.5L)	0.1	2	0.9	0.074
packaging (plastics- Polyethylene)	0.2	4	1.8	4.32
disposables (preferred over ceramics)	0.1	2	0.9	3.06
small clothings	0.01	0.2	0.09	0.189
Glass	0.01	0.2	0.09	0.756
Paper-Not recycled	0.15	3	1.35	1.431
Metals				
Aluminium cans	0.08	1.6	0.72	0.878
Copper wires	0.02	0.4	0.135	0.106
Garden and Wood Chippings	0.03	0.6	0.27	0.486
total GHG potential on daily basis				55.6 kg of CO2e

- *Daily food habits:* Starting with the primary food item consumed in North America, meat is included in daily food items. The GHG potential of meat preparation is 27 times, whereas leafy vegetables have twice GHG potential of a kg of CO2e (Food's Carbon Footprint,). Hence taking this into consideration, an individual can think to change the food consumption pattern from inclusion to meat to turn into consumption of green leafy vegetables. Individuals can utilise mobile-based applications to track the daily purchase and the amount saved subsequently.
- *Minimise the use of Plastics:* An individual is encouraged to take his/her own cloth-jute bag to fetch the grocery everytime. This will not only reduce the usage of plastic at both the ends (consumers as well as retail shops/stores), rather make space in the kitchen which is taken over by the plastic bags on a monthly basis.
- *Make out of waste:* An individual, depending upon the food habits can practice reduction of waste generation at kitchen level. Utilising a product after completion of its life cycle as a raw material is the essence of Circular Economy as well. For Example; used tea bags and coffee powder can be utilised as an natural fertiliser for your kitchen garden. Practice optimisation in kitchen works as well, water used for washing the vegetables and fruits can be utilised in the kitchen garden.
- *Try composting once:* Data published by EPA shows that food scraps and yard waste comprise 28% of a waste generated from a household. This 28% can be composted at household level (United States Environmental Protection Agency, 2014). All vegetable waste, fruit scraps can be included in the compost along with dead leaves, branches and twigs. Having the right amount of water also assists in development of compost in appropriate time.

Table 3. Total GHG Potential

Catégories	Areas to reduce GHG potential based on certain assumptions	% contribution	Generation in Pounds/day	Greenhouse potential / carbon footprint(kg of CO2e)	Total potential in kg of CO2e
Food					
meat products	consumption of meat is reduced by 10%	0.05	1	0.45	12.15
Dairy products	consumption of dairy products is reduced drastically	0.02	0.4	0.18	2.43
Plant products	consumption of plant products is increased by 10%	0.15	3	1.35	2.7
leafy vegetables	increase in consumption of leafy vegetables.	0.08	1.6	0.72	1.44
Plastics					
empty bottles(0.5L)	try to take your own bottle and reduce the usage by 50%	0.05	1	0.45	0.03
packaging (plastics- Polyethylene)	recycled plastics	0	0	0	0
disposables (preferred over ceramics)	reduce disposables by 50% at least	0.05	1	0.45	1.53
small clothings		0.01	0.2	0.09	0.189
Glass		0.01	0.2	0.09	0.756
Paper-Not recycled	recycled paper can be utilised- at least 5%	0.1	2	0.9	0.954
Metals					
Aluminium cans		0.08	1.6	0.72	0.878
Copper wires		0.02	0.4	0.18	0.106
Garden and Wood Chippings	utilisation of wood chippings as a compost within the garden	0	0	0	0
total GHG potential on daily basis					23.21 kg of CO2e

Know your Supply Chain well: It is an important aspect to know the product life cycle as well. For example; tissue paper- check recyclability, organic mark on the food products. Ensure to purchase food products approved by Food & Drug Administration (FDA) and properly labelled.

Introduce being a Minimalist: Individuals can rely upon having a mindset of keeping the things not beyond its requirements in day to day life. The lifestyle as a minimalist leads a person to keep things which are essential only and buy the things necessary ones. Being a minimalist does not require any radical change to embrace it fully. Turning off lights and utilisation of natural light which provide a sense of positive change and fulfillness (Sheila,).

According to data published by the World Resource Institute (WRI), it takes around 2,700 liters of water to make one cotton shirt which is sufficient amount of water for one person to drink for 2.5 years. Considering these facts, an individual can strive for repairing the clothes to use them for a second time. Individuals can also sign up for the exchange programs running locally, wherein clothes are picked for recycling. The discarded wearables are recycled to transform them into raw material for new clothing or pellets for fuel. One such program is run by Uniqlo Sustainability based out of Seattle, Washington, USA (UNIQLO Sustainability, n.d.).

Modeling Methods and Data

We employ the widely used GTAP (Global Trade Analysis Project[1]) data base and model for our analysis. This is a multi sector multi country Computable general Equilibrium (CGE) model. Using a base year of 2014, this version 10 of the database is compiled from several data sources across the world, in terms of production, consumption, emissions, trade, protection, domestic support, taxes, etc. We use a special energy-environment version of this model, named GTAP-E. It contains the emissions tracked across the economy for several activities like production, consumption and trade. It also allows for tradeable permits, carbon taxes and other methods of carbon mitigation. Based on our calculations above, compared with the base data of CO2 emissions in GTAP, we impose a 50% reduction in CO2 emissions, by keeping carbon tax endogenous.

Modeling Results

Our results suggest that to achieve such a dramatic reduction in emissions, we would have needed a high carbon tax of 46 $ per tonne of carbon, if the households were not to voluntarily reduce their emissions as discussed in this paper. Such a steep increase in carbon tax may have led to over 22 billion $ in economic damage, in terms of GDP reduction. It may have also hurt production and trade seveely: almost 42 billion $ reduction in exports and a 1.4% higher inflation rate. Use of coal would have almost dimished to 3% of what it is today, while gas may have witnessed a 30% reduction. Electricity and energy intensive industries may have had to cut their production by 20% and 4% respectively. Therefore, a voluntary reduction in emissions by consumers would have achieved all these without having to forcefully inflict damages to these sectors to this extent. In contrast, the consumers may increase their savings by about 0.6%, which could result in an investment of 0.3% higher than the baseline. This could slightly boost the economy, instead of hurting it, which may have been the outcome of a command and control policy to cut emissions to this extent.

CONCLUSION

This chapter focuses on initiating the concept of circularity and reducing generation of household based waste. This initiative does not induce any extra cost to an individual, rather improves the budget with increase in savings. This will enable the positive society- wide- benefits as well. Therefore, we conclude that incentivizing zero waste lifestyle among households through tax sops may go a long way to reduce emissions without hurting the economy, and rather boosting it.

REFERENCES

BBC News. (2020, January 31). *Australia fires: A visual guide to the bushfire crisis*. Retrieved February 5, 2020, from https://www.bbc.com/news/world-australia-50951043

Circular Economy. School of Thought. (n.d.). Retrieved February 15, 2020, from https://www.ellenmacarthurfoundation.org/circular-economy/concept/schools-of-thought

Climate Change. (n.d.). Retrieved February 11, 2020, from https://www.un.org/en/sections/issues-depth/climate-change/

FCC Environment CEE. (n.d.). *From Linear to Circular Economy – closing the loop*. Retrieved February 14, 2020, from https://www.fcc-group.eu/en/fcc-cee-group/news-and-media/stories-of-waste/from-linear-to-circular-economy-closing-the-loop.html

Food's Carbon Footprint. (n.d.). Retrieved February 16, 2020, from https://www.greeneatz.com/foods-carbon-footprint.html

Kennedy, L. (2015, May 17). *What's the difference between global warming and climate change?* Retrieved February 10, 2020, from https://www.climate.gov/news-features/climate-qa/whats-difference-between-global-warming-and-climate-change

Ornes, S. O. (2018, August 14). *Core Concept: How does climate change influence extreme weather? Impact attribution research seeks answers*. Retrieved January 25, 2020, from https://www.pnas.org/content/115/33/8232

Sheila, S. (n.d.). *How Minimalism Can Help You Live A Sustainable Lifestyle*. Retrieved February 17, 2020, from https://www.practigalblog.com/minimalism-sustainable-lifestyle/

UNIQLO Sustainability. (n.d.). Retrieved February 18, 2020, from https://www.uniqlo.com/en/sustainability/recycle/

United Nations. (n.d.). *Cities and Local Action to Combat Climate Change*. Retrieved February 12, 2020, from https://unfccc.int/topics/education-youth/youth-engagement/global-youth-video-competition/global-youth-video-competition-2019/cities-and-local-action-to-combat-climate-change

United States Environmental Protection Agency. (2014). *Municipal Solid Waste Generation, Recycling, and Disposal in the United States: Facts and Figures for 2012*. Retrieved from https://www.epa.gov/sites/production/files/2015-09/documents/2012_msw_fs.pdf

United States Environmental Protection Agency. (n.d.a). *Managing and Reducing Wastes: A Guide for Commercial Buildings*. Retrieved February 15, 2020, from https://www.epa.gov/smm/managing-and-reducing-wastes-guide-commercial-buildings

United States Environmental Protection Agency. (n.d.b). *National Overview: Facts and Figures on Materials, Wastes and Recycling*. Retrieved February 15, 2020, from https://www.epa.gov/facts-and-figures-about-materials-waste-and-recycling/national-overview-facts-and-figures-materials

What are the long-term effects of climate change? (2002, May 29). Retrieved February 11, 2020, from https://www.usgs.gov/faqs/what-are-long-term-effects-climate-change-1?logstash-usgs-pw%3Apalladium_root_topics=&logstash-usgs-pw%3Apalladium_root_publication_year_date=&sort=&qt-news_science_products=4#qt-news_science_products

What is the difference between global warming and climate change? (n.d.). Retrieved February 10, 2020, from https://www.usgs.gov/faqs/what-difference-between-global-warming-and-climate-change-1?qt-news_science_products=0#qt-news_science_products

ENDNOTE

1 Visit www.gtap.org for more details.

Chapter 3
Climate Change and the Circular Economy:
Analysis of Policy and Individual Behavior in the Indian Ecosystem

Aakriti Mathur
University School of Law and Legal Studies, Guru Gobind Singh Indraprastha University, India

Kanwal Deepinder Pal Singh
University School of Law and Legal Studies, Guru Gobind Singh Indraprastha University, India

ABSTRACT

The world is presently facing a climate catastrophe of its own making through the unabated increase in greenhouse gas emissions. Global consumption patterns are to blame, as presently, the global annual demand for resources outpaces the annual rate of the earth's ability to regenerate those resources. Thus, there is an urgent need to reduce the global demand for resources to a sustainable level, through the adoption of a circular economy. Individual consumption behavior habits form the basis of global consumption patterns, and therefore, adoption of sustainable consumption habits and lifestyles are necessary for addressing the climate crisis. In this chapter, the authors assess the potential for addressing the climate crisis through the adoption of a circular economy and sustainable consumption behavior. The authors also evaluate the extent of adoption of sustainable consumption behavior in India and make recommendations for adopting a circular economy in India.

INTRODUCTION

The impacts of climate change ranging from increasing extreme weather events to increased droughts and wildfires to massive flooding serve as a stark forewarning of the times to come in case the world does not act now. It is estimated that even if countries comply with their Intended Nationally Determined Contributions (INDC's) under the Paris Agreement, the world is unlikely to be able to reduce emissions consistent with a 1.5 degree rise in temperature. Linear economy with its make-take-waste approach

DOI: 10.4018/978-1-7998-4990-2.ch003

leads to an ever increasing and unsustainable demand for resources. Calls for degrowth and adoption of circular economy have become particularly relevant in the circumstances.

Any efforts to address climate change must necessarily include efforts to reduce production and consumption to sustainable levels, for the simple reason that individual consumption is responsible for a large share of green-house gas emissions. This is true across industries but more the impact is much more significant in areas such as transportation, food production and consumption and plastic production and consumption. The rise of consumerism and corresponding increase in expected level of convenience and comfort translate directly into increased per capita consumption of materials and energy. In a linear economy this creates problems of not only unsustainable extraction of resources and excessive waste generation, but also contribute to climate change due to the green-house gas emissions associated with these processes.

Degrowth which can be defined as "the equitable downscaling of production and consumption that increases human well-being and enhances ecological conditions at the local and global level" and the adoption of circular economy which aims at the de-linking of "value creation from waste generation and resource use by radically transforming production and consumption systems" are concepts that are gaining international recognition as a new sustainability paradigm. Circular economy focuses on restoration and regeneration and looks at value creation from waste. The United Nations in 2015 adopted 2030 Agenda for Sustainable Development and adopted 17 Sustainable Development Goals (SDGs). Two of these goals that is SDG 12 of responsible production and consumption and SDG 13 of taking urgent action to combat Climate Change and its impacts can be directly addressed by adopting a circular economy.

The plastic packaging industry is expected to become one of the largest contributors to green-house gas emissions if current trends of production continue. Clearly the largest driver of single use plastic production is the consumer demand. Owing to the paucity of time and increase in the buying capacity of people, plastic packaging has become convenient. Also, buying packaged version and readymade goods is far easier than preparing it for hours. The plastic packaging does not add much to the manufacturing cost which makes it a favorable choice for the companies too. The companies using the plastic are also flouting rules like Extended Producer Responsibility for plastic. In fact, businesses have repeatedly blamed consumers for unsustainable demands on resources and the problems of mismanagement of waste. Coca Cola company was recognized as the largest plastic polluter in an audit of plastic waste in 2019 and despite having this dubious distinction, during the World Economic Forum in Davos, Switzerland, in January 2020, Coca Cola's head of sustainability Bea Perez cited continued consumer demand as the reason for not ending its production of single use plastic bottles. Sustainable consumption behavior on part of consumers and conscious rejection of unstainable business models then contributes to adoption of business models which foster sustainable consumption and promote a circular economy.

There has, however, been some change in the attitude of companies wherein they are partnering with entities which get their plastic wastes collected. These collected plastics are then supplied to the cement kilns where they are utilized. The management of plastic waste is much different from the wet waste management. There are some companies for example Saahas and Tetrapak which are helping in the management of plastic waste through different methods like collecting the plastic waste from companies and waste-pickers and then using them in either making new products or providing it to the companies which can use it in their manufacturing process (Saahas, n.d.).

Another major issue resulting from increased consumerism and linear economy is the solid waste generation and the landfills where most of this untreated waste ends up at. More than one hundred thousand tons of Municipal Solid Waste, which does not include sewage, is generated by cities in India every day. It is estimated that out of this huge amount of waste, two-thirds is food waste whereas medical waste, e-waste, packaging papers, etc. constitute the remaining one-third. Leachate, which is the liquid that trickles down the piles of landfills gathering all the toxins, is a major issue in waste disposal system. This liquid contains poison from lead batteries, medical waste etc. This liquid when it percolates down and reaches the underground water, it results in several diseases including respiratory issues, cancers and birth defects. These leachates affect the people living in surrounding areas more severely, and this is not the only threat that landfills pose. These mountains of waste serve as a perfect breeding ground for insects, specially mosquitoes. These mosquitoes result in life threatening diseases. One of such disease was Zika virus which resulted in birth defects like microcephaly. A great threat is posed to the waste-pickers who work in highly unhygienic and inhuman conditions. They come directly in contact with the germs and catch diseases. Landfills also lead to the production of Methane, which is a very powerful Greenhouse gas which directly contributes to climate change. A bacterium is found in these landfills which produces Methane gas. The amount of greenhouse gases produced from waste all over the world, is one and a half times the total emissions that in produced by India's electricity. This production can essentially be utilized in generation of electricity.

According to United Nation's Food and Agriculture Organization (2015), "The global annual food waste is equivalent to junking 7.2 million blue whales". Per year, 3.3 billion tons of carbon dioxide is produced in growing this amount of food. According to these figures, 'food waste' after US and China is the third largest emitter of carbon dioxide. It is expected that a substantial amount of global water resources are also wasted by being used for the production of this wasted food. Sustainable food consumption behavior and minimizing of food waste can therefore contribute to climate change mitigation efforts as well as reduced resource demand consistent with a circular economy.

Individual consumption behavior habits form the basis of global consumption patterns and therefore adoption of sustainable consumption habits and lifestyles are necessary for addressing the climate crisis. However, the role played by sustainable individual consumption behavior has largely been ignored in discussions surrounding the adoption of circular economy.

The objectives of this Chapter are to assess the potential for addressing the climate crisis through the adoption of circular economy and to evaluate the role played by individual sustainable consumption behavior. The concept of circular economy have been discussed in the context of India. The methodology adopted in this Chapter is empirical and primary data was collected through a questionnaire administered to a random sample of 300 respondents aged 18-75 years from urban India. The authors have evaluated the attitude to sustainable consumption and the extent of adoption of sustainable behavior in India relating to travel and mobility and in the context of consumption of electricity, plastic, paper, water and food. The authors have also discussed the potential for adoption of a circular economy in India through the adoption of sustainable consumption habits.

BACKGROUND

The climate crisis is a direct result of the extractive linear economy of "take-make-waste" which not only results in increasing green-house gas emissions but also generates massive amounts of waste. Unsustainable consumption patterns in the linear economy further tax the resources with the global demand for resources outpacing the earth's regenerative ability. Materials from the earth extracted by companies and energy and labor is used to manufacture the desired product. When the purpose is served it is all disposed- off adding to an enormous amount of waste on earth. This is called the liner-approach. It relies heavily on fossil fuels and the natural resource of water, minerals etc. is heavily used for producing products that in turn produce vast quantities of Greenhouse Gases. Thereby, essentially the natural resources are depleted to manufacture products that will further destroy the environment. This whole cycle further exacerbates the problem of Climate change. The (World Economic Forum, 2016) identifies climate change as the "The most important long- term risk facing the global economy, both in terms of probability of occurrence and economic gravity." As per the expert reports the global estimate for economic damage is US$ 54 trillion with 1.5 degree increase by 2100. Severe flooding and spells of drought have been identified as a great risk by World Bank (2013) for India. It has also been indicated by another study that economic burden of 20% will be borne by India owing to the climate change along with having carbon social cost being the highest in the world.(K. Ricke, 2018).

Nitish Arora, Souvik Bhattacharjya, Avishek Goel, Pallavi Gulati, Chandan Bhavnani, Arnesh Sharma and Shekhar Himanshu published a Report on "Circular Economy: A Business Imperative for India, 2018". This report has laid stressed on the principle of "5Rs – Reduce, Reuse, Recycle, Re-produce and Refurbish". The report identifies the stages of a product's life cycle. It also discusses policies like Zero effect for adoption of a circular economy. At the stage of manufacturing principle of Zero Defect can also be adhered to. Along with this if technology is used efficiently, the circular economy will be easily tweaked into the economic fabric of India. However, the report also recognizes the importance of collaboration between different stakeholders.

The draft of Niti Ayog on "*Strategy for Secondary Materials Management for promoting Resource Efficiency (RE) and Circular Economy (CE) in Electrical and Electronic Equipment Sector, Ministry of Communication & Information Technology (2019)"*, points out how increase in consumption has led to straining of the accessible resources. Efficient utilization of resources and an economy circular in nature will resolve the disputes which arise at the junctions of political, economic and social relations owing to the dearth of resources. Resource efficiency has to be met while shifting for a circular economy so that the requirement of resources is met.

Ellen MacArthur Foundation, (2016) has published a report "Circular Economy in India: Rethinking Growth for Long-Term Prosperity". According to this report, in 2050 an annual benefit of US Dollar 624 billion will be brought if it chooses the path of circular economy. The key areas of concentration in the report are infrastructure, agriculture, manufacturing of automobiles. India can put its reliance upon the circular economy for development and an efficient and effective economy.

Jessica Klaver in an article titled "Individual Sustainable Consumption and the Circular Economy: Research challenges and Opportunities" (2018) has carefully scrutinized the position and importance of consumer in a circular economy. As per this article the sustainable consumption is a perfect fit into the Circular economy at microlevel.

A paper by Ellen Macarthur Foundation in (2019) titled "Completing the Picture" in "*How the Circular Economy Tackles Climate Change"* focuses on the relation between the greenhouse gases and circular economy. It attempts to prove that adoption of circular economy will greatly lessen the emissions of greenhouse gases.

A comprehensive report by the European Commission (2015) titled "Closing the loop: Commission delivers on Circular Economy Action Plan" was adopted in 2015. The report extensively discusses the route towards a circular economy which is competitive in nature. The focus is on how a plan can be designed which reduces the strain on natural resources and the ecosystem.

Seonaidh McDonald, Caroline J. Oates, Panayiota J. Alevizou, C. William Young & Kumju Hwang have written a paper titled "Individual strategies for sustainable consumption" in the "*Journal of Marketing Management*" (2012). The paper deals with the consumer roles and how choices of consumers can help in the meeting of the targets set by governments for waste management, environmental impacts etc. The consumers can play a very important role in helping the State reach its target for better environmental results.

The World Economic Forum published a paper titled "Circular Economy in Cities: Evolving the model for a sustainable urban future" (2018). The paper thoroughly goes through the impacts that "urbanization, industrialization and globalization" has made on the environment and how the development has been affected by them all around the world.

A Final Report by European Economic and Social Committee titled "Circular economy strategies and roadmaps in Europe, identifying synergies and the potential for cooperation and alliance building" (2019) analyzes the circular economy and goes through the strategies in support to the European Circular Economy Stakeholder Platform (ECESP).

There has been a positive shift in the focus of environmental philosophies from creation of only recyclable materials for production to a radical redesigning of services and the products themselves around environmental, financial and societal considerations for a future which is sustainable.

As per World Economic Forum (2018), the circular economy has two dimensions, namely Upstream circularity (before use) and downstream circularity. While Upstream circularity pertains to the efficient management of resources and bettering the production and consumption processes, reducing wastage and ensuring cost effectiveness, Downstream circularity (after use) pertains to saving of the inherent value in an otherwise "waste" material and increasing the extraction of this latent value within the system. An example of Downstream circularity is the reintroduction of the valuable components of the used products as input into the economic cycle.

The three principles given by The Ellen McArthur Foundation (2016), characterizing the circular economy are, "Value Preservation, Resource Optimization and System Effectiveness". Value preservation refers to the retention of the maximum possible value of input materials during the process of production and creation of new products. For example, to repair, reuse, repurpose, remanufacture components in order to attain extension of product life and value.

Resource optimization refers to the efficient, limited and reduced usage of primary resources together with a better waste collection system as well as usage of renewable energy sources and resource recycling. System effectiveness refers to the maximum possible reduction of leakage whatever is useful to mankind (e.g. health, education) in its production as well as consumption cycle and addressing the related externalities (e.g. pollution, climate change)

According to the Ellen MacArthur Foundation (2016) a circular city is one which has all the functions, economic systems, its establishments embedded in the fundamental of circular economy. It is by its very design, regenerative and restorative. There is no concept of 'waste' in a circular city and has the maximum utility of every asset.

The World Economic Forum (2018) has identified Amsterdam as a circular economy. A circular city is one which promotes the use of mechanisms to administer financial, societal and ecological advantages to its people along with giving them a better quality of life.

Warde(2005) has shown that Individual Consumption and environmental sustainability have a strong link and therefore states that the underlying reasons behind a consumer's choice should be read and understood.

Per capita consumption is increasing every year and according to Meadows(1972), this is driven both by "the positive feedback loops of population growth and of capital growth" and thus the environment is bound to get greatly affected by over-consumption. Meadows has pointed out that natural resources suffer depletion, deterioration and degradation due to over-consumption.

According to Merli et al (2018), to overcome the linear economy and its "take-make-dispose" path from producing and consuming resources Circular Economy has been designed. It is proposed that "a circular system in which the value of products, materials and resources is maintained in the economy as long as possible". The idea of Circular economy has been fast spreading and has become common amongst both, scholars and practitioners.

J.B. Schor & D.B. Holt (2005), state that the technological advancements will not being change to the overall structures production and consumption and in order to strive for sustainability via consumption and productivity, these overall structures need to be altered.

Lewis Akenji (2014) argues that the sustainable consumer policy is drawn out with a micro vision. It is expected from the consumers to force manufacturers and retailers to carry out more sustainable production by consuming products which put much less pressure on the environment.

The idea of sustainable consumption is being promoted through "Green consumerism", which puts obligation on the consumer to consume more purposely the sustainable products, what can be called as consumption of 'green' or 'eco-friendly' products. It what is consumed is changed being towards 'eco-friendly' and the quantity of consumption remains the same, the economic growth will not be adversely affected, which is an important aspect. Akenji (2014) defines Green consumerism as the "production, promotion, and preferential consumption of goods and services" based on their environmental sustainability. There are a number of novel ideas being used to promote Green consumerism like labelling the products, certifying them as 'eco-friendly' according to their recycling, waste management and other eco-friendly activities. Even the governments have being promoting eco-friendly methods and start-ups and companies which use eco-friendly methods.

The EU Strategy for "Plastics in a Circular Economy" is the first EU policy framework adopting a material-specific lifecycle approach to integrate circular design, use, reuse and recycling activities into plastics value chains. This EU strategy regarding Plastics will act like a catalyzer as by 2030 all plastic packaging placed on the EU market is to be either reusable or recyclable. The report states, that the EU strategy has identified core actions that would enable collaboration between the various stakeholders in the value chain, in this regard.

The European Commission (2019) has been instrumental in taking initiatives with respect to plastic use such as taking actions on Single-Use Plastics, taking initiatives like the Global Plastics Platform with UN Environment and International Partnership on Plastic Waste in the context of the Basel Convention. EU is also helping developing countries in talking with the plastic pollution. EU has played a key role and has kept up the momentum in the agenda of plastic pollution.

The steps and measures that have being undergoing final legislative procedures, such as, a ban of single-plastic-use products which have been detrimental to the environment for a long time and have been a big reason for rapid climate change. A ban on oxo-degradable plastic is an important step in that direction. Steps for reduction of use of products like food containers and beverage cups which are made from plastic and add up to the huge piles of plastic use each day. Labelling of certain products is also to be undertaken in order to decrease the use of the plastics. One of the most important targets is "to incorporate 30% of recycled plastic in beverage bottles as from 2030 and 25% for PET bottles as from

2025 as well as a 90% separate collection target of plastic bottles by 2029 and the introduction of design requirements to connect caps to bottles". EPR schemes covering the cost to clean-up litter, applied to products such as tobacco filters and fishing gear. Effective measures have been taken up for reduction of plastic litter from ships. (European Commission 2019)

The authors in this chapter have discussed the importance of adoption of circular economy in India as also its benefits. The extent of individual sustainable consumption behaviors adopted by urban Indians have also been discussed.

CIRCULAR ECONOMY IN INDIA

The Indian economy today is marching towards growth because there is an alleviation in demand of means to cater human ambition for improved lifestyle, however the challenge lies in the fact that such economic development has to be not only affordable but also environment friendly. According to Arora Nitish Et al (2018) the policymakers find it challenging to draw an equilibrium between the need for development and zeroing down the negative impact associated with such use of resource. It is on policy maker to come up with such idea which provide framework to ensure resource efficiency, thereby fulfilling the goal of circular economy.

Given the population of India our economy has mostly been consumption-based with restricted manufacturing capacities. This can be substantiated by the fact that import to India exceeds far more than the exports. One of the main reasons for such trade imbalance is lack of availability and maintenance of resources like Gold, Oil, rare earths, etc.

As per Ellen MacArthur Foundation Report, (2016) various features of circular economy are penetrated in daily activities of Indian, for example in India Vehicles are used exhaustively, they are repaired time and again, an once they go completely out of use there are parts are recycled. All such activities though managed informally, are source of income of many poor families. Another example will be that, India recycles 60% of discarded plastics while US recycles 6%, and 95% of this activity happens informally. Having said this it is equally important to understand that these practices occur towards the finish of value-chains and more often acts as a tool to manage scarcity rather as a technique to have quality production, because of which idea of circular economy becomes distraught. Another major issue associated with Indian practices is lack of safeguards or standards rendering negative results, including health risks, open waste, leaking into rivers and oceans etc.

Since India is a growing economy therefore lot of its lower economic class is turning into middle class signifying improved living standards which also means less use of recycle techniques as that originated from necessity. This change could result in reduction of circularity in the system.

The circular economy provides answer to many resource related challenges, for example the natural capital is enhanced by encouraging creation of environment for regeneration of soil and other living systems. When resources are needed, the circular system favors more efficient technologies and renewable energy processes.

Regarding the amount of waste being generated in India, government data (CPCB Report, 2016) states that the country is generating around 50 million tons of municipal solid waste or even more annually and at this rate it is expected to reach 150 million tones by 2025. Such huge amount of waste not only threaten the environment but also cause long term health issues.

India requires development in a number of industries. The three primary areas in which circular economy can prove fruitful are "cities and construction, food and agriculture and mobility and vehicle manufacturing". As per Business Standard report urbanization is taking place in India at increasing rate and if such pace is maintained 60% of India's population will move to cities by 2050 as compared to current 30%. In such a scenario, development of cities based on Circular economy principles could result in benefits of ₹4.9 lakh crore annually in 2050, at the same time not harming the environment. (ICAR 2011)

World Bank (2013) states that the pressure on the system has been increasing due to growing population, food demands and various environmental challenges. A system based on Circular Economy can not only improve the Indian food system but would also create "benefits of ₹3.9 lakh crore annually in 2050".

One of the major aspects of economic growth is mobility as it enables individuals to access goods-services and employment thereby increasing business productivity. As per K. Button (2009) a development framework based on Circular economy for mobility and manufacturing of vehicle could generate benefits of ₹31 lakh crore annually by 2050. Circular economy principles can very well help in development of innovative, environment friendly and efficient mobility system.

A circular economy would open new areas of business services, like "reverse logistics, remarketing, remanufacturing, and refurbishment". Circular economy would provide such services which would keep the consumer satisfied and engaged. Ellen MacArthur Foundation (2012) has discussed assured profit avenues, for example, through food-waste processing and repair of vehicle, remanufacture have been identified. Circular economy can go long way in promoting Government policies like Digital India and Make in India, etc.

Such an economy has turned out to be fruitful at other places as well, for example Circular Economy has helped EU substantial annual net material cost savings. In a country like India where largest population is that of middle-class material-intensive consumption is likely to increase at much greater rate. Since circular economy focus more on complete or exhaustive use of product ("looping of products, components, and materials") it is more likely to generate greater revenue. Although certain sectors like material extraction industry would face reduction in activities but, overall there will be boast in economy.

Circular economy would result in reduction of GHC emission in all the three focus areas identified above. Such a system would lead to reduced consumption of "virgin, non-renewable materials of 25% in 2030 and 38% in 2050", since for example in construction industry Circular Economy would replace brick, steel etc. which are concrete, non-renewable material with renewable material like plastic waste. (ICAR 2015) Similarly, food industry will also be enhanced by implementation of circular economy as such a system would promote land productivity, nutrients etc. and reduce waste production. It would also lead to reduced inner-city pollution as zero-emission vehicles and regenerative farming techniques will be used which would also reduce the health issues associated to pollution considerably.

SUSTAINABLE CONSUMPTION BEHAVIOR IN INDIA

The Concept of circular economy was introduced to the world in 1970 however its existence in India predates that. Although Circular Economy as an economic system or developmental framework was never formally introduced by the Government as policy or rule but the same was inherent in the "common man's" household culture.

There is various day to day activities of middle-class Indian households which fit well within the concept of circular economy. For example, it was a common practice to give away old clothes in exchange of new utensils. This practice ensured, that no waste would be generated and in fact, the clothes which otherwise would have been thrown away, would get refurnished and sold at a lesser price. Another example would be that of paper waste. All the newspapers or used pages were collected and given away for a fixed price per kilogram to the ragman. A very common day to day habit of our ancestors was to carry jute bags while going for shopping. This reduced the necessity of taking multiple plastic bags for carrying each item bought. Similarly, earlier, various food commodities were not sold in a packed form and one was supposed to carry his own bag or utensil to carry it back, for example, milk and milk products. Similarly, Cold drink bottles were made of glass and one was supposed to return it to the shop after consuming it for reuse. There was an understanding that durability of plastic was valuable and plastic was used judiciously and almost all households did not dispose of even single use plastic bags and instead reused it multiple times not only as carry bags but also to waterproof household items including notebooks.

Through the means of an online questionnaire, the authors have evaluated the sustainable consumption behavior practiced by individuals. The questionnaire was responded to by 300 respondents aged 18-75 years, living in various cities of India. Out of these 222 respondents (74%) of the respondents were under the age of 37 years, thereby disproportionately representing the urban youth due to the questionnaire being administered in English and through online means only. The questionnaire had questions related to various areas of sustainable consumption in everyday life such as those related to water consumption, paper and plastic consumption, electricity usage, sustainable travel consumption behavior, food consumption and waste as well as attitude towards importance of sustainable consumption. Responses in each of these areas are analyzed and discussed below.

As regards the attitude to sustainable consumption behavior, the majority of respondents have a positive attitude towards sustainable consumption behavior as also its importance. It is evident from the Figure 1 that 92% of the respondents believe that the role played by individual consumption behavior impacts the total green-house emissions of India. 86% respondents take positive steps to reduce their individual greenhouse gas emissions and almost all (99%) respondents reported that they would make

Figure 1. Attitude to Sustainable Consumption Behavior

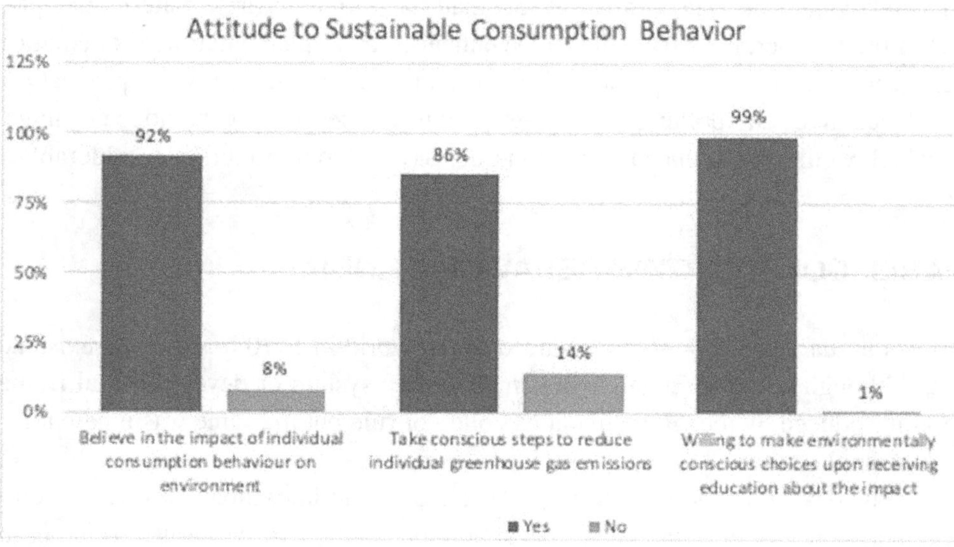

an extra effort to make environmentally conscious choices if they are educated about the impact of their choices. It is therefore clear that majority of urban Indians are happy to adopt sustainable consumption behaviors consistent with a circular economy.

As regards the attitude to sustainable travel consumption behavior, again, majority of the respondents show positive travel consumption behavior. As is evident from Figure 2, more than 80% respondents try to reduce their greenhouse gas emissions by walking, cycling, car-pooling, etc. whenever possible, avoid cars for short journeys and try to limit speeding. More than 67% try to reduce the number of flights taken by them whenever possible.

Figure 2. Sustainable Travel Consumption Behavior

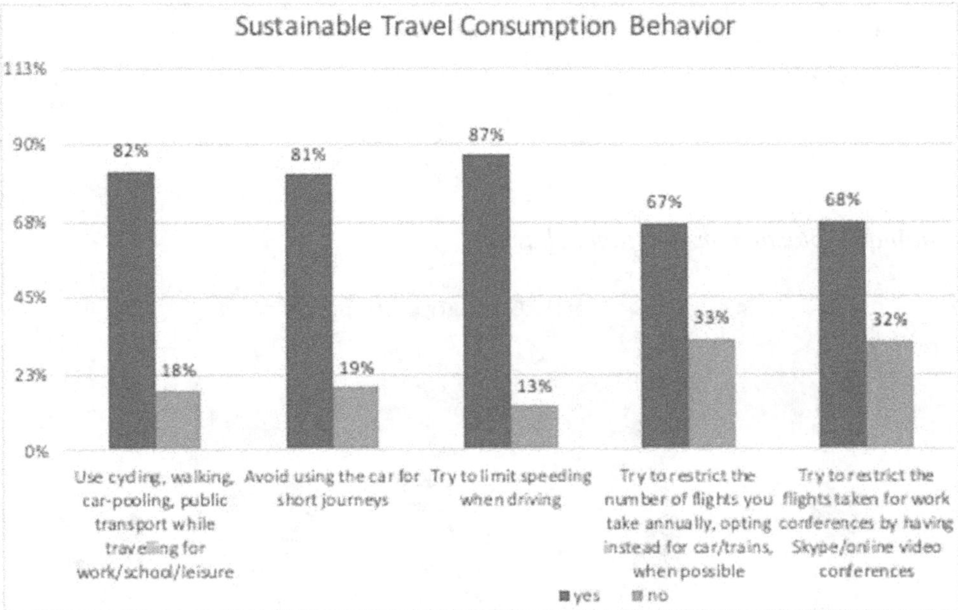

As regards to adoption of sustainable electricity consumption behavior also majority of respondents (more than 88%) practice sustainable behavior including by limiting air conditioner use and using energy efficient air conditioners. An over whelming majority of respondents use energy saving light bulbs, and switch off their lights, fans and geysers when not in use (more than 95%).

As regards sustainable plastic consumption behavior, as is evident from Figure 4, more than 80% of the respondents carry their own reusable bags and reusable water bottles while travelling/shopping. However, only 44% have boycotted single use plastic and only 40% practice plastic recycling. Therefore, there is a need to improve plastic consumption behavior in India. Further, it can be seen that government intervention through ban on single use plastic will be fruitful in this regard. Further still, initiatives for promotion of and facilities for households to recycle plastic are also expected to improve plastic consumption behavior as currently there is lack of awareness regarding how to recycle plastics.

As regards sustainable paper consumption behavior as is evident from Figure 5 more than 80% respondents practice sustainable behavior including reducing paper use and waste, including in packaging, as well as reusing paper. However, only 56% respondents recycle newspapers at home. It is clear that

Figure 3. Sustainable electricity consumption behavior

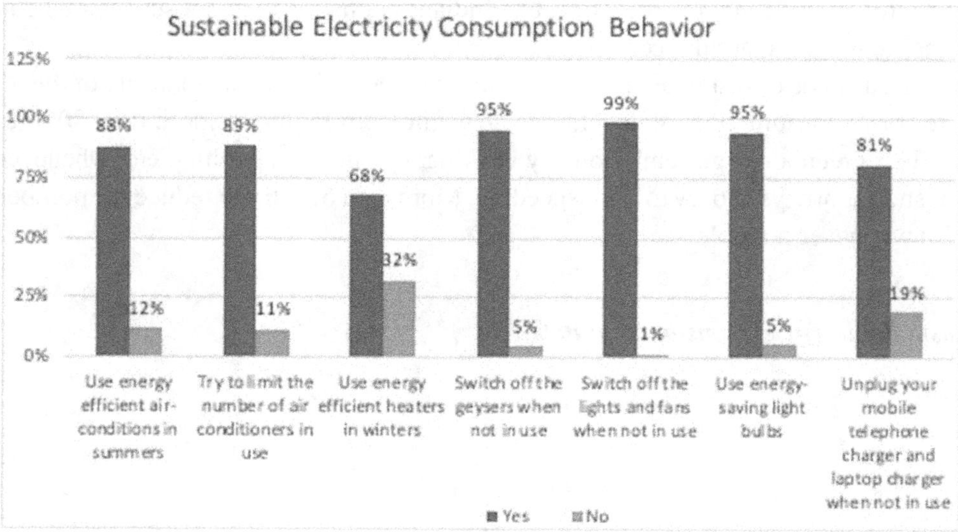

Figure 4. Sustainable plastic consumption behavior

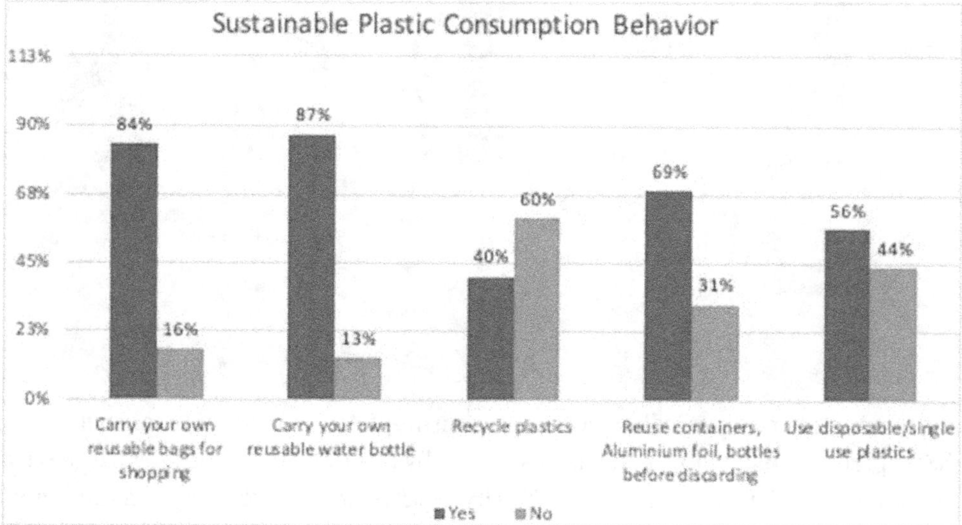

urban Indians need to be educated to adopt recycling behavior. Government initiatives relating to the same would be useful.

As regards sustainable water conservation behavior, as compared to other areas, there is less adoption of positive consumption behaviors. It can be observed from Figure 6 that less than 55% respondents conserve and reuse household water and/ or have installed a low water volume/dual flush toilet in their house to save water. Further, 77% respondents do not harvest rainwater also. More positive behavior however is shown regarding water use for brushing, bathing and washing utensils and clothes with more than 67% adopting positive behavior in each area.

Figure 5. Sustainable paper consumption behavior

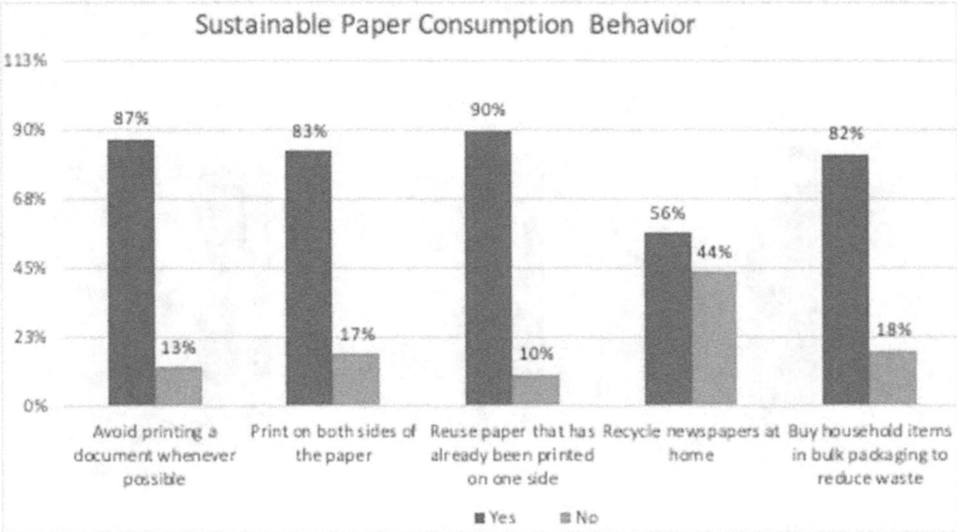

As regards sustainable food consumption behavior, as is evident from Figure 7 an overwhelming majority of respondents have adopted positive sustainable consumption behavior, with more than 95% respondents making a conscious effort not to waste food and eat local and seasonal produce.

Figure 6. Sustainable water conservation behavior

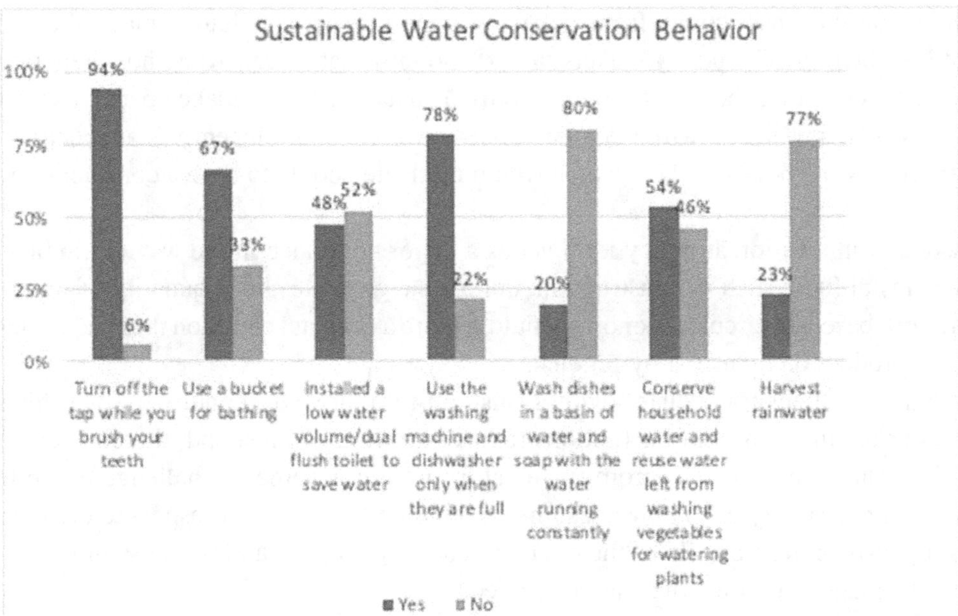

Figure 7. Sustainable food consumption behavior

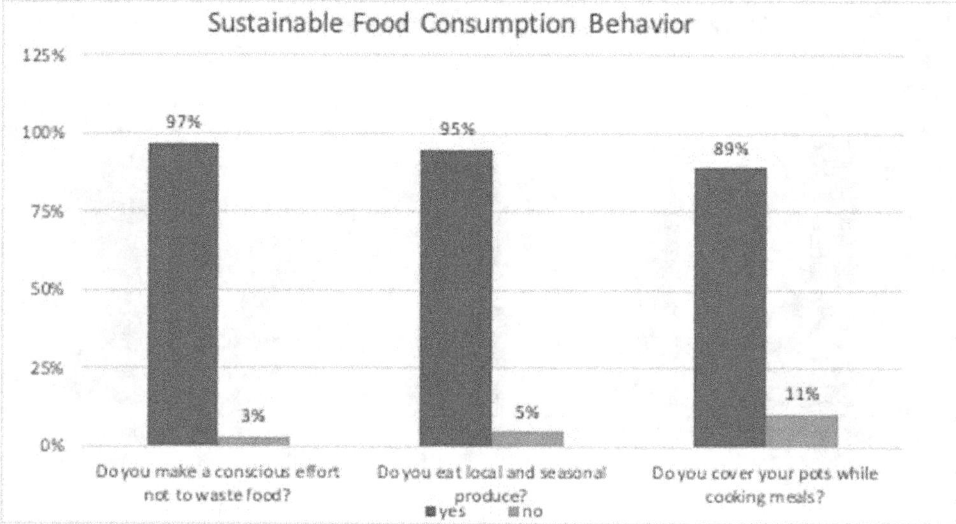

CHALLENGES IN ADOPTION OF CIRCULAR ECONOMY IN INDIA

It is safe to say that everyday lifestyle of a poor or middle class man in India has various facets of circular economy. From repairing an old bicycle for next generation to re using cookies plastic or tin boxes in kitchen, the regular Indian household has natural tilt towards the 3R's. However, this tilt does not emerges from an environmentally conscious mind rather, it is more of an habit which has come down through generations and there lies the problem. Proper implementation of Circular economy requires more systematic approach for example one of the major challenge is waste Segregation at source in the value chain, one may often finds C&D waste mixed with Municipal waste, which makes the work much more tedious and expensive.

This lack of consciousness comes from lack of awareness, people are hardly made about the circular economy and it's benefit. The policy makers provide no information regarding how beneficial circular economy can be, not just for the country but for individual as well. They make no active efforts to bring about policies which are in sink with Circular economy, there are no incentives attached to the use of circular economy by the policy makers which would motivate people to have a conscious shift towards the same.

The absence of innovation at policy level act as a major hindrance in the way of circular economy. Various activities in India such as construction, mining etc generates huge quantity of waste. A proper policy framework based on circular economy would require a constant check on these activities to ensure minimal waste production by use of by-products.

Another major challenge associated with Transition to a circular economy is that this shift from linear to circular requires financial institutions to also innovate and respond, thereby act as a catalyst facilitating this transition. This help from financial institution becomes a challenge in the light of the fact that there is no certainty as to how consumers are going to react with respect to circular products. Given the unique risk-return profile of the circular economy projects and business models, there is no one-size-fits-all financial product that can be availed.

SOLUTIONS AND RECOMMENDATIONS

The material consumption per capita in India has a slow growth as compared to other growing economies like China (CISRO 2013). In 2009 the consumption rate in India was "7% of all the materials used in the world, despite having around 14% of the world's population" (IGEP 2013). Indian consumers practice sustainable consumption habits in all areas of their daily life as a result of being a traditionally frugal society. The consumption behavior patterns seen from the data discussed in this chapter also support this view and therefore, it would be much easier to have an economic system based on circular economy model in India. The practices of the majority of Indians are in sync with this system. It is the Government of India, which needs to provide an effective mechanism to ensure systematic application of circular economy in their national life. People in India already practice - use, repair, reuse in their day to day consumption, however it is at the stage of recycle that the Government intervention is essential. For example, an individual buys an electronic item, he uses it, then gets it repaired whenever required, again reuses it and finally either throws it away or as is common in most middle-class households, gives it to the ragman. In such a case if the government doesn't provide any mechanism for recycling, it would result in an increase in waste. An effective system from the Government's end would go a long way in making India a model for circular economy.

Circular economy will give space for new innovative ideas for growth of businesses leading to exploration of new arenas of work and with cost effective investment, greater returns will be ensured and in order to build a circular economy knowledge and capacity and to avail its many advantages, it is important that the same people who are associated with decision making should also have an in depth understanding of this concept and its varied aspects. Therefore, there is a need for special training and practice for all employees in all government as well as private organizations. Innovation in any field plays a big role in the creation of new products and business models which provide a demonstrable success. A circular economy provides a wide horizon for innovation competitiveness and technology. This would give equal opportunity to both the start-ups as well as established businesses to come up with new ideas and make India an attractive outlet for entrepreneurship.

With regard to the waste industry, there is tremendous potential for growth. If waste segregation at source is resorted to, this waste can be reduced to a substantial amount as then it will be of major use. Wet and dry waste once segregated make it easier to be reused. This segregation should start from the primary level, i.e. from the household waste. This felt was strongly felt by citizens in Bengaluru. A PIL was filed in the High Court of Karnataka, asking for better waste management. The High Court had ruled that the bulk generators of wastes like householding, hospitals, households, etc. have to segregate their waste and this waste could be directly handed over to private contractors. This was a big step and led a far better waste management system in Bengaluru. Same policy needs to be implemented in whole the country because right now only 20% of the waste is being managed.

Once the waste is segregated into wet and dry waste, dry waste can then further be segregated. For this purpose, many dry-waste centers are using technology. There are also start-ups like Carbon Masters which use the wet waste to generate biogas or compost. This segregated wet waste is provided by companies like Saahas. Carbon Masters also provides for what can termed as 'green transportation', biogas cylinders on which vehicles, even trucks can run. If the dry waste is seen in three divisions, the first is Paper waste and PET Bottles which can be very well utilized in Paper industry and textiles industry respectively. The second category consisting of plastic which can be converted into granules and be converted into switches, pipes etc. Third is the very low-quality of plastic which can be mixed in the bitumen to lay roads.

If the waste management industry is properly built up, it will also generate employment. The people will also be working in better environments and direct contact with waste will also be lessen. There are also managers, marketers and trainers. The administration and supporting staff like watchmen will also be employed. Therefore, if this industry is allowed to thrive it will result in a lot of employment generation. If waste is managed properly, it will be a major push in the direction of circular economy. The people who are already working as rag pickers will get a more dignified job and better working situations. Given the large amount of municipal waste India generates, it will be able to provide a substantially large amount of jobs geared towards the betterment of the environment and thereby improve the working conditions of thousands of people. It is therefore time that India starts 'managing' waste than 'dumping' it.

Recycling initiatives must also be emphasized, and the population made aware regarding the potential and importance of recycling towards adoption of a sustainable economy.

FUTURE RESEARCH DIRECTION

The need for adoption of circular economy cannot be overemphasized in area of mitigation of climate change as demand for resources is a key driver of greenhouse gas emissions that lead to climate change. The role played by sustainable individual consumer behavior for the reducing overall greenhouse gas emission is also substantially important for the same reason. The individual sustainable consumption behavior can lead to adoption of sustainable business model by companies and as a result reduce the overall greenhouse gas emission associated with production processes. It is therefore necessary to study the linkage between sustainable consumption behavior in development of s businesses consistent with circular economy model and research can be conducted in this area.

Further the present study focuses on young urban Indian population therefore research opportunity exists for evaluating the kind of Individual Consumption habits and behavior adopted in rural economy as well as the scope for adoption of circular economy in rural area for reducing overall greenhouse gas emissions. Further still, one important area of research relates to adoption of circular economy within waste management especially in the context of plastic and food waste management in India.

CONCLUSION

With the average per capita consumption increasing annually at exponential rates, the problem of over consumption and unsustainable consumption behaviors has reached alarming proportions. It is clear that these consumption patterns both emerge from and fuel the linear economy. Any shift from a linear economy to a circular economy is therefore contingent on the change to more sustainable individual consumption patterns. Majority of urban Indians already practice sustainable consumption behaviors consistent with a circular economy. However, it is pertinent that the Government also develops a comprehensive policy at the central, state and grassroots levels to support the shift to completely circular economy. To be able to achieve this goal, it would have to, set a clear direction and show its commitment on a regular basis by creating platforms for collaboration among all stakeholders for creation of a proper enabling regulatory framework. Any policy barriers that are encountered would also have to be done away with.

The Government would also have to support the circular model through public procurement and developing proper infrastructure as well as by creating awareness about circular economy. The corporate sector also needs to take a lead in adopting sustainable production methods. In pursuit of the same developed countries must assist developing countries by sharing technologies for capacity building for transition to sustainable patterns of consumption and production. Other stakeholders, such as higher educational institutions, NGO's and international organisations, must also extend a hand to all corporates and governments for adoption of a circular economy especially through awareness campaigns to help in disseminating information among individuals about the Circular economy and the importance of sustainable consumption behavior.

REFERENCES

Akenji, L. (2014). Consumer scapegoatism and limits to green consumerism. *Journal of Cleaner Production*, *63*, 13–23.

Ayog. (n.d.). *Strategy for Secondary Materials Management for promoting Resource Efficiency (RE) and Circular Economy (CE) in Electrical and Electronic Equipment Sector.* Ministry of Communication & Information Technology.

Button, K. (2009). Social change and demand for mobility. *Transportation Engineering and Planning*, *II*, 13–35.

Commonwealth Scientific and Industrial Research Organisation (CSIRO). (2013). *Recent trends in material flows and resource productivity in Asia and the Pacific, UNEP*. Retrieved from http://hdl.handle.net/20.500.11822/9318

Circle Economy (2019). *The Circularity Gap Report: Closing the Circularity Gap in a 9% World.* The Platform for Accelerating the Circular Economy (PACE).

Ellen MacArthur Foundation. (2012). Economic and business rationale for an accelerated transition. *Towards the Circular Economy*, I.

Ellen MacArthur Foundation. (2016). *Circular Economy in India: Rethinking growth for long-term prosperity.* Retrieved from https://www.ellenmacarthurfoundation.org/publications/

Ellen MacArthur Foundation. (2019). *Completing the Picture: How the Circular Economy Tackles Climate. Material Economics*. III.

Environmental Information System CPCB. (n.d.) *National Air Quality Monitoring Programme.* Ministry of Environment, Forests & Climate Change. Retrieved from http://cpcbenvis.nic.in/airpollution/finding.htm

European Commission. (2019). *Closing the loop: Commission delivers on Circular Economy Action Plan, Press Release 4th March 2019.* Retrieved from https://ec.europa.eu/commission/presscorner/detail/en/IP_19_1480

Geels, F., McMeekin, A., Mylan, J., & Southerton, D. (2015). A critical appraisal of Sustainable Consumption and Production Research: The reformist, revolutionary and reconfiguration positions. *Global Environmental Change*, *34*, 1–12.

International Cooperation Division. (2019). *Office Memorandum F.No. 3(4)/5/2019-IC-II(pt.1)*. Delhi: Ministry of Environment, Forest & Climate Change.

Jessica, K. (2018). *Individual Sustainable Consumption and the Circular Economy: Research challenges and Opportunities*. Retrieved from https://www.schumacherinstitute.org.uk/download/pubs/res/201810-Individual-Sustainable-Consumption-and-the-Circular-Economy-Research-Gaps-and-Opportunities-Jessica-Klaver.pdf

Juana, O. C., Casper, B., & Ida, P. N. (2018). Consumption in the Circular Economy: A Literature Review. *Sustainability*, *10*, 2758.

McDonald, S., Oates, C. J., Alevizou, P. J., Young, C. W., & Hwang, K. (2012). Individual strategies for sustainable consumption. *Journal of Marketing Management*, *28*, 3–4, 445–468.

Meadows, D. H. (1972). *The Limits to growth; a report for the Club of Rome's project on the predicament of mankind*. Universe Books.

Merli, R. (2018). How do scholars approach the circular economy? A systematic literature review. *Journal of Cleaner Production, 178*, 703-722.

Nitish, A., Souvik, B., Avishek, G., Pallavi, G., Chandan, B., Arnesh, S., & Himanshu, S. (2018) Report on *Circular Economy: A Business Imperative for India*. Retrieved from https://wsds.teriin.org/2018/files/teri-yesbank-circular-economy-report.pdf

Ricke, K. L. D. (2018). Country-level social cost of carbon. *Nature Climate Change*, *10*(8), 895–900. doi:10.103841558-018-0282-y

Sahaas. (n.d.). *Alag Karo, Har Din Teen Bin, 2020*. Retrieved from https://saahas.org/our-work/programs/sensitization-and-behavioral-change/alag-karo,-har-din-teen-bin

Salvatori, G., Holstein, F., Böhme, K., Wills, T., & Hans, S. (2019). *Circular economy strategies and roadmaps in Europe Identifying synergies and the potential for cooperation and alliance building*. The European Economic and Social Committee (EESC). Retrieved from https://mail.google.com/mail/u/0/#inbox/FMfcgxwGDNWQqjxBjKqBcspNKTnvvqjr?projector=1&messagePartId=0.1

Schor, J. (2005). Prices and quantities: Unsustainable consumption and the global economy. *Ecological Economics*, *55*, 309–320.

The Commission to the European Parliament, The Council, The European Economic And Social Committee And The Committee Of The Regions. (2019). *Report on the implementation of the Circular Economy Action Plan*. European Commission.

The Indo-German Environment Partnership programme. (2013). *India's Future Needs for Resources*. Retrieved from http://www.hrdpnetwork.com/live/hrdpmp/hrdpmaster/igep/content/e48745/e50194/e58089/ResourceEfficiency_Report_Final.pdf

Warde, A. (2005). Consumption and Theories of Practice. *Journal of Consumer Culture*, *5*(2), 131–153.

WBCSD & IEA. (2013). *Technology Roadmap: Low-Carbon Technology for the Indian Cement Industry*. World Business Council on Sustainable Development and International Energy Agency.

World Bank. (2013). *Turn Down the Heat: Climate Extremes, Regional Impacts, and the Case for Resilience, A report for the World Bank by Potsdam Institute for Climate Impact Research and Climate Analytics*. World Bank.

World Economic Forum. (2018). *Circular Economy in Cities Evolving the model for a sustainable urban future*. Retrieved from http://www3.weforum.org/docs/White_paper_Circular_Economy_in_Cities_report_2018.pdf

ADDITIONAL READING

Ackerman, F. (2000). Waste management and climate change. *Local Environment*, *5*, 223–229. https://pdfs.semanticscholar.org/313c/b8d850e66d725bee1b7e924586595760835f.pdf

Bohringer, C. (2007). Measuring the immeasurable: A survey of sustainability indices. *Ecological Economics*, *63*, 1–8.

Ellen MacArthur Foundation (2013). Opportunities for the consumer goods sector. *Towards the Circular Economy*, II.

Münzel, T. (2014). Cardiovascular, Effects of Environmental Noise Exposure. *European Heart Journal*, 829–836.

NRDC-ASCI. (2012). *Constructing Change*. Retrieved from http://www.indiaenvironmentportal.org.in/files/file/Constructing%20Change.pdf

Serenella, S., Biagio, C., & Peter, N. (2015). A systemic framework for sustainability assessment. *Ecological Economics*, *119*, 314–325.

United Nations Environment Programme. (2018) *Single Use Plastics: A Roadmap for Sustainability*. Retrieved from https://wedocs.unep.org/bitstream/handle/20.500.11822/25496/singleUsePlastic_sustainability.pdf?sequence=1&isAllowed=y

KEY TERMS AND DEFINITIONS

Circular Economy: A system in which emphasis is supplied to the exhaustive use of the product which means that a product is not simply thrown away after its use rather the same should be repaired and put to reuse and one's it becomes completely nonfunctional the parts of same should be sent for recycle thereby generating minimum waste, and making the product more cost effective.

Climate Change: Rising of Earth's average temperature due to human activities, especially burning of fossil-fuels which in turn results in changing climate pattern.

Degrowth: An unconventional, environment-friendly concept that does not adhere to the general notion of development, which is synonymous with abundant production, consumption and high-greenhouse-gas-emitting living. It suggests reasonable reduction in production and consumption that does not mean stagnation, but sustainable growth with respect to natural resources so as to meet the requirement and cut down the surplus.

Green Consumerism: Consumer behavior under which the consumer purchases a product which is more environment friendly than the alternatives and is least harmful to the environment.

Linear Economy: A system which extracts a resource, make a product and then sell it. In the process whatever non-required is produced and also the final product at the end of its shell life is disposed of as waste, disregarding the concept of reuse or recycle.

Sustainable Consumption Behavior: Human behavior in which an individual use the goods resources and services in a reasonable amount so as to meet the basic requirement of quality life. Such behavior stands for reducing the use of natural resources, and products which are not environment friendly so as to ensure better quality for future generations.

Sustainable Development: Economic development which does not take place at the expense of environment. It is a development which meets the requirement of present generation without reducing the opportunities for future generation to come thus balancing economic growth and that satisfies the needs of the present without compromising the capacity of future generations, guaranteeing the balance between economic growth, and environment protection

Sustainable Development Goals (SDGs): A set of 17 goals which United Nations General Assembly has outlined in 2015 in order to achieve end of poverty, protection of planet and promotion of peace by 2030.

Chapter 4
Circular Economy:
A Critical Understanding of Anti-Waste Politics

Dipanwita Jena
University of Delhi, India

ABSTRACT

The ongoing discourse of zero-waste and the circular economy in recent time have been underscored by key players, such as the European Commission, NGOs, INGOs, academia, and multinational companies. The discourse revolves around the fact that capitalist form of development has pushed the environment to the brink of destruction. The need of the hour is sustainable growth through the model of the circular economy. Thus, the idea of growth is being de-politicized by a post-growth narrative. This chapter wants to delve into the critical aspect of circular economy which propounds itself as a solution to capitalism driven growth. The first theme it addresses the actual materialization of circular economy whether it is actually a possible phenomenon or not. The second theme it deals with the concept of social sustainability and fulfillment of human wants. The last theme revolves around ideological dimension of post-growth, how the circular growth in the garb of post-growth ideology propels and legitimizes a more growth -driven society.

Circular Economy: A Critical Understanding of Anti-waste Politics

The idea of a perpetual growth economy is the product of modern capitalist system. The notion of a perpetual growth is there both in the tenets of economic thought as well as in economic institution[1]. This idea of continual growth has been subjected to a lot of criticism both within the economic theory[2] as well as in the environmental sciences[3]. Against this scenario, there have been a will among the policymakers, academicians and Non-governmental Organizations (NGOs) for the sustainable economy beyond growth[4]. The negative fallout of the growth is not new; it has been well highlighted by many[5].

DOI: 10.4018/978-1-7998-4990-2.ch004

There has been a shift of interests for looking into the alternatives of the current way of organizing of our society. Nevertheless, to criticize the past and imagining an alternative future are not two separated intellectual activity- rather it is intertwined. Critique and creativity goes together- only through critical engagement with the present we can think of a different future. In this context, critical and creative thinking should try to look into the relationship between growth and sustainability and try to go beyond a commonsensical idea.

Imaginations of alternatives and critiques are still negligible[6]. In a broader academia, post-growth and de-growth have not been paid attention in management, organization and entrepreneurship studies. The scholars of post-growth and de-growth studies asserts that we need to problematize the nature of ever-growing growth. And there is a need to reclaim and re-politicize discourses, theory, and practices around sustainability and post-growth. Some have suggested research in alternative economic organizations that is not based on perpetual growth model[7].

Adjusting Sustainability- In the World of Business.

The United Nations(U.N.) held a conference in Stockholm in 1972 on the Human Environment, which laid emphasis on the problems associated with climate change and its harmful effect on environmental degradation. During the same year, an international think tank, the Club of Rome, came out with a Report called The Limits of Growth, which called into questions of environmental problems related to perpetual growth economy which included depletion of natural resources and relentless pollution of the ecosystem. The report focused that the ' Earth is finite' with only a limited quantity of natural resources, an underlying fundamental fact that creates pertinent constraints on the overall economic growth and the ecosystem cam bear. Taking into account the speed of economic development that shaped industrial development-and the related accelerated consumption of natural resources- the authors of the report stated that we would reach the threshold point within a period of 100 years. This would lead to 'in a sudden and uncontrollable decline in population and industrial capacity'[8]

With the increased focus on climate change and environmental degradation, the United Nations promoted the publication of a report which is called *Our common future* in 1987. The report was spearheaded by the Commission on Environment and Development (WCED), guided by the former Norwegian Prime Minister Gro Harlem Brundtland. The report brought into focus for the first time about the concept of sustainable development[9], defining as 'development that meets the needs of the present without compromising the ability of future generations to meet their own needs'[10]. This focal point on reconciling economic growth with the ecological balance has remained in focus in more current endeavor to rethink sustainable developments[11]. During the 1990s the idea of sustainable development entered into the management and organization discourse[12]. Nevertheless, the concept of sustainable development remained 'fuzzy, elusive, contestable'[13].

Current Trend in Circular Economy and Sustainability

Popularity of circular economy is wide, cutting across policy makers, corporations and environmental groups. This idea of circular economy necessitates a fixed set of practices for transitioning towards a sustainable ecosystem. Some examples include reuse of organic waste, product design to churn out from waste; integrated heat infrastructure in industrial as well as residential designs; repair cafes in urban locality; or digital sharing platforms[14]. Circular economy evokes an inspiring and revolutionary concept;

it is defined mostly in opposition to the 'linear economy', which is based on a 'make-use-dispose' pattern of thinking. Environmental economists lay stress that a circular economy offers us a road to a post growth/consumerist society, in which material demand are retrieved from the existing sources[15].

The idea of circularity has found much wider acceptance in national and local governments in all over Europe. Thus, the concept of circularity has started to be materialized in development policies combining urban development, reorganization of utilities, and energy-policies undertaken in city-regions. Examples- *Be Circular* Brussels redevelopment plan; *Copenhagen Model* for circular bio-waste streams; *Paris Circular Economy Plan* for valorizing waste; the Dutch Plan *Netherlands Circular 2050*, among other things Circularity is the main idea propelling urban development projects integrating waste, heat and energy networks such as Tampere's Eco3Business park, London's old Oak and Park's royal and Gent's old Dockyard[16] .

Despite its popularity in city-regional governance, the proponents on the circular economy is concerned mostly with its instrumental aspects or in other words the micro-aspects of sharing, living and reusing of waste among households. As Hobson and Lynch asserts 'frameworks for, and examination of, the circular economy have arguably remained all silent about its broader socio-economic horizons, mostly on how a circular economy might look like'[17]. The more optimistic among them have argued that circular economy promotes social reciprocity, sustainable consumerism, sharing of product and eco-manufacturing[18]. The others eulogize the concept for its potential to address the resource scarcity, waste and ecosystem services[19]. But the critique of circular economy defines it as 'the latest and the most sophisticated version of the 'sustainable' fetishized commodity[20]. Finally, some others discard circularity as a 'bundle of ideas' that transforms the existing idea into a newer morality of ecologically-driven economic consumption[21].

This chapter will take into account a critical dimension of circular-economy which propounds itself as a solution to capitalism-driven growth. The first, theme would look into account the possibility of actual materialization of circular –economy. Whether it is actually a possible phenomenon or not? The second theme, will deal with concept of social sustainability and fulfillment of human wants. Though circular economy speaks of sustainability mostly from an economic vantage point, it hardly addresses the issue of social sustainability. The last theme would revolve around ideological dimension of circular –growth. How the circular-growth in the garb of post-growth ideology propels and legitimizes a more growth –driven system.

The concept of Achievability and Feasibility

One of the pertinent challenges faced by the circular economy framework is related to the achievability of the idea. At the core of the concept, is the idea of minimizing waste. In certain sectors, such as manufactured goods the implementation of the idea can be possible globally and the materials can be used and reused before dismantling them completely. However, with respect to other sectors, the existing limitations might make it impossible to close the loop indefinitely; for instance, paper re-cycling is limited to a certain number of cycles. Also, certain particular hazardous waste such as mercury or asbestos might also reach a dead end and cannot be recycled further and had to be contained off the cycle. As per the second law of thermodynamics states "all spontaneous processes irreversibly disperse energy (and as a consequence, matter) into ever more chaotic" which ends in loss of quantity and quality of substances and idea of complete closure of loops hardly achievable[22]. In current recycling process, the impurities can be removed up to a certain limit. These shortcomings are well perceived by legislators; the European

Commission for example, in its first endeavor to frame a Circular Economy, framed long term recycling goals up to 70%, the remaining 30% being considered as non-recyclable entities.

Beyond the question of achievability is the idea of feasibility for business. In the current scenario, trying to achieve 100% recyclability might prove counter-productive, if for instance the price of recovered material being higher than the value of the material obtained. Further, lack of incentives in the regulatory framework makes it a less desirable pursuit. The certain aspiration for circular economy objectives i.e. usage of 100% renewable energy, may stand in opposition with other tenets related to resource efficiency. For example, in using present day technologies – the amplification of solar energy uses more scant resources. *"Without effective usage of produced energy, [it] might also further increase the resource scarcity"*[23]

So the question arises that is a fully circular economy really achievable? Very likely not. Does it mean it is not worth pursuing for? Answer is not at all. We have a very long path to go before we come up against the limitations of what is achievable, and we can surely make enormous economic and environmental gains on the journey. However, there will be numerous instances when trying to achieve to be circular can be counter-productive. Trying to go after every last minuscule of recycling in the waste conduit could be too exorbitant in relation to the value of the material to be recovered – you reach a certain point when the marginal cost of striving to recycle a bit more turns out to be prohibitive.

Prices are basically static and that the current permutations and combinations of taxation, incentives and regulation, which rule the economics, cannot be altered. However in practical terms, of course, government (in the broadest sense) can strive to make re-use more attractive, or disposal costs restrictive, or even completely shun some disposal routes altogether, and so try to move waste up in the hierarchy ladder or even out throw out of existence. It has been in practice now for quite a number of years: the recent waste market, and the current waste industry, has been designed mostly in response to regulation, from Europe. So if a minister is of the view that a circular economy is not achievable because the economics do not support it. Then one could retort that it is the economic and regulatory structure should be altered so that they really do hold up the apex of the waste hierarchy and the circular economy.

It is mostly believed that market forces will itself create its own circular economy with time, without the intervention of the government. That might be a possibility if demand for goods grows faster than the supply chain, pushing the prices of the raw materials up. Then relatively, it will be a force multiplier to look for secondary resources and alternative ways and pushing its way forward to circular economy. Nevertheless, all the discussions around resource scarcity, it would be still difficult to exactly foresee or predict how market forces will align itself to circular economy. It is a difficult task to evaluate the argument that to strive for a fully functional circular economy could lead to environmental dis-benefits, for instance excessive energy use, extra greenhouse gas emissions, or other kinds of pollution. As a more of a general rule and not axiom, recovering secondary raw materials are preferable over the use of primary raw materials for environment. Although this logic becomes more difficult in cases of renewable resources, for example wood. Thus, this idea of achievability of circular economy would merit further rigorous scientific investigation.

The Question of Social Sustainability: - The Unaddressed Element in the Cycle?

Circular economy is strongly rooted in the idea of eco-sustainability. The framework of circular economy remains silent about the social dimensions of sustainability (e.g. fulfillment of human wants). The principles are mainly from the vantage point of business that tries to strive equally for both environmental and economic benefits. Social benefits are often not addressed. Additional manufacturing processes in circular economy –e.g. restoring or recycling –requires more human labor than the normal manufacturing of things as these processes are not standardized[24]. Even if this has the potential of employment creations, it is not sure that jobs will be created locally- a vast centralized recycling facility created on a massive scale, might also be an outcome of the circular economy hence, would totally fall short in creating job opportunities locally[25]. Moreover, people's basic requirement at a global level still can be relegated to corner by abuses of power, unfair labor laws and living conditions or disregard for human rights. As such, in totality, the circular economy does not fulfill all the facets of sustainability. Also, in the current scenario, the circular economy framework does not give a clear picture for selection of actions or specific guidelines for implementation. Since, the implementation of circular differs for different products, drive for a general guideline becomes problematic. Also, engaging in a circular-economy framework might bring into surface some difficult trade-offs. Circular economy can tend to discard materials which are not fully recyclable.

The main drawback of the concept as it is currently being propagated is that it views the world through a purely instrumental lens while (ironically) completely relegating the economic part of the system. Recent research has probed whether closing material and product loops does in fact intercept primary production. The researchers concluded that "circular economy activities can increase overall production, which can partially or fully offset their benefits"[26]. This tells us that the circular economy has the well-reported rebound effect which is known from energy efficiency strategies. The current approach with which the circular economy is propagated creates the false impression that we can handle all our ecological problems with technical engineering approach. It is well clear that the strategy was created to make it lucrative for large global corporations to become partners and contribute to circular economy. It pledges growth for business — and this is exactly the main systemic flaw. Though technical or instrumental solutions can have a lower per-unit impact, overall the environmental benefits will be largely neutralized by economic growth.

One of the intellectual trailblazer of the circular economy, Walter Stahel, architect and economist came up with the idea of shifting the tax burden instead of taxing labor we have to tax non-renewable resources as a way of providing incentive and accelerating innovation to a circular economy and create jobs. Such a strategy could help mitigate the systemic flaws of the circular economy and can try to offer a way out to structural unemployment. But in this process it would make the idea quite unattractive for big corporations and is therefore not promoted by the advocators of the circular economy.

Civil society organizations who are putting an effort to identify and promote more systemic remedies to current social and ecological problems should particularly avoid falling into the narrative of supporting and promoting the circular economy as it is currently taking place. The environmental crises are also linked with the problems of migration, inequality and democracy. None of these crises can be sufficiently addressed in *cetris paribus*, but the circular economy does not take into account the exorbitant inequality inherent to financial capitalism or the fact that there is ongoing democratic erosion we are facing as a result of the market society that we have metamorphosed into.

A more in depth analysis of the economic system and of the main causes of global crises is therefore required. It would give us insight to different solutions, leverage points and strategies. An economic system looking towards the future has to find solutions to the dire problem of economic growth and current wasteful consumerism, also to the undemocratic power relations in the global economy. The circular economy can only come up as a positive concept to a new economic system if it is intertwined in a vision and discourse of a post-growth and post-neoliberal economy.

A much more insightful and in-depth critical engagement with the circular economy is urgently needed. The novel ideas behind the circular economy are without an iota of doubt important blocks of the Great Transition, but the concept is constantly being advocated in isolation as a comprehensive framework for a new economy — which surely it isn't.

Civil society organizations that are keen to change the system should be cautious of magic win-win formulas to mitigate our global crises. Instead, confrontation with the deeper problems is required which can't be fixed with technical quick fix. Undoubtedly, the novel ideas of circular economy will only show results if its deeply integrated with other strategies and with the economic systems.

Circular Economy: Is it Really Post Growth?

The ideological drive of circular economy lies in the idea of post-growth. Post –growth politics aims to rupture the power relations and also shows the futility of the debate of the cultural ideology of capitalist expansion[27]. This also means that rejecting the fact that capitalism blooms upon the promise of ever-developing, secular cosmopolitan geographies, while relegating an over-exploited, 'necropolitan' space into a corner where agonizing people live, "The same causes which develop the expansive power of capital, also develop the labor-power at its disposal. The relative mass of the industrial reserve army thus increases with the potential energy of wealth. But the greater this reserve army in proportion to the active labor-army, the greater is the mass of a consolidated surplus population, whose misery is in inverse ratio to the amount of torture it has to undergo in the form of labor. The more extensive, finally, the pauperized sections of the working class and the industrial reserve army, the greater is official pauperism. This is the absolute general law of capitalist accumulation (Marx 1990 [1976]:798, emphasis in original)"[28]. This will remain a domain of political struggle. Yet, the utmost problematic is not among the inconsistencies between the narratives of post-growth, trying to provide an alternative to capitalism, as some authors have posited[29]. The actual problem seems to be appears in the picturisque grip that narratives and cultural elements demanding on capitalist growth have increasingly shown over working and consuming subjects, halting their identification with an active and critical political stance[30].

Ideals of growth project have been always perceived as the 'safe haven' during economic crises. They have also permeated and absorbed representations that stand otherwise, admitting the premise of permanent growth and celebrating it as a sort of Fukuyamean 'end of history' for socio-economic governance, psycho-social development[31]. Such de-politicization stance has been mainly advocated by the discourse of 'sustainability'. Once a radical denouncer of the un-sustainability of capitalism[32], the notion of 'sustainable growth' now encourages more of the same rather than departing from the economic growth of model[33]. Sustainability is well accepted when it is turned into the fetishized content of the so-called 'ethical' and 'green' products. And thus, essentializing part of the narrative (and practice) through which capitalist economy legitimizes itself.

The green-practices of the 'circular-certified' company Apple Inc. can be discussed here. Zero-waste practices can essentially divert our attention from the well-devised obsolescence that has gone into the building and producing and marketing of Apple products[34]. Apple brand proudly declares its achievements in complying with green practices and recycling standards of production. The public thus, turn oblivious to the competitive marketing design of the Apple, which seeks for the consumers to discard their old model as soon the new model is launched. This is so because the 'circular' as marketed by

Apple propels the consumer to conceive the purchase of Apple commodities as the ideal antidote to Apple's own wasteful logic.

Conclusion

Circular economy though has its merits, but it is not devoid of short-comings. The challenges to circular economy remain on various levels. Despite all these shortcomings, the principles carried out by the circular economy offer lots of hope. Firstly, it permits reconciling environmental preserving with business concerns, stating that value creation can still be possible within strong planetary boundaries. While taking inspiration by nature principles, the propagaters of circular economy have achieved to actualize the benefits of the circular economy into clear business goals (Lacy, 2014), making it much more nuanced than the idea of sustainable development, a notion which is tend to be often criticized for lacking a fine balance between environmental and economic goals. As the notion still bears shortcomings, it makes it a concept worth studying from an academic angle as well as in practical terms, in order to grasp how at the practical level, the notions and tenets of circular economy can be effective in the implementation of current business practices.

REFERENCES

Bechtel, R., Marans, R., & Michelson, W. (2013). *Methods in environmental and behavioral research.* Academic Press.

Berg, A., & Hukkinen, J. (2011). The paradox of growth critique: Narrative analysis of the Finnish sustainable consumption and production debate. *Ecological Economics, 72*, 151–160. doi:10.1016/j.ecolecon.2011.09.024

Binswanger, H. C. (2013). *Die Wachstumsspirale: Geld, Energie und Imagination in der Dynamik des Marktprozesses.* Metropolis-Verlag.

Bjorn, A., & Strandesen, M. (2011). Absolute versus Relative Environmental Sustainability: What can the Cradle-to-cradle and Eco –efficiency Concepts Learn from Each Other? *Journal of Industrial Ecology.*

Easterlin, R. A. (2005). Feeding the illusion of growth and happiness: A reply to Hagerty and Veenhoven. *Social Indicators Research, 74*(3), 429–443. doi:10.100711205-004-6170-z

Ellen Macarthur Foundation. (2013). *Towards the circular economy, economic and business rationale for accelerated transition.* Retrieved from https://www.ellenmacarthurfoundation.org/assets/downloads/publications/Ellen-MacArthur-Foundation-Towards-the-Circular-Economy-vol.1.pdf

Geissdoerfer, M., Savaget, P., Bocken, N. M. P., & Hultink, E. J. (2017). The circular economy: A new sustainability paradigm? *Journal of Cleaner Production, 143*, 757–768. doi:10.1016/j.jclepro.2016.12.048

Girardet, H. (2014). *Creating regenerative cities.* Routledge. doi:10.4324/9781315764375

Gregson, N., & Crang, M. (2015). From waste to resource: The trade in wastes and global recycling economies. *Annual Review of Environment and Resources, 40*(1), 151–176. doi:10.1146/annurev-environ-102014-021105

Heinberg, R. (2011). *The end of growth: Adapting to our new economic reality*. Clairview.

Herod, A., Pickren, G., Rainnie, A., & McGrath-Champ, S. (2013). '*Waste, commodity fetishism and the ongoingness of economic life'*. *Area*, *45*(3), 376–382. doi:10.1111/area.12022

Hobson, K. (2015). Closing the loop or squaring the circle? Locating generative spaces for the circular economy. *Progress in Human Geography*.

Hobson, K., & Lynch, N. (2016). *Diversifying and de-growing the circular economy: Radical social transformation in a resource-scarce world*. Academic Press.

McIntyre, M., & Nast, H. (2011). Bio(necro)polis: Marx, surplus populations, and the spatial dialectics of reproduction and "race". *Antipode*, *43*(5), 1465–1488. doi:10.1111/j.1467-8330.2011.00906.x

Meadows, D. H., Meadows, D. L., Randers, J., & Behrens, W. W. (1972). *The limits to growth*. Universe Books.

Reike, D., Vermeulen, W. J. V., & Witjes, S. (2017). (in press). The circular economy: New or Refurbished as CE 3.0? *Resources, Conservation and Recycling*.

Savini, F., & Dembski, S. (2016). Manufacturing the creative city: Symbols and politics of Amsterdam North. *Cities (London, England)*, *55*, 139–147. doi:10.1016/j.cities.2016.02.013

Sennett, R. (1999). Growth and failure: The new political economy and its culture. In M. Featherstone & S. Lash (Eds.), *Theory, culture and society: Spaces of culture: City, nation, world*. SAGE publications. doi:10.4135/9781446218723.n1

Stahel, W. R. (2010). *The Performance Economy* (2nd ed.). Palgrave Macmillan.

Stahel, W. R., & Reday-Mulvey, G. (1981). *Jobs for Tomorrow, the potential for substituting manpower for energy*. Vantage Press.

Valenzuela, F., & Böhm, S. (2017). Against wasted politics: A critique of the circular economy. *Ephemera*, *17*(1), 23–60.

Williams, J. (2019). Circular cities. *Urban Studies (Edinburgh, Scotland)*, *56*(13), 2746–2762. doi:10.1177/0042098018806133

ENDNOTES

1. Binswanger, H.C. (2013) *Money, Energy and Imagination in the Dynamics of the Market Process.* The central idea proposed by the author that conventional economics still believed in the idea of static equilibrium. But modern economics manifests itself in growth spiral. The two main drivers of growth spiral is, firstly, banking system for steady growth of money. Secondly, exploitation of natural resources for raw materials.
2. Richard Heinberg (2013), Herrera, R (2011) – main idea that policy makers, politicians try to make an economy on earth's limited budget rather than trying for ever unattainable GDP goals. These thinkers critiqued the ever-growing notion of growth economy.

3 Rockstrom, et al., 2009a; Rockstrom et al., 2009b)- In 2009, former centre director of Stockholm Resilience Centre Johan Rockström led a cohort of 28 internationally renowned scientists to study the nine processes that regulate the stability and resilience of the Earth system. Scientists proposed nine planetary boundaries within which humanity can strive, crossing these boundaries will led to disruptions.

4 Eisenstein, 2011; Gorz 1999;North, 2010; Paech, 2012.

5 The criticism against an idea of quantitative growth already had started. This de-growth movement sometimes is given credit to Rachel Carson. Her book The story of silent spring was advocated against technological growth especially against the usage of DDT and pesticides.

6 Wright et al 2013 *Future Imaginnings*- Though this article talks about climate change but it asks us to question the prevalent sanitized market oriented interpretations of growth. Then only we can imagine an alternative way of future.

7 D'Alisa et al., 2015; Bohm et al., 2015; Parker et al., 2014- advocates to focus mainly on waste which will be the resource of consumption and production further. They mainly focuses on the urban policies in Netherlands (Amsterdam) where the agenda of green growth is based on valorization of waste.

8 Meadows et al., 1972:23

9 Mebratu (1998) focuses that with the publication of *Our common future* has had enormous influence on the discourse of sustainability and the concept of sustainability has shaped our idea how we now perceive growth and environmental degradation.

10 WCED, 1987: 2,4.

11 Rockstrom et al., 2009a; Rockstrom et al., 2009b

12 Galdwin, T.N., J.J. Kennelly, and T.S. Krause (1995) –they claimed that modern management is based on fractured epistemology and there is a separation of humanity from nature. Reintegration is pertinent if organizational sciences is to support ecologically sustainable models.

13 Galdwin et al., 1995; 876

14 W.J.V. Vermmuellen, D. Reike and S. Witjes (2013): *Circular Economy 3.0: Getting Beyond the Messy Concepyualization of Circularity and The 3R'S, 4R'S and More* …The authors have tried to clear up the conceptual cacophony around the 3Rs (Reduce, Reuse and Recycle). Came up with a 10R's hierarchy (starting with the R0 which is 'Refuse' from the perspective of the consumer and finishing with R9, the re-mining from old land fill.

15 see, for example, Ellen MacArthur Foundation, 2015; Geissdoerfer, Savaget, Bocken, & Hultink, 2017; Ghisellini, Cialani, & Ulgiati, 2016; Mathews, 2011; Murray, Skene, & Haynes, 2017. In January 2016, the World Economic Forum and the Ellen MacArthur Foundation with the assistance from Mckinsey and Company, came up with report *The New Plastics Economy- Rethinking the future of Plastics* at the WEF in Davos For the first time research introduced the idea that plastics never become waste.

16 see Savini & Habdank, 2018, for a complete list).

17 Hobson & Lynch, 2016, p. 16-advocates that though Circular Economy (C.E.) is quickly becoming the key to design regional and international plans. But it has embedded challenges around consumption and consumer. The role of consumer is de-politicized and technologically mediated engagements are given more priority.

18 Girardet, 2014-He posits the central contradiction that is being faced. Mankind is building an urban future, yet urbanization threatens the very future of the mankind and the natural ecosystem. With

ever-growing people living in urban-spaces and resource-hungry cities, we are at risk of long-term well –being and even human longevity. He puts up the question that what positive steps can be taken to address such fundamental flaw? He introduced the concept of regenerative urbanization which is supposed to give answers to this problem. It is just not about greening of urban areas, however these step might be important, it is a call for citizens to create regenerative systems of production, transportation and consumption.

19 Williams, 2019- posits that taking an circular approach can help address many other socio-economic problems grappling the cities, for instance, allocation of accessible accommodation, enlarging and diversifying of the economic base, constructing more enlarged and synergetic communities in the cities.

20 Valenzuela & Böhm, 2017, p. 28- mainly concerned with the attempt of de-politicizing in the quest for reform. This de-politicization is problematized by Valenzuela and Bohm and calls for re-politicizing of the waste which drives towards more consumption.

21 Gregson, Crang, Fuller, & Holmes, 2015, p. 220- according to these thinkers concept is disseminated as an ideal. Actual implementation is weak. Majorly circular economy is implemented through global recycling circuits which serves as a primary means for recovering wastes as resources. But European policies shun these networks. Extracting waste as a means to use as resources is considered illegal.

22 Robèrt et al. 2010 cited in Bechtel, 2013

23 Bjørn and Hauschild, 2011

24 Walter, R. Stahel - In their research report in 1976 to the European Commission in Brussels 'The Potential for Substituting Manpower for Energy', Walter Stahel and Genevieve Reday tried to design the vision of an economy in loops (or circular economy) and its subsequent impact on creation of job, economic competitiveness, resource economizing and prevention of waste. The report came out in 1982 as a book "Jobs for Tomorrow, the Potential for Substituting Manpower for Energy". In today's time these factors are commonly called as the three main pillars of sustainable development: ecologic, economic and social compatibility. In 1981, Stahel organized these ideas in his prize winning paper "The Product-Life Factor" and came out with the idea that selling utilization instead of products as the ultimate sustainable business model of a loop economy: selling out utilisation helps to create sustainable profits without requirement of an externalization of the costs of risk and costs of waste.

In their 1987 report "Economic Strategies of Durability – longer product-life of goods as waste prevention strategy", Stahel and Börlin showed to the world that economic actors in a circular economy can strive a higher profitability than their competitors in the linear economy. With the help of 30 cases, the report showed that for a loop economy to be fully functional, a re-designing of the industrial economy and its framework conditions would be of massive help.

As a response to this report in 1987, some experts came forth with the idea of a product responsibility "from cradle to grave" as an alternative to a circular economy, with the edge that cradle to grave was also compatible with the current linear economic model.

25 Ellen MacArthur Foundation, 2013

26 T,Zink R, Geyer 2017 *Circular Economy Rebound*

27 Sennet, 1999.

28 Mcintyre, Michael & Nast, Heidi. (2011). Bio(necro)polis: Marx, surplus populations, and the spatial dialectics of reproduction and "race". Antipode. 43. 1465 - 1488. 10.1111/j.1467-8330.2011.00906.x.

29 Berg and Hukkinen, 2011; van den Bergh, 2011- asserts that academic discussion around economic growth and the environmental protection has revived under the aegis of the degrowth debate. Till date discussions around de-growth has been mainly theoretical actual empirical policy discussions are very few. Narrative policy analysis is the most suitable tool for complex policy cases. By examining and comparing the various stories, non-stories and counterstories in the discourse, the analysis tries to intellectually pave for solution. It is a common knowledge even among business and ministry representatives to criticize the present growth-bound economic structure. From the lens of narrative policy analysis, however, this critique only strengthens uncertainty and complexity in the policy area which, ironically, leads to more strengthening of the dominant growth structures. Thus, constructing a complete narrative de-growth is important so that policy work on it gets started.

30 Swyngedouw, 2009; Žižek and Hanlon, 2001

31 Easterlin, 2005; Levy, 2014; Velasquez-Brust and Sarkis, 2012

32 Meadows, et al., 1972

33 Victor, 2008: 19

34 Herod et al., 2013- Waste in general and e-waste in particular have become a topic of academic discussion. How the goods are handled at the end of their cycle and again used as inputs for different product creation. This led to the concept of economic continuity as how wastes are again re-used to the point that it cannot be ascertained. Herod asserts that though this talks about waste utilization but ultimately leads to commodity fetishism which precisely this de-growth movement stand against, it essentializes it.

Chapter 5
Innovation With Competitive Risk:
A Locus of Sustainable Competitive Advantage in the Circular Economy

Hergovind Singh
Maulana Azad National Institute of Technology, Bhopal, India

ABSTRACT

This is the dawn of an innovation and knowledge-driven economy, and the volatile business environment is forcing the industries to undergo a paradigm shift. This is causing volatility of business parameters from value creation to value maximization through reduction of value loss., instead of merely focusing on the value creation. This value maximization gels with quality, binding the end outcomes of enterprise, and quality of these end outcomes cumulatively shows the dependability towards the various inputs like man, money, material, machine, and information to innovate and re-innovate and measure continuously. Without saturation and to create value continuously in circular motion for spiral growth in circular economy all dimensions needs to be innovative to gain sustainable competitive advantage (SCA). The chapter is a study of concepts and models to impel the SCA. It analyzes innovation as a measure driver for SCA with various types of risk associated with it in the context of the circular economy.

INTRODUCTION

The search for a sustainable competitive advantage keeps the scholar of strategic management as well as Managers of high profile corporate houses in India and elsewhere glued to the stock exchange rumblings vis-à-vis top level conclaves of CII and business schools all over the globe (Savarova & Vrchota, 2014). Incessant fall of dollar value in recent times forces OPEC to cut back production and mark up price to avoid heavy loss of revenue. Expected hike in tourist traffic both inbound and out bound opens up new hope for those playing in this sector yet sustainability eludes. Could there be a mantra to safeguard the sustainability feature of any particular strategy. The paramount question that persist is how could India

DOI: 10.4018/978-1-7998-4990-2.ch005

continue to hold on to its hangover of 10% growth in the last quarter of 2003-04 or for that matter how does any organization sustain its market share – or profitability or any other parameter it may choose to hold on over a long period in the face of ever changing external and even the internal context of the organization (Sharma, 2003). The whole perspective of industrial engineering spanning over more than 150 years is seized with this organizational illusion. It expressed some times through augmented efforts of method study, formulation of problem such that they can be solved analytically and sometimes through quality movement. Fundamentally this search for a permanent sustainable edge is continuous, unbroken, uninterrupted, discernible yet sometimes undecipherable musings of some of the scholars who are yet at the job of undoing the complex knot of politics, economics, mathematics and even physics all embedded into one with a sobriquet of management (Rezaee, 2016). One way of viewing this reality is to accept the fact that sustainability cannot be ever permanent feature of any strategic competitive advantage as all strategic move will be subject to imitation by competitors. External context that exists is ever changing and ever widening as witnessed today. This basically turns today's advantage into disadvantage of tomorrow it not taken serious cognizance of it early. Organizations are required to create value. The concept of value creation is so primitive & so basic that it sunk into even the simple transactions. Yet all transactions do not create value. In many cases the transaction itself defines the value that is captured by the GAAPS. From one station to another the business process is supposed to yield additional value to sustain the process viability. Yet this process miserably fails and instead of creating additional value the process embarks on value destruction – a phenomena not well perceived by many new breed of Managers. Recrudescence of value destroying disease may finally eat away the total vitality vis-à-vis the viability of any organization. As such value destruction recurs with unimaginative organization structure, friction between processes and uncooperative and uncoordinated outsourcing of business processes. Similarly fierce competition in an oligopoly or free market also reduces value to a very large extent. It is reported that a number of organizations have spun off their process to marginalize this crucial & devastating phenomena of value destruction. While organizational culture plays a pivotal role in retaining & creating the value. While organizational culture and Learning Capability of Organization (LCO) (Cabrera, 2005).

Spic-n-Span

In today's challenging global market, enterprises must innovate to survive. Business innovation must occur in all dimensions – product process and organization – to improve competitiveness and business performance. To creating more value the quality and reengineering as the wave of previous decade and innovation as the wave for the next millennium. As describe by the Sumantra Ghoshal, an INSEAD, professor and Chris Bartellet a Harvard Professor today's Manager must focus on new dimension, the flow of intelligence. Idea and Knowledge-Innovation this in addition to the traditional flow of parts, components and Finished good,/funds, skills & other scarce resources, managers have awakened to the fact that their real responsibility/ opportunity is leveraging the intellectual capability of their individual employee and the organization as a whole (Martín, 2015).

In some industries, such as pharmaceutical and computer, for competitive advantage the critical parameter is Innovation, the with saturation of competition on the ground of Money, material, man & Information, and technology because every firm rivals having the same, hence innovation is increasing its importance in 21st century

In to day global economy research suggest that innovation in both product and process is becoming linked with above average return in a growing number of industries Innovation is vital to the develop-

Figure 1. Conceptual relationship of SCA and Innovation with other strategic elements.

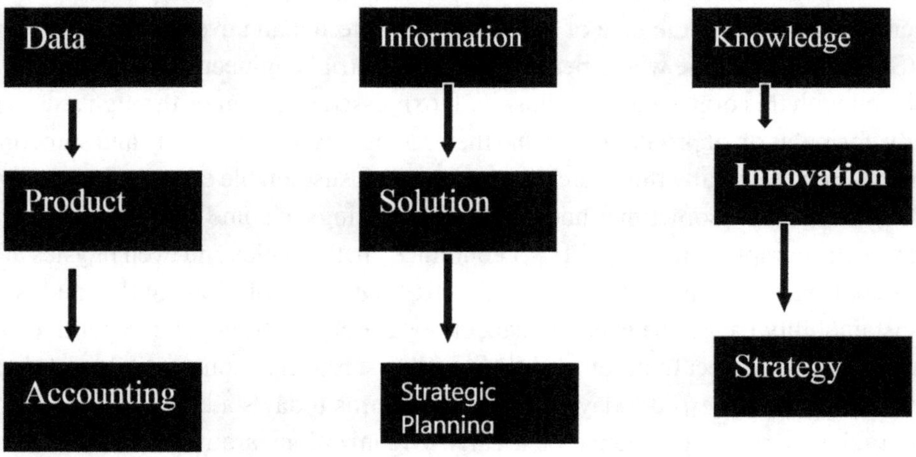

ment of competitive advantage in the services sector as it in the sector manufacturing sector. Although certainly Importance to day innovation has long been recognized as vital to the competitive success. The competitive advantage of global value chain is that enterprises can seek involvement at their level of Technological competence, competing on global value chain can build a foundation for the industrial innovation and learning with the different dimension of innovation with both the categories of innovation as radical and incremental innovation:-

- **Process innovation**

Improving the efficiency of Transforming inputs, into output, internal process because significantly better that those of rivals.

- **Product Innovation**

Leading to better quality, lower priced and more differentiated products as well as shorter times to market for few products.

- **Functional innovation**

assuming responsibility for new activity in the global value chain that can involve extending involvement from contract manufacturing to design and marketing of incorporating logistics within the contracted work.

- **Inter-Chain Innovation**

Moving to new and more profitable chain Enterprises in Taiwan province of china moved from the manufacture of transistor radio o calculator to television, to computer monitor, to laptop, and now to

Figure 2. Conceptual diagram of value creation and value capturing.

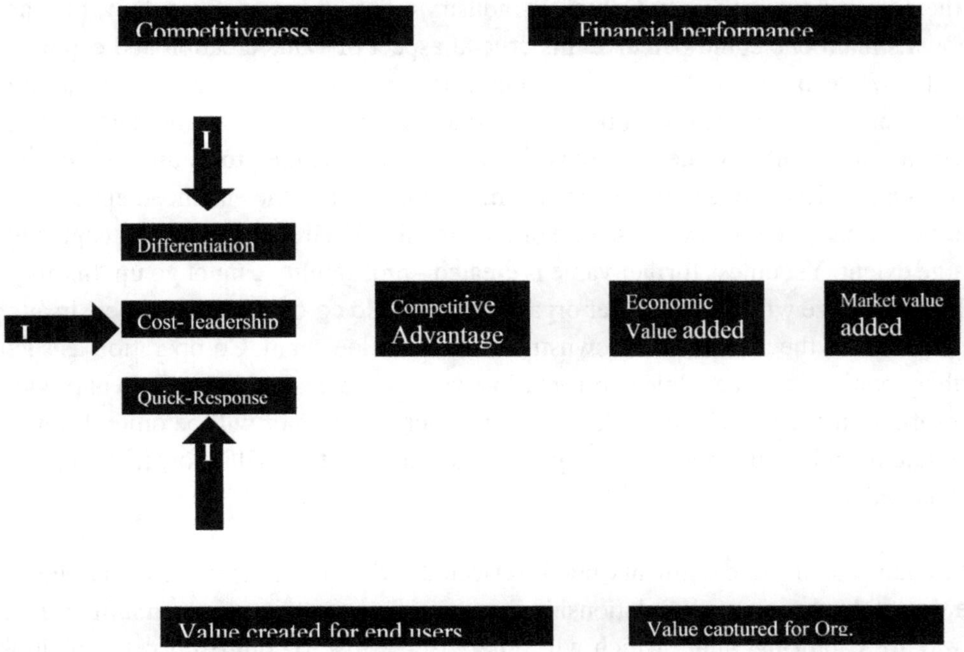

wireless application protocol telephones. The lead organization play a major role in organizing trade to computer monitor (Abernathy & Wayne, 1998).

a part of the value or even mitigating the effect of value destruction it cannot altogether nullify the effect.

Value as known to us is the surplus the consumer is willing to leave for us. Same product or service can create varied surplus depending on the consumers preference for a particular goods. Restricted supply of a particular goods can also create additional surplus. In the latter case it is the market that determines the surplus available from a particular product or service. Competition in any segment of the value chain will reduce the value created for a particular producer. In general value creation will depend on several factors like

1. Cost of the process.
2. Economics of scale.
3. Market structure – Competition
4. Entry barrier in a particular Industry.
5. Available Substitutes
6. Surplus earning of the consumer
7. Taste of consumer
8. Time of consumption
9. There will be several other factors that will have direct or indirect impact on the phenomena of value creation by any organized activity. It is also a fact that all those factors narrated here may not have equal influence. The organization looking at the strategy for creation and retention of value needs to have a set of desperate ideas in its quiver. In a way, total value created by any organiza-

tion will be partly captured by the competitor, suppliers, consumer, employees, shareholders and even the government agency. In Computer industry today, if one analyses the value chain both up and down stream one could perceive this crucial aspect of value creation and capture by various segments. While Intel and Microsoft are capturing most of the value – the local computer assemblers can hardly cover the cost because of intense competition from numerous manufacturers. Value creation as well as value capture will help in enhancing the profitability of any organization (Amara et al., 2015). Value creation is very important so far as the enhancement of profitability is concerned. A particular market structure or the organizational position help in capturing the value to a large extent. Yet unless further value is created - profitability cannot go up. In this perspective one should analyze whether his or her organization should co-operate or compete in any particular value segment in the upstream or downstream of the value chain. Co-operation as such will lead to further creation of value while confrontation will dissipate and will not help in productivity vis-à-vis profitability. Value chain model of a fish seller or a farmer will be quite different from the value chain model of monopoly industry. A limited competition will allow the industry to capture additional value.

In a value chain, usually one segments gain is reflected in the loss of other segment as nobody as such can capture the total value created. Relationship in terms of contract or memorandum of understanding is another way for capturing value, which will otherwise be lost to competitors. Let us look at a tyre plant located in Gwalior and supplying tyres to Chennai. Let us assume the cost of production of tyres is Rs 5000/- per piece and cost of transportation is Rs 500/- per piece. In other words opportunity cost of supply of each tyre is around Rs 5500/- and it sells the tyres at the price of Rs 7000/- per piece to the automaker. Let us now assume that another business house set up a plant near the automakers establishment and starts providing tyres at a cost of Rs 6000/-. He also makes an offer to the automaker to sell the tyres at Rs 7000/- per piece. However in all likelihood the automaker will not accept the offer. Rather it will exercise buyer power to lower the price as he is fully aware that the tyre manufacturer has sunk in a large investment and he does not have any alternate channel to sell. Under this circumstances the tyre manufacturer may be compelled to sell the tyres just covering the opportunity cost or even lower than this. Tyre manufacturer will fail to capture the value it creates. To capture the value what was required was to establish a contractual agreement with the automaker before investing fund for tyre manufacturing. This contractual relationship would have protected the value being created by the company. Enron while investing in Dabhol power company exactly did this so that it can capture the full value it creates.

Let us consider the value chain of production and distribution of Rice, which happens to be one of the most essential commodity.

Figure 3. Indicative value chain of farming.

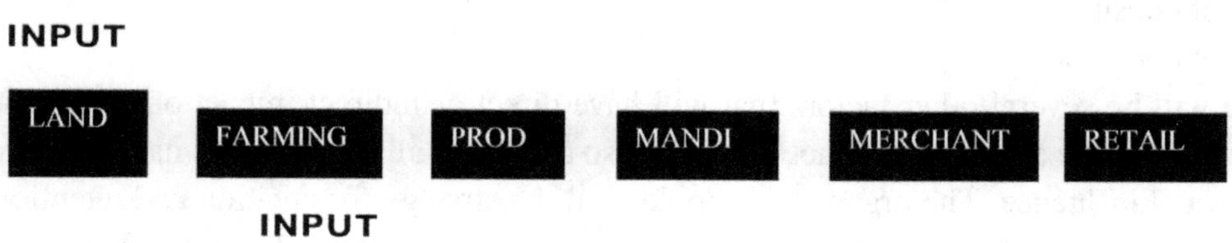

Let us assume that there is a monopolistic hold over land, which fundamentally forbids any competitive interference. As there is no competition – the landowner will try to extract as much value as possible through rent. Similarly the input supplier usually multinationals will extract the highest possible value through branding that cut across competition. Here Farmer is assumed to be engaged in only activity and that is tilling the land and producing grain. At the end of the season the farmer will harvest the crop and in absence of his internal ability to store or further process the grain he will move to a Mandi where in all likelihood he will sell his grains to a rich merchant who will exert as much buyer's power as possible to pay less for the commodity or in other words the merchant will enhance his own value capturing ability by using his market power. This will finally lead to a situation where the farmer will sell at the opportunity cost that barely covers his cost of production wherein the landowner exerts supplier's power and extract maximum value from this chain. In effect out of the total value created at the end of the chain everybody tries to capture as much value as possible and this is aided by the position or capability of the organization or the individual. In a changed scenario where there are multiple suppliers of land or the farmer has the capacity of integrating some other segments like production of input material or logistics or storage, their capacity or capability to capture value from this chain will change. To restate, by value we mean the value of the product or services to the final consumers and value creation is the total value perceived by the consumers minus the opportunity cost of the resources to produce the value. Though every segment in the chain will create value yet no segment is capable to capture the whole value chain. Nevertheless it is not necessary that he – who contributes higher value can capture higher value from the chain. As stated in the above example- farmer cannot capture a very high value because:-

1. They are numerous and have no option to work in any other segment of the value chain.
2. High level of competition among them will restrain their capacity to capture value.
3. Low level of skill required for doing farming does not pose any serious entry barrier to new entrants- thus competition grows.
4. Low capital requirement also helps farmers to join the occupation without much threat and in the process make substitute farmers easily available. High level of supply pushes down the price of labour.

On the other hand the landowner extracts higher value for

1. Supply of land is restricted- it cannot be created easily.
2. Higher level of capital is required to procure land. As the cost of capital increases – the supply reduces.
3. The land can have alternate use.
4. Entry barrier is high.
5. Land cannot be substituted. If may need high level of capital investment on R&D and technology.

However in the second example the farmer can capture higher value if he can integrate some of the value segments and in the process exert supplier or buyer power in down & upstream segment of the value chain. Sometimes intervention by statutory bodies help capture reasonable value by the framers as is in the case of minimum support price for paddy or wheat.

Nevertheless it is almost impossible to determine how much value is created by each segment in the chain and what should be their ethical share in any sense. Positional strength of the organization will always play a mediating role in fixing the share of value by the players involved.

Let us consider another example where land is fragmented and there are numerous owners. The cultivators are the member of a strong producers association who have their own land, farming equipment, logistics support, storage space and also distribution channel. Union is well capable of bargaining for the wages of the farmers in such a case. In this case the workers would capture the most of the value the chain creates. In all these cases, one may notice, the value each segment creates does not differ at all though the value captured by each segment differs significantly.

Most important factors in this scenario are supplier's power as well as buyer's power as enunciated by Michael Porter. In a particular market if the suppliers can demand higher prices exceeding the opportunity cost of its resources – it is said that supplier is exerting their power to grab the so called PIE or potential industry earning. Similarly buyer power is the ability to demand low price for the commodity it might be buying.

To the reader it might be now clear that competition as such circumvent the buyer or supplier power as mooted by Michael Porter An individual marginal farmer cannot exercise any power whatsoever and as such he can not bargain for any higher share of the value created by the chain. The computer assemblers in this country face the same challenge. The plurality of the suppliers – low entry barrier - all add to their incapability of grabbing value. In thirty's when Pt. Jawharlal Nehru gave an idea of farming cooperative – it was with this idea of empowering the farmers so that they can grab a higher value from the value chain of farm products. This view was not shared by many and as such this experiment could not take off. Yet later the sugar co-operatives of Maharashtra have successfully gained both power and profit through this model.

****** ******				
Completely outsourced	Alliance	Jt. Venture	Segmented	Highly Integrated

This is the same phenomena that operate in the labour market, in the agrarian market, in the coal mining sector, in the unorganized small industry sector and push down the value capturing capability of the market players. Management scholars will recognize the spectrum of Industry continuum that interplay in the market to capture more value.

Figure 4. Schematic diagram of risk sources.

Industry spectrum shown here will have disparate capacity to grab value from the numerous value segments contained in the chain. While fully integrated organization as shown in the right of continuum will capture almost the whole value created in the value chain – the business organization with every function outsourced will never be able to capture the whole value created by it. Rather business on the left of the continuum will have to share more and more value with other partners. Quantum of the value capture will be guided by several factors – prime among them is the buyer or supplier power (Bhattacharya, 2002). In addition any shift on this continuum also entails movement of enterprise risk as exhibited. This spectrum also brings forward another point i.e. higher risk does not necessarily help capture higher value. Negotiation is also another means to capture value to a large extent. Negotiation individually reflects the positional strength of the business organization. One cannot carve out a large value segment through negotiations unless he operates from a strong position. Organization with a unique capability as a particular strength is also helped by negotiation. We go back to the discussion on the industry continuum where we said that a large integrated firm can capture maximum value. But a large integrated firms also needs very high level of co-ordination that increases the chance of value loss during transmission. In fact much of the value loss reported today is from these large integrated firms where co-ordination and co-operation play a very vital role in capturing value. This is apparently one of the reasons why monolithic organizations have spun them off into smaller business unit called SBUS. In general value loss takes place through executive friction, lack of foresight, lack of analytical capability and communication loss. Value capture minus value loss should be positive to maintain the organizational viability. In a value chain it is always conjured up that some segment gains at the cost of other segments. This will be true in general until every segment operates in a strong competitive environment. Competition usually limit buyer as well as supplier power and pushes down the captured value to the marginal level that covers only the opportunity cost. Nevertheless the organization can replace competition by co-operation and create more value so that absolute value retained by them is more than the value captured earlier. Let us consider a firm in one segment of the value chain that has buyer power or supplier power which in effect mean it has sufficient market standing to dictate the output price. OPEC as a cartel resembles such an organization that can exert enough power to set the output price. Price discrimination may be resorted by organizations to capture more value. In fact a number of airlines now a days offer price discrimination in an attempt to capture maximum value from a particular operative flight. Sometime price discrimination by a particular firm is not possible neither it is possible to prevent buyer from capturing some of the value created.

If all firms in every segment of a value chain operate in a highly competitive environment – the firm can only charge a price for its products or services that will equal to its marginal opportunity cost and thereby is unable to capture the value it creates. Final consumer in such a case will capture the maximum value though it does not have any buyer or supplier power. Firms usually may resort to price discrimination to capture some of the value. Yet more often than not a firm with a monopoly in a particular segment of a chain in which all other segments are competitive cannot improve its profits by obtaining a monopoly in another segment as well "The firms with supplier or buyer power will be better off when the other firms in the value chain are in perfectly competitive industries. Firms will also prefer their buyer who have no supplier power. If a firm can increase its own supplier power or reduce supplier power elsewhere in the chain, it can increase its profits".

Apart from this, product and price differentiation may be resorted to capture higher value. Brands help in capturing value through this differentiation. Both horizontal as well as vertical differentiations are resorted with a single object of shifting the demand curve so that even for a lesser demand, price recovery can be affected. Conceptually horizontal differentiation means that all consumers are not unanimous in ranking the product as superior wherein in vertical differentiation the consumers are unanimous in their opinion regarding the product quality. Similarly low cost strategy of a exploiter firm can help in capturing more value in a highly competitive market.

Any business without a concern for capturing value in its own segment will have a bleak fortune as a whole. Value analysis –particularly the strategy deployed to capture the value being created must be an essential activity for a strategy planner. In a competitive market, value creation cannot be the be all and end all of any organization. The business must play a wholesome game – when it creates value and maximizes the value capture and finally retain the same. Value destruction needs to be looked into.

In so far as the discussion is done – the reader might have realized that value creation is definitely not the only option for value capturing and value retention. The organization need to maneuver through a special context either internal or external and sometimes try to change some of the rules of the game so that value is not captured by rivals are even the consumers (Goswami, 2002).

Sometimes this is the gist of a complicated game that every organization needs to play in the market. In fact this is the only game some of the organizations are trying to impose on others. Ramification of this strategy is evident in the market, which is more liberalized. Some of the ploy resorted to in this strategy is to create a veil, a confusion in the market and even creating situations that compels a favorable policy so that the incumbent firm or its opponent win. These extraneous factors often become overarching goal of quite some of the organizations paying in the field. Telecom sector of today is witnessing some of the phenomena issuing from the scenario as depicted here. In this complex world of multiple forces – the resultant vectors are not always favorable to the firm trying for a foothold into an established market. To combat – the organization may sometimes need to align with somebody, may allow somebody to enter the market without much fuss, may encircle some other organization in some market, may resort to direct conflicts in another market. All these strategic decision will eventually lead to mastering the position in the market so that it can exercise its suppliers or buyer power. Engaging a rival in one market or giving walkover to another in another market will be commonplace decision in a market that might operate in a near saturation point. Entrepreneurship and innovations are some of the value contributing factors that will run the risk of its own kind.

It is a fact that in the name of free market nobody wants anarchy. Everybody including the strongest organizations believes that some kind of regulation is needed to control the market behavior. Everybody takes a risk when he purchases a fridge or a Television. Strangely nobody perceives the risk associated with this purchase. Might be there is a need to differentiate between risk and hazard in a way the market hazard should not be synonymous with market risk. While entrepreneurs will pick up some of the market risk through innovations to gain a bit of competitive advantage they need not face a market hazard that may terminate the whole operation. As the history opens up, Strategic decisions will be more and more sought after as a protective cover for the value created by any organization.

In conclusion it can be maintained that value creation is not synonymous with value capture or value retention. While it is important to crate value it is also necessary to ensure that proper mechanism is set up so that value loss is minimized. Organizations may require to resort to some strategy that gives it a sustainable edge for some time. It is true no strategy will last for even to keep the organization afloat. Yet human search for a strategy of alchemies continues.

REFERENCES

Abernathy, W. J., & Wayne, K. (1982). Limits of the Learning Curve. In Management of Innovation. Pitman.

Amara, N., Halilem, N., & Traoré, N. (2016). Adding value to companies' value chain: Role of business schools scholars. *Journal of Business Research*, *69*(5), 1661–1668. doi:10.1016/j.jbusres.2015.10.035

Bhattacharya, K. K. (2002). A Model of Integration of Information Technology in Agriculture Extension for Improving Crop Production. *2nd Global Conference on Flexible System Management.*

Emerson, R. W. (1996). Achieving competitive advantage through strategic innovation. *The Essence of Corporate Strategy*, 1-36.

Martín, G. (2015). Knowledge management and innovation in knowledge-based and high-tech industrial markets: The role of openness and absorptive capacity. *Industrial Marketing Management*, *47*(May), 143–146. doi:10.1016/j.indmarman.2015.02.032

Omkar, G., Arun. A.K. Vishal, M., & Arindam, D. (2002). Competitiveness of Indian Manufacturing –results from a firm level survey. CII Report.

Porter, E. M. (1985). Competitive advantage. The Free Press.

Rezaee, Z. (2016). Business sustainability research: A theoretical and integrated perspective. *Journal of Accounting Literature*, *36*, 48–64. doi:10.1016/j.acclit.2016.05.003

Savarova, M., & Vrchota, J. (2014). Influence of competitive advantage on formulation business strategy. *Procedia Economics and Finance*, *12*, 687–69. doi:10.1016/S2212-5671(14)00394-3

Valle-Cabrera, R. (2005). Organizational learning capability: A proposal of measurement. *Journal of Business Research*, *58*(6), 715–725. doi:10.1016/j.jbusres.2003.11.002

Chapter 6
Policies for Promoting the Circular Economy in India

Namita Kapoor
Rabindra Nath Tagore University, Bhopal, India

Sangeeta Jauhari
Rabindranath Tagore University, Bhopal, India

Deepti Maheshwari
Rabindranath Tagore University, Bhopal, India

ABSTRACT

The demand for resources is increasing in India because of growth, changing lifestyles, and aspirations of people for improving lifestyles, but the major challenge for the economy is to provide these economically without hampering the ecology and society negatively. The negation of externalities resulting from the use of resources is the major challenge for the policymakers along with providing balanced developmental avenues to the society. The framework to achieve efficiency in resource use can be appropriately designed through innovative ways and policies. The Indian economy over the last few years has clearly moved to controlled regulation from command through the practice of economic instruments for regulations. The policy adopted by India to achieve circularity includes the financial support and guidance for research and development, formulation of standards like ECOMARKS, public procurements, and certification and self-regulation, which are discussed in the chapter.

INTRODUCTION

The gap between the availability of finite resources and the demand is a caution highlighted by the trends in Global Demand- Supply. Environmental degradation, volatility in prices and depletion of resources has emerged from the rising competition (Di Maio & Rem, 2015). The burden on resources has increased tremendously as a result of various reasons:

DOI: 10.4018/978-1-7998-4990-2.ch006

i. **Population growth** (EMF,2013, Tse, Esposito& Soufani, 2015),
ii. **Linear economy model** based on the doctrine of "take-make-dispose" approach (Ellen MacArthur Foundation 2013; World Economic Forum 2014). The demand for resources is expected to reach two and three planet's worth by 2030 and 2050 (Tse, Esposito& Soufani, 2015). This basically poses question on the reality of the linear model that countries and business are being following globally.
iii. **The rules and regulations** followed in different countries are varied: Various socio- cultural, economic and psychological factors that hinder the shift in the global plan for transforming a linear economy to a circular economy.
iv. **The developing countries** are highly populated, which is a major challenge for requirement and implementation of systematic intervention in the concept of circular economy.

World Economic Forum and Ellen Mathur Foundation are the driving forces for initiating the transformation of the linear economy to circular economy through various interfaces, research and best practices. The focus of circular economy is on efficient management of resources by integration of reverse logistics and innovation in design and business models development of an ecosystem based on collaborative efforts. The main goal of circular economy is to reduce waste (disposal) and decrease in primary raw material because of their significantly high environmental impact and global scarcity.

Indian society has always practiced circularity involving repair, reuse and recycling products. With the rise in consumerism and increase in affordability there has been frequent replacement of assets which has increased the waste as well as retarded the adoption of circular economy (Kumar A. et al, 2020). At every stage of value chain there is requirement of the application of 5Rs.The success of adoption of circular economy depends largely on consumer's awareness, mindset and readiness to participate in it. The tradition growth model of India was basically predicted through the "linear Model" economic model which is functioning against the limited resources of our planet. Also, this model generated massive waste in every stage of the product life cycle. For the growth of manufacturing sector, it is required that we should not only use the scarce resources diligently but also substitute the primary resources with secondary through the efficient management of secondary resource. Circular Economy can help in achieving this through operating in a closed loop to minimize the leakage or wastage of resources as less as possible through Sharing, Leasing, Repairing, Refurbishing and Recycling.

Circularity concept is not just recycling it is basically a system which is restorative in the industrial processes which treats the waste as a resource. It implies that once a in the product life cycle the product's life ends attempts should be made to utilize them by creating a value of it (Ellen Mc Arthur 2015). The transition from tradition to circular requires the changes in the functioning of organizations and reshaping of the supply chain process by infusing the mindset of sustainability in product designers (Thelen et al. 2018)

Circular Economy is an upcoming field providing opportunity and profitable business. It is now an agenda for discussion on the political mainstream discussion (One of the agenda for G20 was circular economy) and G20 countries are formulating and implementing strategies to achieve SDG through integrating Circular economy processes. In India Government has launched many programs to achieve the committed Sustainable Development Goals and Paris Accord which are aligned the discussed aspects of circular economy. These approaches are although fragmented and lack systematic approach, challenging the business to adopt circular economy practices or models.

The demand for resources is increasing in India because of growth, changing lifestyles and aspirations of people for improving lifestyles but the major challenge for the economy is to provide these economically without hampering the ecology and society negatively. The negation of externalities resulting for the use of resources is the major challenge for the policy makers along with providing the balanced developmental avenues to the society. The framework to achieve the efficiency in resource use can be appropriately designed through the innovative ways and policies. The development of recycling economy needs to form a social resultant force in the Government promotion, enterprise entities, public participation, with the clarification for the responsibility and obligation in the three parties (Huiqiang Chengan and Xiang-Yun Du 2010). *Sustainable manufacturing considers use of reusable, recyclable material with less energy consumption in production to develop a high-quality product reaching to end user with minimum damage to environment. Saving of resources is same as producing of resources (Alok Khatri, D. Garg and G. S. Dangayach, 2010)*. The most significant policy initiated by India to instigate the sustainability concept was NEP, 2006. As per the National Environment Policy, 2006 development which includes the social justice imperatives and considers the constraints of ecology should only be considered as sustainable. Indian Economy over the last few years has clearly moved to controlled regulation from command through the practice of economic instruments for regulations. The policy adopted by India to achieve circularity includes the financial support and guidance for research and development, formulation of standard like ECOMARKS, public procurements, and certification and self- regulations. There is a global commitment to achieving resource efficiency in order to establish sustainable consumption and production patterns. It is important for the Government to announce policies related to this aspect. The various policies like Atma Nirbhar Bharat, Made in India, Zero Effect- Zero Defect Scheme, smart cities, Swachh Bharat and Ganga Rejuvenation mission are some of the steps in this direction. which is It is also a priority for the Government of India, and is reflected in various policies/programme announcements like Make in India, Zero Effect-Zero Defect Scheme, Smart Cities, Swachh Bharat, and Ganga Rejuvenation Mission The key policies undertaken by India for resource efficiency and sustainable consumption are presented in this chapter.

KEY POLICIES DURING THE PRODUCT LIFE CYCLE

1. Practicing Resource Efficiency in mining:

More than 95% of the requirement of materials in India is covered by the internal sources. The substantial amount of savings can be achieved through improvements in efficiency of resources for the economy as well as sector.

The improvements in resource efficiency means the improvements in the mining practices that would lead to the wastage minimization, beneficial through better transportation through less clashes in the environment and society.

1.1 National Mineral Policy 2008

The National goal highlighted through the National Mineral Policy, 2008was achieving zero waste in mining and providing importance to conservation of resources. The suggestions as per the policy include the value addition with the help of latest technologies through blending of products, beneficiation, sizing, concentration, customization, palletization and purification of product. The policy also suggested use of the mechanical instruments that will enhance efficiency and make mining economically viable. It is also suggested that the technical organizations must strengthen research under the guidance of Ministry of mines for mineral beneficiation. The policy suggests the methods for preventing and mitigating the negative effects on environment which includes the closing of mines in order and systematic way acknowledging the environmental problems.

The **framework for sustainable development of mining sector** was published in2011, which outlined the requisite during the mining lease grant as environmental and social sensitization. The policy framework envisages Mining to Viable not only financially but should be responsible socially, environmentally and technically correct to ensure mineral resources optimally are used optimally, and ensures sustainability.

1.2 MMDR, Minerals and Mining Development Regulatory Act, 2016

The sectoral sustainable development framework is assessed and implemented by MMDR Act 2016. The Act directs the Central Government to issue the directions to adopt measures to reduce waste and practice waste management, promote material recycling, mitigation of adverse effects on ecology and minimization of effects on habitat, bio diversity including flora and fauna. The Act empowers the authority in formulation of strategies for activities that would ensure the optimum use of mined resources. Other policies relevant to these issues also include guide-lines on Management of Sustainable Sand and Mining (2017) and the issues for rating the mining industries.

2. Achieving and enhancing Resource Efficiency - Phase during Product design

To achieve Sustainable development goal it is necessary to design products which are environmentally benign. Efficiency of resources during the designing phase of product can be in any form like- enhancing product durability, using recycled materials, labelling of product for re use and recycle potential. The parameters which are the key factors for product sustainability under the three pillars of Sustainable development – Economical, Environmental and social are explain in Table1. The Economical aspects include Product life cycle, Innovativeness, Carbon trading, Profitability, Return on Investment and Green Supply Chain Management.; the Environmental Aspects include the 5R concept, Biodegradable material, waste minimization, carbon foot print and the social aspect include housing and service infrastructure, Health and education, Job opportunity, Social capital, Legislation and enforcement.*(Gupta et.al 2015)*

2.1 National Design Policy, 2007

To make a positive effect on economy and quality of life, National Design Policy was introduced by Department of Industrial Policy and Promotion knowing the importance of design in the competitiveness of the product. Indian Design mark has been made a Brand Image for designers in India which meets the requisite criteria of design like innovation, originality, aesthetic, safe, user friendly and ecofriendly. (DIPP2007).

At the Design Stage, policies like National Housing and Habitat Policy,2007 and the Pradhan Mantri Awas Yojana (PMAY),2015 emphasize on developing appropriate ecological design Standards for

Table 1. Sustainability Aspects: Economical, Environmental and Social

Economical	Environmental	Social
Product Life Cycle	1. 5R concept	1.Housing and service infrastructure
Innovativeness	2. Biodegradable material	2.Health and education
Carbon Trading	3. Waste minimization	3.Job opportunity
Profitability	4. Carbon foot print	4.Social capital
Return on Investment	5. Energy conservation	5. Legislation and enforcement.
Green Supply Chain Management	6. Clean development mechanism	

Source: Gupta et.al 2015

building components, materials and construction methods and there is a urgent need to introduce such components in the sector policies.

DST, MST is promoting research and development in the area of waste management and there is a need to further enhance the funding for resource efficiency and Secondary Raw Material related research and development. (NITI AAYOG,2017)

2.2 Science, Technology and Innovation Policy (2013)

Sustainable Growth which is inclusive is the main objective of this policy. The main aim of the policy is to increase the employment opportunities through research and development in the field of science and technology. The main purpose of the policy is to encourage optimization of resource, efficient innovations different domains of technology. The policy also includes the provision for incentives to commercial innovations with green manufacturing as a major agenda. (Department of Science and Technology 2013)

2.3 Bureau of Indian Standards Act, 2016

BIS Act 1986 was replaced by BIS Act 2016 in the year 2017 by the Government of India. This Certification is provided for a large number of goods across different sectors including chemicals, machines, construction materials, textiles, packaging and their effects on environment. The Government can issue for any product or good or item any mandatory obligations or certification from any listed industry, system, service or process which is deemed to be important for protection of human health, life and safety including protection of flora and fauna along with preventing the unfair trade practices and threat to national security.

3 Enabling Resource Efficiency- Manufacturing

One of the most important sectors in Indian Economy is manufacturing. **National Manufacturing Policy, 2011** has been a guiding policy to bring about the transformation in the sector. The earlier Manufacturing Policy has been redesigned to cover the new promises of the Government on "Make in India", "digital India" and "Skill India". This policy aims to elevate environmental sustainability and also to improve the global competitiveness of India's manufacturing along with achieving inclusive growth.

3.1 National Manufacturing Policy of 2011

The National Policy of 2011 aims to increase the share of manufacturing in the total output in Indian Economy .The policy supports the technologies that are sustainable, environment friendly and controls the use and consumption of the scarce resources particularly water and energy.

3.2 National Policy of Electronics (2012)

The National Policy of Electronics (2012) is designed to make India more competitive in manufacturing globally that cannot just meet the national growing demand for electronics but also can cater to the rising demand of other countries. The policy also aims to align the implementation of the rules pertain to e –waste including the extended responsibility of the producer under the e water Rules of 2011.

3.3 National Policy on Electronics (2019)

The aim of National Policy for Electronics is to make India a global hub for ESDM (Electronics System Design and manufacturing) by creating an enabling environment for the industry. This Policy is important in terms of increasing electronic imports, higher potential for electronic manufacturing, and higher domestic demand for electronics and so on. This policy aims to achieve the growth in the domestic electronic manufacturing by US$ 400 Billion by 2025 along with more focus on technical advancement of domestic manufacturing and exports. Major support mechanisms under NPE 2019 include first, interest subvention scheme, under which an interest subsidy of 4% on loans up to Rs10, 000 Crores would be provided and the loan should be spend on Plant and machineries. Second is Credit Guarantee Fund Scheme, Upgrading of Existing Manufacturing Clusters scheme into Electronic Manufacturing2.0 Sovereign Patent fund to upgrade technology and to ensure that chips and components can be made available to all Indian firms at low cost. The policy also focuses on the latest technologies like Artificial Intelligence, Medical and defense electronics and consumer electronics. The policy aims to create an Ecosystem for the development of the ESDM Sector and reduce import dependence and develop a growth platform for this sector.

3.4 National Manufacturing Competitiveness Program, 2014

To improve the competitiveness of MSME in the year 2014, National Manufacturing Competitive Program was launched. The resource efficiency in this sector is the most important one which can be made effective through the policies aiming for this sector specifically. The main policies under the National Manufacturing Competitive Program'2014 include Credit linked Capital Subsidy and Technological Upgradation, Reimbursement for ISO 9000/ ISO 14001 Certification, Assistance and support for Marketing, Lean Manufacturing competitiveness for MSMEs – Aims to reduce waste, increase productivity, introducing innovative practices for improving overall competitiveness, imbibing culture of continuous improvement; Support and consultancy for design; Support for improving quality and upgrading technology ; Incubators for Entrepreneurial and managerial development of MSMEs; ***Enabling competitiveness of manufacturing through the adoption of QMS and QTT.***

Table 2. Schemes under National Competiveness Development Program

1.	Credit linked Capital Subsidy and Technological Upgradation	For upgrading the technology, the scheme entitles MSME for subsidy of 15% on additional investment upto 15 Million INR
2.	Reimbursement for ISO 9000/ISO14001 Cerification ISO 9000/ISO 14001	Provides incentives to MSME to acquire the certification: ISO 9000/ISO 14001 and also reimburses the expenses
3.	Assistance and support for Marketing	Encourages adoptions of International number standards: Bar Codes/ E commerce applications
4.	Lean Manufacturing Competitiveness for MSMEs – Aims to reduce waste, increase productivity, introducing innovative practices for improving overall competitiveness, imbibing culture of continuous improvement.	For the implementation of Lean Manufacturing techniques financial assistance may be provided ((20% from the beneficiaries and 80% by Government of India)
5.	Support and consultancy for design	Support MSME through i. Support of Rs.60,000 for each seminar and for each workshop 75% to a maximum of ii. Consultancy to be provided to MSME for product or strategy design
6.	Support for improving quality and upgrading technology	To reduce the manufacturing cost the MSME are advised to use energy efficient technology and adoption of clean development procedures.
7.	Incubators for Entrepreneurial and managerial development of MSMEs	1. It finances the innovative business ideas – in the early stage which could be materialized in an year. 2. Providing financial support for setting up business incubators.
8.	***Enabling competitiveness of manufacturing through the adoption of QMS and QTT***	Encourage MSME for adoption of the Standards that are latest in Quality Management (QMS) and adoption of latest Quality Technology (QTT)

Source: MSME 2019

3.5 ZED Certification Scheme 2017- Providing financial support to MSME

This certification is to promote ZERO DEFECT ZERO EFFECT in all producing industries in India including services with more focus and attention to MSME. This certification includes all the manufacturing mechanisms and processes they have zero defects in the process of production and also have zero negative effect on environment and ecology. Under this scheme financial assistance is provided to MSME and a PAN India awareness campaign is being done to promote this certification in MSME. This is going to have a significant growth in India's MSME sector in terms of decrease in waste and enhanced productivity in the global supply chain.

4. Resource efficiency during Consumption:

The offering of savings has the main association with the resource efficiency. In order to have responsible consumption and production to achieve sustainability the Government has introduced and re designed new policies.

4.1 List of Schemes for Labelling:

4.1.1 ECOMARK (1991)

ECOMARK is one of the initial labels used for identification of the products which are environment friendly. The Ministry of Environment and Forests launched the scheme and BSI (Bureau of India's Standards) managed and implemented the scheme.This scheme of labelling standardizes the product as ecofriendly which is produced, consumed and disposed in such a way that the effect on environment is minimum. This scheme defines and considers the "cradle to grave" approach which includes till disposal from material extraction.

4.1.2 Energy Labelling- Star Labelling Program (2006): Bureau of Energy Efficiency

The label for energy efficient good was launched under this scheme in the year 2006 to keep consumers awarded about the products and choices there by save their expenses on electricity bills. A significant amount of energy can be saved through household and commercial buildings in the coming years. All key domestic and Industrial appliances (White goods) covered under this scheme (BEE.2017)

4.2 National Policy on Biofuel 2009

The National Policy on Biofuels of 2009 was announced with the objective of providing energy security and meets the increased energy demands. *The main purpose of this policy was the development and utilization of domestic waste land, emphasizing on R&D on farming, processing as well as manufacturing of biofuels and developing the blends of Ethanol and development of Bio diesel mandate.*

4.3 Renewable Energy Certification, 2010

The process and ways of increasing renewable energy composition in the total National energy generation capacity was provided by 2003 India's Electricity Act and other policies under the Act along with NAPCC (National Action Plan on Climate Change). The extra capacity produced by the states having abundance of renewable energy can be sold to less energy producing states. The Renewable Energy certificate program was introduced by the Central Electricity Regulatory Commission to enable the distribution of renewable energy by companies who meet the criteria or purchase obligations and to provide incentives for generation of green energy.

4.4 Market Based Scheme- Perform Achieve and Trade (PAT) 2012

The basis aim of this scheme was promotion of energy efficiency in industries which were energy intensive. The scheme was introduced under the NMEEE, National Mission on Enhanced Energy Efficiency and is being administered under the BEE, Bureau of Energy Efficiency. The energy consumption by the selected industries is provided specific targets, the industries gain certificates for their efficiency which can be traded in the energy –intensive sectors.

4.5 Auto Fuel Policy (2015)

To promote the improvement in quality of fuel as well as strict emission norms in the year 2015, Vision for the year 2025 was formulated as Auto Fuel Policy 2015.

4.6 National Electricity Mobility Mission Plan (2020)

To bring the paradigm shift India launched plan for automotive and transport sector under the Plan. The plan envisaged that by the year 2020 the number of battery operated or hybrid cars in India would be six to seven million. The benefits of e vehicles are not just on environment but it will also help in favorable trade balance through importing less crude oil. Government of India in order to promote the adoption of e vehicles is providing incentives in the areas where population is more than 1 lakhs. Every single automobile provider has plans to offer hybrid and electric versions by 2025.

Under the National Electric Mobility Mission (NEMM) in 2015 various policies have been adopted for the Fast Adoption of Manufacturing (of Hybrid) and Electrical vehicles in India (FAME, India). In the Budget of 2019, INR10, 000 Crores is being allocated to FAME II schemes besides announcing the tax deduction of Rs1.5 lakh on the interest paid on loans taken to buy Electric Vehicles. The GST council has also announced to reduce the rate from 12% to 5%. It has also been highlighted in the Economic Survey of India 2019 to emerge as a EV manufacturing hub. FAME I scheme was successful increasing the share of hybrid and electric passenger from 0% in 2012 to 1.3% by 2016. In February 2019, Government announced subsidies of $1.4 Billion for both buyers and manufacturers of EVs and also to promote indigenous automotive companies to manufacture EVs.

5. Achievement in Resource Efficiency in Disposal of Waste:

5.1 Batteries Amendment Rules 2010 for Management and Handling

In the year 2010 the earlier regulation of 2001 were revised and amended for the selling of batteries through the registered channels and assigning the responsibilities to the bulk buyers. The regulations were implied for importers, assembler's, re conditioners, dealers, recyclers, auctioneers and bulk consumers to ensure not only the sale but also recycling and transportation along with the collection of batteries.

5.2 Solid Waste Management Rules Amendment (2019) of Solid Waste Management Rule 2016

The old rules were replaced by new Solid Waste Management Rules in 2016 by releasing the notification and finally amended in the year 2019 by The Government of India. To create the opportunities for value addition and promote recycling, recovery and re use the new rule mandates the segregation of waste. The powers have been assigned to the local authorities to impose fines or charges that violate and do not segregate waste or litter waste. During the development phase the estate agents have to area for waste management – resource recovery as well as recycling not less than 5% of the total area. It is the responsibility of waste segregation is with the local bodies and they have to build in the infrastructure so that waste pickers get easy access and the segregated waste reaches the recyclers. Solid Waste Management Rules was further amending ended in 2019 for the color of bins. As per the 2019 amendment the bins for storage of biodegradable waste shall be painted green, storage of all recyclable wastes shall be printed blue and those for storage of other waster shall be printed black

5.2.1 Waste Management Rules of Construction and Demolition (2016)

The notification regarding the management of waste from demolition and construction was been done in 2016.The responsibility of the waste generators is to store and transport the waste to the collection centers and hand over it to the authorized processing facilities.

5.2.2 Rules for Management of E- Waste (2016)

The objective of E waste rules notified in the year 2016 was to channelize the treatment of e-waste and the resource recovery. It is made mandatory by rules that collection centers would be set up which were earlier not part of extended producer responsibility authorization, recycling and resource recovery should be done environment efficiently.

5.2.3 E- Waste (Management) Amendment Rules 2018

The E-Waste (Management) Rules (2016) were in 2018 amended to facilitate and effectively implement the environmentally sound management of e –waste in India with the objective of channelizing the E-waste in the country towards authorized dismantlers and recyclers in order to formalize the e- waste cycling sector. The collection targets under the provision of Extended Producer Responsibility (EPR) in the rules have been introduced for the new products that have started the sales operations recently.

5.2.4 Plastic Waste Management Rules (2016) and Amendment (2018)

In year 2016, Government issued notice to make responsible system of proper utilization of waste through the proper system of collecting waste; using plastic was for construction of roads as per the guidelines provided by Indian Road Congress or energy recovery.

5.3 Hazardous and other waste Rules Act 2016

To ensure the proper management of hazardous and other waste materials generated from the rule desires the reuse and recovery of materials.

5.4 Hazardous and other waste Rules Amendment Act 2019

Under the Amendment solid plastic waste has been prohibited from import into the country including SEZ and EOU. Exporters of silk waste are exempted from requiring permission.

5.5 GST on Waste Products- Reduced (2017)

The Government had drastically decreased the rates on the scarp of glass and rubber to 5% as earlier from 18% e waste to 5% as earlier from28%

6. Technical and Financial Infrastructure for Circular Economy

Issues regarding sustainable development can be addressed through R&D in resource efficiency. It not only helps in development of the processes, goods and services through transforming knowledge but also employment opportunities can be created. One of the largest Government supported Research and development organization is CSIR.DST has been the supporter of circular economy and has been channelizing the resources to CSIR.

Technical Development Board (TDB) has been set up under for provided support for development and commercialization of not only local and indigenous technology but also the faster adaption of the technology from abroad. For the promotion of technology startups through Business Science and Technology Incubators, Science and Technology Parks "Speed Support Scheme" is also being launched.

The shift from linear to circular present before the managers and decision makers the opportunities and challenges to enforce the policies to innovate and develop disruptive businesses models. The financial institutions infuse the necessities to innovate and respond for transforming from linear to circular. The financial institutions wish to minimize the risk in the transition from linear to circular to get the maximum returns on investments. The financial institutions can support this transition in two ways: first, can support it through financing project and the second way is to provide clearance to the companies after assessing their internal process and operations to imbibe the principles of circularity.

There must be awareness of risks and opportunities that will come along with the shift to circularity. The development of the innovative financial instruments and methods far from the traditional system is required for the creation of new business perspectives and serving the new horizons of business viz C2C and C2B. It is projected that the country would gain by moving to the circular model would be 30% of its current Gross Domestic Product.

The sectors emerging to provide favorable environmental, social and economic impacts require apparent understanding of these risks which are inherited and require the development of new pricing and evaluation methods and procedures for building internal capacity. This can be a special contribution of financial institutions in the Growth of the nation by developing this type of competency and thereby help the economy in achieving Sustainable development Goals and Paris Agreement. The internal sustainability targets involving the social as well as environmental concerns in the formulation of business strategies can be achieved, which is the most import area of functioning of financial institutions. The projects aligned to the climate sectors are been provided access to capital at ow cost by Development Financial Institutions which includes Supranational and Green Climate Funds.

The opportunities thus provided should create a positive environment for financial circular models with changing cash flows and material flows and because of this the financing of these business models have a unique set of risks as well as challenges. The risks as perceived by the financial institutions include – uncertainty in consumer's acceptance of the innovative circular products, risks related with payments, no surety of success of new products, absent of risk analysis for financial institutions, the residual value of second hand or refurbished products, issue of ownership of product – particularly business model involving product as a service, the creditworthiness of consumers requires a serious attention as it may lead to the risk of bankruptcy of the consumer to supplier and financial institutions. The contract or legal risk also exists in lease agreements. There is no unique financial product that may be availed by circular economy projects or business models given the profiling of risks. The appropriate financial mechanism depends on the inherent risk, the level of advancement in the product life cycle of the business model and the current life cycle stage of the business. In the initial stage of product life cycle the capital risk

Table 3. Forms of finances availed for different capital requirements

Banking and Non-Banking Financial	Debt Finance, Supply Chain Finance Blended Finance Credit enhancements
Development Finance Institutions and Multilateral Development Banks	Green mortgages
Capital Markets	Green bonds, SDG bonds
Foundations and Impact Investors	Seed funding, impact bonds
Venture Capital and Private Equity Funds	Private equity
Crowd Funding Platforms	Seed funding
Institutional Investors	Pension funds
Specialized funds like Green Climate Fund	Debt, grants

Source: Circular Economy: Business Imperative for India- TERI and Yes Bank

is higher as compared to the latter stages of product life cycle. The various sources of funds across the different stages of product life cycle are also different mentioned in the table 4

7. CONCLUSION

The policies in India are still focusing on the themes relating to individual areas and the approach followed in not well structured and systematic. Most of the policies related to extraction and mining of minerals does not focus on resource efficiency and secondary resource management (NITI AYOG, 2017). The National Design Policy of 2007 directly relate with resource efficiency and secondary resource management but is related to value the strategic content of material in the product, which is crucial for resource recovery. The National Design Policy (2007) does not directly relate to the need for enhancing RE and secondary resource management but valuing the strategic content of material in a product is crucial to enhance resource recovery. Integration of science, technology and innovation and emphasis on RE and SRM can go a long way in achieving sustainable and inclusive growth. This poses a challenge for businesses that want to adopt circular economy models. Business involving circularity approaches viz, substituting the scarce and hazardous material/ resources with the restorative, cleaner and more regenerative ones involves huge financial resources which they lack. There is an urgent required for not only technological but financial eco system also that can help India to adopt circular economy. For sustainable growth along with the creation of job opportunities manufacturing sector is gaining. Enhancement in resource efficiency and promotion of use of SRM has tremendous potential to create environmental

Table 4. Sources of funds across the different stages of product life cycle

CONCEPT -Grand Subsidy Crowd funding	**START** Venture / Seed capital New entrants	**GROWTH** Debt: banks Public capital Impact investor	**MATURITY** Institutions (pension funds)

Source: *Circular Economy: Business Imperative for India- TERI and Yes Bank*

benefits and economic opportunities in the manufacturing processes. Enhancing RE and promoting the use of SRM has the potential to create both economic opportunities and environmental benefits in the manufacturing process. Despite these benefits most of the policies fail to promote resource efficiency and SRM in the manufacturing sector.

The promotion of Circular Economy cannot be solely done by the Government only. An approach involving the partnership of consumers, retailers and investors jointly is required. Circular Economy is a concept that brings management, resources and residues together for the wellbeing of Economy, Livelihood and Environment. If this concept of Circular Economy is implemented properly it will encourage innovations and will channelize investments. Circular Economy is India's hope towards a smart and sustainable growth.

REFERENCES

Bureau of Energy Efficiency. (2015). *Perform, Achieve and Trade*. Retrieved from https://www.beeindia.gov.in/content/pat-3

Bureau of Energy Efficiency. (2017). *About Standards & Labelling Program*. Retrieved from https://www.beeindia.gov.in/content/pat-

Bureau of Indian Standards. (2016). *Operation of ECO Mark Scheme*. Retrieved from http://www.bis.org.in/cert/echo_mark_scheme.htm

Circular Economy. (2017). *Business Imperative for India*. Retrieved from https://www.teriin.org/sites/default/files/2018-03/TERI-YES_BANK_Circular_Economy_Report.pdf

Confederation of Indian Industry. (2014). *Innovation Ecosystem in India*. Retrieved from https://www2.deloitte.com/content/dam/Deloitte/in/Documents/technology-media-telecommunications/in-tmt-innovation-ecosystem-of-india-noexp.pdf

Department of Heavy Industry. (2012). *National Electric Mobility Mission Plan 2020*. Retrieved from https://www.dhi.nic.in/UserView/index?mid=1347

Department of Industrial Policy and Promotion. (2017). *National Policy Design*. Retrieved from https://dipp.gov.in/sites/default/files/CFPC_2017_FINAL_RELEASED_28.8.17.pdf

Department of Science and Technology. (2013). *Science, Technology and Innovation Policy, 2013*. Retrieved from http://dst.gov.in/sites/default/files/STI%20Policy%202013-English.pdf

Di Maio, F., & Rem, P. C. (2015). A robust indicator for promoting circular economy through recycling. *Journal of Environmental Protection*, *6*(10), 1095–1104. doi:10.4236/jep.2015.610096

Ellen Mac Arthur Foundation. (2016). *Circular Economy in India: Rethinking growth for long term prosperity*. Retrieved from https://www.ellenmacarthurfoundation.org/assets/downloads/Summary_Circular-economy-in-India_5-Dec_2016.pdf

Ellen Mac Arthur Foundation. (2016). *Money makes the world go round*. Retrieved from https://www.ellenmacarthurfoundation.org/assets/downloads/ce100/FinanCE.pdf

Ellen MacArthur Foundation & GRANTA. (2015). *Project Overview: An Approach to Measuring Circularity*. Ellen Mac Arthur Foundation.

Gupta, D. S. (2015). Key Determinants ofSustainable Product Design and Manufacturing. Procedia CIRP, 26. doi:10.1016/j.procir.2014.07.166

ING. (2015). *Rethinking finance in a Circular Economy*. Retrieved from https://think.ing.com/uploads/reports/Financing_the_Circular_Economy.pdf

Khatri, Garg, & Dangayach. (n.d.). Critical Success Factors of Sustainable Manufacturing and Procurement: An Empirical Study. *International Journal of Social Ecology and Sustainable Development, 10*(3).

Kumar, A., Wasan, P., Luthra, S., & Dixit, G. (2020). Development of a framework for selecting a sustainable location of waste electrical and electronic equipment recycling plant in emerging economies. *Journal of Cleaner Production*, *277*, 122645.

Kumar, A., Wasan, P., Luthra, S., & Dixit, G. (2020). Development of a framework for selecting a sustainable location of waste electrical and electronic equipment recycling plant in emerging economies. *Journal of Cleaner Production*, *277*, 122645.

Ministry of Electronics & Information Technology. (2019a). *National Policy for 2019*. Retrieved from "https://meity.gov.in/writereaddata/files/Notification_NPE2019_dated25.02.2019.pdf

Ministry of Electronics & Information Technology. (2019b). *National Policy for 2012*. Retrieved from https://meity.gov.in/writereaddata/files/NPE_Notification.pdf

Ministry of Environment and Forest. (2003). *Corporate Responsibility for Environmental Protection (CREP)*. https://hspcb.gov.in/Charter%20on%20corporate%20responsibility%20for%20Env.%20Protection.pdf

Ministry of Environment and Forest & Climate Change. (1999). *The Fly Ash Notification, 1999*. Retrieved from http://envfor.nic.in/legis/hsm/flyash.html

Ministry of Environment and Forest & Climate Change. (2006). *National Environment Policy 2006*. Retrieved from http://www.moef.gov.in/sites/default/files/introduction-nep2006e.pdf

Ministry of Environment and Forest & Climate Change. (2010). *Batteries Management and Handling) Amendment Rules 2010*. Retrieved from http://enfor.nic.in/legis/hsm/SO1002.pdf

Ministry of Environment and Forest & Climate Change. (2016). *Waste Management Rules*. Retrieved from http://envfor.nic.in/sites/default/files/waste%20Management%20Rukes%202016pdf

Ministry of Environment and Forest & Climate Change. (2016). *Waster management Rules*. Retrieved from http://www.mppcb.nic.in/proc/Batteries%20(Management%20and%20Handling)%20Rules,%20 2001.pdf

Ministry of Environment and Forest & Climate Change. (n.d.). Retrieved from http://moef.gov.in/environment/waste-management/

Ministry of Environment Forest and Climate Change. (2016). Retrieved from http://www.indiaenvironmentportal.org.in/files/file/BMW%20Rules,%202016.pdf

Ministry of Environment Forest and Climate Change (MOEFCC). (2015). Retrieved from http://www.ismenvis.nic.in/Database/Fly-Ash-Amendment_Draft-MoEF_3366.aspx

Ministry of Micro, Small and Medium Enterprises. (2017). *National Manufacturing Competitiveness Programme*. Retrieved from http://dcmsme.gov.in/schemes/nmcp.scm.htm

Ministry of Mines. (2017). *The Mines and Minerals (Development and Regulation) Amendment Act 2016*. Retrieved from https://prsindia.org/billtrack/the-mines-and-minerals-development-and-regulation-amendment-bill-2016-4228

Ministry of New and Renewable Energy. (2009). *National Policy on Biofuels*. Retrieved from http://mnre.gov.in/schemes/new-technologies/biofuels

Ministry of Petroleum and Natural Gas. (2019). *National Auto Vision Fuel Policy 2025*. Retrieved from http://petroleum.nic.in/sites/default/files/autopol.pdf

Ministry of Steel. (2019b). *National Mineral Policy, 2008*. Retrieved from https://www.nepa.gov.jm/documents/NATIONAL_MINERALS_POLICY_DRAFT_JULY_2008.pdf

Ministry of Steel. (2019a). *National Steel Policy 2017*. Retrieved from https://steel.gov.in/sites/default/files/draft-national-steel-policy-2017.pdf

On the Dynamic Mechanism of Developing Recycling Economy for Enterprises in China. (2010). *International Journal of Social Ecology and Sustainable Development*, 20–29. www.igi-global.com/article/dynamic-mechanism-developing-recyclingeconomy/41957?camid=4v1a

Press Information Bureau. (2011). *National Manufacturing Policy*. Retrieved from https://dipp.gov.in/policies-rules-and-acts/policies/national-manufacturing-policy

Renewable Energy Certificate Registry of India. (2010). *Renewable Energy Certification (RECs) 2010*. Retrieved from https://www.recregistryindia.nic.in/index.php/publics/AboutREC

Thelen, D., Van Acoleyen, M., Huurman, W., Tom, T., van Brunschot, C., Edgerton, B., & Ben, K. (2018). *Scaling the Circular Built Environment: Pathways for Business and Government*. World Business Council for Sustainable Development & Circle Economy.

Tse, Esposito, & Soufani. (2015). Why the circular economy matters. *European Business Review*.

World Economic Forum. (2014). *Reorganize and streamline pure materials flows*. Retrieved http://reports.weforum.org/toward-the-circular-economy- accelerating-the-scale-up-across-global-supply-chains/reorganize-and-streamline-pure-materials-flows

Chapter 7
Visualising the Prospective Circular Economy:
Closing the Economic Loop – The Case of India

Varun Chotia
Jaipuria Institute of Management, Jaipur, India

Vranda Jain
Jaipuria Institute of Management, Noida, India

ABSTRACT

In contrast to the traditional linear economic model, which is primarily based on the 'take-make-consume-throw away' pattern, the concept of circular economy is based on the principles of sharing, leasing, reuse, repair, refurbishment, and recycling, revolving in a closed-loop, where the value focus is on products and the materials which these products contain. In simple words, it focuses on waste reduction to a minimum level. From an Indian perspective, the idea has immense potential as it could deliver numerous opportunities like less pressure on the environment, a higher level of competitiveness, better security in terms of supply of raw materials, more innovation, higher growth, and more jobs. At the same time, this shift also brings along certain challenges like financing issues, the need for key economic enablers, skill requirements, consumer behaviour and business models, and the need for multi-level governance.

Background of Circular Economy Concept

The concept of Circular Economy (hereafter CE) is usually defined as the one in which the products and materials contained in these products are highly valued. This is in complete contrast to the linear economic model followed traditionally which is based on a 'take-make-consume-throw away' philosophy. CE concept is primarily a production and consumption model which finds its base in two complementary

DOI: 10.4018/978-1-7998-4990-2.ch007

loops drawing inspiration from biological cycles. One of these loops is identified as existing for 'biological' materials (that can be decomposed by living organisms) and the other one containing 'technical' materials (that cannot be decomposed by living organisms). CE aims at minimizing the resource usage in each of the loop.

In practical sense, CE concept follows the approach of waste reduction to the minimum. CE works towards keeping the materials/ resources in circulation even when the products are approaching the final stage in their life cycle. Hence, these resources can be re-used productively and contribute in creation of value, yet again. The measures which lead towards CE concept work on the pattern of reusing, repairing, refurbishing and recycling existing materials and products. The CE philosophy rests on the strong fundamental that what is considered as *waste* in linear economy has the potential to be converted into a *valuable resource* using the CE framework.

Various examples can be seen where companies across the globe have implemented CE concept in various sectors for their own specific products. In CE approach, different types of indicators can be used for resource use. One of most commonly used indicator is Resource Productivity. Productivity of a resource at the country level involves two parameters- gross domestic product (GDP) and domestic material consumption (Blomsma and Brennan, 2017). Few other indicators employed by researchers and practitioners (MacArthur, 2013) for monitoring CE implementation and its progress are resource efficiency, recycling rates, the amount of waste per GDP output, the amount of municipal waste per capita and eco-innovation index.

Figure 1.

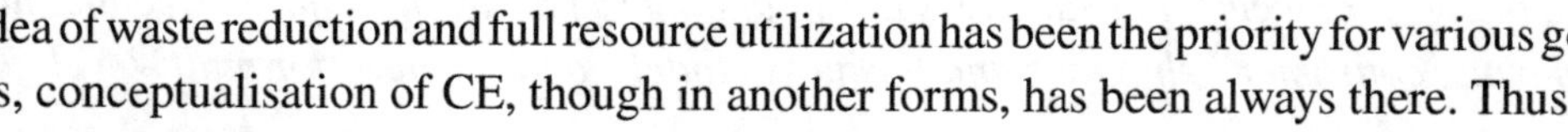

The Upsurge of Circular Economy Concept

Since the idea of waste reduction and full resource utilization has been the priority for various governments for decades, conceptualisation of CE, though in another forms, has been always there. Thus it becomes relevant to understand the emergence of CE concept and its gaining importance in recent scenario. The present section brings forth the main drivers of CE.

- **Rapid Changes in the Pattern of Consumer Demand**

Off late, it has been observed that sustainability practices pursued by businesses have gained importance in purchase decision of consumers (Coderoni & Perito, 2020). Products made using environment friendly/ socially sustainable materials are in demand. What catches buyers' attention these days is not the catchy advertising slogans or campaigns but the sustainable practices pursued by companies leading to environmental benefits and the enhanced product life, leading to its use over a longer duration

Figure 2.

and hence generating personal savings. To sum up, sustainability has become an important aspect for consumers, driving the move towards adoption of CE.

- **Shortage of Resources**

Companies across the globe involved in the production of goods from different sectors use a variety of resources. Since earth's resources are limited in quantity and the present thrust on linear economic model, most of the resources are used just once. According to government estimates, 20% of the raw material types currently in use will run out in the next 50 years and 35% of them within the next 100 years, considering the most important fact that most of these are not re-used even once. This is an alarming sign as earth's population is growing and the need for resources is increasing day by day. As per the rising population and growing demand of our country, the absolute requirement of food, water and energy would go up by 35 per cent, 40 per cent and 50 per cent respectively by 2030. Since the supply of some of the resources is relatively inelastic, our existing resource availability may not be able to catch up with this increased level of demand. This increased pace of consumption forces us to infer that effectively, we are "borrowing" the raw materials that should be used by our future generations. The situation is alarming and hence recycling of resources and moving towards CE adoption appears to be the need of the hour. The continuous depletion of raw materials is a major issue, not only from an availability perspective, but also from a financial prospective as it creates volatility in the prices of raw materials, thereby generating instability and financial consequences for businesses involved.

- **Technological Development**

Since quite some time, economies have been functioning in one direction (refer Figure I). This unidirectional flow involved extracting resources manufacturing products as per the market demand and disposing off the waste Presently, we are in midst of the fourth industrial revolution, which is motivated by technological development and built on pillars of digitalization and data intelligence. There is no doubt in accepting that while the first industrial revolution introduced waste to the world, the world is now collectively working towards if not eliminating, but certainly reducing the present levels of waste generation. The fourth industrial revolution completely supports CE concept and promotes resource sustainability by keeping the discarded materials in perpetual circulation and reusing them. Section IV will discuss how technological development apart from being a major driver of CE, is also an enabler of CE adoption.

Potential Opportunities

If we envision this concept of CE from an Indian prospective, the idea has immense potential (environmental and economic rationale) as it can deliver numerous opportunities. These potential opportunities are being discussed below:

- **Reduced Pressure on Environment**: CE approach would involve lesser consumption of natural resources (like water, land) and would generate effective waste management, leading to a favourable impact on climate, reduction in Greenhouse Gas (GHG) emissions and limiting the biodiversity loss by reducing habitat disruption and marine littering.
- **Enhanced Security of Supply of Raw Materials**: Risks and uncertainties in the supply of raw materials ranging from their availability, price volatility and import dependency would be put to rest using the CE concept.
- **Higher Level of Competitiveness**: Improved resource efficiency as an outcome of adoption of CE approach would generate higher savings for businesses and consumers. This could result in reducing the net resource spending which would again have a positive impact on total benefits. If the government adopts for much stricter environmental legislations, this shall too provide a competitive advantage to businesses.
- **Innovation Drive**: Implementation of CE model would necessitate redesigning materials and/or products for circular use. This would initiate an innovation drive across different sectors of the economy. Under this approach, the redesign principle shall apply even to those sectors which are usually not considered to be innovative.
- **Growth and Jobs**: CE would lead to a strengthening of economic growth trajectory and creation of new jobs. The increasing pace of technological advancement may further complement and in specific sector supplement jobs.

Enablers for Adoption of Circular Economy in India

As discussed in previous sections, at the country level, the adoption of CE would enhance benefits of industrialization, promote socio-economic wellbeing, minimize vulnerability to environmental shocks and subsequent adverse impact on prices and will thus invoke beneficial socio-economic and environmental transformations. To achieve these benefits arising out of sustainable production and consumption, global organizations, academicians, researchers and environmentalists have initiated discussions for aligning CE strategies in accordance with United Nation's Sustainable Development Goals (SDGs), global climate change discussions and global treaty on biodiversity protection (Reike *et al.,* 2018). Embedding sustainable resource use through closing the loop would act as a catalyst for global economic growth.

In spite of these underling benefits and efforts, the progress in the direction of implementation of CE as a new development paradigm is far from satisfactory. The recent Circularity Gap Report (2020) draws attention to the fact that the global economy is at present only 8.6 per cent circular. This highlights two issues. First being the poor transmission of improved energy efficiency and resource productivity in absolute resource usage. De Wit *et al.* (2018) estimates that less than one-tenth of the global waste generated in 2015 was recycled. The second aspect being the alarming difference in adoption levels between developed and developing countries. Extant literature (e.g. Turkeli *et al.* (2018) has paid minimal attention to CE analysis in developing countries, with China being an exception. Having legislated CE in 2016, China developed an Industrial symbiosis- an ecosystem leading to an industry's by-product being utilized by another industry as raw materials. Researchers (e.g. Govindan *et al.*, 2016, Mukherjee and Mondal, 2009; Sharma *et al.*, 2016) have shown that developing countries like India, Bangladesh, Bhutan, Brazil and Sri Lanka are in infancy stage of executing their remanufacturing processes.

The slow pace of adoption of CE paradigm by developing countries is unsupportive of these economies emerging as global production hubs and future consumption centres. It is estimated that out of an additional 1.8 billion consumers by 2025, 55 per cent would belong to the emerging world, with major concentration in India and China, implementation of CE framework would be imperative to achieve desired output growth while responding to growing demands in these emerging and developing countries (Winans *et al.,* 2017). Empirical studies in Indian context (Nason & Wiklund, 2018) have found a positive correlation between domestic economic growth and internal resource requirements, suggesting an increase in demand for resources and underlining the dire need to enhance the pace of development of circular value chains.

The concept of CE has evolved differently across different nations. While developed nations like EU and Japan have adopted CE as a bottom-up approach (Winans *et al.*, 2017), China implemented it as a top-down strategy (Yu *et al.*, 2015). What is commonly accepted amongst nations is that the implementation of CE is challenging and thus requires a detailed discussion and deliberation on its enabling mechanism. Since enabling factors already exist in the system, they can support and clear the way for other factors. India, at present, is witnessing a higher demand for resources which is posing a challenge to optimal resource utilization while ensuring maximum positive social impact and minimum environmental damage. This section discusses the enablers that will assist the transition from a linear to a circular model in Indian context.

- **Creating Awareness**

Numerous studies in marketing literature have established a shift in consumer behavior in favour of ethical and sustainable products. This can be an opportune time for companies to generate greater awareness about benefits of CE paradigm and the cleaner, resource efficient options it has to offer. With the intention of influencing mindsets and have a wider reach, it is suggested to adopt multi stakeholder programs, comprising of consumers and producers in general and entrepreneurs, engineers, product and procurement managers, designers, academicians, dealers, refurbishers and resident welfare associations (RWAs) in particular. Educating about the emerging new business models through workshops, seminars, knowledge sharing sessions, engaging in collaborative activities and using other ways to enhance outreach like organizing collection drives can generate awareness. Ministries and departments may launch stand-alone awareness programs or may collaborate with industrial associations. To equip trainers with desired skills, government can also consider setting up specialized institutions and drive CE adoption to scale. To achieve wider application over the medium and long term, integrating CE model and practices in school and higher education curriculum can be considered. Encouraging informal participants to implement proper waste disposal, adopt sustainable practices in procurement and production can also be a step in the right direction.

- **Access to Technology**

Disruptive technology like Internet of things, block chains, artificial intelligence, machine learning, Satellite based GPS, wireless technology and advances in big data can facilitate implementation of CE paradigm. These technological interventions having digital, physical and biological facets can act as enablers towards shared platforms, extended lifecycles and cleaner resources, thereby improving supply chain traceability and ensuring a closer monitoring of external environment. In Indian context, technology support towards CE implementation is subject to two challenges. One, arising out of the digital divide with close to 14 per cent people without a mobile phone and around 59 per cent of population not having Internet access (figures as per government statistics), coupled with inadequate government mechanism towards universal access to digital and communications networks. Importing cheaper hardware from developed countries as a short term solution to bridging the digital divide would have health and environmental risks over the longer horizon. The other challenge emerges from ad-hoc government support towards the development and commercialization of local and indigenous technologies. Facilitating technology startups by setting up technology business incubators, extending seed support and partnering with domestic and international R&D institutions would provoke grassroots technological innovations and facilitate knowledge transfer into process and product development, promoting output growth and employment generation.

- **Access to Finance**

Transformation from a linear to a CE necessitates adequate access to finance. This has been most one the most challenging and concerning issue for smaller firms to implement CE compatible industrial processes and innovation priorities. In a study of developing countries, Humphrey (2018) estimated an infrastructure investment gap of $1 trillion a year for developing countries in the 12-year period till 2030. Before suggesting the measures to overcome this gap, it become relevant for the financial community to evaluate risks and opportunities arising out of such transition. Adoption of CE framework can provide an opportunity to leverage new businesses created, develop innovative financial instruments and cater to new markets so emerged. On the other hand, an assessment of risks and challenges in financing CE business models may include investment restrictions on new and unproven business models, multiple forms of capital requirement for the unique risk-return assessment of CE projects, scaling up finance for CE activities, uncertainty in consumer preferences towards CE products and uncertain residual value of CE products in second-hand market. Apart from provisioning budgetary allocation and extending financial support and subsidies to private sector, government should develop regulatory framework to attract venture capitalists and private equity firms for mobilizing CE funds. Financial institutions will have to innovate and respond while maximizing returns on investments and minimizing switching costs and risks. At the micro level, companies would be required to allocate appropriate capital funds for research, innovation and development.

- **Enabling Policy Landscape**

Policymakers in developing countries are faced with the challenge of shifting businesses and consumers towards resource efficient CE paradigm. Indirectly, it also calls for extending support towards system and product innovation, thereby developing markets for sustainable products. Due to complex interactions among participants in a CE, the policy landscape engulfs different production and consumption components, making it complicated. Comprehensive policies can be an answer towards facilitating better resource productivity and accelerating CE adoption by overcoming implementation barriers. In Indian context, a mix of policy tools and instruments comprising of regulations (e.g., permits, sanctions, inspections); economic instruments (e.g., subsidies, taxes, rebates, tradable permits); information based measures (providing information through public campaigns, disclosures etc.) and voluntary incentives (voluntary agreements between government and private sector/households) can provide a balanced approach towards tailoring efficiency issues at local and national levels.

- **Building Institutional Capacity**

In the absence of strong governance frameworks and inappropriate CE specific regulations/standards, the rapid pace of urbanization in developing countries has posed risk in terms of installing cheaper technologies and devices. There is also growing concern over the repeatedly recycled products and plastics that may contain toxic and hazardous substances, leading to health related risks. One such example is the poorly regulated informal building sector in India where close to 90 per cent of the residential building stocks is not regulation compliant, leading to lower asset lifetime (Jawaid *et al.,* 2018). Institutional frameworks comprising of varied platforms and structures can support coordination across different sectors and levels. Researchers (e.g. Healey, 1998) have defined Institutional capacity as stakeholders' engagement and participation in collective actions to solve everyday problems and have laid stress on institutional capacity building as an important constituent for developing an industrial symbiosis network. In Indian context, a centralized or distributed coordination amongst different ministries will foster greater usage of sustainable resources. It should be the prerogative of Environment Ministry to undertake industrial and innovation strategies and work in sync with other ministries while generating a deeper government ownership.

- **Promoting Collaboration and Partnerships**

Niesten *et al.* (2017) identified lack of collaboration between businesses and within a business as factors hindering the closure of loop. For example, gaps may arise in the requirements of product designers and recyclers, leading to inadequate support in adoption of CE model. Researchers (e.g., Mishra et al., 2019) have highlighted that since businesses cannot achieve full circularity on their own, the network of collaborating organizations holds great importance. Fostering internal and external collaborations and partnerships in value chains, within industry, government authorities, MSMEs, NGOs, consumers can enable the implementation of CE framework. Businesses should act as belonging to a wider operating system and extend cooperation along the value chain. Such collaboration will reduce the potential economic risks and costs associated with desired investments. For example, a collaboration between industries associated with hydropower- like marine industries, agriculture and processing industry- can enhance economic and environmental sustainability. Within an industry, a company can consider partnering with upstream suppliers and downstream customers for designing new processes and products and contribute towards closing the loop.

- **Overcoming Infrastructural Deficits**

It is known that a well-developed infrastructure comprising of transportation networks for goods and people, distribution of energy, power stations, sewage systems, etc. forms a country's backbone and contribute to economic growth and stability. Provisioning of this critical infrastructure builds the demand for raw materials and energy. Further, due to rapid urbanization in India and consumption pattern getting increasingly influenced by counterparts in developed countries (Ahmed *et al.,* 2016), there is an increasing pressure on infrastructure. However, the absence of required infrastructure has led to an expansion in slum areas and increased density of population in slums. Hence the need of the hour is to complement the wave of growth by focusing on investing in new infrastructure and building stock. CE can provide an important pathway to overcome the smaller stocks of raw materials through reuse and recycling. For instance, resources available in unused assets, products, Infrastructure and at other places can be drawn back to circulation and value chains.

- **Assisting Standardization and Research & Development (R&D)**

CE aspires towards zero waste and closing the loop in production processes. However, in Indian context, the resource efficiency requirements have been inhibited by absence of required standards. Guidelines and standards such as registration with BIS, declaration of CE practices and materials used in production, details on possibility of virgin materials getting replaced by secondary materials can address recyclability, reusability and recoverability. In other words, well-defined standards to be pursued by companies while at different stages of product cycle- ranging from product, material use, recycling, collection, disposal, etc. would aid not only in ensuring efficient usage of resources but also would work towards maximizing stakeholders' benefits. It would also be helpful if adequate attention is paid towards the development of R & D infrastructure in sync with the rapidly changing technological and material composition. Technological innovations like IOT, 3D printing, censors and controls; sharing platforms and resource recovery technologies can contribute towards implementation of CE models. Hence a continued public and private sector support is needed for identifying the key technological areas in line with the CE framework.

Policy for Achieving Waste Reduction in Circular Economy

The discussions in previous sections necessitate the formulation and implementation of a policy framework towards CE adoption for all stakeholders, exclusively for Indian setting. This policy should serve as a benchmark towards implementation of sustainability and waste reduction and its management. The prime thrust of such a policy should be on:

- Setting new waste management targets for the future. Along with this, also increasing the share of municipal waste and packaging waste prepared for reuse and recycling, and steadily limiting the municipal waste landfill. Each of these reduction targets can be achieved by putting a certain optimal value to be achieved and a specific time frame.
- Adhering to monitoring compliance along with the development of an early warning system.
- Devising producer responsibility schemes, setting minimum requirements, segregating producers' contribution and specifying products' treatment in later stages of product life cycle.
- Endorsing food waste prevention and its reuse.
- Restructuring the provisions for by-products and the end-of-waste status when products are no longer deemed to be re-used.
- Aligning definitions, calculation methods for the set targets, reporting obligations and provisions on delegated and implementing acts.

Closing the Loop: Action Plan

The action plan for CE approach has to be in sync with the schemes and directions laid out by different institutions and bodies towards achieving sustainability. 'Closing the loop' CE approach is compatible with the waste reduction policy. Countries across the globe are striving towards attaining the United Nations Sustainable Development Goals (SDG), with India being no exception. Goal 12 of SDG stresses on sustainable consumption and production. The present section brings forth the action plan while focusing on several broad areas, besides waste management.

- From **consumption** perspective, the action plan should work towards better dissemination of information pertaining to green consumption and generating consumer awareness on the same. Consumers attention can be drawn towards usage of sustainable materials in the product via product labelling. Spreading the benefits of shared products and encouraging innovative forms of consumption like preferring the consumption of services over products and promoting CE in green public procurement can be the steps in right direction. This would require setting up markets for secondary raw materials and establishing quality standards for materials derived from waste while keeping an eye on toxic recycles. Treated waste water should be considered for reuse.
- From **production perspective**, the action plan should promote products' reparability and durability. Attention should also be given products' upgradation, recyclability and extended producer responsibility schemes. All of this would call for improving the product design. The synergy arising out of *Industrial Symbiosis* should be channelized well. In Indian context, this would generate business opportunities for small and medium enterprises (SMEs).

- From **Innovation** perspective, the action plan should involve engagements with stakeholders at different platforms and at different levels. This would infuse innovation in the existing structure and would foster development of newer skills and socio-economic benefit for the nation.

Suggestive Measures Under the Action Plan

In Indian context, the following five sectors have been identified as priority sectors due to their contribution in the economy and relative significance in CE framework.

- Food Waste
- Plastics
- Biomass and Bio-based products
- Critical Raw Materials
- Construction and Demolition

A brief outline of varied indicative measures pertaining to the priority sectors is as under.

- Legislative measures like proposal on water reuse for irrigation.
- Communication measures like information sharing on waste-to-energy, plastics and critical raw materials.
- Standards measures comprising of forced regulations like recycling of electronic waste and voluntary standards like recycling of construction and demolition waste.
- Implementation and enforcement measures like waste shipments, end-of-life vehicles, and use of former foodstuffs for animal feed.
- Support measures like better communication between manufacturers and recyclers.
- Indicator measures like developing indicators for measuring wastage of food.
- Guidance and best practice measures like integrating waste management and resource efficiency in terms of using the best available technique.

A well laid, coordinated approach with effective legislations, government leadership, adequate awareness, financial support and incentives to businesses adopting sustainable practices can enable India to reap the benefits of CE and overcome the challenges arising out of resource shortages in years to come.

REFERENCES

Ahmed, M. E., Khan, M. M., & Samad, N. (2016). Income, Social Class and Consumer Behaviour: A Focus on Developing Nations. *Journal of Applied Business and Economic Research*, *14*(10), 6679–6702.

Blomsma, F., & Brennan, G. (2017). The emergence of circular economy: A new framing around prolonging resource productivity. *Journal of Industrial Ecology*, *21*(3), 603–614. doi:10.1111/jiec.12603

Coderoni, S., & Perito, M. A. (2020). Sustainable consumption in the circular economy. An analysis of consumers' purchase intentions for waste-to-value food. *Journal of Cleaner Production*, *252*, 119870. doi:10.1016/j.jclepro.2019.119870 de Wit, M., Verstraeten-Jochemsen, J., Hoogzaad, J., & Kubbinga, B. (2019). The Circularity Gap Report 2019. *Circle Economy*. Available at https://www.circularity-gap.world/

Govindan, K., Shankar, K. M., & Kannan, D. (2016). Application of fuzzy analytic network process for barrier evaluation in automotive parts remanufacturing towards cleaner production–a study in an Indian scenario. *Journal of Cleaner Production, 114*, 199–213. doi:10.1016/j.jclepro.2015.06.092

Healey, P. (1998). Building institutional capacity through collaborative approaches to urban planning. *Environment & Planning A, 30*(9), 1531–1546. doi:10.1068/a301531

Humphrey, C. (2018). *Channeling private investment to infrastructure: What can multilateral development banks realistically do?* ODI Working paper 534, London: Overseas Development Institute Available at https://www.odi.org/sites/odi.org.uk/files/resource-documents/12176.pdf

Jawaid, M. F., Pipralia, S., & Kumar, A. (2018). Review of environment responsiveness of building regulations in Jaipur. *Journal of Urban Management, 7*(2), 111–120. doi:10.1016/j.jum.2018.06.001

MacArthur, E. (2013). Towards the circular economy. *Journal of Industrial Ecology, 2*, 23–44.

Mishra, J. L., Chiwenga, K. D., & Ali, K. (2019). Collaboration as an enabler for circular economy: A case study of a developing country. *Management Decision, ahead-of-print*(ahead-of-print). Advance online publication. doi:10.1108/MD-10-2018-1111

Mukherjee, K., & Mondal, S. (2009). Analysis of issues relating to remanufacturing technology–a case of an Indian company. *Technology Analysis and Strategic Management, 21*(5), 639–652. doi:10.1080/09537320902969174

Nason, R. S., & Wiklund, J. (2018). An assessment of resource-based theorizing on firm growth and suggestions for the future. *Journal of Management, 44*(1), 32–60. doi:10.1177/0149206315610635

Niesten, E., Jolink, A., de Sousa Jabbour, A. B. L., Chappin, M., & Lozano, R. (2017). Sustainable collaboration: The impact of governance and institutions on sustainable performance. *Journal of Cleaner Production, 155*, 1–6. doi:10.1016/j.jclepro.2016.12.085

Reike, D., Vermeulen, W. J., & Witjes, S. (2018). The circular economy: New or refurbished as CE 3.0?—exploring controversies in the conceptualization of the circular economy through a focus on history and resource value retention options. *Resources, Conservation and Recycling, 135*, 246–264. doi:10.1016/j.resconrec.2017.08.027

Sharma, V., Garg, S. K., & Sharma, P. B. (2016). Identification of major drivers and roadblocks for remanufacturing in India. *Journal of Cleaner Production, 112*, 1882–1892. doi:10.1016/j.jclepro.2014.11.082

Türkeli, S., Kemp, R., Huang, B., Bleischwitz, R., & McDowall, W. (2018). Circular economy scientific knowledge in the European Union and China: A bibliometric, network and survey analysis (2006–2016). *Journal of Cleaner Production, 197*, 1244–1261. doi:10.1016/j.jclepro.2018.06.118

Winans, K., Kendall, A., & Deng, H. (2017). The history and current applications of the circular economy concept. *Renewable & Sustainable Energy Reviews*, *68*, 825–833. doi:10.1016/j.rser.2016.09.123

Yu, F., Han, F., & Cui, Z. (2015). Evolution of industrial symbiosis in an eco-industrial park in China. *Journal of Cleaner Production*, *87*, 339–347. doi:10.1016/j.jclepro.2014.10.058

Chapter 8
International Trade in the Realm of the Circular Economy

Isha Jaswal
Delhi Metropolitan Education, Guru Gobind Singh Indraprastha University, India

ABSTRACT

A circular economy advocates the use of resources for the longest time possible and to further regenerate materials when such resources are at the end of their service life. The movement towards a circular economy brings structural changes in an economy, and this, in turn, can potentially impact the international trade regime. Consequently, the aim should be to achieve material circularity among various countries of the world. While transiting towards a circular economy, nations introduce superfluous trade restrictions and at times enter into trade disputes with trade partners. It is imperative that circular economy policies and trade policies are reciprocally supportive. International cooperation on circular economy value chains should thus be explored for coordination of quality standards of materials, promoting demand for second-hand goods and secondary raw materials, removing unnecessary regulatory barriers, and to avoid environmentally harmful activities.

'Waste can become a valuable resource.' This is the driving force behind the concept of circular economy. Waste is rather the result of how the natural resources have been put to use during the life-cycle of the product. With prudent policy initiatives, this waste can become important means of furthering the production at low cost and yet enhancing the growth rate of the economy.

It is thus important to device policies for development of materials, designing of products and industrial processing which are conducive for smooth transition towards circular economy. This entails that the resources are put to use for as long as possible, thus reaping the maximum value from them during their usage life term and thereafter recovering and regenerating products and materials at the end of each service life (figure 1).

This means that circular economy not only demands lesser use of natural resources to ascertain their supply longevity, but also highly efficient manufacture and use of materials throughout their life cycle. Nevertheless, world economies are not self-sufficient since raw materials, semi-finished and second hand goods and other are traded amongst countries within a product's entire value chain.

DOI: 10.4018/978-1-7998-4990-2.ch008

Figure 1.
Source: Waste and Resources Action Programme (WRAP). Available at: https://www.wrap.org.uk/about-us/about/wrap-and-circular-economy

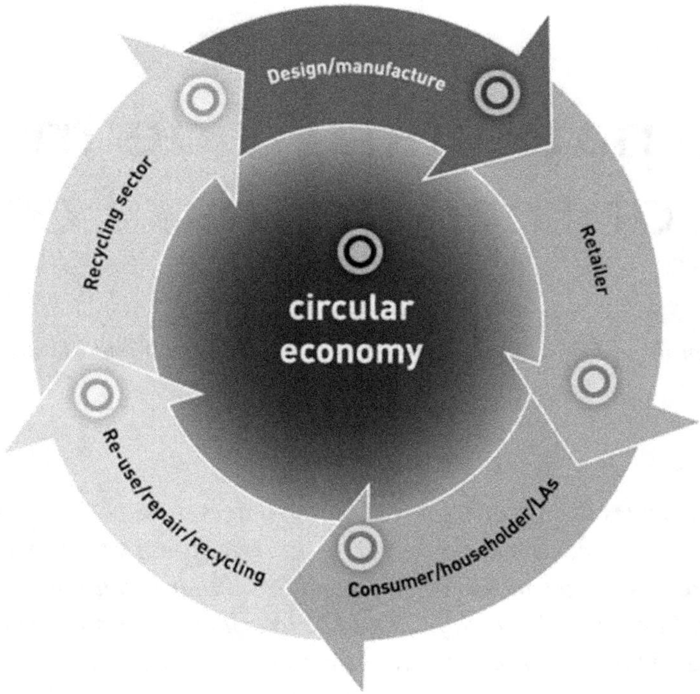

Consequently, the material circularity within the boundaries of domestic economy intersects with global trade at various junctures of the product value chain (figure 2). For instance, trade in goods for restoration and remanufacturing, trade in materials and waste for recycling and energy recovery, trade in secondary raw materials and trade in second-hand goods.

However, trade barriers impede the process and can pose hurdles in shifting towards a global world of circular economy. For example, remanufactured products undergo cross border issues while shipping across different domestic boundaries on account of varying standards and regulatory requirements.

Plastic waste is one such commodity which is traded because the exporting nations do not have adequate capacity to recycle or reprocess it. Usually developing economies are observed to import waste materials on account of economic value attached to it. Also, plastic waste is exported to less developed economies, where lack of standardized mechanisms result in mismanagement of this waste.

Importantly, production of plastic in itself depend upon fossil fuels. Thus, the entire value chain from production of plastic to disposition of its waste in open landfills and water bodies has caused threatening challenges to the natural environment round the world. In fact, since 1950 more than 60 percent of global plastic production had ended up in landfills, oceans or in natural surroundings.

Additionally trade of plastic waste is also on a rise. This entire scenario is worrisome because environment takes around over hundred years to consume the disposed plastic. Consequently, it has damaged the biodiversity and ecosystems worldwide. This makes adoption of circular economy imperative, and calls for harmonized efforts in international trade to transit towards a global circular economy. Further, the following segment discusses the case of EU export of plastic waste and related issues.

Figure 2.
Source: OECD. (2018). International Trade and the Transition to a Circular Economy. Available at: https://www.oecd.org/environment/waste/policy-highlights-international-trade-and-the-transition-to-a-circular-economy.pdf Notes: Solid arrows indicate domestic flows; dotted arrows indicate international trade flow

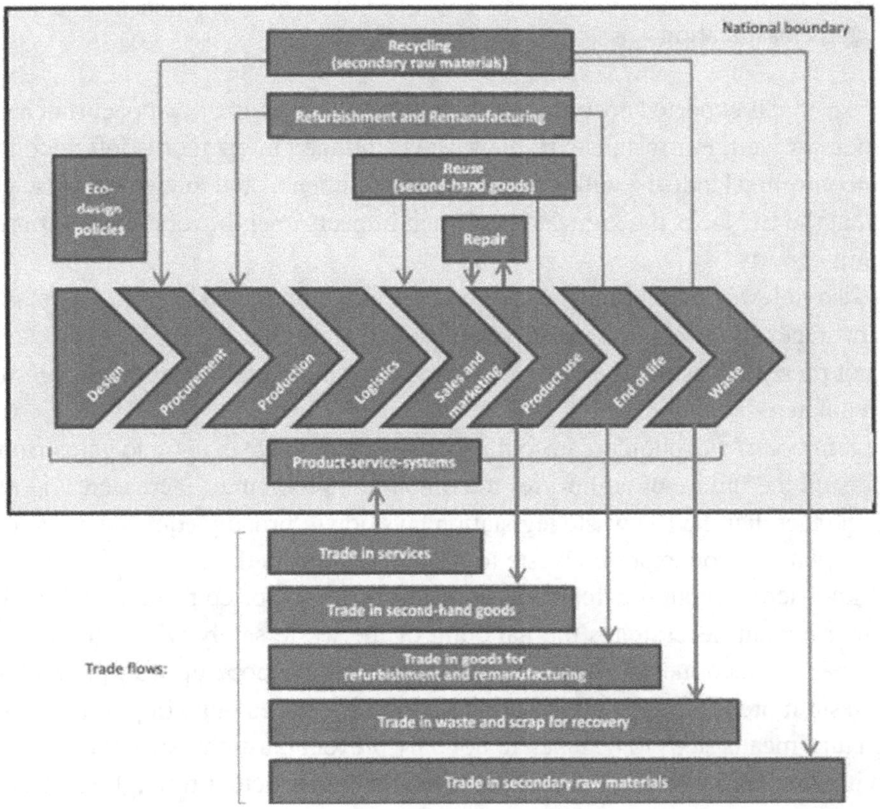

The Issues in Exporting Plastic Waste: Case of European Union (EU)

The EU is majorly deficient in reusing, recycling and recovering its plastic waste and challenges involved in managing the latter relative to paper, metal and glass is a matter of recent awareness. This is the reason why EU prefers to rather export this waste plastic. Not only due to lack of capacity, but plastic waster is exported on account of its import demand. This import demand exists due to the economic value or profits attached to it.

It is noteworthy that the EU law restricts the export of plastic waste for its disposal from the EU to non EU nations. However, Asian economies import it in large quantities because of profit making avenues. Additionally, the regulations pertaining to treatment of waste in these countries is different from the EU and are rather less stringent. Thus, the importing Asian economies witness an influx of plastic waste form the EU.

The determining factors of exporting plastic waste from the EU to other countries (in terms of volume and direction) include:

- tariff and non-tariff barriers and differences in gate fees at treatment facilities
- transport costs
- environmental taxes and policy stringency
- treatment capacity
- legislation and classification

The plastic waste that is exported not only has environmental and climatic impacts but has burgeoning social consequences as well. For instance, if this waste is dumped in open or is left uncollected or may be disposed in uncontrolled landfills; will only lead to environmental and related hazards. The downside of the matter is that the EU lacks the knowledge of such impacts or spillover effects with regards to the plastic waste that it exports.

Further, it is also noteworthy that most of the nations to whom the EU exports its plastic waste are still in their infant stages of developing effective and sound waste management. Also, the share of imported waste is not processed as per the European standards and to additional dismay, it might even be discarded in unregulated methods.

As a result, a number of stakeholders in south-east Asia reap huge economic gains from deficiency of legal operators and the failure of authorities to combat the problem of increased imports. This is in stark contrast to the fact that the EU waste legislation lays down 'broadly equivalent conditions' which apply to recovery operations on exported waste to economies within the EU.

Thus, lack of knowledge about the treatment of plastic waste exported from the EU and its resultant impact on the environment necessitates the handling of the waste safely within the EU. Given these concerns, the EU has initiated mechanisms in order to manage and cope up with the problems of plastics and plastic waste more efficiently. The European strategy places huge importance on the circular economy. This in turn means steps to be taken to not only prevent plastic waste but to manage the waste in consonance with the paramount environmental standards, in particular through reuse and recycling.

In this regards many novel and aspiring targets for plastic recycling had been incorporated in the waste directives of 2018. For instance, the Single Use Plastic Directive which bans single use plastic form 2021 is a transitional step towards handling plastic and resultant plastic waste in a circular manner.

Specific to trade in plastic waste, the EU nations are regulated by the Waste Shipment Regulation which forbids the export of plastic waste for disposal to non-EU countries (except those in the European Free Trade Area, which are party to the UN Basel Convention) and of hazardous plastic waste for recovery to countries that are not part of the Organisation for Economic Co-operation and Development (OECD).

Moreover the UN Basel Convention makes provision for including tainted, mixed or hard-to-recycle plastic waste. This shall more likely lessen the trade of plastic waste with economies not part of the EU and can act instrumental in plastic waste management. Nevertheless, in the short run, this may increase the landfilling. Nonetheless, this will simultaneously put pressure in EU countries to transit towards a more circular plastic economy.

In fact, the following figure (figure 3) evidences the enormous potential on part of the EU nations to boost the process of plastic recycling. It is clear from the figure the from 2007 to 2016, the recycling and recovery of plastic packaging waste — which accounts for the largest fraction of plastic waste— grew significantly. With recycling rates less than 50% in the EU till 2016 depicts the probability of gravely increasing the process.

Figure 3. Plastic packaging recycling and recovery in the EU-28 (2007-2016)
Source: European Environment Agency. (2019). Plastic waste trade in circular economy. Available at: https://www.eea.europa.eu/themes/waste/resource-efficiency/the-plastic-waste-trade-in

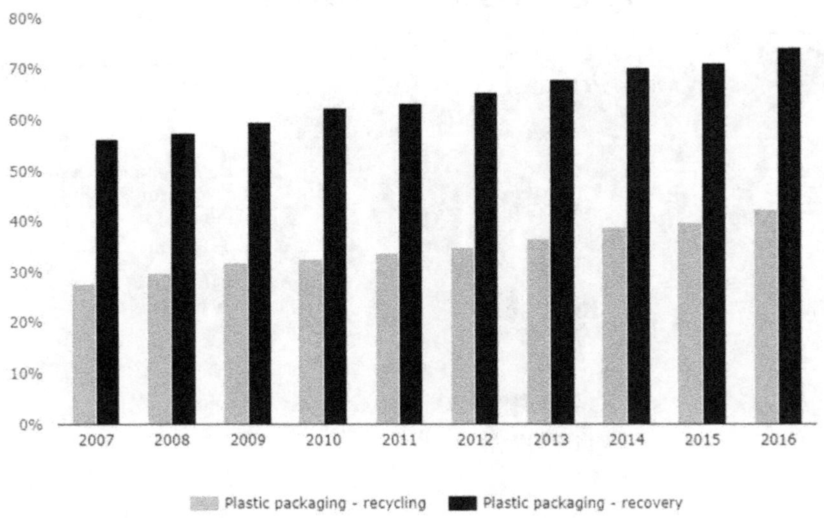

This means that plastic waste can provide huge opportunities to manufacturing units for processing secondary resources. Additionally, waste management and recycling initiatives will generate employment opportunities as well.

Trade in Waste and Secondary Raw Material

The world is becoming rapidly conscious of the resource potential of the waste material and hence the attached trading possibilities as well. It is important to understand that waste material can be processed to generate material and energy resource. This gravely enhances the significance of trade in waste. For instance, 13 percent of the world's second hand steel production took place in India in 2014. This was when the domestic supply of steel scrap was relatively less in India, only to indicate the imperativeness of trade of waste material to enhance the production of second-hand good in the importing economy. In fact, trading this waste to those countries which have better know-how of its processing and efficient regulatory mechanism can eventually push up the rates of recycling globally.

Nevertheless, where on one hand, production potential on part of developing nations can suffer due to imposition of trade barriers; on the other hand, concerns have been raised time and again with regards to mismanagement of imported waste and hence its harmful impact on the environment. Moreover, it has become apparent through global evidences that less stringent policy controls and liberal environmental standards have actually boosted the trade of waste material and scrap products. This scenario is rather common to advanced developing nations and other emerging economies where capacity and strategy of waste management is quite limited and underdeveloped.

The important concern that needs to be addressed is whether this traded scrap and waste is being processed in tune with the goals and purposes of circular economy. For instance, the policy of 'reduce, reuse and recycle' can prove to be extremely critical in this direction. Thus, enhancing the scope of

Figure 4.
Source: OECD. (2020). Environment at a Glance Indicators – Circular economy, waste and materials. Available at: https://www.oecd.org/environment/environment-at-a-glance/Circular-Economy-Waste-Materials-Archive-February-2020.pdf

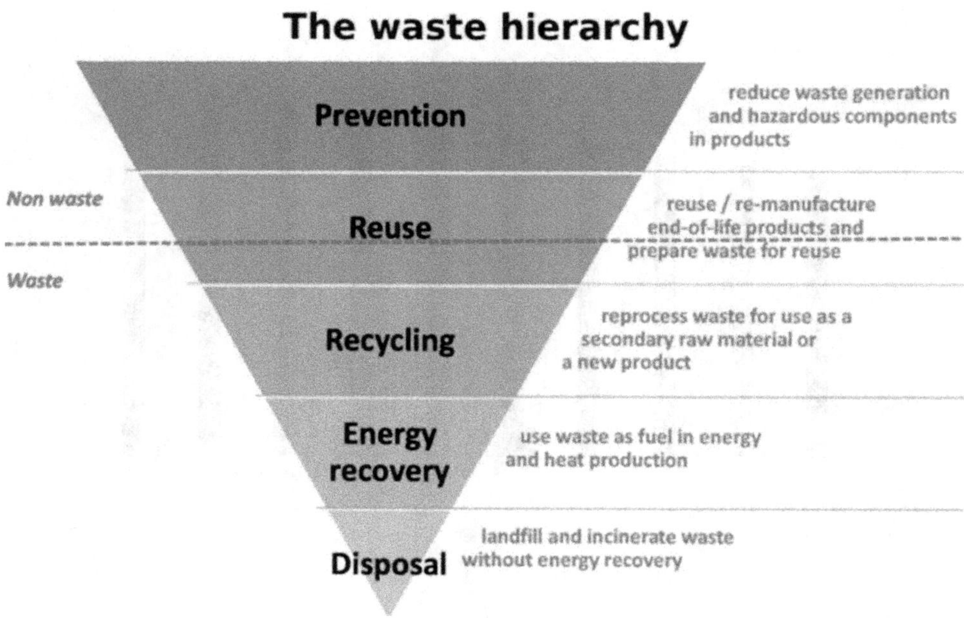

management of waste according to the hierarchy depicted in the figure can ensure the effective and efficient use of materials throughout the stages of their life cycle.

However, what adds to this concern is the difference in the classification of secondary material, waste and scrap amongst various economies of the world. Thus the objective of circular economy may call in for standardized trading norms in this regard and near uniformity in definition and classification of such products.

Further, out of the total worldwide production of iron ore, 43 percent of it was exported from producing nations in 2013. This fact highlights that economies round the world are differently endowed with natural resources and minerals. In turn this leads to significant implications on international trade of primary raw materials. Nevertheless, its international demand can be replaced by secondary raw materials.

According to international economic theory, traded goods have a net positive economic value attached to them. Considering the fact that much of the waste generated globally is non-toxic or non-dangerous; this waste can rather be used as a resource. Circularity essentially perceives the waste as a resources which can be converted and traded just like primary resources which are obtained from mother nature. Taking the example of the EU, waster plastic, paper and glass's combine market was worth 85.2 billion euros between 2002 and 2012 whereas this was much less than the full capacity or EU's potential.

However, just like primary raw materials, secondary raw materials also witness a skewed concentration globally. Moreover, this trade observers trade restrictions as well. For instance, an OECD report highlights the fact that one-third of restrictions on exports were imposed on scrap and waste between 2009 and 2014. Therefore removing trade barriers on such commodities will attune international trade with the circular economy targets. This further calls for taking steps to design products first hand in such a way that they are easily recyclable and free from hazardous chemicals and other contents. Eco-designing coupled with global value chains can rather play a vital role in moving towards a circular economy at global level.

Second-hand marketplace is an important which needs a definite mention. It hold importance because it is highly circular in nature and this type of market place has grown rapidly in the past decade and a half. Second-hand marketplace is usually operational through online medium and stakeholders can trade remanufactured products or pre-owned, pre-used goods or even left over materials. For instance OLX group operates in over 40 nations and bring buyers and sellers together through online platform to trade second hand goods ranging from apparels and fashion items to electronics and household goods to cars and bikes.

Similarly, exchange between traders of residual and recycled raw materials is facilitated by material-trader.com. United Wardrobe is another such example for trading second-hand clothes. Thus these kind of marketplaces help in retaining the good's value rather than they being disposed to litter the environment and moreover it provides economic gains to both buyer and sellers.

CONCLUSION

In order to transit towards global circular economy, it is imperative to make collaborative efforts through multilateral trade negotiations. There is a need to identify priority materials from trade point of view and subsequently formulate uniform and quality standards for the same. It is equally important to encourage the trade of second hand goods, waste and scrap by addressing the existing bottlenecks like stringent trade barriers, lack of data etc. and hence promoting the goals of circular economy. Consequently, this will lead to advent of new technologies and production processes thus generating employment.

REFERENCES

European Environment Agency. (2019). *Plastic waste trade in circular economy*. Available at: https://www.eea.europa.eu/themes/waste/resource-efficiency/the-plastic-waste-trade-in

OECD. (2018). *International Trade and the Transition to a Circular Economy*. Available at: https://www.oecd.org/environment/waste/policy-highlights-international-trade-and-the-transition-to-a-circular-economy.pdf

OECD. (2018a). *Improving Markets for Recycled Plastics: Trends, Prospects and Policy Responses*. OECD Publishing. Available at: https://www.oecd-ilibrary.org/environment/improving-markets-for-recycled-plastics_9789264301016-en

OECD. (2020). *Environment at a Glance Indicators – Circular economy, waste and materials*. Available at: https://www.oecd.org/environment/environment-at-a-glance/Circular-Economy-Waste-Materials-Archive-February-2020.pdf

Pacini, H. (2018). *Circular Economy: The New Normal*. Policy Brief No. 61, United Nations Conference on Trade and Development (UNCTAD). Available at: https://unctad.org/en/PublicationsLibrary/presspb2017d10_en.pdf

Sell, M., & Pajunen, N. (2018). *The circular economy – What's trade got to do with it?* International Centre for Trade and Sustainable Development. Available at: https://www.ictsd.org/opinion/the-circular-economy-

Valles, G. (2016). *The circular economy in international trade*. UNCTAD. Available at: https://unctad.org/fr/pages/newsdetails.aspx?OriginalVersionID=1400

Waste and Resources Action Programme (WRAP). (n.d.). Available at: https://www.wrap.org.uk/about-us/about/wrap-and-circular-economy

Chapter 9
Sustainable and Circular Mango Farming Through Redesigning Sales Contracts

Santosh Kumar
Chandragupt Institute of Management, India

ABSTRACT

Mango orchards in Bihar are managed through four different types of sales contracts, namely fully self-managed, short-tenure sales contract, long-term sales contract, and last quarter sales contract. This study has attempted to appraise the impact of different types of sales contracts on mango yield and farmers' income. Results indicate that last quarter sales contract is most sustainable followed by fully self-managed contracts. The remaining two contracts are neither sustainable nor financially viable. The higher sustainability of the last quarter's sales contract is attributed to clean landholding of the owners, optimal use of flowering inducers (PBZ), and segregated rights of merchants and owners.

1. INTRODUCTION

India is endowed with huge varieties of mangoes with sizeable value of produce (INR 385681.7 million) and significant value of export of mangoes from India (INR 4455.4 million). The total cultivable area of mangoes is 1.19% of the total area under cultivation in India and only 30% of mango orchards are irrigated. More than four fifths of the farmers in mango orchards are marginal and small farmer with less than one hectare land holding. Bihar is also significant contributor in mango production with average productivity of 9.82 metric ton per hectare. The harvest season of mangoes hovers between June and July. Bihar produces different varieties of mangoes namely Bombay green, Chausa, Dashahari, Fazli, Mallika, Amrapali, Gulabkhas, Kishen Bhog, Himsagar, Zardalu, Langra, Dhudhia Maldhah, Sinduria etc. Major mango producing districts are Darbhanga, Samastipur, Muzaffarpur, Purbi Champaran, Vaishali, Bhagalpur etc. Total value of mangoes produced in Bihar is approximately INR 59828.3 million underscoring its importance in national production. This study attempts to investigate various sales contracts (Table 3) in vogue among farmers and merchants and its degree of sustainability in future generations in Bihar.

DOI: 10.4018/978-1-7998-4990-2.ch009

2. USE OF CULTARS (PBZ) IN MANGO ORCHARDS AND LINKAGES WITH SUSTAINABLE FARMING

Rahim et al. (2011) highlight the controversial effect of paclobutrazol (PBZ) in North Sudan in floral induction of mangoes and suggest to use it if the temperature is lower than 20 ^{0} C. In Indian context, Reddy and Kurian (2008) conclude that the application of paclobutrazol at 5 gram a.i per tree as soil drench for three consecutive years and then discontinuation for three years seems to give higher yield in Alphanso mango trees. Yeshitela 2006) advocates the positive impact of PBZ in South Africa and Euthopia mango trees with improved yield and quality. Singh et al. (2012) adds that PBZ 7.5 ml is most effective in Litichi for higher yield. Yeshitela (2004 also suggests that PBZ has suppressed vegetative growth and augmented fruit yield of 'Tommy Atkins' mango in Ethiopia. Costa et al. (2012) argue that radioactivity level of fruits is abysmally low with application of PBS in mango trees. Various studies highlight that use of PBZ is useful in increasing yield of mangoes and still it need to be confirmed in Bihar on different varieties of mangoes. On the other side, merchants or traders owning mango orchards use excessive dose of PBZ resulting into excessive yield with severe ramifications for the primary stakeholders.

Reganold et al. (1990) advocate that the resource conserving methods with modern agriculture with less dependency on chemicals can achieve sustainable agriculture. Horrigan et al. (2002) also argue that sustainable agriculture is not only necessary for food security but also very important to the health of human and environment. Wezel et al. (2014) suggest that organic fertilization, reduced tillage, drip irrigation and biological pest control have high potential for better food production with less detrimental impact on human and environment. D'Souza and Ikerd (1996) pose various questions for sustainable farming and size cum attributes of small farms. Pretty (1994) also adds that better livelihood of farmers can only be achieved through paradigm changes in professional norms and practices. Kirsten and Sartorious (2002) suggest that the new institutional economic framework is required for timely supply of inputs to small farmers and for better price of their produce from traders. Robertson (2015) highlights that several environmental issues namely climate change, loss of biodiversity and increasing pollutions have serious repercussions food security. He also argues that the socio ecological models through right incentives and political will can only pave the way for sustainable agriculture with better trade off between farming and society. The producer and trader share three different types of contract in the farming (Rehber, 1998; Wolz & Kirsch, 1999) with varying degree of control between producer and trader. First type of contract has empowered producers with high decision making ability. Second type of contract has shared decision making due to partial contribution of resources. Third type of contract is more skewed towards traders and aggregators. In the last two decades, there is increasing focus on food security with resource conserving methods with sustainable status of environmental and human health which can be better achieved with more decision making authority with producers rather than traders and aggregators of crops. Especially in mango farming, Indian farmers have experienced various types of contractual relations with traders right from exclusive rights of orchards management to limited rights of post harvest activities only. Further section will explain the rational followed by the prevalent modes of contract in mango farming in India for better understanding.

3. RATIONALE OF THE STUDY

The flowering and fruit inducers are useful as long as they are used with prescribed dose and the users are aware of this information. In practice, most of the mango orchards are sold to long term and short term sales contracts where the pre and post harvesting rights are vested in merchants. Merchants have the sole motive of maximum profit for the contract period. This system incentivizes the merchants to exploit the mango orchards as much as possible for the maturity period of the contract reducing the life of orchards to 10-15 years. Therefore, it is important to investigate the viability for the different types of prevailing sales contracts in mango orchards in Bihar.

4. PREVALENT CONTRACTS IN MANGO ORCHARDS

There are four types of sales contracts in mango orchards in vogue in the market described as below.

Fully Self-managed Mango Orchards (FSM)

This mode is more prevalent in marginal farmers having less one hectare land and less than 4-5 trees in mango orchard. Technically speaking, farmers have exclusive rights on pre-harvesting, harvesting and post harvesting activities in orchards. Therefore, soil cum nutrient enrichment, flowering, pest control and sale of mango produce are managed by small and marginal farmers. Farmers himself sell mangoes in local market on scattered days to retail buyers. Variety of different types of fruits is very common in this category with spread harvesting period from May to July. This type of farming practices and contracts are more in vogue with small and marginal farmers with spare land in the vicinity of their houses. Hardly, any soil nutrient enrichments and pest controls are found. Very few farmers use any chemical or green manures for orchards. They also don't use flowering stimulator known as Cultar (PBZ). Farmers are only dependent on natural production capacity of the trees.. Most of the harvesting requirements are met manually through family members. Security and soil hygiene are completely neglected. The produce of mangoes is sold in nearby local market with lower price spread as compared to other models. But these plants are highly vulnerable to monkey menace and stone peltors because of scattered harvesting period of different varieties of mangoes. Family structure of the owners of this contract is mixed

Long Terms Sales Contract in Mango Orchards (LTSC)

This contract is more prevalent in farmers having cultivable areas more than one hectare where the orchards are sold to merchants consecutively for 2-3 years. This incentivizes merchants to maximum productivity and maximum benefits for three years from orchard. Farmers are paid 20-30% of the booking amount and the remaining payments are due one month before the harvesting period. These annuities are either for two years or three years depending on the agreement between farmers and merchants. Thus, merchants have the exclusive rights in pre-harvest and harvest activities of the orchard. This leads to the maximum exploitation of trees through higher dose of Cultars beyond permissible limits for inducing flowering in mango trees beyond permissible limits. Soil enrichment is negligible but pest controls are used frequently. Trees are loaded with maximum fruits and highest bamboo support in lower branches. Harvesting period is concentrated in one month due to one or two varieties of mangoes. This leads to maximum harvest and benefits for merchants for three years. These short of contracts are more prevalent in joint families where orchards are owned by more than ten people on an average but onus on none leading to long time sales derivatives with merchants. Security is sufficient but soil hygiene is highly compromised due to open defecation in orchards fields. Most of the harvesting requirements are met mechanically by merchants. It is very obvious that farmers have no roles in orchards for three years but merchants are doing all farming and sales activities of the mango orchards with maximum exploitation of the orchards for three years. These contracts keep the orchards in most vulnerable condition in 10-12 years leading to drying of trees and loss of livelihood for farmers and indirect stakeholders.

Short Term Sales Contracts in Orchards (STSC)

This contract is very akin to LTSD except the maturity period of the contract reduced to one year. Payment structure, exploitation of orchards and ownership pattern of the families are also exactly similar. Farmers opine that this will also keep the orchards in most vulnerable condition in next 15 years leading to drying of trees and loss of livelihood for farmers and indirect stakeholders.

Last Quarter Sales Contract in Orchards (LQSC)

This sales contract is more popular in aware and active farmers having cultivable area more than one hectare where the orchards are sold to merchants only for four to five months in the month of January every year. This contract is most competitive among merchants from bid's perspective. Pre- harvest activities of the orchards are controlled by farmers and the only four month period from flowering to harvest is in merchants' control. Merchants have no incentives to induce trees with Cultars (PBZ) in last year rainy season since they have no clue about owning the orchards in coming year. Therefore, farmers engage in farming activities and merchants engage in harvest and trade activities. Thus farming and trade ownership is separated. In this contract, most of the farmers receive 100% payment within seven days of the agreement in contracts. Thus, farmers are rewarded four months well in advance for the care of mango orchards. On the other hand, merchants are also rewarded with optimal produce in quantity and value without abnormal exploitation of the orchards. Soil is most enriched through green manure by farmers. Soil hygiene is also well maintained through complete security of the orchards from open defecation. Security is partially shared among farmers and merchants. However pest control is still doubtful as the farmers explained that they have no knowledge of pest control. It is also noticed that this sort of contract is with 5-10% of the farmers with nuclear families or clearly demarcated land ownership with trusts or religious authorities. Plants are optimally loaded with fruits and can tolerate moderate shocks of storm with reduced vulnerability. These orchards are most sustainable with maximum life span of plants accruing benefits to farmers, merchants and other stakeholders.

5. FINANCIAL VIABILITY AND SUSTAINABILITY OF THE RESOURCES

In four different sales contracts in mango orchards, initial investments are almost same but the yearly investments are relatively higher in LQSC where the owner has the right of managing the mango orchards. In LQSC, owners have the highest motivation for future generation and sustainability and they intervene in mango orchards for first 8 months with optimal combination of inputs. From financial viability perspective, only FSM and LQSC are viable where as long tenure and short tenure sales contracts are not viable owing to zero or almost negligible net present value in forty years of mango orchards. FSM and LQSC have the highest life span of plants but the internal rates of returns are 9% and 13% respectively. In LTSC and STSC, resources are highly strained due to highest exploitation by the merchants using higher dose of Cultars (PBZ). One can argue that FSM and LQSC have sustainable future owing to less dependency on Cultars similar to the arguments of Reganold et al. (1990). LQSC contracts are likely to generate more payoffs to different stakeholders for longer duration without compromise on human health and environment. Horrigan et al. (2002) has also highlighted the same issue of sustainable farming where food security must be clubbed with human health and environment. LQSC contracts have limited interventions from aggregators and traders and have better prospects for farmers congruent to the other studies (Pretty, 1994: Kirsten and Sartorious, 2002)

6. APPARENT RISKS AND CONCERNS

Out of four different sales contracts, FSM has the lower price spread owing to direct sales by the farmers in the nearby market. Remaining three contracts have price spread as high as 100 percent to 150 percent. Farmers require huge investment in LQSC for first eight months having higher financial risk as compared to no outlay made by the farmers in other three contracts. However the returns are commensurate with risk in LQSC mode. It is also observed that farmers in the joint family with land conflicts are more prone to LTSC and STSC leading to unviable practices in the long run. These types of families have many owners but onus on none leading to the merchants' controlled regime in mango orchards. Many times it is observed that the trusts or religious bodies or family with delineated land holdings fall in the LQSC regime with clear demarcation of responsibilities of owners and merchants. In case of force majeure, merchants will exit out of contract and forego the investments made in the orchards. From resources and livelihood perspective, LQSC is far better than any other contract in mango orchards with sustainable income for next 60-65 years after maturing of plants. These findings are in conjugation with the observations of other studies (Rehber, 1998; Wolz & Kirsch, 1999). It is highly likely that LQSC contracts have higher decision making authority entrusted with producers contrary to that of LTSC and STSC contracts. Division of rights and responsibilities in mango orchards can help to decide the optimal dose of PBZ or Cultar for optimal yield on sustainable basis in LQSC mode. These contractual variations and different practices are partly due to the lack of knowledge about the nutrients requirement and pest control techniques. Similarly most of the owners are not aware of the impact of open defecation and soil deterioration. On the other side, mango orchards owners are still dependent on merchants due to lack of integration with the online portal of national agricultural marketing. (e-NAM).

7. RECOMMENDATIONS AND SUGGESTIONS

This study has compared the four different prevalent sales contracts in the market and found that LQSC regime is the most sustainable practice followed by FSM regime. Long tenure and short tenure sales contracts are neither sustainable nor financial viable in the long run. The better performance of LQSC regime is attributed to clearly delineated land holdings, green manure, and segregation of rights of farmers and merchants leading to optimal use of resources. There is further scope of raising income to LQSC owners if three specific requirements are made. Firstly local markets are integrated with online portal of national agricultural marketing (e-NAM) for better discovery of price. Secondly famers shall have direct or feeder based air cargo or train cargo facility for the mango produce. Finally the department of agriculture should acquaint the farmers about the requisite dose of nutrients and chemicals in order to avoid the exploitation from merchants.

REFERENCES

Costa, M. A., Torres, N. H., Vilca, F. Z., Nazato, C., & Tornisielo, V. L. (2012). Residue of 14C paclobutrazol in mango. *IOSR J. Eng*, *2*(05), 1165–1167. doi:10.9790/3021-020511651167

D'souza, G., & Ikerd, J. (1996). Small farms and sustainable development: Is small more sustainable? *Journal of Agricultural and Applied Economics*, *28*(1), 73–83. doi:10.1017/S1074070800009470

Horrigan, L., Lawrence, R. S., & Walker, P. (2002). How sustainable agriculture can address the environmental and human health harms of industrial agriculture. *Environmental Health Perspectives*, *110*(5), 445–456. doi:10.1289/ehp.02110445 PMID:12003747

Kirsten, J., & Sartorius, K. (2002). Linking agribusiness and small-scale farmers in developing countries: Is there a new role for contract farming? *Development Southern Africa*, *19*(4), 503–529. doi:10.1080/0376835022000019428

Pretty, J. N. (1994). Alternative systems of inquiry for a sustainable agriculture. *IDS Bulletin*, *25*(2), 37–49. doi:10.1111/j.1759-5436.1994.mp25002004.x

Rahim, A. A. O. S., Elamin, O. M., & Bangerth, F. K. (2011). Effects of paclobutrazol (PBZ) on floral induction and associated hormonal and metabolic changes of biennially bearing mango (Mangifera indica L.) cultivars during off year. *Journal of Agricultural and Biological Science*, *6*, 55–67.

Reddy, Y. T. N., & Kurian, R. M. (2008). Cumulative and residual effects of paclobutrazol on growth, yield and fruit quality of'Alphonso'mango. *Journal of Horticultural Sciences*, *3*(2), 119–122.

Reganold, J. P., Papendick, R. I., & Parr, J. F. (1990). Sustainable agriculture. *Scientific American*, *262*(6), 112–121. doi:10.1038cientificamerican0690-112

Rehber, E. (1998). *Vertical integration in agriculture and contract farming*. Regional Research Project No. NE-165: Private strategies, public policies, and food system performance. Department of Resource Economics. Amherst, MA: University of Massachusetts.

Rehber, E. (1998). *Vertical integration in agriculture and contract farming* (No. 1299-2016-102484). Academic Press.

Robertson, G. P. (2015). A sustainable agriculture? *Daedalus*, *144*(4), 76–89. doi:10.1162/DAED_a_00355

Singh, B., Singh, S., & Sandhu, S. (2012). Effect of growth retardants on vegetative growth, flowering and fruiting of litchi cv. Calcuttia. *HortFlora Research Spectrum*, *1*(1), 29–33.

Wezel, A., Casagrande, M., Celette, F., Vian, J. F., Ferrer, A., & Peigné, J. (2014). Agroecological practices for sustainable agriculture. A review. *Agronomy for Sustainable Development*, *34*(1), 1–20. doi:10.100713593-013-0180-7

Wolz, A., & Kirsch, O.C. (1999). *Equitization of agribusiness in Vietnam: options for small-scale farmers with special emphasis on coffee production in Daklak Province*. Discussion Paper No. 69. Heidelberg, Germany: Research Centre for International Agrarian and Economic Development.

Yeshitela, T., Robbertse, P. J., & Stassen, P. J. C. (2004). Paclobutrazol suppressed vegetative growth and improved yield as well as fruit quality of 'Tommy Atkins' mango (Mangifera indica) in Ethiopia. *New Zealand Journal of Crop and Horticultural Science*, *32*(3), 281–293. doi:10.1080/01140671.2004.9514307

Yeshitela, T. B. (2006). *Effect of cultural practices and selected chemicals on flowering and fruit production in some mango (Mangifera indica L.) cultivars* (Doctoral dissertation). University of Pretoria.

APPENDIX

Table 1. Abbreviations

Notations	Meaning
FSM	Fully self managed mango orchards
LTSC	Long term sales contract in mango orchards
STSC	Short term sales contract in mango orchards
LQSC	Last quarter sales contract in mango orchards
PBZ	Paclobutrazol called as Cultars
NPV	Net present value
IRR	Internal rate of returns
NAM	National agricultural marketing
MT	Metric tons

Table 2. Mango Statistics at a Glance

Particulars	Response
India's rank in mangoes production in world	First (40% share of the world output)
Total area in India (2016-17) for mango production	2262.8 thousand acres (1.19% of the cultivable area and 30% of the horticulture area) and only 1/3 of the mango area is irrigated
Number of holdings in India	5055485
% of holdings in marginal holding (less than 1 hectare)	84%
% of holdings in small holding (1-2 hectare)	8%
% harvest and post harvest losses of mangoes	9-12%
Total production in India	19686.9 thousand MT (2016-17)
Productivity in India for mangoes	8.7 MT per hectare
Productivity in Bihar for mangoes	9.82
Highest productivity state in India	Uttar Pradesh (17.14 MT/Hectare)
Compound annual growth rate	6%
Exports from India (Quantity)(2016-17)	53.17 thousand MT
Exports from India (Value)(2016-17)	44554.54 lakh rupees
Total value of mangoes (2013-14) in India	3856817 lakh INR
Total value of mangoes (2013-14) in Bihar	598283 lakh INR
Peak harvest season in Bihar	June-July
Varieties of mangoes produced in India	Bombay green, Chausa, Dashahri, Fazli, Mallika, Amrapali, Gulabkhas, Kishen Bhog, Himsagar, Zardalu, Langra, Dhudhia Maldhah, Sinduria
Major producing districts in Bihar	Darbhanga, Samastipur, Muzaffarpur, Prubi Champaran, Vaishali, Bhagalpur

Table 3. Attributes of Different Sales Contracts in Mango Orchards

Particulars	Different Types of Sales Contracts			
	FSM	LTSC	STSC	LQSC
Assets	Mango orchards	Mango orchards	Mango orchards	Mango orchards
Seller or Owner	Farmers	Farmers	Farmers	Farmers
Buyer	Farmers	Merchants	Merchants	Merchants
Maturity period	NA	2-3 years	1 years	4 months
Exit option	NA	Buyers can exit but forgo the amount paid	Buyers can exit but forgo the amount paid	Buyers can exit but forgo the amount paid (limited time option of one week)
Category of produce	Higher variation	Few varieties	Few varieties	Few varieties
Contractual payments	Not applicable	20-30% booking amount with remaining payment one month before harvest	20-30% booking amount with remaining payment one month before harvest	100 percent payment three months well in advance (January-February)
Who owns post harvest activities	Retail Traders and Farmers	Merchants	Merchants	Merchants
Who owns pre harvest responsibilities	Farmers	Merchants	Merchants	Partially shared among merchants and traders
Type of Farmers	Marginal farmers	Landlords	Landlords	Landlords, Trusts, Maszid, Samiti
Family ownership	Nuclear and joint	Joint	Joint	Nuclear or clearly delineated land ownerships
Incidence of Cultar (PBZ)	Negligible	Extremely high and beyond permissible limits	Extremely high and beyond permissible limits	Less than requirement
Fruit bearing capacity of orchards	Normal	Highest with bamboo support	Highest with bamboo support	Moderate with scattered bamboo support
Prominent fruit season	Scattered from May to July	June	June	May-June
Crop Insurance	Negligible	Negligible	Negligible	Negligible
Soil and nutrient management	Negligible	Negligible	20% of the requirement	Bio fertilizers are used but lacks scientific methods
Factors of loss	Stone peltors, Monkeys, Street boys	Monkey	Monkey	Monkey
Who owns security of fruits	Farmers	Merchants	Merchants	Shared responsibility (60% Farmers and 40% Merchants)
Security and soil hygiene	Highly vulnerable	Highly vulnerable and open defecation	Highly vulnerable and open defecation	Guarded and better soil hygiene due to no open defecation
Bids	Not applicable	Highly competitive	Competitive	Highly competitive
Price spread (Difference between farm price and market price)	Low (30%)	Very high (150%)	Very high (150%)	Higher (80-100%)
Access to market	Nearby local market	Different districts	Different districts	Different districts and export use
Access to e-NAM	Not yet	Merchants driven	Merchants driven	Merchants driven
Life of plants	90 years	10-12 years	15 years	90 years
Impact on livelihood	Sustainable mode	Farmers receive cash flows for 10-12 years without any investment in that period	Farmers receive cash flows for 15 years without any investment in that period	Farmers have perpetual income till 80-100 years with 25% of the receivables invested in orchards
Gross income to owners with 25 years aged plants @ 10% growth per year for next 20-25 years	Rs 10000 per acre	Rs 20000 per acre	Rs 20000 per acre	Rs 30000 per acre
Gross income to merchants with 25 years aged plants @ 15% growth per year for next 20-25 years	Not applicable	Rs 80000 per acre	Rs 80000 per acre	Rs 80000 per acre
Internal Rate of Return of Owners or Farmers	9%	6%	8%	13%
Net life time value of annuities (INR) of orchards	116563	-25901	23418	1513778
Comments on viability	Subsistence	Abandon	Approximately no profit no loss	Highly viable
Impact on farmers	No impact	Debt trap and loss of livelihood	Debt trap and loss of livelihood	Fully sustainable
Job creation (man days)	60	30	30	40
Job creation (tractor hours)	NA	6	6	10
Overall sustainability and financial viability	Yes	No	No	Yes
Risk to Farmers	Natural risk	Short term risk negligible. Long term risk very high because of reduced plant life	Short term risk negligible but long term risk very high because of reduced plant life	No long term risk but short term financial risk with the farmers because of fixed fund outlay irrespective of flowering
Risk to Counterparty (Merchants)	Not applicable	Merchants have low risk because of long term tenure of the contract.	Merchants have moderate risk	Merchants have higher risk in the short term because of investment irrespective of flowering and fruit.
Risk to resources (orchards)	Not	Very high	High	Not

Table 4. Challenges and Suggestions for better management of Orchards

Challenges	Suggestions
Lack of knowledge about nutrient management and high yield varieties	KVK should conduct the demonstration of high yield varieties mangoes in farmers' plot and update about the nutrient requirements of the orchards at different stages. Farmers are very stressed due to high incidence of Cultars (PBZ) for good flowering.
Water requirements	The department of horticulture should provide subsidy for irrigation in mango orchards with minimal wastage of water. Electricity department may coordinate with revenue departments for quick disposal of irrigation permits on subsidized rates.
Land rights and family types	Nuclear family or family with delineated land ownership take better care of the mango orchards.
Contracts violations by merchants	Merchants also violate the contract in second year if the lean flowering prevails. This can be avoided through escrow account and merchant registration in Panchayats and PACs.
Open defecation by residents	Higher incidence of insects is observed in mango orchards due to open defecation and consequent soil purification. It can be reduced by community toilets provided by Panchayats.
Difficulty in reaching market	Dedicated air cargo and train cargo facility with refrigeration logistics
No registration in e-NAM	Local mandi should be registered in e-NAM so that outside merchants can be invited for better price.

Chapter 10
Sustainable and Green Human Resource Practices

Mitali Dohroo
Amity Business School, Amity University, Noida, India

Taranjeet Duggal
Amity Business School, Amity University, Noida, India

ABSTRACT

Two topics, circular economy and human resource practices, have been in separate baskets. However, recent studies have shown that both have a major impact either directly or indirectly on each other. Human resource management or human management is largely associated with a behavior of an economy. It has been largely debated and accepted that human resource management has a major role in creating sustainable organizations. Human resource management as a function involves a lot of postulates of sustainability in the scope of an organization. We all understand that the role of human resources has widened throughout time, and there is a need for more innovations in better management with various stakeholders and employees to create HR as a more solution-based function.

For the longest years the two topics circular economy and Human Resource Practices has been in separate baskets and never thought of bringing both together. However, the recent studies has shown that both has a major impact either direct or indirect on each other.

Human Resource Management or Human management is largely associated with a behavior of a economy. It has been largely debated and accepted that Human Resource Management has a major role in creating sustainable organisations.

The transition is taking place in many organizations where the practices are largely affected through the concepts of circular economy as it helps in optimum utilization of resources or gaining more value from the employees and providing better experiences and outputs to the stakeholders. Human Resource Management as a function involves lot of postulates of sustainability in the scope of a organistion. (Vickers, 2005). We all understand that the role of Human Resource has widened throughout the time

DOI: 10.4018/978-1-7998-4990-2.ch010

and there is a need of more innovations in better management with various stakeholders and employees to create HR as a more solution-based function.

To develop this chapter we have reviewed 53 research and empirical papers along with 15 articles referring to Green HRM and Sustainability along with focused discussions with HR professionals of leading think tanks working on Sustainability. The research gave as an understanding of relationship between Green HR practices, Sustainability and employee development along with the outlook on potential areas to be explored in future to meet the developing needs.

The chapter presents the concepts highlighted in research and adaptation of various Sustainable Human Resource Practices in organisations widely along with the development of the human potential by implementing the relevant practices.

While the widely discussed parameters of Economic, Social and Environmental focus in regard to sustainability are addressed, the chapter takes closer look in developing and applying the same to enrich employee development and providing a Green Work environment to the staff.

INTRODUCTION

Over the years Human Resource function of organisations has evolved from becoming felicitator to a Strategic arm of developing organisations. Since 1980's there had been numerous debates on better management of humans or employees in the organisations and tremendous research shows us direct and positive relationship between Human Resource Management Practices and Organisation Performance.

With the urgent requirements of increasing environmental and sustainability issues around the world, organisations are developing and introducing relevant strategies to focus and address the same.

Research shows that the focus of organisations is growing in terms of demonstrating their commitments to sustainability.

The Think Tanks, Government and other stakeholder bodies are making certain conscious attempts to make these changes through corporate consultative groups and bring a radical change.

We understand that to make Human Resource Practices more sustainable, the functions shall work around economic performance, social performance, and environment performance.

- Economic Performance here means that we analyse the appetite of the organisation to be more innovative in terms of its functions and Products.
- Social Performance would mean effectiveness to manage diversity of resources and human potential.
- Environment Performance is to introduce functions and processes which are more environment friendly and help in providing the conducive work environment to the staff.

Sustainable Human Resource Management has been tried to define through various research studies and the recent rising interest on the topic has shown varied definitions of the same.

Sustainable HRM can be defined as the adoption of HRM strategies and practices that enable the achievement of social, financial and ecological goals by creating an impact inside and outside of the organisation and over a long term time horizon while controlling for the unintended side-effects and negative feedback. (Michel, Muller-Camen, 2016)

The above definition highlights two vital points:

1. The recognition of multiple, potentially contradictory, socially, economic, ecological and social goals such as human sustainability (Dorchery, Kira and Sherry, 2009)
2. Complex Interrelations between HRM systems and impact on internal and external environments with the long term impact on resources and externalities.(Mariappandar, 2003)

"Sustainable human resource management (SHRM) refers to the concept which combines the idea of sustainability with the soft approach to human resources. This approach promotes basing an HRM strategy on fostering a culture of trust and cooperation and on developing employee involvement, one component of which is loyalty to one's employer. The soft approach to HRM aims to achieve adequate financial results, but through the policy of building a good "employer–employee relationship." A soft strategy – according to the research – is effective in retaining an employee for a longer period of time in an organization and encouraging them to share knowledge, work more productive, act with passion and commitment, generate creative ideas in order to achieve the business goals" (Smaliukienė et al., 2017; Ogbeibu et al., 2018; Kim and Shin, 2019; Meier et al., 2019).

"sustainable HRM is the pattern of planned or emerging human resource strategies and practices intended to enable organizational goal achievement while simultaneously reproducing the HR base over a long-lasting calendar time and controlling for self-induced side and feedback effects of HR systems on the HR base and thus on the company itself"(Ehnert I., Parsa S., Roper I., Wagner M., Muller-Camen M. Reporting on sustainability and HRM: a comparative study of sustainability reporting practices by the world's largest companies. Int. J. Hum. Resour. Manag. 2016;27:88–108. doi: 10.1080/09585192.2015.1024157)

Green HRM is defined that socially responsible human resource management function in an organisation helps in building employee-oriented practices which increases overarching sustainability goals in terms of employee retention, performance, and measurement and all other valid HRM Practices. *(Dyllick T., Muff K. and López-Fernández M., 2016)*

The Green or Sustainable Human Resource Practices are not focussed only around the representation of environment and social concerns but also developing a trustworthy culture which helps in providing a conducive and productive workplace environment to the employees.

In the diverse pool of HR principles and sustainability, development of HR is one of the basic elements of the function (Gladwin,1985).

With the growing awareness of the organisation in sustainability, lot of organisations are reporting their social, economic and ecological standards(Schaltegger & Wegner,2006) and the same are further reported in Global Reporting Initiative (GRI).

Sustainability and Human Resource Management are further studied and analysed in relation to gather practices and strategic decisions for implementing Sustainable practices in corporates and organisations (Chen-Taylor, Muller-Camen, 2012).

In this relation it was further found that key role of Sustainable Human Resource Management and Green practices contribute to sustainable business organisations economically, socially and ecologically and evidently making HRM system more sustainable (Enhert & Harry, 2012)

The conclusion of a diverse research and literature review quotes and confirms that Sustainability and HR are not two different directions but a spoon and fork of a same dish. The principles defined by different authors can be put into separate buckets as to the development of concept of the sustainability and specific or intentional practices which can be functioned and adopted by HR in the organisations for employees.

With the changing world, we have understood that how vital is to make an organisation sustainable in nature which is very clear that the function shall be such that it caters the current generation without affecting the resources for future. To develop a more sustainable HRM it is important to bring in more ethical and strategic Human Resource Management. Human Resource Management is a biggest stimulator to bring sustainability in organisation through innovation.

The sustainability in Human Resource Management to understand the social behaviors at large around the world and strategically implementing decisions as a part of process and management of Human Resource within our organisations.

The below given table articulates principles widely and the translation to development of HRM practices.

Social Issues	Human Resource Policy
Freshers or Inexperienced employees who are vulnerable to layoffs	Re-design junior jobs to enable employees to be expected variety of tasks that involve complexity.
Skill differentiation by Gender, Age, Caste and Orientation	Reform policies to accept more diversity. Be inclusive in forming a culture
Inequity related to progression and succession plans	Periodic review of individual needs of training linked to their development plan and career paths.
Employee Participation and Empowerment	Involvement of Employees in Decision Making and providing right platforms
Long Term Perspective and addressing social exclusion of Marginal Employees	Developing Employee Competencies through training and development and Regular Training, Learning and Development for the employees to increase a competency base.
Flexibility	As future of work and to build more conducive culture, the contemporary organisations must encourage flexibility. Flexibility offerings to organisations and individuals as well.
Fair and Equal Opportunities	Reaching to the Unreachable and provide equal opportunities to employees and people reaching out to your respective organisations.
Protection of Human Resources	Employee Retention and Regeneration of your staff in order to take care of people associated with you.
Environment Protection	HRM designs the policies and practices and communicate the same to all employees in order to design and work on initiatives of protecting ecological environment.
Partnership with outer world	To bring collective actions in the atmosphere and environment, organisations must partner with external world and stakeholders.

(Stankevičiute Ž., Savanevičiene A. Designing Sustainable HRM)

Sustainability cannot ignore the important component of Profitability; literature cites that more sustainable principles in practice will bring longevity and profitability to the organisations.

In the further section we are going to analyse vital Human Resource Practices bucketed in different section and how they implement sustainability or learning from circular economy in the function.

1. **Human Resource Planning:** To bring sustainability in organisation through innovation, the practices followed shall be such which makes employees to think, create and reflect. The Employee behavior shall foster the following:
   a. High Degree of Creativity- Organisations shall focus on bringing more creativity in terms of sustainability of the organisation. Sustainability is not just focused on the longetivity of the organisation but also the approach and functionality. Sustainability talks about bringing more green approach. As a HR function it holds the right to develop a culture which focusses on the creativity in sustainability. For example- There are organisations which are making it a part of the policy to not use papers or prohibiting the use of paper in digital era which brings both efficiency and sustainability.
   b. Long Term of Focus – The planning should be taking into consideration the longetivity of the organisation in changing times and era. There should be an increased attention to sustainable development and green organisations in managerial plans (Gonzalez-Benito & Gonzalez-Benito, 2006). The main purpose of sustainable development is to integrate economic, social and environmental objectives to optimaly maximise the benefits and provide welfare to Human capital of the organisation.
   c. High Level of cooperative and interdependent behavior- To bring any change and also in terms of sustainability it is important to conduct a cooperative and interdependent behavior towards the practices, process and people.
   d. High Degree of risk-taking appetite – Sustainability is being explored from various angles recently and also Green HRM, there are changes which may impose risk on the organisations, it is vital to plan the financials and processes in such a manner so that organisations can bear any risk if there is any.
   e. High tolerance to unpredictability- Business Environment is highly unpredictable in nature. Therefore, in terms of changing environment and adaptability of ecological friendly practices is giving birth to many concepts and research which are pot to practice.
2. **Talent Acquisition and Retention:** With the introduction various technological functions in place there is more suitability and means to maintain the whole cycle of employment from acquisition to retention. The technological solutions with the regular update on the functionality are more sustainable in nature, though there has been numerous debates around the same but still Technological innovations and Artificial Intelligence Systems are more effective in implementing sustainability in the process. The manual procedures are more time taking and also effect the Turn Around Time. While we are doing a Human Resource Planning, keeping the circular economy impacts in mind following are expected;
   a. Creating a balanced skill mix in the teams to achieve efficiency.
   b. Opportunities for Voluntary team assignments
   c. Placing right people at the right job.
3. **Talent Development:** Talent Development is one of the key function of Human Resource Practices. To make your employees more efficient and effective at the workplace, it is of utmost importance to invest on your employees. As sustainability is a central theme of circular economy, the talent development not only makes employees equipped to match the market trends and need of the economy but also helps in succession planning.
4. **Performance Management:** Human Resource Management function while focusing on the performance management and performance appraisals, they foster encouragement to take risks,

Employees shall themselves demand innovation in the processes, Making the workforce open to generation and adoption of new ideas, Continuous peer evaluation, frequent evaluations and auditing of innovation practices.

5. **Reward and Recognition:** The practices are evolving and to recognise and reward the employees in context of factors of circular economy and encourage them to more sustainable ideas, the reward and recognition system has to be planned strategically where following shall be covered majorly;
   a. Freedom to employees to do research and bring their ideas into the practice
   b. No Judgements on the failure of ideas which are put into testing
   c. Employees shall form teams as per their own will and ideas; such freedom shall be encouraged
   d. The Pay parity shall be taken as utmost serious agenda and bringing pay and pride in action
   e. Developing dual career tracks
   f. Promoting from within which shall have a consensus to the promotion and equal motivation leading to higher employee quotient factors
   g. Recognition and Rewards shall be continuous in nature.
   h. Maintaining the balance of team and individual rewards

To bring sustainability in the nature of functioning of Human Resource Practices, the function has to be evolved and bring postulates of social performance in the strategy.

a) The performance Management systems shall be developed more on the basis of equity, distributive justice, autonomy and respect.
b) Organizations shall ensure they take care of employees both physical and Mental Health at the workplace.
c) One must ensure there is transparency in the systems and respect towards each other.

Building Green Cultures:

The above also articulates how organisations through their evolving practices are developing Green Cultures. One of the important point which appeared with consultation amongst the think tanks and corporate groups is to promoting and sensitizing human resources on forming green organisation cultures through deliberate and responsive attempts in employee behavior.

This all begins with first stage of recruitment and comes down the employee development where you define the green culture of organisation in your talent acquisition process and train the staff further on implementing the same.

The goal by which circular economy runs is the environment. Most of the organisations re now adopting Green Human Resource Practices to become more environmentally inclined. Human Resource policies which make the culture of the organisation greener and environment friendly shows their sustainability in the longer run.

With the change in times and urgency at our environment due to depletion of natural resources, it is of primary importance to imply environment friendly Human Resource Practices. The result of the same can be seen in the kind of benefits organisations are reaping out of it. There are more attraction of environment friendly consumers and making more in house or national productions which result in cost deuteriations.

The literature and researches shows that to have a successful Environment Management System at place, it is of vital importance that the same shall be supported by strategic Human Resource Management System.

Therefore all the Practices as listed above shall have the environment backing to it. The organisations shall focus on the principles and strategies as listed below:

1. **Talent Recruitment and Onboarding:** Recruitment of people is done on the basis where people are environment friendly.

On the onboarding organisation may gift a sapling to take care of during their entire tenure with the organisation. They can plant the same as tree in the organisation campus or take along with them as a sign of farewell when they leave the organisation.

Environmentally motivated activities can bring major impact to their engagement and relation with organisation. The organisarions shall put into practice the concepts of using public transport and less and also fuel less vehicles to reduce pollution and help the environment. This in terms halps in making practice more green and sustainable.

The question arises how is HR doing the same or can make it Green, HR can commit to green practices through virtual or telephonic screening of candiadtes than holding Face to Face interviews. The range of this effort can include simple methods such as using Skype for initial screening interviews, and even more complex electronic methods for the purposes of undertaking group interviews and expansive virtual business exhibitions (Rokos et al., 2012).

2. **Talent Development:** Promote and give more and more trainings on environmentally friendly practices they can conduct in the organisations. The employees can receive environment credits for the same and some reward for the maximum rewards earned.

The concepts must focus on bringing Financial performance and environmental balance. This study was given by (Daily & Hung, 2001; O'Donohuea et al., 2016).

HR must guarantee that preparatory programs in the early stages of recruitment will include information regarding organization's green goals and methods as well as the manner of employees' participation in voluntary and environment improvement programs (Bauer et al., 2012)

The training and development shall not only hold green environment trainings but also focus on building the methodologies to provide such trainings such as reducing paper and transportation.

3. **Reward Management:** Engage your employees in more environment friendly activities and link the same to performance and reward management. HR chas the rights to persuade managers where employees could be drawn towards environment friendly goals. Such goals could be marked as special achievements and foster the culture of sustainability in the organisation. Green Award and Compensation Mechanisams shall be fostered in the organisation where the culture of Green and sustainability could be amplified.
4. **Environmental Team Meets-** As an employee engagement activities try to coordinate and arrange more and more environment talks and open interactions so the synergy remains there. the management must try to establish a workplace in which the employees are able to freely express their opinions regarding green issues because it's them who are really in charge of realization of ethical

guidelines in the routine life of the organization (Collier & Esteban, 2007). A study on 214 British organizations shows that managers' support and employees' possibility of participation result in interest in the environment as the most prevalent encouragement methods (Ahmad, 2015).

In addition to the above practices, it is of immense importance to work on the full structure of organisation. While quoting this we mean catering to Management Development and Leadership and increasing knowledge base on Green Leadership.

Management and Leadership Development-

Human Resource Management function is not just a gatekeeper of the organisation functions but a developer and a strategic force to make sure the correct implementation of the same to bring effective results.

It is a key aspect to pay our details on enforcing changes, which are primarily driven through leadership. The green and sustainable practices define that we must consciously attempt to not make any negative reinforcement as they might result in creating dis-engagement and hostile environment for employees, whereas we can make attempt in environmentally educating the employees and connecting the sustainable practices to employee life cycle.

Let us try to understand more functions of Human Resource and its relation to make it Green.

A. **Job Analysis**- While we do the analysis the most important thing which we focus on the responsibilities and dimensions of particular employment and job. In addition to that it is of prime importance to consider green competency as special component of recruitment and job analysis.

B. **Recruitment**- Environmental Criteria's and focus of the organisation towards the same shall be brought up in the recruitment notices.

C. **Selection-** The candidate selection shall not be just restrictive to job specifications but also look at the awareness of the candidate about environment. The candidate shall be focused and aware about the green issues in their job and also take into consideration their complete behavior being green consumers in personal lives as well.

D. **Socialisation –** HR shall focus on informing their employees about the organisation's green initiatives and development upon the same. Building a culture which promotes green citizenship could be done by arranging more socializing events for the employees.

E. **Training and Performance Evaluation:** As discussed earlier, programs on promoting knowledge and skill regarding green roles could be developed and allocated to employees. The goal designing of employees shall include the green goals and the parameters to study their progress on the same should be assessed to allocate a specific training program to employees. The green goals should be studied and developed for all the levels of the organisation.

F. **Reward Management:** Recognizing and rewarding employees who has gone an extra mile in setting and achieving the green goals. Both financial and non financial rewards could be designed for the employees such as introducing them as green employees.

G. **Management of Discipline and Procedures:** Development and Compilation of the green rules and procedure for every employee to adhere for. The induction trainings of the new employees shall have a major session on green practices so as to ensure sustainability throughout in their behaviors.

Green Initiatives that Organisations can build upon: Future of Green HRM

Human Resource being a backbone of a organisation, play an important role from talent acquisition, talent development to exit of an employee. Organisations being socially responsible and moving towards creating ecological friendly policies brings HR at a position to be more responsible in creating a culture and policies in the organisation which are green in nature.

The future of Green HRM bring sustainability in approach and looks promising and with bright future. The practices will prove beneficial for everyone from a researcher/academician to a practitioner.

Though the future is promising we still need to focus more on the academic front on Green HRM practices. Organisations are still working on various policies to bring Green HRM in practices as organisations are focussing more on environment and are designing such practices to meet the same.

Hence we need to bridge the gap between professional and academic front to bring immense parity and understanding in the practices.

Green HRM not only promoted sustainability but has also been ecological, economical and practical at the same time.

Recycling of products and Sustainability Workshops: Encouraging staff to recycle the products and run continuous sustainability workshops to embibe the practice and behaviour which is continuous in nature. This is also encouraged by asking employees to create sustainable practice goals.
Promotion of using public transport: More and more organisations are encouraging to use public transport and reduce the carbon footprint. The same is supported by providing Public Transport Allowances. **Car pooling:** Car pooling is new cool collaboration, it brings different teams and people together from their neighbourhoods and support environment. Organisations are encouraging by announcing Car Pool Champions.
Green Manufacturing: Industries are making conscious efforts to do green and sustainable manufacturing whether it is cloth industry or products. The conscious efforts are made by using more sustainable available resources.
Online training: Technology is a blessing where we can make a conscious effort of reaching to unreachable and developing online content and delivering the same. Training is widely seen as the most effective method of making employees aware about sustainable and environment friendly approach. The staff can be trained on how to collect waste data, build eco literacy. The well trained employees help in bringing radical and effective change sin the organisations over a period of time.
Telecommuting and Teleconferencing: Communication is the key to effectiveness and constant engagement helps in building better performances. The emerging technologies cover the organisations from missing any communication and help in maintaining constant clear communications.
Energy Efficient Office Spaces: As a practice organisations shall look into the physical spaces in order to maintain Green environment. Organisations shall foster on creating energy efficient spaces with sensing electricity, water saving technology, sustainable utensils and No food waste policy initiatives.
Green Office Furniture: Many organisations at present are opting for more sustainable spaces and providing green office furniture's.
Green Work Culture: This is an interesting work area where lot of work has already been quoted and there is still a scope to explore the subject more. Green Work Culture defines the spaces not only physically environment friendly but also the practices which are deliberate to provide conducive work environments to staff. For an instance; Transparent functions, Pay Parity, Employee Friendly policies, Inclusive Decision Making and many more.

We have highlighted some of the initiatives organisations has taken into account to count their practices as green.

With the above mentioned points, it clearly brings out numerous opportunities and ways for organisations to develop Green Human Resource and Sustainable Management practices.

CONCLUSION

The above has been derived from the methodological studies of articles and papers published in the reputed journals and presented in the conferences. The chapter shreds the extensive capacity of Human Resource Management functions for making organizations, operations and employees practices green in nature. We have tried to cover all functions from job design to employee relations. HR professionals in this era of environment fostered economy towards circular sustainability are facing a major challenge to study the depth and scope of green HRM practices in transforming or developing organisations as green entities. More efforts into strategizing the same is leading to make better environmental performance of the organisation. The creation, practice and maintainence of green human resource practices and foster environment lead innovative behaviours of employees coupled with right perceptions and attitudes towards building organisations as green entity, the green HRM practices hold a critical place.

Existing Human Resource Practices, Environment Management and sustainable practices literature suggest that employee behaviors and practices contribute majorly to the goals of a organisations towards sustainability and Green Entity resolutions.

It has been proved and understood that employees only contribute and enjoy to the goals when they feel that it adds to their value profile and certainty. Studies proved that 86% of the employees feel more engaged when they are more related and responsible towards environment practices and understand their organisation fosters a behaviour and practices which is more environmentally aligned and sustainable in nature of functioning.

Green HR contributes to organization building in positive steps and approach to develop organisation reputation, the green practices also promote in developing high degree of engagement of employees and eliminating their negative environment impacts. the Chartered Institute of Personnel and Development (CIPD) thinks that "a green employer may improve employer branding, company image and is a useful way to attract potential employees who have environmental orientation" CIPD(2007).

Green HRM practices contribute in making organisations and their operations green. The green recruitment practices, performance, attitude, and green competencies of human resource management can be designed by following and adapting green HRM practices. Talent Acquisition and Talent Inductions are the first stages of creating green awareness among all the employees working for organisations and making green entities. Such adaptations lead to causes of environmental degradation. The awareness among the talent and practices can lead to green movements, green programs and practices and also retention of resources for future generation.

The Green Human Resource Practices develop inspiration and commitment of employees to contribute their ideas and efforts for the awareness and implementation of Green Human Resource Management Practices in their respective organisation.

These practices result in increased efficiency, cost feasibility, less wastage, sustainable use of resources, improved work life balance as their would be more use of technology for communication and efficiency. The world should eventually move towards Green HRM practices with the change in world towards environment efficiency and sustainability.

We have also discussed about how organisations apart from taking Green HRM responsibility can turn green in various ways. The world is strongly moving towards more sustainable practices and yes, the approach of organisations and HR would play a major role in bringing the behavioural change amongst employees and people.

REFERENCES

Ambec, S., & Lanoie, P. (2008). Does it pay to be green? A systematic overview. *The Academy of Management Perspectives.*

Bashford, S. (2008). *Brownie points for green workers.* Human Resources.

Beardwell, I., & Holden, L. (1997). *Human Resources Management. A Contemporary Perspective.* Pitman Publishing.

Blanco, T. M. (2014). The meaning of employability in the new labour relationships between company-employee: A model of training in companies. *Procedia: Social and Behavioral Sciences, 139*, 448–455. doi:10.1016/j.sbspro.2014.08.039

Davies, A., Fidler, D., & Gorbis, M. (2020). *Future Work Skills.* University of Phoenix Research Institute.

Eccles, R. G., & Serafeim, G. (2013). The performance frontier: Innovating for a sustainable strategy. *Harvard Business Review.*

Egri, C. P., & Herman, S. (2000). Leadership in the North American environmental sector: Values, leadership styles, and contexts of environmental leaders and their organizations. *Academy of Management Journal.*

Ehnert, I. (2009). *Sustainable Human Resource Management.* Springer.

Fernandez, E., Junquera, B., & Ordiz, M. (2003). Organizational culture and human resources in the environmental issue. *International Journal of Human Resource Management.*

Fryxell, G. E., & Lo, C. W. H. (2003). The influence of environmental knowledge and values on managerial behaviours on behalf of the environment: An empirical examination of managers in China. *Journal of Business Ethics.*

Green Human Resource Management: A Review and Research Agenda. (2012). *International Journal of Management Reviews.*

Gupta, B. (2011). *A comparative study of organizational strategy and culture across industry. Benchmark Int. J.*

Human resources development as an element of sustainable HRM – with the focus on production engineers. (2021). *Elseiver- J Clean Prod.*

Innovation and growth: how business contributes to society. (2010). *Acad. Manag. Perspect.*

Kramar, R. (2014). Beyond strategic human resource management: Is sustainable human resource management the next approach? *International Journal of Human Resource Management.*

Mael, F., & Ashforth, B.E. (1992). Alumni and their alma mater: a partial test of the reformulated model of organizational identification. *Journal of Organizational Behaviour.*

Marcus, A., & Fremeth, A. (2009). Green management matters regardless. *The Academy of Management Perspectives.*

Milliman, J., & Clair, J. (1996). Best environmental HRM practices in the U.S. Academic Press.

Pfeffer, J. (2010). Building sustainable organizations: The human factor. *The Academy of Management Perspectives.*

Philpott, J., & Davies, G. (2007). *Labour Market Outlook.* CIPD/KPMG.

Ramus, C. A. (2002). *Encouraging innovative environmental actions: What companies and managers must do. Journal of World Business.*

Redman, T., & Snell, S. (Eds.), *The Sage Handbook of Human Resource Management*. Sage.

Russo, M., & Harrison, N. (2005). Organizational design and environmental performance: Clues from the electronics industry. *Academy of Management Journal.*

Singh, S.K., & Singh, A.P. (2019). Interplay of organizational justice, psychological empowerment, organizational citizenship behavior, and job satisfaction in the context of circular economy. *Manag. Decis.*

The Gallup Organization. (2010). Employers' Perception of Graduate Employability. Author.

The greening of Euro-pean management education. (n.d.). InWehrmeyer, W. (Ed.), *Greening People: Human Resources and EnvironmentalManagement* (pp. 289–300). Greenleaf Publishing.

UNEP. (2014). International Declaration on Cleaner Production: Implementation Guidelines for Facilitating Organizations. UNEP.

Wagner, M. (2004). Sustainable reporting? The link of environmental reports and environmental performance. *Corporate Environmental Strategy.*

Wilkinson, A., Hill, M., & Gollan, P. (2001). The sustain-ability debate. *International Journal of Operations and Production Management, 21*, 1492–1502.

Chapter 11
Impact of Sustainable Banking (E-Banking) on the Organisational Commitment Level of Bank Employees in Delhi

Sweety Gupta
Amity University, Noida, India

Anshu Yadav
Amity University, Noida, India

ABSTRACT

The growing awareness among the society has led to a demand of a sustainable banking. Sustainable development promotes society betterment, and it also benefits the bank in several ways. One such factor is an increase in organization commitment among bank employees as a result of sustainable banking. This study revolves around finding the impact of sustainable banking towards the organization commitment level of bank employees in Delhi. For this study, 550 questionnaires were sent to the respondents. Out of the questionnaire sent, only 450 were found useful for further study. Convenient sampling was used to gather data from bankers. Correlation and regression analysis were done in AMOS to study the relationship between both the stated variables.

INTRODUCTION

Deforestation, global warming, climate change are some of the major issues that need to be addressed urgently. Deforestation is the result of cutting of trees for meeting various human needs. It is defined as the mass cutting of trees for the facilitation of human activities One such need for which we chop trees is the need for paper. Going paperless or reducing paper consumption can reduce deforestation. One

DOI: 10.4018/978-1-7998-4990-2.ch011

way of resolving these issues is moving towards a sustainable way of development. Through sustainable development, we plan to take care of not only present generation but also the coming generations. Sustainable banking is one way through which we can promote Sustainable development.

Sustainable banking refers to "Any form of financial service that brings together environmental and social criteria into the banking field or investment decisions for the benefit of society at large". Sustainable banking is all-round development as it takes into consideration all the stakeholders of the organization. Bankers devote major time of their lives in banks and therefore can be considered to be one of the important stakeholders of banks. Sustainable banking can be understood in simple terms as a process of modifying banking products and services in a way that they help create more prosperous society. Even after a great interest shown by different levels of society in a sustainable business, there has been no study found to be showing the impact of Sustainable Banking on the organisation commitment level of bank employees in Delhi region.

Objectives of the Chapter

The Banking sector is one of the busiest and stressed sectors in most parts of the world. The employees in banking sector are required to work for long hours in the banks. Apart from that, their work requires a lot of attention as dealing with public is involved. As such, sustainable banking has become the need of the hour. Sustainable banking and organization are two important variables for study in the banking sector. Numerous researches have been done in the world on sustainable banking and organization commitment, but the studies are limited in the India. Moreover, the relationship between the two needs to be established in a stronger manner. Therefore, it is crucial to study the relationships between Sustainable banking and organization commitment. Therefore, through this study an attempt has been made to check the impact of sustainable banking on the organization commitment. Based on the purpose of study following objectives are framed:

1. To understand the benefits of Sustainable banking.
2. To check the impact of Sustainable banking on organizational commitment in banking sector.

BACKGROUND

Electronic banking has made the traditional banking system more sustainable and future oriented. The traditional system of banking revolved around documentation and paper work. But the electronic banking system of today has replaced the queue system with a press of button.

Sustainable Banking

Electronic banking is sustainable banking in the nature that it reduces paper (like cheques, withdrawal slip, deposit slip), reduces the carbon emission (by reducing the need for transportation/ travel for customers), reduces deforestation (reducing the need for notes printing). The benefits of sustainable banking are as follows:

1. Conserves energy for the future and present generation.

2. Saves paper and reduces deforestation.
3. Takes into consideration all the stakeholders.
4. Reduces carbon emission
5. Environment friendly

With the execution of sustainable banking, the bank tends to achieve the below objectives:

1. Increase in goodwill.

We understand that today the customer is highly knowledgeable and smart. They are very careful about where they want to invest their money and look forward for environment friendly option. As such, sustainable banking helps in increase of goodwill and loyalty towards the bank. Today the customer want to choose paper less mode of transaction over paper as it is more eco-friendly.

2. Reduces number of queues

There is no doubt about the fact that electronic banking has considerable reduced the number of queues in the bank. The presence of automated Teller Machines at different location has also eased up the queues in the bank. Moreover, the e-payment systems have significantly improves due to the presence of new payment methods such as paytm, Phonepe etc.

3. Reduced manpower

Taking into account, the huge population of India, the manpower requirement has not increased in proportion with the increase in population. This has been made possible by electronic banking which has made operation possible without visiting the bank.

4. **Increase in Job Satisfaction and productivity**

Sustainable Banking has resulted in reduces work pressure, reduced number of queues in the bank, more efficiency in banking operation, faster banking operation. All these benefits has resulted in increase in job satisfaction. Reduced work load makes it possible for bankers to focus on more important task at hand. As such, they can be more productive by completing the urgent task with sufficient time in hand.

5. Faster operations

There is no doubt that the paperless way of doing transaction is faster, safer than the paper form of doing transaction. Now, with the help of electronic banking, the customers can take care of regular banking work from home at the click of buttons. Mobile banking has resulted in tremendous increase in the speed of doing operations.

6. Reduction in operating cost.

Green Banking (Sustainable Banking) leads to transactions being faster with less paperwork. It has resulted in less number of employees being required at bank branches (saving salaries), less number of cheque books/passbook/statements being issued (saving paper cost), faster operations in less time (saving time), reduced the number of branches required (saving fixed cost).

7. Customer Oriented

Besides being environment friendly, sustainable banking focuses on customer satisfaction. It is a viable option in the long run as electronic banking makes the transaction faster, more convenient, secure and hassle free for the customers. Sustainable Banking focusses on customer satisfaction in every possible manner and increases their loyalty towards the bank in long run.

8. Reduction in work load

Electronic banking has resulted in revolutionary facilities such as NEFT, ATM, Mobile Banking etc. All these facilities together have resulted in less number of people visiting bank for cash withdrawal, cash deposits, cheque deposits etc. As such electronic banking has resulted in tremendous reduction in work load of the bank employees which would have never been possible otherwise.

9. Innovation driven

Technological innovations are a necessity for every business today. Sustainable banking supports technology in the form of mobile banking, NEFTs, Electronic Clearance System, Online Banking. The new way of banking is highly driven by technology and therefore is faster, safer and more sustainable in nature.

10. Corporate social responsibility

Sustainable Banking fulfills the objective of corporate social responsibility. In every society, bank constitute as one of the most important organization as they directly deal with the members of the society. In light of the same, it becomes crucial for the banks to work towards the betterment of the society. Sustainable Banking makes it possible for the banks to perform the duty of corporate social responsibility by being more socially responsible for their different acts.

Organisation Commitment

Commitment is related to the sincerity of the employee that develops his ability to work hard and produce good results in any scenario. Organizational commitment gained popularity as the organizations began to gain interest in understanding the role of organization commitment in influencing the stability in the organization (Lumley 2010). Organizational commitment is considered an attitude as it relates to the perception of the employees working in the organization (Allen & Meyer 1990).

It can also be defined as an effective response of the employee towards the organization and the inclination, attachment or loyalty towards the organization. There are three main constructs of organization commitment which include affective, normative and continuance aspects of commitment (Coyle-Shapiro et al., 2006). These three constructs of organization commitment represent the mental state of employee that decides their loyalty remains with an organization.

Organizational commitment is defined as belief of the employee towards organization's objectives, an effort by employee as a representative of the organization in reaching these objectives and strong desire to maintain membership in the organization.

Raju and Srivastava (1994) described organizational commitment as a contributor towards promoting the attachment of the employee towards the organization. Organizational Commitment is said to have been achieved if the employees are willingly to continue being associated with an organization and are devoted towards achieving organizational goals and hold a belief in the values of the organization. Also, greater levels of effort shown by employees are associated with high levels of organizational commitment, thereby promoting higher job performance and higher productivity at both the employee and the organizational level. (Raju and Srivastava (1994)).

Becker et al. (1995) has defined organizational commitment in three dimensions. First, the research stated it a strong desire to remain as a member of a particular organization. Second, it is a willingness among the employees to exert high levels of efforts on behalf of the organization and third dimension was that it is a belief in the values and goals of the organization and acceptability of the same.

Organizational commitment has three dimensions related to the attitude of employee in the organization. First is the extent to which the employee demonstrates a desire to remain part of the organization. Second is the extent of willingness to exert efforts for organization. Third is the belief and acceptance of the employee towards the goals and value of the organization. These are three dimensions of Organizational Commitment. (Mowday, Porter, and Steers (1982))

i) Affective Commitment

Affective commitment is the psychological or emotional connection of the employee and his identification with and participation in the organization (Meyer & Allen 1997).The employees with affective commitment towards the organization carry on working for it as they want to and because of their familiarity with the principles of the organization(Meyer & Allen 1991).In addition, employees with affective commitment remain with the organization because their employee-employment relationship are in harmony with the goals and values of the organization. The Affective commitment is present when there is a positive interaction between the individual and the organization as a result of similar values (Shore and Tetrick, 1991). The employees with affective commitment retain their position in the organizations not only because they need the occupation but also because they want it (Meyer et al., 1993).

ii) Continuance Commitment

Continuance commitment is defined as the awareness of the employees towards the costs associated with leaving the organization. Continuance commitment is considered to be calculative as it is associated with the awareness or consideration of the employee about the expenses and threats linked to leaving the organization, (Meyer & Allen 1997).

Continuance commitment is the opposite of affective organizational commitment as it is based on the idea that employee's do not leave the organizations for fear of losing their benefits, taking a pay cut, and not being able to find another job (Murray, Gregoire, & Downey, 1991). It states that the employee face difficulty in leaving the organization due to the unknown or having less or no alternatives. According to it, employee's with a strong continuance commitment stay with the organization because they need it and based on the costs associated with leaving the organization. The two subsets of continuance commitment are personal sacrifice and perceived lack of alternatives (Dunham et al., 1994; Meyer et al., 1990). Both these variables increase the costs associated with leaving the organization.

iii) Normative Commitment

Normative commitment can be explained as a sense of responsibility to continue employment with the organization (Meyer & Allen 1997). It states that responsibility and commitment allows employees continued membership that is appreciated by a specific organization (Allen & Meyer 1990). It explains that employees with normative commitment stay with the organization due to the belief that it is the right and moral thing to do (Meyer and Allen, 1991). Wiener and Gechman (1977) argued that this commitment develops based on the belief that arises during their early socialization from family and culture and during their socialization as newcomers to the organization. In addition, normative commitment might also develop because of the psychological contract between an employee and the organization (Roussenau, 1995).

It increases when an individual feels more loyal towards his organization or responsible towards work to compensate for the benefits received from the organization (Meyer et al., 1993). It concerns the belief of the employee about his responsibility to the organization.

CONCEPTUAL FRAMEWORK

To conduct this study, a conceptual model of Sustainable Banking and organization commitment was established with the help of literature review. However, there were very few studies present that showed the relationship between the two variables. No exact study was found showing the impact of Sustainable Banking on organization commitment in Delhi. Based on the literature review, a conceptual model which explains the relationship between both the variables was proposed.

INITIATIVES TAKEN BY INDIAN BANKS TOWARDS SUSTAINABLE BANKING

The banking sector has taken many initiatives

1. State Bank of India (SBI)

SBI has made tremendous efforts to make the banking system more sustainable and viable. For this, they launched 'Green Channel Counter' (GCC) facility at various branches throughout the country. This new system launched by them was more eco-friendly and convenient. Not only this, they were the first bank in the country to enter into generation of renewable energy by installing windmills for wind energy. To take this to another level, they also installed ATM working on solar energy all over India.

2. Bank of Baroda

Bank of Baroda is known for giving high weightage to loan proposals and projects focusing on renewable sources of energy thereby helping in reduction of carbon emissions. .The bank of baroda also attempt to get water treatment plant installed at customer's site while dispensing loan to manufacturing units for industrial water treatment. Tis step taken by the bank goes a long way in reducing water pollution. In addition to getting the treatment plant installed, they ensure that their client obtain a No Objection Certificate from government agencies responsible for keeping check on pollution of industries. For their work, the Bank of Baroda was appreciated by Excellence award by Institute of Development and Research in Banking Technology (IDRBT). This bank is also working towards constructing its bank branches that satisfies all green building norms.

3. Punjab National Bank

The bank has also contributed towards sustainable banking by introducing Core Banking solutions that are eco-friendly. Punjab National Bank regularly conducts green audits at various bank branches and they also promote the use of 4 star/5 star electrical appliances that conserves energy. The bank has proper system in place for providing loan to industrial units involved in generation of renewable energy such as wind energy, solar energy etc. PNB also promotes the use of electronic banking to cut the use of paper and ensure faster, safer and hassle free banking. PNB has successfully installed green practices at various bank branches to save energy and cut down operational cost. The bank is also installing Automated Teller machines at selected places that work on solar energy.

4. Bank of India

The bank is successfully using all the latest electronic banking modes such as ATMs, NEFTs, mobile banking, Electronic Clearance System to cut down on the use of paper and reduce deforestation. They educate their customers to switch to electronic banking from traditional banking to make the entire banking system more efficient and sustainable in the long run. Bank of India encourages customers to use e statements and electronic payments by keeping the system in place. The bank has taken various green drives by planting small tree saplings and increasing the green cover. The bank regularly promotes campaign aimed at creating awareness towards the benefits of planting trees and conserving energy for future generations.

5. ICICI Bank Ltd

ICCI Bank has launched the famous scheme of automobile financing aimed at going green. Under this scheme, they provide a waiver of upto 50% to their clients who are interested in purchasing automobiles that are more eco-friendly. Coming to home loans, the bank provide reduced processing fees to clients that buy energy efficient buildings. The bank has initiate a programme to educate different industrial bodies and bank institutions involved in green projects for conserving wild life, for conserving energies etc. at different levels. The bank has also successfully installed water treatment plants and solar panels at different locations.

6. HDFC Bank Ltd

HDFC bank has actively added green feature to its various bank branches aimed at promoting water management through green water harvesting, use of energy efficient electric appliances to conserve energy The also implemented a phase out policy under which they reduced all old lighting system with the latest LED lighting. They also use technologies that are approved by Central Pollution Control Board (CPCB) for conserving energies wherever possible. Installation of service points, ATMs by the bank at various location also aims at reduction of carbon emission (less use of paper, less transportation required).

HDFC bank successfully runs awareness campaigns to create green awareness among its employees and customers. While dispensing loans they conduct proper screening to eliminate projects with high environmental cost using Social and Environmental Risk Management System

7. Axis Bank Ltd

Axis Bank is also contributing towards sustainable banking by using Environment and social safeguard policy" (ESSP) wile dispensing loans for various projects to its clients. Axis Bank also give priority to green projects that are based on clean technologies, promote the use of renewable source of energy, has less industrial wastage. The bank achieved a milestone in the year when it received a credit of US $70 million from international finance corporation (IFC) to ease loan dispersal to green projects.

The building of the head office of Axis bank is based on green design where they have installed all measures aimed at reducing the carbon footprints such as latest LED lights, energy efficient appliances to conserve energy etc. They also dispose of the electronic waste (old printers, Air-Conditioners, monitors etc) with the help of approved government bodies. They have also initiated a green technology mission aimed at green banners that have massively cut down on their waste. In addition, they planted over 1 at over a thousand locations across India.

8. YES Bank

The initiatives taken by Yes Bank also go a long way in the promotion of sustainable banking. It became the first bank to sign the carbon disclosure project in UN Global Compact to declare the carbon footprints and is taking suitable efforts to reduce them Not only this, it is the first Private sector bank to sign the UNEP statements on sustainable development. YES BANK has undertaken the Environmental and Social Policy (ESP) through which the Bank compiles the environmental risks into banking risk structure. They are well known for funding India's biggest solar project i.e. The Welspun Neemuch solar PV project in Madhya Pradesh at a huge capacity of 130 MW. Yes Bank is the first bank in India to get ISO 14001:2004 certification. This certification is aimed at environment management.

MAIN FOCUS OF THE CHAPTER

Indian banking industry is in undergoing massive changes. The Banking industry in India is the support system of Indian financial system. In the present era of globalization, keeping pace with the changes in the society has become very important for the successful functioning of the banking sector. Without science and technology, banking industry will fall apart in the present times. Electronic Banking has enlarged the role of banking sector in India. Electronic Banking has helped us create a fast and efficient banking system that responds to the needs of growing banking users. In the last three decades banks in India are investing heavily to meet the global standards in terms of technology. The innovations of electronic banking such as Online banking, mobile banking, tele-banking, National Electronic Fund Transfer (NEFT), automated teller machines (ATMs), credit cards, debit cards, smart cards, Real Time Gross Settlement (RTGS), customer relationship management (CRM), other electronic payment systems etc have become an integral part of Indian Banking System. These financial innovations have bought improvements in quality of banking services by reducing the time and energy required in the completion of a banking transaction. The main focus of the chapter is to highlight the changes associated with Impact of Sustainable Banking (E-Banking) on the Organization Commitment level of bank employees in Delhi.

Issues, Controversies, Problems

Sustainable development is not very easy to practice as it takes patience to practice. However, it is the right way. The biggest issue faced by the banking industry in practicing Sustainable development is the *low acceptance* among people towards Electronic Banking. People feel that it is cumbersome, less secure and they still want to use the traditional banking practices.

Even in the 21st century, it is easy to find strata of society who are not comfortable using the modern banking practices such as debit card, credit cards, ATMs, NEFTs etc. There it becomes difficult to make development 100% sustainable. In addition, change is never easy for anyone. Bank customers *resist practicing the e-way of banking*. Long queues can still be found to get passbooks updated at various bank branches despite the option of accessing e-statements. It is high time that awareness is created among this group to make the shift from traditional banking t sustainable banking easy for them.

Sustainable banking (Electronic banking) is *difficult to practice in villages and small towns* where the customers are less educated and tech-savvy. The acceptance rate towards electronic banking is very low among villages and small towns. More efforts need to be made by the government, banking authorities and banking employees to make electronic banking more inclusive.

RESEARCH METHODOLOGY

i) Tools and implementations

The questionnaire was made up of three parts. First part obtained demographic details of the respondents, second part obtained information about sustainable banking and the third part was based on organisation commitment.

ii) **Hypotheses**

H1. Sustainable banking positively affects organisation commitment

iii) Sampling process

The questionnaire was sent to 450 employees working in banks in Delhi/NCR. Convenient sampling was used while sending questionnaires and obtaining the data. Quantitative analysis was used to analyse the data on 9 point Likert scale. Demographic characteristics of respondents, descriptive statistics and testing of hypothesis were reviewed with SPSS. Correlation and regression between the studied variable was established through AMOS.

iv) Analysis and Interpretation

Table 1. Demographic Profile of the respondents

DEMOGRAPHIC PROFILE OF THE RESPONDENTS			
	Classification of variables	**No. of respondents**	**Percentage**
GENDER	Male	258	57.3
	Female	192	42.7
MARITAL STATUS	Married	324	72.0
	Unmarried	126	28
EDUCATION	Graduate	200	44.4
	Post Graduate and above	250	55.6
INCOME	Between 20,000-Rs 40,000	35	7.8
	Between 40,000-Rs 60,000	115	25.6
	Above Rs.60,000	300	66.6
EXPERIENCE	Less than 5 years	90	20
	Between 5-10 years	60	13.4
	Between 10-15 years	160	35.5
	More than 15 years	140	31.1
BANK	Private Sector Bank	245	54.4
	Public Sector Bank	205	45.5

Table 1 shows the information about the respondents. It indicates that 57.3% were males and 42.7% of the 450 respondents were female. The married percentage was 72%, while unmarried were only 28%. The percentage of graduate was 44.4% and post graduate constituted 55.6%. Respondents earning between 20,000-Rs 40,000 is 7.8%; between 40,000-Rs 60,000 is 25.6% and that of above Rs. 60,000 is 66.6%. Of all the respondents, 20% had experience of less than 5 years; 13.4% had experience between 5-10 years; 35.5% between 10-15 years and 31% had experience more than 15 years. The percentage of respondents working with private sector bank is only 54.4 and that working with public sector bank is 45.5.

Table 2 shows the results of reliability test. To check the internal consistency of items, reliability test was conducted. In general, the value of cronbach alpha above .60 is considered acceptable. As seen

Table 2. Reliability statistics

Cronbach Alpha Items
Sustainable Banking .883 7
Organisation Commitment .914 8

in above table, the value of cronbach alpha for both the variables is above 0.60, the data is considered consistent for further analysis.

Table 3. Model Fit Indices

Chi - square	D. F.	CMIN/DF	GFI	CFI	IFI	RMSEA
91.703	89	1.03	.976	. 999	.999	.009

Table III depicts the indices of model fitness showing different fitness criteria. As shown in the table CMIN/DF is 1.03 which shows that model is good as its acceptable limit is below 4. All values were near to their traditional criteria which showed that model was fit for that study.

Regression Analysis

Table VI illustrates the regression weights of the study model. The result presents a positive and considerable impact of job satisfaction on organizational commitment.

Table 4. Regression Weights: (Group number 1 - Default model)

			Estimate	S.E.	C.R.	P	Label
OC	<---	SB	.467	.064	7.288	***	par_14
SB6	<---	SB	1.000				
SB5	<---	SB	.933	.068	13.802	***	par_1
SB4	<---	SB	.848	.065	13.077	***	par_2
SB3	<---	SB	.845	.066	12.870	***	par_3
SB2	<---	SB	.889	.064	13.814	***	par_4
SB1	<---	SB	.869	.063	13.869	***	par_5
OC6	<---	OC	1.000				
OC5	<---	OC	.813	.054	15.126	***	par_6
OC4	<---	OC	.893	.059	15.145	***	par_7
OC3	<---	OC	.784	.055	14.353	***	par_8
OC2	<---	OC	.878	.059	15.000	***	par_9
OC1	<---	OC	.842	.058	14.486	***	par_10
OC7	<---	OC	.828	.055	15.002	***	par_11
OC8	<---	OC	.889	.059	15.165	***	par_12
SB7	<---	SB	.974	.067	14.569	***	par_13

MEASUREMENT MODEL

In the below diagram, Job Satisfaction and Organisation Commitment are the two constructs. SB1, SB2, SB3, SB4, SB5, SB6 and SB7 are the statements predicting Job Satisfaction among the banking employees in Delhi and OC1,OC2,OC3,OC4,OC5,OC6,OC7, OC8 are the statements predicting the Organisation Commitment among the banking employees in Delhi.

Figure 1. Correlation between Sustainable Banking and Organization Commitment using AMOS

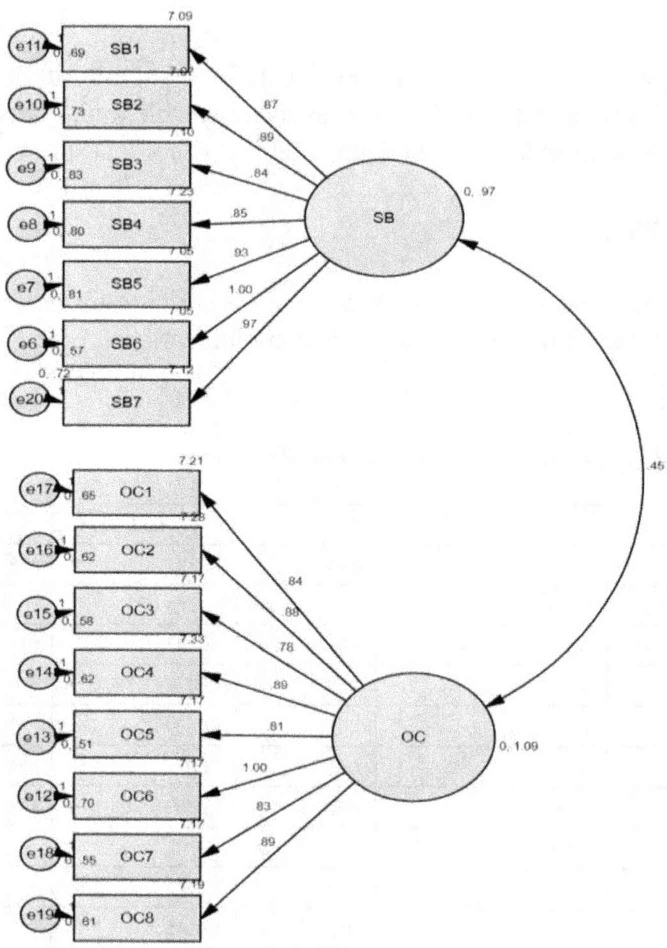

The above figure shows the correlation between Sustainable Banking and Organization Commitment. The value of correlation is 0.45. As we know that the value of correlation lie between -1 to 1. So, we can say that there is high level of correlation between Job Satisfaction and Organization Commitment among banking employees in banking sector. In addition, the level of correlation between the statement and the construct is greater than 0.5 in each case, thereby showing that the statements have good level of correlation with the constructs.

The above figure shows the regression between sustainable Banking and Organization Commitment to be 0.47. The above figure proves that Sustainable Banking has a significant impact on Organization Commitment among banking employees in banking sector.

LIMITATIONS OF THE STUDY

1. The limitation concerns regarding the nature of the measures used in this research study. The measures included in the study are based on the perceptions of the respondents. Therefore, the inaccuracies in data due to misrepresentation in any item or predisposition to certain responses on the part of respondents exist in the study.
2. This research study had sampled population which was restricted only to Delhi and therefore the outcome might not be banking employees working in the other parts of the country and therefore recommendations may not be generalized to other banks. It was due to limited time only that the banks of only Delhi region were considered. Therefore, study in other cities is required to generalize the outcome of the present study. Secondly, the banking sector was chosen as the area for investigation, so the findings may not be applicable to the organizations outside the banking sector. However, the findings of this research were largely consistent with the earlier research findings carried out in other parts of the world.
3. The top level management and the concerned branch of banks were sometimes reluctant to share the required information for the study. In addition, there are always chances of the biasness on the part of respondents. There are possibilities that some respondents may not be ready to reveal the exact information.
4. The major issue encountered during the course of this research was that the respondents were bankers who are quite busy due to the demanding nature of their jobs and therefore difficulty was faced at the time of distributing and collecting data from them. This also made the sample size of the study limited in comparison with the population of bankers in Delhi. Moreover, it was found that at the time of collecting data from the bankers, the employees were occupied with work and were not able to provide much time to fill the questionnaire.
5. The financial resources and time frame also posed many limitations on the researcher to do a more in-depth study on the topic.

DISCUSSIONS

Sustainable Banking has provided huge competitive advantage to banks by reducing the overall cost structure. Not only this, there has been a substantial increase in customer satisfaction as they don't need to step out of their homes and complete the transactions at click of buttons. Customer satisfaction has gone up as payments, withdrawal, transfer, fixed deposits, recurring deposits, NEFTs etc can be done online. This has led to low carbon emission also which is good for the environment. (manohar & kumar, 2013)

However, more needs to be done in the area of Sustainable Banking as still there is immense scope of reduction of carbon emission. Some bank customers still prefer the conventional/traditional form of

Figure 2. Regression between Sustainable Banking and Organization Commitment using AMOS

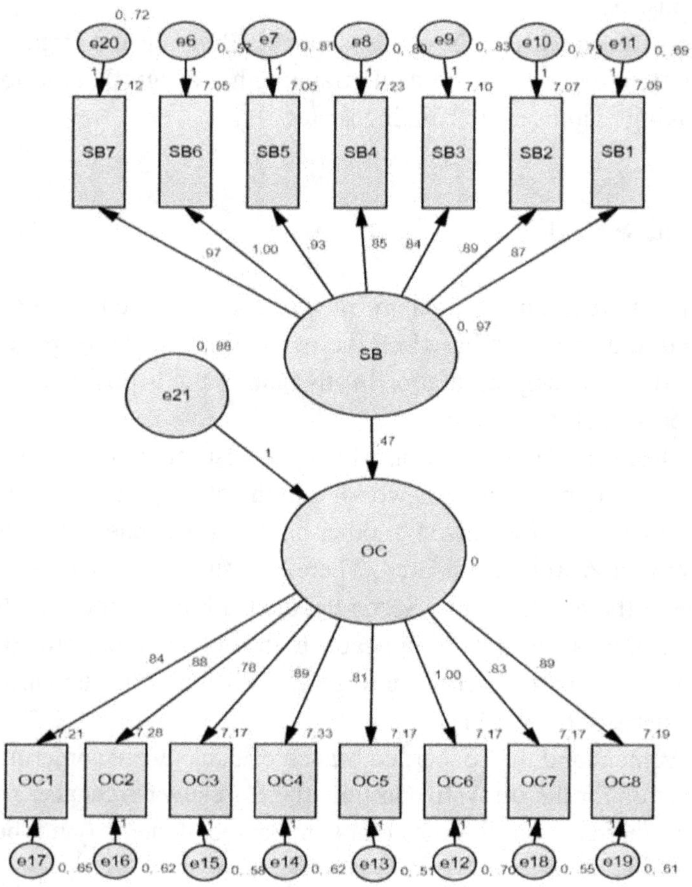

banking over electronic banking. As such, more awareness needs to be created among the society about the benefits of electronic banking so the switch to the same can be made swiftly. Moreover, there are customers who resist the use of debit card/credit card over safety issues. Even in that regard, the bank should create awareness and address all safety related issues (queries) of the customers. We as society can definitely have a better and more secure future if we work together towards Sustainable Banking. Needless to mention, the benefits of Sustainable Banking has been found on the employees of banking sector as well. There has been significant increase in their commitment level of bank employees which has benefitted the banking sector.

SOLUTIONS AND RECOMMENDATIONS

Electronic Banking itself is a solution to many problems. It has multiple benefits for all stakeholders. It benefits the banking industry by reducing the operative cost. It benefits the bank employees' by increasing their commitment level and job productivity levels. It benefits the customers by making transactions faster and secure. It benefits the environment by reducing cutting of trees. It benefits society by giving them a better place to live with better air quality (result of reduction in cutting of trees). It is however, recommended to make electronic banking more inclusive by raising awareness and education in villages and small town about how to use it. More government campaign needs to run to create a better understanding about the benefits of paperless banking so the society can benefit from it at a larger level.

CONCLUSION

Sustainable Banking and organization commitment are two crucial job related attitudes that should be properly understood by banking organizations. This is because committed employees have higher productivity and contribute more towards organizational productivity. This study provides valuable insights about sustainable Banking that leads to organizational commitment and thereby increasing productivity. Increased employees productivity is largely related to their level of their organizational commitment level.

REFERENCES

Abdullah, A., & Ramay, I. (2012). Antecedents of organizational commitment of banking sector employees in Pakistan. *Serbian Journal of Management*, *7*(1), 89–102. doi:10.5937jml201089A

Al Shaikh, F. N. (1995). Organization Commitment in the banking sector in Jordan: An Empirical Investigation. *Journal of Administrative Science & Economics, 6*.

Allen, N. J., & Meyer, J. P. (1990). The measurement and antecedents of affective, continuance and normative commitment to the organization. *Journal of Occupational Psychology*, *63*(1), 1–18. doi:10.1111/j.2044-8325.1990.tb00506.x

Bank of Baroda. (2013-14). Annual Report-Bank of Baroda. Vadodara.

Bank of India. (2013-14). *Annual Report*. Bank of India Mumbai.

Becker, T. E., Randall, D. M., & Riegel, C. D. (1995). The multidimensional view of commitment and the theory of reasoned action: A comparative evaluation. *Journal of Management*, *21*(4), 617–638. doi:10.1177/014920639502100402

Bihari, S. C. (2010). Green banking-towards socially resonsible banking in india. *International Journal of Business Insights & Transformation*, *4*(1).

Bouma, J. J., Jeucken, M., & Klinkers, L. (Eds.). (2017). *Sustainable banking: The greening of finance*. Routledge. doi:10.4324/9781351282406

Brundtland, G. H. (1987). Our common future—Call for action. *Environmental Conservation*, *14*(4), 291–294. https://doi.org/10.1017/s0376892900016805

Chadichal, S. S., & Misra, S. (2012). Exploring the online service quality dimensions in service sectors impact on developing e-CRM in Indian banking sector. *Global Journal For Research Analysis, 2*(1), 115-117. doi:10.15373/22778160/january2013/8

Coyle-Shapiro, J. A., Morrow, P. C., & Kessler, I. (2006). Serving two organizations: Exploring the employment relationship of contracted employees. *Human Resource Management, 45*(4), 561–583. https://doi.org/10.1002/hrm.20132

Deniz, O., & Kirmizi, A. (2009). The organisational commitment of IT professionals in private banks. In *European and Mediterranean Conference on Information Systems* (pp. 13-14). Academic Press.

Fiorita, J. A., Bozeman, D. P., Young, A., & Meurs, J. A. (2007). Organization Commitment, Human Resource Practices, and Organization Characteristic. *Journal of Managerial Issues, 19*(2), 186–207.

Gelder, J. W. V. (2006). The do's and don'ts of Sustainable Banking: A BankTrack Manual. *BankTrack.* Available from: https://www.banktrack.org/download/the_dos_and_donts_of_sustainable_banking/061129_the_dos_and_donts_of_sustainable_banking_bt_manual.pdf

Global Alliance for Banking on Values (GABV). (2012). *Strong, Straightforward and Sustainable Banking: Financial Capital and Impact Metrics of Values Based Banking.* Available from: https://www.gabv.org/wp-content/uploads/GABV-Summary-final.pdfi

Hawken, P. (2013). *The Guide to Sustainable Banking 2013. Blue and Green Tomorrow.* Available from: http://blueandgreentomorrow.com/wp-content/uploads/2013/10/guide-to-banking-2013-10MB.pdf

HDFC Bank. (2014). *Sustainability Report 2013-14.* HDFC Bank Mumbai.

Imeson, M., & Sim, A. (2010). *Sustainable Banking: Why Helping Communities and Saving the Planet is Good for Business?* SAS White Paper Issued by SAS Institute Inc. World Headquarters.

Jeucken, M. (2010). *Sustainable finance and banking: The financial sector and the future of the planet.* Earthscan.

Lalon, R. M. (2015). Green banking: Going green. *International Journal of Economics, Finance and Management Sciences, 3*(1), 34-42.

Lumley, E. J. (2009). *Exploring the relationship between career anchors, job satisfaction and organisational commitment* (Doctoral dissertation). University of South Africa.

Manohar, B., & Kumar, C. V. (2012). Green Banking: Bye-bye cheques, hello electronic payments. *Asia Pacific Journal of Management & Entrepreneurship Research, 1*(3), 60.

Meyer, J. P., Stanley, D. J., Herscovitch, L., & Topolnytsky, L. (2002). Affective, continuance, and normative commitment to the organization: A meta-analysis of antecedents, correlates, and consequences. *Journal of Vocational Behavior, 61*(1), 20–52.

Mowday, R. T., Steers, R. M., & Porter, L. W. (1979). The measurement of organizational commitment. *Journal of Vocational Behavior, 14*(2), 224–247.

Park, H., & Kim, J. D. (2020). Transition towards green banking: Role of financial regulators and financial institutions. *Asian Journal of Sustainability and Social Responsibility, 5*(1), 1–25.

Rajput, N., Kaura, R., & Khanna, A. (2013). Indian banking sector towards a sustainable growth: A paradigm shift. *International Journal of Academic Research in Business and Social Sciences, 3*(1), 290.

Raju, P. M., & Srivastava, R. C. (1994). Factors contributing to commitment to the teaching profession. *International Journal of Educational Management*.

Ramnarain, T. D., & Pillay, M. T. (2016). Designing sustainable banking services: The case of Mauritian banks. *Procedia: Social and Behavioral Sciences*, *224*, 483–490.

Ramnarain, T. D., & Pillay, M. T. (2016). Designing Sustainable Banking Services: The Case of Mauritian Banks. *Procedia - Social and Behavioral Sciences, 224*, 483-490. doi:10.1016/j.sbspro.2016.05.424

Renn, O., Jager, A., Deuschle, J., & Weimer-Jehle, W. (2009). A normative-functional concept of sustainability and its indicators. *International Journal of Global Environmental Issues*, *9*(4), 291–317.

Soundarrajan, P., & Vivek, N. (2016). Green finance for sustainable green economic growth in India. *Agricultural Economics*, *62*(1), 35–44.

Sustainable banking: The Greening of finance. (2001). Greenleaf Publishing.

Weber, O., & Feltmate, B. (2016). *Sustainable banking: Managing the social and environmental impact of financial institutions*. University of Toronto Press.

Yip, A. W., & Bocken, N. M. (2018). Sustainable business model archetypes for the banking industry. *Journal of Cleaner Production*, *174*, 150–169.

KEY TERMS AND DEFINITIONS

Bank: A bank is a financial institution that accepts deposits from the public at a certain interest level and lends loan to the needy at a higher interest level.

Commitment: the act of engaging/dedicating yourself emotionally or mentally to something (someone).

Electronic Banking: Electronic banking (online banking) is a form of banking in which funds are transferred electronically with the help of internet instead of cash, cheques, or other types of paper documents.

Organisation Commitment: Organisational commitment is the employee mental and/or attachment towards the organisation.

Sustainable Development: It is the development that takes place while considering the needs of the upcoming generation and present generation at the same time.

Chapter 12
A Study of Consumer Switching Behaviour in the Indian Context With Respect to Recycled Products

Charul Agrawal
Amity University, Noida, India

Taranjeet Duggal
Amity Business School, Amity University, Noida, India

ABSTRACT

In recent years, the need of every corporation to address the environmental issues has grown multifold. The corporate social responsibility concerns are growing, and it has become an indicator to judge a business performance. In the context of increasing environmental concerns where issues of pollution, generation of wastes, use of toxic substances for packaging, etc. are gaining strong ground, the consumers have also become alarmed and they fully understand the implications of such issues both on nature and earth. The chapter aims to study the behaviour and the change therein of Indian consumers. It is true that all the efforts and policies targeted towards initiative of green marketing cannot be realised if it is not received by the consumers. The chapter proposes to cover the concept of green marketing and its relation to the circular economy, the green marketing practices in Indian context, the attitude and preference of the Indian consumer towards green products, and the switch in the purchase pattern of the Indian consumers with respect to green/recycled products.

INTRODUCTION

The business organisations globally have become very sensitive to the environmental concerns. Not only has the realisation to save the Earth dawned on the business corridors, these issues have found their presence in all aspects of business functions, be it production, packaging or advertising. In recent years the

DOI: 10.4018/978-1-7998-4990-2.ch012

need of every corporate to address the environmental issues has grown multifold. The Corporate Social responsibility concerns are growing and it has become an indicator to judge a business performance. In the context of increasing environmental concerns where issues of pollution, generation of wastes, use of toxic substances for packaging etc. are gaining strong ground the consumers have also become alarmed and they fully understand the implications of such issues both on nature and Mother Earth. Green Marketing is a practice where the companies strive for sustainability and adopt environment friendly practices and methods for production, packaging and distribution of their products.

Bhattacharya (2011) The paper discusses the today the major issue confronting the business world is to maintain the ecological balance because the world has already reached the threshold where the limits are alarming and resources are fast diminishing. The negative developments like generation of e-wastes and its poor management, the biodegradable pollutants are shooting. Amidst all such issues Green Marketing can be one such imitative which can bring about a change. The terms like re-use, re-cycle and re-generate are keywords of future and can bring back the environment to friendly terms. However, the term Green Marketing should not be limited to mere products alone the purview can be extended to services also.

Wastes and pollution do not happen by chance rather they are the result of the decisions taken at the product design stage. From the time when the economy witnessed the Great Industrial Revolution where goods were being produced in masses as the labour was cheap and the resources were infinite to till date where this mass production has brought extensive depletion of the natural resources. The situation has even endangered the future generations where they might be completely devoid of these resources. Basically, this functioning of the production mechanism works on Linear Economy which is based on three principles of TAKE-MAKE-WASTE, which simply put means the resources are taken from the nature, made or converted in to goods and then when they are no longer in use they are wasted or dumped. This process is subsequently followed by the similar pattern of TAKE-MAKE-WASTE. The need of the hour is a complete turnaround from the concept of Linear Economy to Circular economy.

WHAT IS CIRCULAR ECONOMY

As per the World Economic forum Circular Economy is defined in the following way.

"A circular economy is an industrial system that is restorative or regenerative by intention and design. It replaces the end-of-life concept with restoration, shifts towards the use of renewable energy, eliminates the use of toxic chemicals, which impair reuse and return to the biosphere, and aims for the elimination of waste through the superior design of materials, products, systems, and business models. "

Simply put, a Circular Economy does not believe in wastes. As per Ellen Macarthur

"A circular economy is based on the principles of designing out waste and pollution, keeping products and materials in use, and regenerating natural systems."

A circular economy believes that wastes and pollutants should not be created in the first place, the design phase should harness the materials and technology in such a way that there is no creation of wastes. Secondly products or components should be such that they be reused, re-manufactured and repaired. It is here that the concept of recycled products come into picture. Recycling is simply turning waste products into useful products; in other words, it is basically a form of Re-Manufacture. The concept of Recycled products and their usage in a developing country like India is explained in the later part of the chapter. The third tenet of Circular economy is based on the concept of Food Chain which says that nothing is waste, the output of one becomes the food for another, In the similar way the wastes should be regenerated back to the economy.

The world can definitely be made a better place if the resources are reutilised and not wasted.

The current market scenario has become sensitive and the consumers are gradually understanding that purchasing environmentally friendly products will make them more responsible towards the cause of Nature Conservatism. Maheshwari (2014) proposes that the Indian consumers do not have enough exposure to green products marketing communication The paper further suggests that there should be high usage of brand promotion to sell environmental friendly products. Though the Indian consumers are still not fully aware of the concept of recycled products or simply put environmentally friendly products but still the change in their purchasing pattern is visible.

It is believed that Indians use a piece of cloth till its last breath, given the fact that we Indians can put the same cloth to multiple uses. The important aspect to realise here is that everyone should understand that the wastes generated after the usage of one product could serve as a raw material for the next product. India is the fifth largest producer of E-wastes.

"According to the Press Information Bureau, India generates 62 million tonnes of waste (mixed waste containing both recyclable and non-recyclable waste) every year, with an average annual growth rate of 4% (PIB 2016)."

With such statistics before us it is essential that Indians in general need to switch to recycled products and reduce the waste generation.

(Biswas, 2015) explains that E-waste management in India is complex due to its multidimensional socio economic and cultural associations with Consumer Disposal behaviour as well as awareness

RECYCLED PRODUCTS IN INDIA

In simple terms Recycling is a process where waste materials could be converted or modified into new products. Not all the materials available with us can be recycled and used again but the good part is that most of the materials or products that we use can be recycled in some way or the other. Most of the products we use as consumers are easily recyclable however in some cases the method of recycling can be less economical. Be it the plastic bottles or the glass crockery all or the cardboard boxes all of them can be recycled. There is a long list of materials which can be recycled but there are many reasons as to why the practices of waste Management and recycling do not have a strong presence in India .

Firstly, there is lack of awareness, most of the people do not even know the concept of recycling. They are not aware which products can be recycled and in what way. In fact in most of the cases the general opinion is that the wastes once generated should be immediately disposed or sold to the local kabadiwala.

Another very prominent reason of low recycling is lack of segregation of wastes. A majority of household consumers in India do not segregate even the kitchen waste. They lack the knowledge and means of differentiating between wet and dry waste. This problem actually makes the waste management all the more cumbersome. Non-segregation of wastes leads to diseases among the rag pickers, many animals are hurt and overall chances of spread of infection accelerate.

Last but not the least the disposal of waste in India is not very efficient. (Dixit, 2013) discusses the effect of demographic variables particularly age, sex, place of residence on the way Consumers There are large dumping grounds in the outskirts of the city where just piling of garbage goes on and the process of recycling is very slow and manual. These dumping grounds also known as Landfill act as a catalyst to increase air and water pollution. The chemicals and non-biodegradable waste in the dumping ground affects the physical environment and at the same time containment of the underground water. There are many other issues also such there is no comprehensive policy regulation from the Governments or strict implementation of the waste segregation. There are many illegal activities associated with the dumping too. With the population of the country increasing every day the problem of garbage is also becoming mammoth and needs immediate attention.

Figure 1.
Source: cnn.com

Recycle is the third R in the hierarchy of Reduce, Reuse and Recycle. These three R's can make a significant change in conserving the environment. There have many instances where consumers have reduced the usage of unwanted materials such as poly bags, plastic and switched over to more environmental friendly products such as organic food, paper bags, and mud utensils for cooking .In fact with increased awareness the consumers have adopted various mean and measures in their own ways to reduce the harmful impact on environment. Rain water harvesting, kitchen gardens, car-pooling, are some of the many ways which Indian consumers are doing their bit for the environment.

Some notable examples in India are:

1. A company called Act Paper Wings uses waste newspapers to make home décor items such as Fridge magnets, key rings, table mats etc.

2.Pepaa uses waste paper to make Pencils and each pencil carries a seedling which is one small bit to make the planet green

3. Goonj, a NGO uses clothes (donated) to make sanitary pads, bags for women in rural areas.

There are numerous other examples where plastic bottles are being converted in to T-Shirts, Used Rubber tyres are being made into pots, Old torn jeans are being used to make bags and the list is long and growing.

INDIAN CONSUMER BEHAVIOUR

It is a matter of concern that the awareness level of recycled products in quite low in the country and moreover it is a general perception that the recycled products are more expensive than the regular ones. A simple example could be taken here of a gift wrapping paper, how a handmade paper is more costly than a normal wrapping paper. The Indian Consumer is a very typical consumer, for him Price is by far the most dominating factor which influences him to take the decision to purchase or not to purchase.

(Prakash, 2017) concludes that in India purchase behaviour towards green packaging material is significantly impacted by personal norms, attitudes and above all willingness to pay.

Some typical characteristics of Indian consumers which shape up the pattern of shopping are:

1. Indian Consumers are highly price sensitive. A change in price of a commodity can either postpone or cancel a decision of purchase by the Indians. Indians are fond of street shopping and they prefer buying in bulk. Bargaining is another important characteristic of Indian consumer personality.
2. Indian consumers are practically new to the concept of E-Commerce. They are still in the exploration phase. There has been a plethora of shopping websites which are offering merchandise in a variety of category from kitchen essentials to Garden equipment. Though there is an increasing trend in the digital payments and more than 40% of Indian Consumers are present on the Internet but still the penetration is low. Most of the Indians use Internet to surf for information or for entertainment through their social media accounts. So it won't be anomaly to say that a majority of Indian shoppers still prefer to shop the traditional way.
3. Indian consumers are savings oriented; they are traditionally known to be attracted by good bargains because value for money is of utmost importance to them. They prefer to save for later for occasions such as upcoming festivals, marriage functions etc. The Indians sometimes look for cheaper substitutes in order to save money. Though they are open to brands both national and International but they will not shy from purchasing cheaper substitutes.
4. Indian Consumers are basically family oriented and they very strongly believe in tradition and culture. For them ownership of home, land, gold still has higher priority rather than buying any other consumer durables. They also prefer to invest in those items which give returns over a longer duration of time and have good resale value rather than recycle value.
5. The Indian consumer mindset adores the values of care, nurture and appreciates quality. They trust brands which communicate such values like TATA and LIC. The trust factor which they have associated with these brands have been for many generations. The Indian consumers take time and for them the past experiences matter a lot.

Overall, we can say that the Indian consumer behaviour is pretty complex, dynamic and unpredictable. (Narula, 2016) stresses that more advance research needs to be conducted so as to address the gap between Consumer Behaviour and the purchase of the green products. The paper further proposes that more insights need to be developed in order to study the willingness to pay for green attributes vis a vis the traditional ones.

The brands really have to work hard to build their footing in the Indian market. The recent scenario of the Indian market is buzzing. With the entry of many foreign brands, ease of accessibility, the expansion of the rural Indian market above all the influence of social media the Indians shopping pattern has undergone some changes. Some of them are:

1. The new generation of the shoppers are experimental as well as open-minded. They don't refrain from trying new brands or new products. From new gadgets to the packaged food materials they are enthusiastic in trying and buying all. They explore new market places and express their opinions frankly on the products and services.
2. There has been an increasing trend on buying durables on Credit. The Indians are buying everything under the sky from a flight ticket to a 3 BHK flat on EMI. With easy financing options available the Indians are buying more and buying more frequently. It has become simple for a Indian consumer to switch to a fully automatic washing machine or a LED Tv. He has ample choices and lucrative financial deals to his advantage. It would not be a felony to say that this has brought a upward shift in the lifestyle and increased standard of living of an average Indian as it has made the consumer durables all the more affordable.
3. The internet has penetrated deep and this has brought the market all the closer to the Indians. The online shopping platform is flooded with e-commerce websites which offer round the clock shopping, with easy payment options and home delivery. If not all but a majority of youngsters prefer to shop online.
4. Another noticeable trend is the shopping centred around information. Today the Indian consumer is aware, he believes in reading reviews and searching on the net before he shops. In such cases he is able to verify his purchase decisions and he is also happy because he thinks he has got the best bargain. Sometimes there are cases of information overload, but the more the information the better it is for him. Information facilitates comparison and he is happy because he thinks himself to be a prudent customer after making rational choices.
5. A consumer's choice set is heavy he has lot of options to choose from. With information at the finger tips, The Indian consumer has also become aware of his responsibilities and he is also aware of the repercussions of his choices. He very well knows the hazards of using plastic containers, he knows that it is not safe to drink water from a Bisleri bottle more than once, he knows what happens when plastic is burned similarly, he also knows that our Nature is in danger with the way these plastic bottles are disposed. The levels of awareness are increasing and so are his concerns.

He is concerned when the leather industries dispose their wastes in water bodies, he is worried when he sees his children's eyes burn due to air pollution, he is sensitive when he sees piled up garbage. All his worries and concerns have only one answer and that one answer is to REDUCE WASTES, RECYCLE PRODUCTS AND REUSE AS MUCH AS POSSIBLE.

This chapter focusses on how and to what extent have the Indian consumers included the recycled products in their shopping baskets. There are various avenues and occasions where he shows interests and prefers Recycled Products.

"In a survey conducted for **Packaging Digest's 2015 Sustainable Packaging Study**, *57% of participants cite a product's recyclability to be top of mind when it comes to the environment and sustainability, a product featuring recycled content and reduced packaging coming up for second and third place. The majority of consumers see recyclability as the most important factor in choosing sustainable products, and it is consumers that ultimately drive company behavior."*

CONSUMER BEHAVIOUR TOWARDS RECYCLED PRODUCTS IN INDIA

According to a report published in The Hindu on August 28, 2018There is much value in waste. The environmental and social gains, are truly remarkable.

, *"one tonne of recycled paper saves approximately 17 trees, 2.5 barrels of oil, 4100 kWh of electricity, 4 cum of landfill and 31,780 litres of water over production of virgin paper from wood.*

Recycling of one tonne of steel scrap saves 1.2 tonnes of iron ore, 0.7 tonnes of coal, 0.5 tonnes of lime-stone, 287 litres of fuel oil, 2.3 cubic meters of landfill, and is achieved through 40 per cent less water and with 58 per cent avoided CO2 emissions.

According to a study by the University of Oklahoma, recycled steel reduces 97 per cent mining waste produced through manufacture of virgin resources, saves 75 per cent of energy, cuts back 86 per cent of air pollution and 76 per cent on water pollution. Similarly, recycling of an aluminium can or producing a glass container saves 95 per cent and 70 per cent, respectively, of the energy required for producing a similar container from virgin material."

The data above is just a fraction of what possibilities are there for us to effectively practice and propagate good waste management practices. With huge amount of trash being generated in our country, it becomes important that we as Businessman and consumers do our bit to recycle the wastes. Our daily lives give us a number of moments where we can take small steps and change our pattern from waste generation to waste management. Some such noticeable instances which have gained huge acceptance are:

1. A lot of residential societies in India have installed water recycle plant, where waste water generated from the bathrooms and kitchen is recycles and then made reusable again. Such recycled water can be used in gardens, washing cars and flushing. Residential societies in metro cities have installed compost making machines where they can treat their kitchen waste daily.
2. India is a country of temples, where people offer almost anything and everything to the deities. There have been profitable ventures where used flowers, incense sticks are recycled and converted in soaps and perfumes. Such products have found easy acceptance with our consumers.
3. Big names like Unilever and Loreal Cosmetics have made their packaging 100% bio-degradable for certain products.

4. Bio-degradable cutlery is another product category which has met ready acceptance from the consumers. Though plastic cutlery was far more affordable and durable but after the compulsory ban on plastic in certain states in India, the consumers have switched to eco-friendly cutlery. Companies like Samanvi and Pappco Greenware are using corn starch and rice husk to manufacture these cutlery items.
5. Another favourable trend seen in the apparel industry is so called "Sustainable Trend" Big designer houses are paying their attention to the discarded pieces and recycling them into wearables. There is no denial to the fact that these recycled clothes are more expensive than the regular ones, but willingness to buy these clothes is clearly visible in the upper-class market. Rejected fabrics, sample strips, stray buttons and worn out clothes are all being used.
6. Sanitary pads are one of the biggest concerns because of their disposal issues. A majority of women in India do not have access while in some cases the pads are affordable. Many NGO's have worked out a way to manufacture bio-degradable pads which are definitely safer than the regular pads. These NGO's perform the dual responsibility to distribute as well as maintain ecological balance.
7. By far the biggest and most observable change which can be seen is the minimised usage of plastic bags. Indians used a lot of plastic especially for buying vegetables and their daily groceries. In certain cases, they used to use multiple plastic bags in single purchase. Slowly and gradually the plastic bags became universal. The were used for almost everything from carrying vegetables, packed food, clothes and the list goes on.

The compulsory ban has brought jute and cotton bags in the homes of Indians which are quite affordable and washable too. Shoppers can be seeing carrying with them a reusable bag with them every time they go to the market.

Above are few of the many cases of recycled products to which Indian consumers are gradually shifting. They use bamboo toothbrushes, recycle Coke and Fanta bottles, use vegetable left overs as manure for their kitchen gardens, indulge in some DIY activities with the waste products of their homes .

Figure 2.
Source: betterindia.com

In a nutshell it can be said that there are many examples which clearly prove that the even if the shift towards recycled products is slow, the change is visible and moreover promising for a brighter future.

Figure 3.
Source: ndtv.com

There are of course some challenges which lie in the path such as lack of awareness, high prices as there is no mass production, low rate of availability of recycled products and above all the mind set which takes time to change and adopt a new product altogether, actually a product made from wastes.

STEPS THAT CAN BE TAKEN TO IMPROVE THE SITUATION.

Spreading Awareness is the first and foremost requirement to speed up the process of recycling thereby speed of waste management.

(Bukhari, 2011) concludes that Companies need to make more effort and increase their communications with the consumers in order to increase the awareness on going green. The paper also emphasises that price and quality are certainly more important parameters for Indian Consumers

There are basically different phases of waste management starting with waste collection and segregation. Further the process is extended to waste treatment and finally the disposal. It is important that consumers are well aware of their responsibilities at every phase.

Segregation of waste leads to correct treatment and modification. Consumers can easily differentiate between toxic and non-toxic and what is bio-degradable and what is not. Recycling can only happen when the materials are segregated as per the parameters decided.

(Rathi, 2006) outlines the role of Community participation and Public private partnership for waste management in a metro city like Mumbai.

There are so many goods available in the market which are a result of recycling, the matter of concern is that most of the consumers do not even know what they are buying, they are not aware of the process used, they are not aware of the effects their purchase or disposal will have on the ecological balance. In simple words they lack the answer to the question as to why they should use eco friendly products? They neither have incentives nor the desire to purchase.

Hence it is required that the corporates should take the following steps to bring about a positive change towards the recycled items:

1. Use Social media platforms to create awareness about eco-friendly products. The advertisements, packaging, processing everything should be eco-friendly. Consumers should be made aware of their contribution when they buy recycled products. The Social media platform will serve by far the most economical and relevant given the fact that today an average Indian does possess a smartphone and has a Facebook or Instagram Account. These social media platforms can serve as information dissemination centre and at the same can work as an interface for buying and selling recycled products.
2. The Business houses should make the promotion of eco-friendly products as a part of their Corporate Social Responsibility Program and adopt a dedicated philosophy towards such campaigns. Biggies like Amazon, Unilever, Proctor and gamble have taken various initiatives in this direction.

Figure 4.
Source: economictimes.indiatimes.com

3. The Government and Financial Institutions should draft a comprehensive policy for the ventures to encourage them so that more and more recycled varieties of products are available in the mar-

ket. There are many instances where small scale NGO and Self-Help Groups have come up with wonderful recycled products. There are a few start-ups in India who have developed their business model around waste management. To name a few Skrap, Sahas Zero Waste, Anthill creations and many more.

4. The educational institutions in our country can play a vital role in the whole process of encouraging Green purchasing. Schools, Colleges, Universities and other professional training Institutes can inculcate a habit of recycling. Formal education needs to be imparted to the future generation so that we can minimise the wastage. Children from a younger age can learn the importance of recycling. Activities and projects which can help children learn and make the recycled projects should be a part of the curriculum.
5. The Consumers too have to shoulder the responsibility. Apart from abiding the rules and regulations imposed by the Government, they should be vigilant and purchase recycled products as much as possible. It has to remembered that even a small purchase of a paper bag, or a recycled pencil can go a long way in restoring the balance in our eco-system.

The Liner economy model will not help our country to survive the environmental threats. We cannot keep on using the resources to make and construct and waste thereafter. This has to be modified and converted into circular economy where there is no concept of waste altogether. Following the philosophy of Circular Economy can bring about a revolution with many added advantages such as waste reduction, stimulation of innovation, increase in jobs and above all it reduces the pressure on the environment., Everything generated within the economic system is put back after modification is how Circular economy works.

CONCLUSION

It is noteworthy to mention here that all the initiatives of the Corporate corridors ultimately boil down to how the consumers perceive these ideologies and how and when do they switch their buying pattern. Given the fact that Indian consumers are both price and quality conscious the task is not easy. More than price and quality the need of the hour is to bring about a change in the mindset of the consumer. It is said that Change is the only constant in Life and it is also true that change is always met with resistance is human tendency to resist change be it workplace or society in which he lives. Actually the change can be brought by following a three step ladder of KNOW, LIKE and TRUST.

The Corporates needs to know what the consumer wants, and how he wants . What makes him happy and what drives him to purchase. Adequate analysis of Consumer Behaviour can definitely reveal some peculiar traits. The next step is to build like factor. He should like the recycled products because then only he will purchase. Preference comes after likeability. The last step in the ladder is building Trust factor which is by far the most difficult and complex to achieve. He may be convinced with the concept of recycling, he may venture out also in search of recycled product but that does not guarantee Trust.

Trust comes only with positive experience which happens after consumption of the goods or services.

Though there is no second opinion that consumers of today have become sensitive to the various ethical and environmental concerns and many of them have shown interests in purchasing organic and environment friendly products. According to economictimes.com around 60% of India's plastic is recycled.

This figure looks promising and positive. It also indicates that we are quite sensitive to this whole issue of waste generation and its management.

It is true that in some of the cases the green buying behaviour is severely impacted by the high prices. Also, that their awareness level about the green products is a major factor which contributes in the decision of green buying. But nevertheless, the situation is not all that bad and steps are being taken by all the stakeholders so as to restore ecological balance of our nature.

REFERENCES

Biswas, A., & Roy, M. (2015). Green products: An exploratory study on the consumer behaviour in emerging economies of the East. *Journal of Cleaner Production*, *87*, 463–468. doi:10.1016/j.jclepro.2014.09.075

Bukhari, S. S. (2011). Green Marketing and its impact on consumer behavior. *European Journal of Business and Management*, 375–383.

Dixit, S. &. (2013). Sustaining environment and organisation through e-waste management: a study of post consumption behaviour for mobile industry in India. *International Journal of Logistics Systems and Management*, 1-15.

Maheshwari, S. P. (2014). *Awareness of green marketing and its influence on buying behavior of consumers: Special reference to Madhya Pradesh. AIMA Journal of Management & Research.*

Narula, S. A., & Desore, A. (2016). Framing green consumer behaviour research: Opportunities and challenges. *Social Responsibility Journal*, *12*(1), 1–22. doi:10.1108/SRJ-08-2014-0112

Prakash, G., & Pathak, P. (2017). Intention to buy eco-friendly packaged products among young consumers of India: A study on developing nation. *Journal of Cleaner Production*, *141*, 385–393. doi:10.1016/j.jclepro.2016.09.116

Rathi, S. (2006). Alternative approaches for better municipal solid waste management in Mumbai. *Waste Management*, 1192-1200. https://www.epw.in/engage/article/institutional-framework-implementing-solid-waste-management-india-macro-analysis

Chapter 13
An Investigation of the Relationship Between Employee Perception of Corporate Citizenship Behaviour and Organisational Sustainability

Anshu Yadav
Amity University, Noida, India

ABSTRACT

Corporate greening practices such as measures to reduce pollution emission, management of waste, use of green technologies, sustainable reporting, consuming removable energy sources, implementation of ISO environment management certification, auditing, etc. are required for sustainability. A lot of studies of stakeholder perceptions of corporate responses towards societal concerns are mostly from the point of view of marketing, existing or prospective customers, and industry at a large, but the employee's aspects is most neglected. This chapter investigates the employee's perception of corporate citizenship (CC) and organisational sustainability and also the interrelationship of these variables.

INTRODUCTION

Corporate Citizenship

Business is like a citizen having rights and obligations towards nation, is predominantly a concept from the field of political science (Drucker, 1964) however provides bases for understanding organisation's behaviour towards (Habisch et al. 2001; Logsdon and Wood 2005) its larger stakeholders as society, country and world ecological environment. Based on the argument under law of company being an "Artificial Person" entails several right to it and so corporate must be having obligation under the territory in which they operate. The term to describe this role and responsibility of business for making differ-

DOI: 10.4018/978-1-7998-4990-2.ch013

ence at the level of individual, society and country is Corporate Citizenship often used interchangeably with corporate social responsibility. Marsden and Andriof, (1998) defined it as managing company's influence on society for gain of both company and society altogether. The term corporate citizenship originated in U.S at the end of nineteenth century (Altman and Cohen, 2000), and later became common in business community discussions and research. This rapidly developing and widespread (Maignan and Ferrell 1999) managerial practice of responsible business (Okoye 2009, Baumgarten and Yucetepe 2009, Wood 1991) is type of self-regulation assimilated in the business model (Grit 2004, Kell 2005, Lam 2009, Maxfield 2008) for "profit maximization" (Bagnoli and Watts, 2003) in terms of benefit to stakeholders such as employee, customer, investor, government and society. Still integrating agenda of citizenship as part of the organisational policy and behaviour is mainly due to legal and political pressure, customer's expectations, credibility, corporate image building and moreover company's tradition and values. It is about balancing of business objectives between preserving profitability for stakeholders and investment in societal welfare. Corporate Citizenship concept is evolving across varied initiatives at different levels, at employees' level its ensuring health and safety, sponsoring training and education programs, profit sharing plans, employee's family welfares initiatives (Maignan and Ferrell, 2000). At the impact level of larger stakeholder these initiatives are sponsoring community initiatives, funding government developmental projects and environment friendly policies (Waddock, 2004).

Most research about CC has adopted an organizational level of analysis and/or focused on external stakeholders (Maignan and Ferrell, 2001a). Few studies have investigated how organizational members (i.e., the ''firm's internal audience'' and one of the most important stakeholders; Maignan and Ferrell, 2001a, p. 471) develop attitudes and behaviors according to the ways they perceive CC of their firms. Most research about CC has adopted an organizational level of analysis and/or focused on external stakeholders (Maignan and Ferrell, 2001a). Few studies have investigated how organizational members (i.e., the ''firm's internal audience'' and one of the most important stakeholders; Maignan and Ferrell, 2001a, p. 471) develop attitudes and behaviors according to the ways they perceive CC of their firms.

Employee's Perception and Corporate Citizenship

Numerous amounts of literature have studied the corporate citizenship at organisational level or concentrated on external stakeholders (Maignan and Ferrell, 2004). Employee are though the most important stakeholders still few studies have focused on their perception and attitudes visa a viz their perceived corporate citizenship. Literature has established that employees want to work with an organisation which is involved and valued for their corporate citizenship initiatives (Turban and Greening, 1997). Employees feels great satisfaction when they do actions that are "discretionary, not directly recognized by the formal reward system" Organ, (1988) i.e. organisational citizenship behaviour, and similarly they appreciate corporate citizenship form the company they work for. This, employees discretionary behaviour that contributes for environmental greening is termed as 'organizational citizenship behaviors for the environment' (OCBE) (Ramus and Killmer, 2007; Daily et al., 2009; Boiral, 2009; Lamm et al., 2013). Studies suggests that corporate citizenship even has a significant influence on employees organisational citizenship behaviour (Linley 2009). In a research Maignan, Ferrell and Hult (1999) studied effect of corporate citizenship and reported that it has positive association with employee's commitment. One of the surveys have found that more than fifty percent of students in America for self-fulfillment wish to be working for socially responsible organisation (Barrett, 2000). Reverchon (2000) found in his study that environment protection is very important criteria for choosing the future employer. In addition employees perception of corporate citizenship is studied in relationship of job satisfaction, job efficacy (Chen 2000, Lin 2010), work deviance (Evans, Goodman and Davis 2010) and commitment (Hofman and Newman 2014) as well but not on employees perception of organisational sustainability.

Organisational Sustainability

Sustainability simply means is that environmental concerns for future generations and can't be separated from the economic benefits for stakeholders (Bowers 2010). The most popular definition of sustainable development as per Brundtland Report (1987) was for "Our Common Future". This approach of business gain is not just for today but has potentials for benefiting business, society and environment at a large for years to come. Environmental concern consists of initiatives such as prevention of pollution, use of green technology, environmental management systems, sustainability reporting, auditing and ISO certifications etc. Environmental sustainability initiatives are complex and diverse and thus their integration with formal management systems is difficult (Lane and Robinson, 2009; Lülfs and Hahn, 2013; Ramus and Killmer, 2007). Businesses bring out citizenship practices for several motive such as linking to corporate culture, response to stakeholders' expectations and profit motives (Kilian and Hennigs 2014). However, having sustainable environment and minimizing disasters are certainly very important motives (Özçelik et al. 2015). Even after the efforts of corporates challenges are still there be it water depletion, deforestation, climate change, loss of biodiversity, threat of bio weapons, income inequality and corruption. Sustainable business practices create economic and societal value by re-aligning their corporate objectives with stakeholder management and environmental responsibility.

The intermittent linkage between the corporate responsibility (if discretionary the citizenship) and corporate sustainability is discussed a lot is academic researches but employees perception for the same is the hypothesized gap that exists. Improving company's internal processes for corporate citizenship initiatives where employee is the instrumental, to its external lasting impact on community, scarce resources and environment is studies theoretically. The present study aims to measure employee's perception of corporate citizenship behaviour and its effect on perceived sustainability.

Facets of Corporate Citizenship

There are several facets of corporate citizenship, first introduced by Carroll (1997, 1991) economic, legal, ethical and a philanthropic face. The bottom line of the business is always to make profit but must be able to sacrifice some for fulfilling economic responsibility towards employees and community. From legal point of view fulfilling legal responsibility of obeying the law. Obeying law is essential but not sufficient so they have to take ethical responsibility. Lastly philanthropy or "give back," is not accountability but normally expected from corporates today. Generally, altruism is the prime motivating factor for this discretionary behaviour, they engage in philanthropy to establish their citizenship. In another study Lin, C (2008) suggested that four dimensions of perceived corporate citizenship, comprising economic, discretionary legal and ethical citizenship which directly influence their engagement with the organisation. Some of the studies have studied the interrelationship of these dimensions as well (Luis and Cristian 2020). In the present research, for the purpose of constructing the questionnaire four dimensions Economical, Legal, Ethical and Discretionary are taken into account to measure employee's perception of corporate citizenship.

Research Methodology

The present study adopts descriptive research designs where in the relationship between Corporate Citizenship (Economical, Legal, Ethical and Discretionary citizenship aspect) and employees perception of organisational sustainability is studied through self-constructed questionnaire consisting total 32 questions on seven-point-Likert scale divided in two parts first part consisting questions on corporate citizenship and second part having questions for perceived organisational sustainability. The questionnaire used for the study is quite reliable as Cronbach-alpha value was calculated 0.86.

A seven-point-differential scale is used to measure the responses. Where score for independent variable employee's perception of corporate citizenship and dependent variable Organisational Sustainability are as below in **table 1**:

Corporate Citizenship	Score Indication	Organisational Sustainability
Score 0-7	extremely low	Score 0-3
Scores 8-14	moderately low	Scores 4-6
Scores 15-21	low	Scores 7-9
Scores 22-28	neutral	Scores 10-12
Scores 29-35	high	Scores 13-15
Scores 36-42	moderately high	Scores 16-18
Score 43-49	extremely high	Score 19-21

Research Findings

For finding out employee's perception corporate citizenship descriptive statistics i.e. mean, median and standard deviation were used. The main predictor of Organisational Sustainability out of the four parameters economical, legal, ethical and discretionary was identified by correlations. Lastly the impact of perceptions on corporate citizenship was calculated using a regression analysis.

Table 2: Descriptive Statistics

Variables	Mean	Median	SD	SE Mean	Minimum	Maximum
Economic	42.412	43	3.179	0.315	34	48
Legal	42.980	43	3.386	0.335	32	49
Ethical	42.588	42	3.745	0.371	28	49
Discretionary	46.627	47	5.254	0.520	31	56

The mean of Economic citizenship is 42.412. This indicates that the employees' perception about the organization's economic citizenship is very good. The employees perceive the organization to be responsible as an economic citizen. The standard deviation of economic citizenship is 3.179. Such a

Figure 1. Economic Citizenship

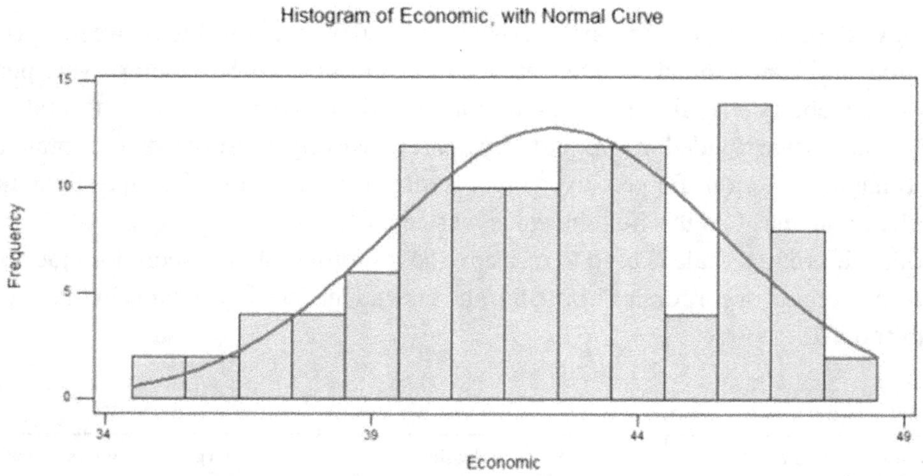

low standard deviation indicates that almost all the employees perceive their organization's economic citizenship similarly. Graph below shows the histogram with normal distribution curve. This indicates that every employee considers that his organization is high on economic citizenship

The mean of Legal citizenship is 42.980. This indicates that the employees' perception about the organization's Legal citizenship is very good. The employees perceive the organization to be responsible as an Legal citizen. The standard deviation of Legal citizenship is 3.386. Such a low standard deviation indicates that almost all the employees perceive their organization's Legal citizenship similarly. Graph below shows the histogram with normal distribution curve. This indicates that every employee considers that his organization is high on Legal citizenship.

Figure 2. Legal Citizenship

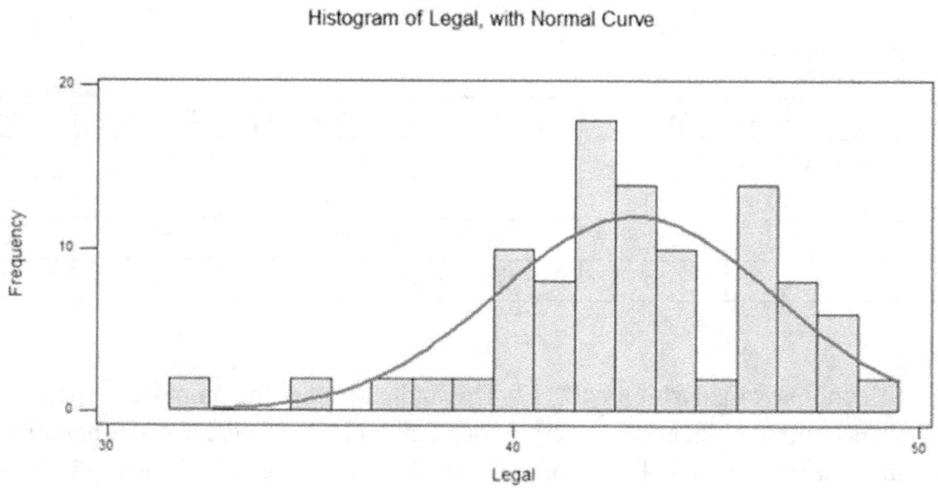

The mean of Ethical citizenship is 42.588. This indicates that the employees' perception about the organization's Ethical citizenship is very good. The employees perceive the organization to be responsible as an Ethical citizen. The standard deviation of Ethical citizenship is 3.745. Such a low standard deviation indicates that almost all the employees perceive their organization's Ethical citizenship similarly. Graph below shows the histogram with normal distribution curve. This indicates that every employee considers that his organization is high on Ethical citizenship.

Figure 3. Ethical Citizenship

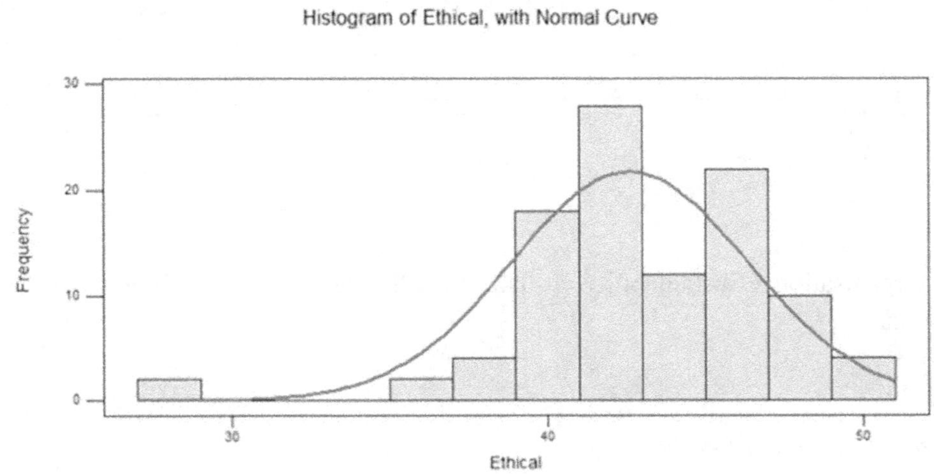

The mean of Discretionary citizenship is 46.627. This indicates that the employees' perception about the organization's Discretionary citizenship is very good. The employees perceive the organization to be responsible as an Discretionary citizen. The standard deviation of Discretionary citizenship is 5.254. Such a low standard deviation indicates that almost all the employees perceive their organization's Discretionary citizenship similarly. The highest and the lowest values are 31 and 56. Same is shown in the graph below shows the histogram with normal distribution curve. This indicates that the employees have varied opinions that his organization is high on Discretionary citizenship.

The inter correlations between the various parameters of corporate citizenship i.e. ethical, legal, ethical and discretionary citizenship are shown below. Also presented the inter correlation of Organisational Sustainability with these parameters.

The above correlation matrix shows us the. Ethical citizenship and discretionary citizenship have a correlation P=0.600 which indicates the correlation as high. These values indicate that the organization's ethical aspects of citizenship have an effect on the discretionary aspects of citizenship. The correlations of the different components of Corporate citizenship on Affective commitment indicate that Economic citizenship and Legal citizenship do not have much effect on corporate citizenship whereas Ethical and Discretionary citizenship have a good effect on Organisational Sustainability shown by P value as .628 and .841 respectively. To study how perceptions of corporate citizenship predict Organisational Sustainability regression analysis has been performed. as shown in the table below.

The Regression equation is:

Figure 4. Discretionary Citizenship

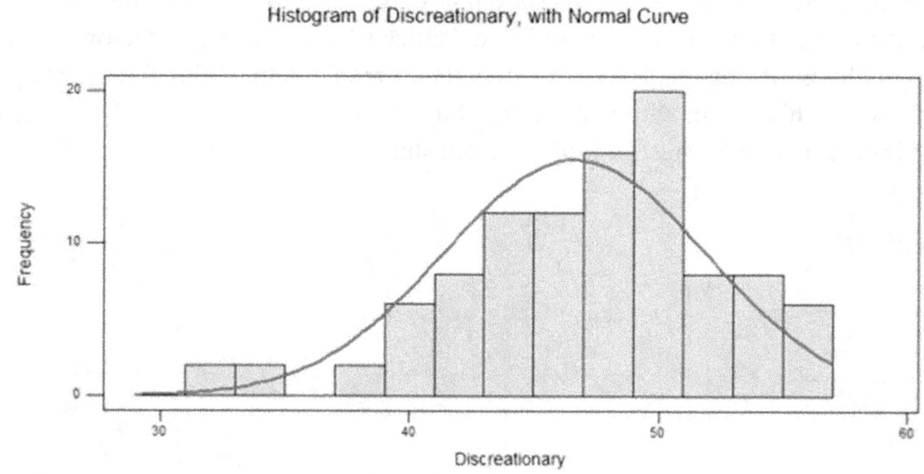

Perceived Organisational Sustainability = -0.40 -0.122Economic + 0.0085Legal + 0.151Ethical+ 0.587Discretionary

Table 3. Pearson correlation, P-Value

	Economic	Legal	Ethical	Discretionary	Perceived Sustainability
Economic	0.512				
Legal	0.410	0.568			
	0.000	0.000			
Ethical	0.377	0.391	0.409		
	0.000	0.000	0.000		
Discretionary	0.250	0.462	0.666	0.600	
	0.011	0.000	0.000	0.000	
Perceived Sustainability	0.333	0.483	0.628	0.841	0.937
	0.001	0.000	0.000	0.000	0.000

Predictor	Coef	SE Coef	T	P
Constant	-0.405	1.787	-0.23	0.821
Economic	-0.12229	0.04289	-2.85	0.005
Legal	0.00851	0.04524	0.19	0.851
Ethical	0.15137	0.04332	3.49	0.001
Discretionary	0.58735	0.0288	20.4	0.000

S = 1.159 R-Sq = 89.8% R-Sq(adj) = 89.3%

Table 5. Analysis of Variance

Source	DF	SS	MS	F	P
Regression	4	1141.97	285.49	212.46	0
Residual Error	97	130.34	1.34		
Total	101	1272.31			

The study finds that discretionary citizenship is the biggest predictor of Organisational Sustainability followed by ethical citizenship, whereas economic citizenship has a negative effect on perceived organisational sustainability. There is no impact of legal citizenship on Organisational Sustainability. R-Sq value indicates that 89.8 percentage of the variance in Organisational Sustainability is explained by Corporate Citizenship. The R-Sq value clearly shows that the Corporate Citizenship has a significant impact on Organisational Sustainability

Source	DF	Seq SS
Economic	1	79.28
Legal	1	193
Ethical	1	310.7
Discreat	1	558.99

Conclusion and Implication

The perception of employees about the organization's Corporate Citizenship is positive. The employees perceive organization are fulfilling the role of a corporate citizen very effectively. As per the findings of the study majority of employees feel that the organization has high Corporate Citizenship on all the parameters of the study. The highest positive perception is on discretionary parameters. The inter correlations between the components of Corporate citizenship are high and the correlations of the parameters in Corporate Citizenship have good correlations with Organisational Sustainability. Therefore, Corporate Citizenship is definitely predictor of Organisational Sustainability. In order to build up organisational sustainability the organisation must put effort towards corporate citizenship activities. Corporate Citizenship has a very good impact on Organisational Sustainability. The Discretionary Citizenship is the major predictor for Organisational Sustainability

REFERENCES

Altman, B. W., & Vidaver-Cohen, D. (2000). A framework for under-standing corporate citizenship: Introduction to the special edition of Business and Society Review 'corporate citizenship for the new millennium'. Business and Society Review, 105(1), 1–7.

Antoine, R. (2000, Nov. 14). Entrepreneuriat, qualité de la vie, citoyenneté: trois tartes à la crème du recrutement. *Le Monde*.

Bagnoli, M., & Watts, S. (2003). Selling to socially responsible consumers: Competition and the private provision of public goods. *Journal of Economics & Management Strategy*, *12*(3), 419–445. doi:10.1162/105864003322309536

Boiral, O. (2009). *Greening the corporation through organizational citizenship behaviors*. Journal. doi:10.100710551-008-9881-2

Bowers, T. (2010). From image to economic value: A genre analysis of sustainability reporting. *Corporate Communications*, *15*(3), 249–262. doi:10.1108/13563281011068113

Brundtland, G. H. (1987). *Our common future: report of the 1987 world commission on environment and development*. United Nations.

Camacho & Salazar-Concha. (2020). Article. *Journal of Economics Studies and Research*. Doi:10.5171/2020.472317

Carroll, A. B. (1979). A three-dimensional conceptual model of corporate social performance. *Academy of Management Review*, *4*(4), 497–505. doi:10.5465/amr.1979.4498296

Carroll, A. B. (1991). The pyramid of corporate social responsibility: Toward the moral management of organizational stakeholders. *Business Horizons*, *34*(4), 39–48. doi:10.1016/0007-6813(91)90005-G

Chen, M.-L., & Lin, C.-P. (2014). Modelling perceived corporate citizenship and psychological contracts: A mediating mechanism of perceived job efficacy. *European Journal of Work and Organizational Psychology*, *23*(2), 231–247. doi:10.1080/1359432X.2012.734455

Chen, Z. X., & Francesco, A. M. (2000). Employee Demography, Organizational Commitment, and Turnover Intentions in China: Do Cultural Differences Matter? *Human Relations*, *53*(6), 869–887. doi:10.1177/0018726700536005

Daily, B. F., Bishop, J. W., & Govindarajulu, N. (2009, June). citizenship behavior directed toward the environment. *Business & Society*, *48*(2), 243–256. doi:10.1177/0007650308315439

Daily, B. F., Bishop, J. W., & Govindarajulu, N. (2009). *A conceptual model for organizational*. Academic Press.

Drucker, P. F. (1964). The Concept of the Corporation. The New American Library.

Evans, W. R., Goodman, J. M., & Davis, W. D. (2010). The impact of perceived corporate citizenship on organizational cynicism, OCB, and employee deviance. *Human Performance*, *24*(1), 79–97. doi:10.1080/08959285.2010.530632

Grit, K. (2004). Corporate citizenship: How to strengthen the social responsibility of managers? *Journal of Business Ethics*, *53*(1/2), 97–106. doi:10.1023/B:BUSI.0000039402.72867.1a

Habisch, A., Meister, H.-P., & Schmidpeter, R. (Eds.). (2001). *Corporate citizenship as investing in social capital*. Logos.

Hofman, P., & Newman, A. (2014). *The impact of perceived corporate social responsibility*. Academic Press.

Hofman, P. S., & Newman, A. (2014, March 09). on organizational commitment and the moderating role of collectivism and masculinity: Evidence from China. *International Journal of Human Resource Management*, *25*(5), 631–652. doi:10.1080/09585192.2013.792861

Kell, G. (2005). The global compact selected experiences and reflections. *Journal of Business Ethics*, *59*(1/2), 69–79. doi:10.100710551-005-3413-0

Kilian, T., & Hennigs, N. (2014). Corporate social responsibility and environmental reporting in controversial industries. *European Business Review*, *26*(1), 79–101. doi:10.1108/EBR-04-2013-0080

Lam, M. L. L. (2009). Beyond credibility of doing business in China: Strategies for improving corporate citizenship of foreign multinational enterprises in China. *Journal of Business Ethics*, *87*(1), 137–146. doi:10.100710551-008-9803-3

Lamm, E., Tosti-Kharas, J., & Williams, E. G. (2013). Read this article, but don't print it: Organizational citizenship behavior toward the environment. *Group & Organization Management*, *38*(2), 163–197. doi:10.1177/1059601112475210

Lane, M. B., & Robinson, C. J. (2009). Institutional complexity and environmental management: The challenge of integration and the promise of large-scale collaboration. *Australasian Journal of Environmental Management*, *16*(1), 16–24. doi:10.1080/14486563.2009.9725213

Lin, C. (2010). Modeling Corporate Citizenship, Organizational Trust, and Work Engagement Based on Attachment Theory. *Journal of Business Ethics*, *94*(4), 517–531. doi:10.100710551-009-0279-6

Lin, C., Lyau, N., Tsai, Y., Chen, W.-Y., & Chiu, C.-K. (2010). Modeling Corporate Citizenship and Its Relationship with Organizational Citizenship Behaviors. *Journal of Business Ethics*, *95*(3), 357–372. doi:10.100710551-010-0364-x

Lin, L. W. (2010). Corporate Social Responsibility in China: Window Dressing or Structural Change. *Berkeley Journal of International Law*, *28*(1), 64–100.

Linley, P. A., Maltby, J., Wood, A. M., Osborne, G., & Hurling, R. (2009). Measuring happiness: The higher order factor structure of subjective and psychological well-being measures. *Personality and Individual Differences*, *47*(8), 878–884. doi:10.1016/j.paid.2009.07.010

Logsdon, J. M., & Wood, D. J. (2005). Global business citizenship and voluntary codes of ethical conduct. *Journal of Business Ethics*, *59*(1-2), 55–67. doi:10.100710551-005-3411-2

Lülfs, R., & Hahn, R. (2013). Corporate greening beyond formal programs, initiatives, and systems: A conceptual model for voluntary pro-environmental behavior of employees. *European Management Review, 10*(2), 83–98. doi:10.1111/emre.12008

Maignan, I., & Ferrell, O. C. (2000). Measuring corporate citizenship in two countries: The case of the United States and France. *Journal of Business Ethics, 23*(3), 283–297. doi:10.1023/A:1006262325211

Maignan, I., & Ferrell, O. C. (2004). Corporate social responsibility and marketing: An integrative framework. *Journal of the Academy of Marketing Science, 32*(1), 3–19. doi:10.1177/0092070303258971

Maignan, I., Ferrell, O. C., & Hult, G. T. M. (1999). Corporate citizenship: Cultural antecedents and business benefits. *Journal of the Academy of Marketing Science, 27*(4), 455–469. doi:10.1177/0092070399274005

Marsden, C., & Andriof, J. (1998). Towards an Understanding of Corporate Citizenship and How to Influence It. *Citizenship Studies, 2*(2), 329–352. doi:10.1080/13621029808420686

Maxfield, S. (2008). Reconciling corporate citizenship and competitive strategy: Insights from economic theory. *Journal of Business Ethics, 80*(2), 367–377. doi:10.100710551-007-9425-1

Okoye, A. (2009). Theorising corporate social responsibility as an essentially contested concept: Is a definition necessary? *Journal of Business Ethics, 89*(4), 613–628. doi:10.100710551-008-0021-9

Organ, D. W. (1988). *Organizational Citizenship Behavior: The Good Soldier Syndrome*. Lexington Books.

Özçelik, F., Öztürk, B. A., & Gürsakal, S. (2015). Corporate Sustainability: A Research on Firms That Issue Sustainability Reports in Turkey. *Business and Economic Research Journal, 6*(3), 33–49.

Ramus, C. A., & Killmer, A. B. (2007). Corporate greening through prosocial extrarole behaviours—A conceptual framework for employee motivation. *Business Strategy and the Environment, 16*(8), 554–570. doi:10.1002/bse.504

Richard, B. (2000). Building a Vision-Guided, Values-Driven Organization. *Triple Bottom Line Conference*, Rotterdam, The Netherlands.

Torres-Baumgarten, G., & Yucetepe, V. (2009). Multinational firms' leadership role in corporate social responsibility in Latin America. *Journal of Business Ethics, 85*(1), 217–224. doi:10.100710551-008-9940-8

Turban, D. B., & Greening, D. W. (1997). Corporate social performance and organizational attractiveness to prospective employees. *Academy of Management Journal, 40*(3), 658–672.

Waddock, S. A. (2004). Parallel universes: Companies, academics, and the progress of corporate citizenship. *Business and Society Review, 109*(1), 303–319. doi:10.1111/j.0045-3609.2004.00002.x

Wood, D. J. (1991). Corporate social performance revisited. *Academy of Management Review, 16*(4), 691–718. doi:10.5465/amr.1991.4279616

Chapter 14
E-Waste Management in India: Need for a Circular Approach

Shinu Vig
https://orcid.org/0000-0002-0063-0470
Institute of Management Studies, Ghaziabad, India

Richa Narayan Agarwal
Institute of Management Studies, Ghaziabad, India

ABSTRACT

E-waste is a rising problem given the volumes of e-waste being generated and the content of both toxic and valuable materials in them. This new kind of waste has raised serious concerns regarding their disposition and recycling all over the world. Having hazardous components in television and computer monitors (lead, mercury, and cadmium) and in circuit boards (nickel, beryllium, and zinc), the recycling and discarding of e-waste becomes a key concern. Disposal of e-waste poses serious environmental and health hazards. However, these problems can be tackled with the help of a circular approach. In this backdrop, the chapter discusses the problem of e-waste management in India, the related environmental and health issues in e-waste handling and disposal. It also discusses e-waste recycling practices in India and the current policy level interventions by the government. The chapter also highlights the possible business opportunities offered by the circular approach to e-waste management.

INTRODUCTION

There is an increasing impact on the environment due to consumerism and the changing lifestyle. The consumption of electronic and electric equipment that have short life cycles and the rapidly developing technology have led to increased e-waste volumes (Gaidajis, Georgios & Angelakoglou, Komninos & Aktsoglou, Despoina,2010). Electronic waste or e-waste generate both toxic and valuable materials, therefore it generates a problem as well as business opportunities (Widmer, Krapf, Khetriwal, Schnellmann & Böni, 2005). E-waste is made of discarded electronic appliances . Currently global production of e-waste is estimated to be 20-25 million tonnes per year . USA and Europe and Australasia are major

DOI: 10.4018/978-1-7998-4990-2.ch014

producers but it is estimated that China, Eastern Europe and Latin America would become the next major producers of E-waste in the coming times (Robinson, 2009).

E-waste contains toxic materials which is hazardous in many ways and causes many diseases(Adhana,2020). The last decade has seen a rise in the consumption of electronic and electrical equipment and it is rapidly producing e-waste. E- wastes may contain gold, silver and other precious metal on one hand and on the other hand it may contain toxin material

It is evident that regulatory approaches are not enough for the management of e-waste, therefore engagement of all stakeholders such as manufacturers, retailers, labours, investors and customers is needed, to develop innovative solutions that will bring the extensive informal sector of e-waste management under guidelines that protect environmental quality and human health .

E- waste in India

India is third biggest producer of e-waste after China and USA (Mohan, 2020). This is produced by both, from domestic generation and illegal imports. India is also used as a dumping ground. These cheap second hand electronic and electrical material lures small business men and they see a great business opportunity in using them. Developing countries lack proper laws and enforcement of laws, which promotes the growth of unstructured economy. Therefore an entire new informal sector breeds in India wherein trading, repairing and recovering materials from redundant electronic devices are thrived. People in India are unaware of the dangers they are dealing in. Informal sector thrives on second hand electronic products as there is lack of awareness and support from the government. The Associated Chambers of Commerce and Industry of India and KPMG studied e-waste management in India and found that computer equipment account for 70%, telephone equipment phones 12% and electrical equipment 8% and medical equipment account for 7% household waste. Though there are no database for the total amount of e-waste generated in India but Basel action network, WA and Toxins India reported that 1.38 million personal computers will become obsolete 1050 tonnes of electronic scrap is being produced by manufactures and assemblers in single year in India.

There is an absence of any comprehensive evaluation regarding the application of a standard approach and methodology to estimate e-waste in India. United Nations published a report in 2017 which claimed that 44.7 million metric tonnes (MMt)of e-waste was generated in 2016 and 2 (MMt) was generated in India only. It is expected to reach to 5.3(MMt) by the year 2020. (Current Affairs,2020).The process of e-waste is accelerated with the advent of liberalisation . The top states in which contributes to e-waste is Maharashtra, Andhra Pradesh, Tamil-Nadu, Uttar Pradesh, West Bengal, Delhi, Karnataka, Gujarat, Madhya Pradesh and Punjab. India loses highly precious elements in e-waste, which could be used for strategic advantage (Mohan,2020). Major issue in India has been the regulation of e-waste management and its implementation aggressively. India requires both government policies and initiatives by social and environmental innovators (Fiksel, Sanjay, & Raman,2020).

Reasons for the Increasing E-waste

There are several reasons for the increase in the amounts of e-waste generated every year. The last two decades have witnessed a significant increase of the e-waste generated in India, which is an outcome of the socio-economic development and is also a characteristic of any developing economy (Borthakur and Govind, 2018). Some of these reasons are increasing consumerism, rise in the disposable income, obsolescence due to fast changing technology, more incentives for consumption and the short lifespan of electronic products. India is witnessing increasing consumption rates of electronic products in the last few years (Agrawal, Singh and Murtaja, 2014).

Figure 1. Reasons for increasing e-waste

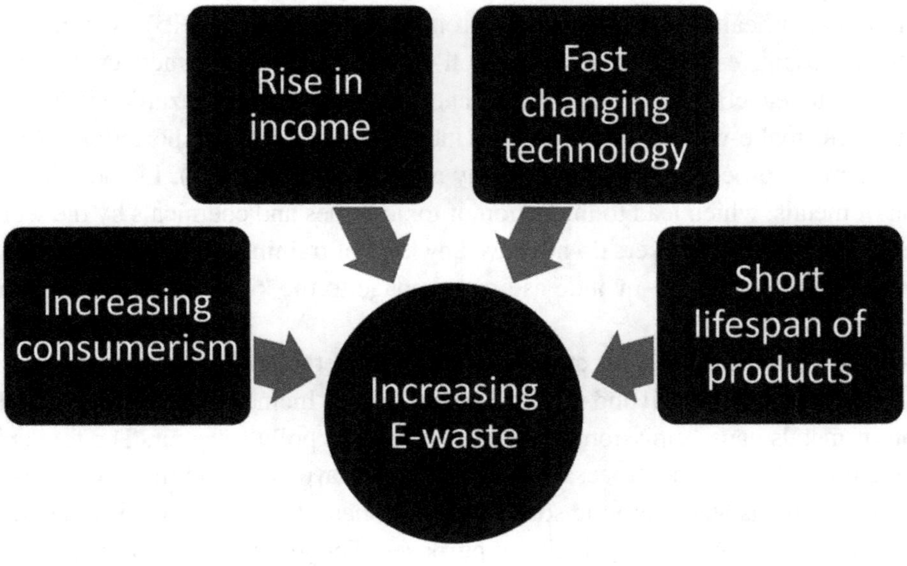

Human behaviour is very important when we talk about environmental problems and it is pertinent that behavioural changes are required if circular economy needs to be implemented to utilize the potential technological innovations which will help environmental sustainability (Steg and Vlek, 2009). It is said that human behaviour is guided by intrinsic and extrinsic attributes (Martin et al., 2017). Knowledge, motivation, beliefs, habits, values, attitudes, intentions and other psychological variables are Intrinsic attributes which guide our behaviour whereas include social and cultural norms, monetary implications, and contextual variables such as infrastructure and institutional constraints make extrinsic attributes (Jackson, 2005; Knussen and Yule, 2008; Young et al., 2009).

It is essential to increase the level of awareness of the consumers to improve their disposal behaviours and to enhance their willingness to improve the current e-waste management system. One of the most frequently disposed type of e-waste is mobile phones. Though the repair and sale of second-hand phones cannot replace the new phones but it may have significant welfare benefits, due to increased connectivity, for the consumers who are unable to afford primary phones (Zink and Geyer, 2017). Borthakur and Govind (2018) in their study reported that some consumers consider the obsolete electric and electronic equipment as 'valuable' and try to find second or third-hand users down the income chain. This behaviour delays the entry of equipment in the growing piles of e-waste and helps in protection of the environment and conservation of precious resources. The policy-makers should create incentives and motivate such behaviour among the consumers to achieve the goal of sustainable cities.

Impact of Recycling E-Waste in the Developing World

All kinds of e-wastes contain components of some recyclable material such as plastic, glass, and heavy metals; however, due to unscientific and primitive disposal methods and techniques these materials cannot be retrieved for other purposes. In India, almost 90 percent of the e-waste is treated in the informal sector in urban slums where it is handled by the workers who are untrained and work in a hazardous manner without any protective equipment. In the process they are exposed to several toxic materials that are detrimental to their health and also to the environment (Annamalai, 2015). According to Julander et al. (2014), though countries like Sweden have well-regulated recycling practices, yet the workers employed in the e-waste recycling in the formal sector are highly exposed to hazardous toxins. The practices followed in the informal e-waste recycling sector include collection, transportation, dismantling of the components, chemical processing etc. (Ragupathy and Chaturvedi, 2013). Incineration of the e-waste for extraction of metals, which lead to inhalation of toxic fumes and chemicals by the workers involved in the processes. Most of the workers do not have any kind of training or experience for such work. The heath hazards of the process may include asthma, damage to the kidney, liver, neurological disorders and cancer.

E-waste recycling in the informal sector by using crude methods can also be harmful to the environment. It may pollute the water, soil and the air in several ways. Incineration of e-waste in the open areas for extraction of metals cause emission of harmful gases that pollute the air. The toxic chemicals that are extracted from e-waste in the process of recycling, but have no economic value are dumped in the landfills. These chemicals leach into the soil and contaminate the underground water sources, thereby making the soil and water unfit for agricultural purposes. The ground water contaminated by leaching of chemicals such as lead, mercury and arsenic, is not fit for human consumption and if consumed, may lead to life threatening diseases. Chakraborty et al. (2019) in their study had reported the increasing concentrations of toxins and heavy metals in the surface soil of some of the metro cities in India, where e-waste was being processed by the informal sector. It also reported that organic pollutants that have a semi-volatile nature are released during into the air during the recycling process.

In India there is an acute shortage of infrastructure for recycling of e-waste, as per the data of Ministry of Environment, Forest and Climate Change. According to the Central Pollution Control Board of India, 304 dismantlers and recyclers having equipment and facilities for environment friendly processing of e-waste, had been granted authorisation by the 18 State Pollution Control Boards/ Pollution Control Committees. The cumulative processing capacity of these authorised units is 7,80,865 tonnes annually.

E-waste Management Policy in India

E-waste management frameworks in India have developed over the years from different rules on the subject of waste. Considering the growing concern of e-waste, the Indian Government supported several initiatives on the assessment of the subject and came up with guidelines around the Environmentally Sound management of e-waste in 2008 wherein e-waste was specifically included in the waste and any person who wanted to process or recycle the same had to register with the Central Pollution Control Board. It was followed by the e-waste management and handling rules, 2011. For the purpose of ensuring that the framework could be made more robust for addressing the challenge of this fast growing waste stream, the rules were revised again in 2016 and Extended Producers Responsibility (EPR) was made a cornerstone of the rules. Extended Producer Responsibility (EPR) is defined as "an environmental protection strategy that makes the manufacturer of the product responsible for the entire life cycle of the product and especially for the take back, recycling and final disposal of the product" (Lindhqvist, 2000). Thus, the producer's responsibility for a product is extended to the post-consumer stage of a product's life cycle (OECD, 2001). There were two original objectives of EPR. First, to reduce the burden of waste management on the local bodies/ municipalities and second, to provide incentives to the producers to decrease the use of resources and to use more secondary materials by introducing changes in their product design to reduce waste (OECD, 2001). Several countries in Europe have implemented EPR based e-waste policies in the past few years (Khetriwal, Kraeuchi and Widmer, 2007).

The Indian Government introduced the E-waste (Management) Amendment Rules, 2018 with an objective to formalize the e-waste recycling sector. The new rules were aimed at channelizing the e-waste generated in the country towards authorised recyclers and dismantlers. The collection targets under the EPR provisions were revised and targets were introduced for the new producers as well. However, there is no evidence or study on the impact of these rules on e-waste management. It has been reported by Bhaskar and Turaga (2018) that despite the implementation of the rules, 85 to 90 percent e-waste is still processed by the informal sector. The major challenges affecting the e-waste value chain in India include lack of data, illegal dumping, insufficient recycling infrastructure and treatment options. Although the government has taken various initiatives in this area yet there are many gaps in the current e-waste management practices like inadequate implementation and administration of the rules, poor awareness among the consumers, non-segregation of waste at household level, reluctance of the corporate sector and dearth of infrastructure for treatment and recycling (Arya and Kumar, 2020).

Circular Approach to E-waste and the SDGs

Lately the businesses and the governments worldwide have become increasingly interested in sustainability issues and have adopted multiple approaches to sustainability. Circular economy practices are also relevant for the 2030 Agenda for Sustainable Development adopted by the United Nations member states in the year 2015 and for the attainment of the Sustainable Development Goals (SDGs). Adoption of a circular approach in e-waste management can contribute particularly towards the achievement of SDG 11 (Sustainable cities and communities) and SDG 12 (Responsible consumption and production). Schroeder et al. (2018) propose that circular economy practices and principles are transversal and adoption of these practices are crucial for achieving several targets outlined under various SDGs. The table below maps the various SDGs with the circular management of e-waste and points out the specific targets that could be achieved.

There are several ways in which the problem of e-waste can be addressed. The potential solutions can be eco-product design, circular resource exchange and management, sharing economy, lifecycle assessment, eco-friendly treatment and development of value-added products (Arya and Kumar, 2020). Instead of subjecting e-waste to crude recycling, it can be introduced back into the assembling enterprises or the same manufacturers under the ambit of EPR. E-waste could be reused for assembly of different products, which will reduce the burden on natural resources. A circular economy approach for management of e-waste can have multiple benefits and opportunities for the developing economies that are demonstrated in the image below:

However, the circular approach of the recycling of e-waste can have several trade-offs with the key targets of the various other SDGs. Such as it may affect the human health of the workers involved in the recycling industry. Thus it may have a trade-off with target 3.9 (Reduction in the number of deaths and

Table 1. Mapping of SDGs with Circular approach of e-waste management

SDG	Target	Target Description
SDG 11- Sustainable Cities and Communities	Target 11.6	By 2030, reduce the adverse per capita environmental impact of cities, including by paying special attention to air quality and municipal and other waste management.
SDG 12- Sustainable Consumption and Production	Target 12.4	By 2020, achieve the environmentally sound management of chemicals and all wastes throughout their life cycle, in accordance with agreed international frameworks, and significantly reduce their release to air, water and soil in order to minimize their adverse impacts on human health and the environment
	Target 12.5	By 2030, substantially reduce waste generation through prevention, reduction, recycling and reuse

illnesses from hazardous chemicals and air, water and soil pollution and contamination) and target 8.8 (promotion of safe and secure working environments for all workers). In order to avoid these trade-offs, the policymakers will be required to devise adequate regulations for protection of the workers. Also there is an urgent need for skills training and capacity building in this area. These needs can be met through effective multi-stakeholder partnerships (SDG 17). Public-private and civil society partnerships can be expedient for mobilizing and sharing knowledge, expertise, technology and financial resources, to support the achievement of the sustainable development goals in developing countries like India (target 17.16) and for building on the experience and resourcing strategies of partnerships (target 17.17).

Figure 2. Benefits of the circular economy approach

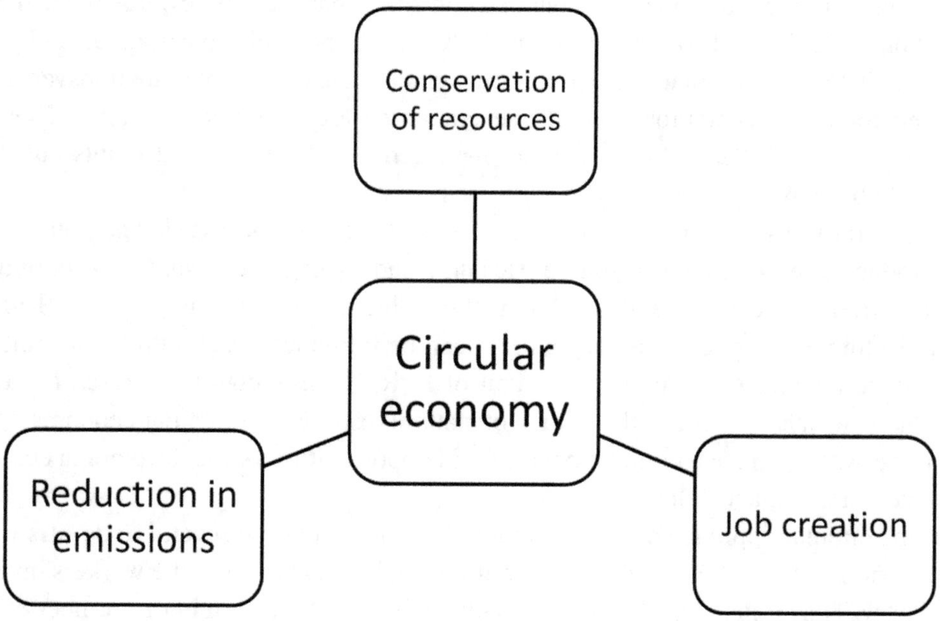

CONCLUSION

The developing economies lack the technical know-how and well-established processes for the e-waste management and face several challenges due to the lack of relevant strategies. But transitioning to a circular economy approach in e-waste management can help them in reducing environmental degradation and preserving the planet, while also delivering on future competitiveness. A holistic circular approach may ensure that the e-waste products are looped back into the production system at the end of use. It will also help in conservation of scarce resources and materials for the future and at the same time presents an enormous business opportunity amounting to around $4.5 trillion by 2030, by creating employment and providing stimulus to business growth (World Economic Forum, 2021). Better utilisation and scientific recycling of e-waste might lead to numerous economic opportunities and savings. Circular economy can help the businesses to remain sustainable by innovating and developing new business models for taking advantage of this unique opportunity (Bhaskar and Kumar, 2019). Efforts should be made to enhance awareness among the various stakeholders-consumers, producers, recyclers and implementation agencies. The governments are required to make additional efforts to forge partnerships in technology, policy and business to explore and devise scalable and sustainable circular solutions that can solve the problem of increasing e-waste.

REFERENCES

Adhana, D. (2020). E-waste management in India: A study of current scenario. International *Journal of Management. Technology And Engineering*, *9*(1), 1–13.

Agrawal, S., Singh, R. K., & Murtaza, Q. (2014). Forecasting product returns for recycling in Indian electronics industry. *Journal of Advances in Management Research*, *11*(1), 102–114. doi:10.1108/JAMR-02-2013-0013

Arya, S., & Kumar, S. (2020). E-waste in India at a glance: Current trends, regulations, challenges and management strategies. *Journal of Cleaner Production*, *271*, 122707. doi:10.1016/j.jclepro.2020.122707

Bhaskar, K., & Kumar, B. (2019). Electronic waste management and sustainable development goals: Is there a business case for linking the two? *Journal of Indian Business Research*, *11*(2), 120–137. doi:10.1108/JIBR-01-2018-0051

Bhaskar, K., & Turaga, R. M. R. (2018). India's e-waste rules and their impact on e-waste management practices: A case study. *Journal of Industrial Ecology*, *22*(4), 930–942. doi:10.1111/jiec.12619

Borthakur, A., & Govind, M. (2019). Computer and mobile phone waste in urban India: An analysis from the perspectives of public perception, consumption and disposal behaviour. *Journal of Environmental Planning and Management*, *62*(4), 717–740. doi:10.1080/09640568.2018.1429254

Circular economy and electronic waste. (2019). Retrieved from: https://www.nature.com/articles/s41928-019-0225-2

Current Affairs Review. (2020). *The scenario of e-waste management in India*. Retrieved from: https://currentaffairsreview.com/the-scenario-of-e-waste-management-in-india/

Fiksel, J., Sanjay, P., & Raman, K. (2020). *Steps toward a resilient circular economy in India.* Clean Technologeis and Environmental Policy. doi:10.100710098-020-01982-0

Gaidajis, G., Angelakoglou, K., & Aktsoglou, D. (2010). E-waste: Environmental Problems and Current Management. *Journal of Engineering Science and Technology Review*, *3*(1), 193–199. Advance online publication. doi:10.25103/jestr.031.32

Garlapati, V. K. (2016). E-waste in India and developed countries: Management, recycling, Business and biotechnological initiatives. *Renewable & Sustainable Energy Reviews*, *54*, 874–881. doi:10.1016/j.rser.2015.10.106

Jackson, T. (2005). *Motivating Sustainable Consumption: A Review of Evidence on Consumer Behaviour and Behavioural Change: a Report to the Sustainable Development Research Network.* Centre for Environmental Strategy, University of Surrey.

Jain, A., & Sareen, R. (2006). E-waste assessment methodology and validation in India. *Journal of Material Cycles and Waste Management*, *8*(1), 40–45. doi:10.100710163-005-0145-2

Khetriwal, D. S., Kraeuchi, P., & Widmer, R. (2009). Producer responsibility for e-waste management: Key issues for consideration–learning from the Swiss experience. *Journal of Environmental Management*, *90*(1), 153–165. doi:10.1016/j.jenvman.2007.08.019 PMID:18162284

Lacy, P., Spindler, W., & Dutton, J. (2021). *The circular economy can help save the planet –if we start innovating now.* World Economic Forum. Retrieved from https://www.weforum.org/agenda/2021/02/the-circulars-accelerator-circular-economy-zero-waste/

Lindhqvist, T. (2000). *Extended Producer Responsibility in Cleaner Production. The International Institute for Industrial Environmental Economics.* Lund University.

Martin, V. Y., Weiler, B., Reis, A., Dimmock, K., & Scherrer, P. (2017). 'Doing the right thing': How social science can help foster pro-environmental behaviour change in marine protected areas. *Marine Policy*, *81*, 236–246. doi:10.1016/j.marpol.2017.04.001

Mohan, V. (2020). India third largest e-waste generator in the world, capacity. *The Times of India.* https://timesofindia.indiatimes.com/india/india-third-largest-e-waste-generator-in-the-world-capacity-limited-to-treat-only-one-fourth-of-its-waste/articleshow/76780611.cms

OECD. (2001). *Extended Producer Responsibility: A Guidance Manual for Governments.* OECD.

Raghupathy, L., & Chaturvedi, A. (2013). Secondary Resources and Recycling in developing Economies. *The Science of the Total Environment*, *461*, 830–834. doi:10.1016/j.scitotenv.2013.05.041 PMID:23768896

Robinson, B. H. (2009). E-waste: An assessment of global production and environmental impacts. *The Science of the Total Environment*, *408*(2), 183–191. doi:10.1016/j.scitotenv.2009.09.044 PMID:19846207

Steg, L., & Vlek, C. (2009). Encouraging pro-environmental behaviour: An integrative review and research agenda. *Journal of Environmental Sciences (China)*, *29*, 309–317.

Wath, S. B., Vaidya, A. N., Dutt, P. S., & Chakrabarti, T. (2010). A roadmap for development of sustainable E-waste management system in India. *The Science of the Total Environment*, *409*(1), 19–32. doi:10.1016/j.scitotenv.2010.09.030 PMID:20951410

Widmera, R., Krapf, O. H., Khetriwal, S. D., Schnellmann, M., & Boni, H. (2005). Global Perspectives on E-Waste. *Environmental Impact Assessment Review*, *25*(5), 436–458. doi:10.1016/j.eiar.2005.04.001

Chapter 15
Water Footprint and Virtual Water Trade of Cash Crops

Sunakshi Budhiraja
TERI School of Advanced Studies, India

Sukanya Das
TERI School of Advanced Studies, India

Badri Narayanan Gopala Krishnan
University of Washington, Seattle, USA

ABSTRACT

Virtual water flows (VWF) among states or countries have been proposed as a viable solution to mitigate water scarcity. The aim of this study is to assess the virtual water content and flows from India, for six cash crops, coffee, cotton, jute, sugarcane, tea, and tobacco, and their derived products over a period 1980-2013. The virtual water trade (VWT) estimates across three time periods show India to be a net exporter of virtual water for all the cash crops, except jute. The quantity of virtual water traded has increased over the decades with the increase in the quantum of crops traded. With free trade policies and the opening up of the economy, export quantities increased during the 1990s and the period thereafter, leading to larger virtual water exports. Sustainable agricultural practices for all crops, and in all countries, can help in reducing the water flow of these crops and help in controlling the water scarcity solution.

INTRODUCTION

Freshwater sustains life on earth, facilitating the functioning of the society, environment and the economy. With increasing population and undisciplined lifestyle, coupled with finite resources, countries across the globe are increasingly facing water shortage and water scarcity. Although India receives ample rainfall, groundwater resources are being depleted at a very fast rate to fulfill domestic and agricultural needs. Being traditionally an agriculture-based country and contributing to more than 60% employment and

DOI: 10.4018/978-1-7998-4990-2.ch015

23% of GDP of the economy, the agricultural sector in India consumes more than 65-70% of freshwater and thus calls for ensuring sustainable use of water in this sector, to ensure food and livelihood security (Katyaini, 2016).

India produces a large number of food crops such as rice, maize, wheat, etc. as well as cash crops such as cotton, coffee, tea, sugarcane, jute, tobacco, etc. (Jain et al., 2007; Kumar & Jain, 2011).

However, such a large volume of production means the consumption of resources in large volumes too. But the supply of water is finite and is not uniformly distributed across regions. Water-rich countries could choose to trade real water with water-scarce countries. But this involves huge transportation costs due to large distances, making direct water transfers impossible. However, water could be traded indirectly, in the form of trade in water-intensive goods, where the water-rich countries could export water-intensive goods to the water-scarce regions and thus reap profits with their 'water wealth'. The water-scarce countries, on the other hand, could import such water-intensive goods instead of producing them, and achieve water security (Hoekstra, 2003).

This trade of 'embodied water' is known as *virtual water trade*. Professor Allan, in the early nineties, researched about the impending water crunch in the Middle-East region and witnessed import of water-intensive agricultural commodities taking place in the semi-arid regions and came up with the concept of 'virtual water', which refers to the water embedded in a product, or the volume of water required to produce a product. It follows the basic economic concept of comparative advantage, where a country with relative abundance in a resource is said to gain from trade in goods in which it has relative abundance. In this case, the water-rich countries are said to have relative abundance in the water resources (Hoekstra, 2003).

Closely associated with the concept of virtual water is the concept of water footprint (WF). The concept, coined by Arjen Hoekstra in 2002, is defined as "the measure of humanity's appropriation of fresh water in volumes of water consumed and/or polluted".

There have been various studies (Singh et al., 2004, Kumar et al., 2005, Kumar and Jain, 2007), that have focused on the VWT of India concerning agricultural commodities and livestock commodities. However, none of them have explicitly focused on the cash crops grown in India. With a growing inclination of farmers towards these cash crops, it becomes imperative to analyze the volume of water consumed in growing these crops and the quantum of virtual water traded through these cash crops. The current study considers six cash crops, namely coffee, cotton, jute, sugarcane, tea and tobacco for observing the trend of VWT during the pre-liberalization and post-liberalization phases of the Indian economy.

Literature Review

The concept of VWT has been of interest not only to economists but also to researchers of various fields such as engineering, ecology, geography, water sciences and the like. It can be looked at from a producer perspective or a user perspective. In the first case, virtual water is described as the volume of water that is used in producing a product, while the user perspective considers virtual water as the volume of water that would have been required had the product been produced at the same place where it has to be consumed (Hoekstra, 2003).

Over the years, various studies have been done to analyze the VWT patterns for different goods and at different scales and scopes. The Middle East and North Africa (MENA) region has been suffering from water insufficiency since the 1970s, making the production of food for domestic consumption difficult. According to Allan (2002), by 2000, 50 million tons of grain were being imported annually, leading to a virtual water import of about 50 billion m^3, playing a major role in averting water conflicts in the region (Kumar & Jain, 2011).

Chapagain and Hoekstra (2004) calculated the WF of different nations. According to the study, Belgium and the Netherlands have a high per capita WF of around 2000 m^3/year/capita. Japan, Mexico, and the USA have an average WF of about 1000 m^3/year/capita and countries such as India, China, and Indonesia fall among the relatively low WF countries, with a per capita WF of about 500m^3/year.

The IHE Delft Institute for Water Education carried out a study to estimate the global VWT for the period 1995-1999. They reported $1040*10^9$ m^3/yr virtual water traded globally. Out of this, 67% relates to international trade of crops, 23% to trade of livestock and livestock products and 10% to trade of industrial products (Hoekstra, 2003).

Chapagain et al (2006a) calculated the Virtual Water Content (VWC) and VWT to the consumption of cotton and cotton derived products, for the period 1997-2001. The global water consumption for cotton products was estimated to be about 256 Gm^3/year, of which blue water accounts for 42%, green water accounts for 39% and 19% is attributed to the grey component. The global average VWC for seed cotton for the 15 largest cotton-producing countries was estimated to be 3644 m^3/ton. The water requirements vary across countries, depending on the climatic conditions. Countries like the USA and Brazil, with low evaporative demand, have favorable climatic conditions and can manage without irrigation, giving high yields. On the other hand, countries like Mali and India have a high evaporative water demand, low effective rainfall, and partially irrigated areas, thus leading to lower yields. Thus, cotton from these regions is water-intensive, whereas cotton from Brazil and the USA is water extensive. The blue VWC is higher in countries like Egypt, Uzbekistan, Pakistan, and India. The global average VWT of cotton products for the period 1997-2001 was about 204 Gm^3/year. There are cross-border effects which can be witnessed. Uzbekistan and India are responsible for about 84% of the WF of cotton in the EU25 region. China, Pakistan, India, and Uzbekistan export the largest amount of blue water. USA is also one of the largest VW exporters, but it exports green water. USA, China, and Pakistan are responsible for exporting the largest volume of greywater, leading to a larger impact on the quality of water in these countries.

Another study assessed the WF, VWC, and VWT of the Dutch consumption of tea and coffee for the period 1995-1999. It suggested that a cup of tea requires about 34 liters and a cup of coffee requires about 140 liters in the Netherlands. The largest WF of these is attributable to the growing stage of the crop. However, the Dutch import their coffee and tea, and hence the study estimates the VWC of tea and coffee for the exporting countries. The global average for VWC of green coffee is estimated to be 17.5 m^3/kg, whereas roasted coffee needs about 20.9 m^3/kg water. The global average VWC of tea leaves is much less at 2.7 m^3/kg, whereas made tea requires about 10.4 m^3/kg volume of water. During 1995-1999, the Netherlands imported 2953 million m^3 virtual water every year in the form of coffee import and 197 million m^3 per year in the form of tea import. Coffee is mostly imported from Brazil, Colombia, Belgium, and Germany. Indonesia, China, Sri Lanka, and India are some of the major sources of tea imports to the Netherlands. Virtual water exports from the Netherlands for coffee and tea are 314 million m^3/ year and 107 million m^3/year respectively. The Netherlands export their coffee to Belgium– Luxemburg, United Kingdom, Germany, and France. Tea is exported to Germany, UK, the USA, Italy, Switzerland, France, the Russian Federation and Belgium-Luxemburg (Chapagain & Hoekstra, 2003a; Chapagain & Hoekstra, 2003b; Chapagain & Hoekstra, 2007). Since the Dutch consume larger amounts of coffee than tea, and because tea has a lower VWC than coffee, the WF of coffee is much larger than the Dutch WF of tea (Chapagain & Hoekstra, 2003a; Chapagain & Hoekstra, 2003b; Chapagain & Hoekstra, 2007).

Leenes & Hoesktra (2009) calculate the green, blue and grey WF of sugar derived from sugar cane in the main producing countries. The total WF of sugar for Brazil is estimated to be 1285 m^3/ton and 1570 m^3/ton for India. The global average WF is 1500 m^3/ton. The VWC of sugarcane varies among countries due to differences in crop water requirements and yields. Countries like India, Egypt, Peru, Pakistan, and Australia have a large blue water footprint since they are mostly dependent on irrigation.

Kampman (2007) analyzed the WF and the international and inter-regional VWT for the Indian states, for the agricultural commodities, for the period 1997-2001. He estimated the average per capita WF of the Indian population to be 777 m^3/year during the period of the study. Out of this average, 227 m^3/capita/year is believed to be the blue WF, 459 m^3/capita/year the green WF and 92 m^3/capita/year is the grey WF. Orissa and Chhattisgarh have the lowest water productivity in producing rice and hence the highest WF. The total interstate VWT of agricultural goods during this period was 106 billion m^3/year, and the net international export amounted to 15 billion m^3/year. Haryana, Punjab, Uttar Pradesh, and Madhya Pradesh were the largest net virtual water exporters and the largest net virtual water importers were Bihar, Kerala, and Jharkhand. According to the author, increasing water productivity is the only long term solution to mitigate water scarcity and remain food self-sufficient.

Kumar & Jain (2011) quantify the VWT at a sub-national level for wheat and rice for the period 2003-04 to 2005-06. They estimated the VWC of wheat and rice for different states using the WF methodology. The VWC of wheat ranged from 745 to 9405 m^3/ton, with the lowest values for high yield states like Punjab and Haryana, and highest values for low yield states like Karnataka and Andhra Pradesh, and that of rice varied from 2502 to 9562 m^3/ton with the lowest value for Punjab and highest for Madhya Pradesh. Punjab, Haryana, Uttarakhand, and Chhattisgarh were net virtual water exporters and states like Maharashtra and Tamil Nadu were net virtual water importers for these two crops.

Methodology and Data Sources

The study involves firstly, the calculation of the WF for cash crops under consideration. Then, the virtual water flows (VWF) are estimated using WF calculations and quantitative trade data. The final assessment involves estimating the VWC and VWT of some of the products derived from the cash crops.

Six cash crops, namely coffee, cotton, jute, sugarcane, tea, and tobacco have been considered in the study. VWF embedded in cash crops from India to the rest of the world and vice versa are considered both for the pre-reform(1980-1990) and post-reform period(1991-2013). Further, the post-reform period is classified into three periods: 1991-2002, 2002-2008 (the boom period) and 2008-2013 (the period after the global financial crisis). This is done to analyze the trend and pattern of VWF under varying economic conditions.

To calculate the VWC of cash crops, data on the crop water requirement (CWR) and the annual yield of these crops is required. The CWR data is taken from Chapagain & Hoesktra (2004), which provides the CWR of various crops for all the countries. Data on a national level annual yield of the cash crops and annual international trade data has been taken from the Food and Agriculture Organisation's (FAO) FAOSTAT database. (www.fao.org/faostat/en/).

To estimate the VWC of cash crops, the methodology has been adopted from the water footprint assessment manual by Hoekstra et al., 2011.

The VWC of crops (in m^3/ton) is calculated by dividing the crop water requirement (in m^3/ha) by the yield of the crop (in ton/ha).

(Hoesktra & Hung, 2002).

Where

VWC= virtual water content (m^3/ton) of crop c in nation n
CWR= crop water requirement (m^3/ha) of crop c in nation n
CY= crop yield (ton/ha) of crop c in nation n

Crop water requirement is defined as "the volume of water that is required to compensate the water that is lost due to evapotranspiration under growth conditions with no constraint by water shortage" (Allen et al., 1998). In other words, the total water required for evapotranspiration from the first stage, i.e. planting, to the last, i.e. harvesting, in a particular climate regime, accounts for the crop water requirement. It is measured in m^3/ha. Calculating the CWR is the first step in calculating the VWC of crops. The CWR for India for the six cash crops under consideration were taken from Chapagain & Hoekstra (2004).

The VWT between countries is estimated by multiplying the quantities of crop traded, with the crop's VWC. The VWC of the exporting country is considered for calculating the VWT (Hoekstra & Hung, 2002).

(Hoekstra and Hung, 2002)

Where

VWT= virtual water trade (m^3/year) from the exporting country to importing country n_i in a given year t, as a result of trade in crop c
CT= crop trade from the exporting to the importing country for crop c in year t
VWC= virtual water content of crop c in the exporting country

It is assumed in the above equation that a crop that is exported from a country was grown in that country itself, and not imported from elsewhere for re-exporting. This is so because all sources of exported products can practically not be tracked. Although there is a chance of certain errors being made this way, it is expected to be small and thus not impact a country's overall virtual water trade balance (Hoekstra and Hung, 2002).

Once we have calculated the VWC of the primary crop, we calculated the VWC of a processed product, derived from that crop. The VWC of a product is defined as the volume of water consumed and polluted throughout its production chain (Hoekstra et al., 2011).

Thus, to calculate the VWC of a product, we need to identify its 'production system', which consists of various processing steps. For example, cotton is grown, harvested, ginned, carded, knitted, bleached, dyed, printed and finished to be made into a cotton shirt. Products often require multiple inputs, due to which there are multiple process steps, thus giving us what is called a 'product tree' (Hoekstra et al., 2011).

The method used for calculating the VWC of processed products is called the stepwise accumulative approach (Hoekstra et al., 2011). Under this approach, the VWC of a product is obtained based on the VWC of the input products necessary in the last processing step carried out to obtain that product, and the process water required in that particular processing step (Hoekstra et al., 2011).

The VWC of a product p derived from a crop is thus calculated as follows:

$$VWCprod\left[p\right]=\left(VWCproc\left[p\right]+\Sigma_{i=1}^{y}\frac{VWCprod\left[i\right]}{fp\left[p,i\right]}\right)*fv\left[p\right]$$

Figure 1. Process to calculate the VWC and VWT of crops. (**source:** *Hoeksta and Hung, 2002)*

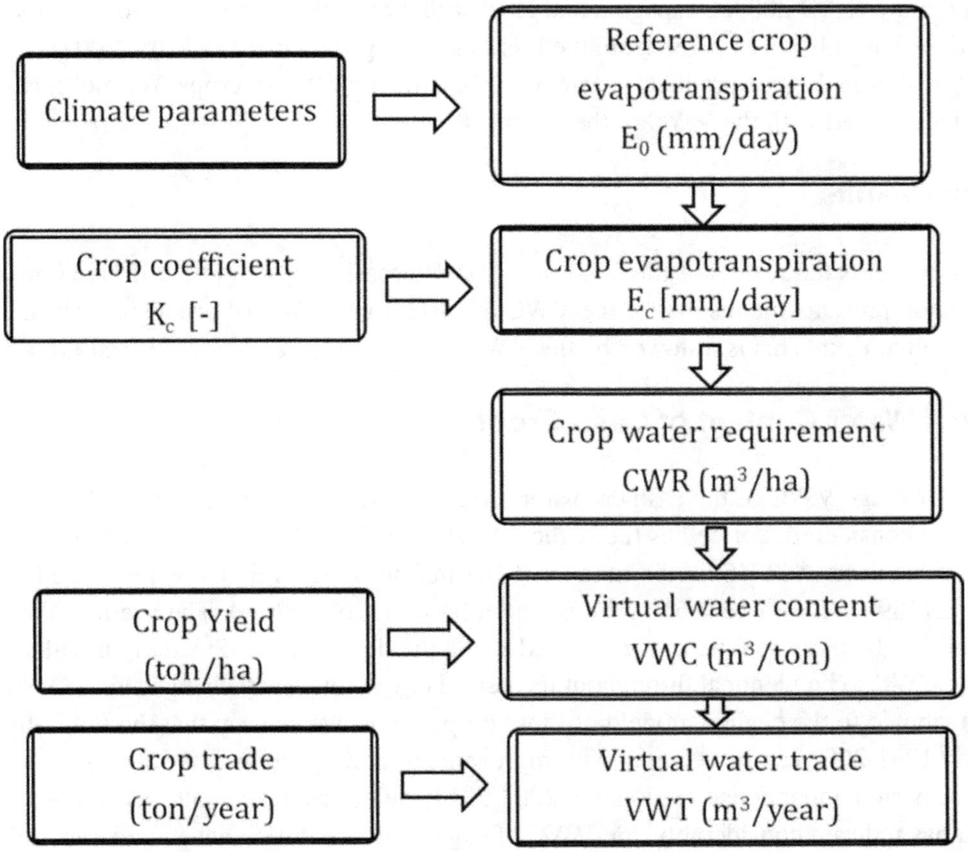

(Hoekstra et al., 2011)
Where

VWCprod[p]= VWC of output product p,
VWCprod[i]= VWC of input i
VWCproc[p]=process water requirement for the processing of the product we are calculating the VWC for.
f_p(p,i)= product fraction
f_v(p,i)= value fraction

The product fractions and value fractions are used when more than one product is obtained from a primary crop, where the VWC of these crops is allocated proportionally to the different products based on their product and value fractions.

Product fraction is defined as "the weight of the primary product obtained per ton of primary crop" (as cited in Chapagain and Hoekstra, 2004). For example, if a 0.8-ton cotton lint is obtained from seed cotton, we say its product fraction is 0.8.

The value fraction is defined as "the ratio of the market value of the product to the aggregated market value of all the products obtained from the primary crop" (Chapagain & Hoesktra, 2004).

The product trees and product fractions for different products derived from cash crops have been taken from the literature (FAO 2003, Chapagain and Hoekstra, 2004 vol 2). They are shown in the annexure. Value fractions have also been taken from the literature (Chapagain and Hoekstra, 2004).

The VWT of crop derived products is calculated like that of VWT of crops. We multiply the quantities of products traded with the VWC of the products.

Empirical Results

This section presents the results of the VWC and VWT of cash crops and their derived products. The first sub-section presents the results for the VWC of cash crops. VWC of products derived from these crops is presented next. This is followed by the VWT of these crops and crop derived products.

The Virtual Water Content of Cash Crops

The national average VWC of the cash crops for different periods are presented in table 1. Among the six cash crops considered, coffee has the highest VWC (16284 m^3/ton) during the period 1980-1990. The VWC of seed cotton (9346 m^3/ton) and tea (8641 m^3/ton) is also relatively high. The least VWC is of sugarcane (189 m^3/ton), jute (3612 m^3/ton) and tobacco (3269 m^3/ton). The average VWC of crops in the period 1991-2001 has fallen, as compared to the previous decade. Since in our calculations, we assumed the CWR to be identical throughout the period of the study, any changes in the VWC of crops are to be attributed to the change in yield of those crops. Thus, we can say that the fall in the VWC of crops during 1991-2001 can be accredited to improvement in the yield over the years.

In the last period under consideration, i.e. 2002-2013, we notice mixed patterns. While the VWC of seed cotton has reduced considerably, the VWC of sugarcane and coffee have increased, although it is only a minor increase. The VWC of the rest of the crops falls, but only by a small amount.

Table 1. National and global averages of VWC of crops for different periods

Cash Crops	National Average VWC in 1980-1990 (m^3/ton)	National Average VWC in 1991-2001 (m^3/ton)	National VWC in 2002-2013 (m^3/ton)	Global average VWC (1996-2005) (Mekonnen & Hoekstra, 2013)
Seed cotton	9346	7485	4493	3589
Sugarcane	189	160	165	197
Tea	8641	7690	7636	8130
Coffee, green	16284	13121	13323	15365
Jute	3615	2893	2441	2389
Tobacco	3269	2728	2436	2226

Global averages given by Mekonnen & Hoekstra (2013) for the period 1996-2005 show that for crops like sugarcane, tea, coffee, jute and tobacco, India's VWC of crops is either less than or very close to the global averages. It is only for cotton that India's VWC is higher than the global average.

The Virtual Water Content of Products Derived From Cash Crops

The VWC of crop derived products is calculated using the methodology described above, and the results are discussed below for each crop individually

Cotton

Cotton has a complex production chain. Before a cotton garment reaches the consumer, it passes through a long process, where the seed of the cotton is sown, harvested, ginned to obtain the cotton lint, carded and combed, then knitted or weaved to obtain the grey fabric, bleached, dyed and wet-processed to obtain the fabric, and finally printed and finished to obtain the final textile. Determining the volume of water consumed or the VWC of the final textile means calculating the VWC of the inputs and the processing water required at every stage of production. Another product obtained on harvesting the cotton is the cottonseed, which is extracted from the cotton lint and then used to produce cottonseed cake, cotton linters, and cottonseed oil.

Table 2. VWC of cotton derived products, for the three-time periods considered

Product	VWC (1980-1990)	VWC (1991-2001)	VWC(2002-2013)
	(m^3/ton)	(m^3/ton)	(m^3/ton)
Cotton lint	18038	14446	8671
Grey fabric	19773	15836	9506
Fabric	20133	16196	9866
Final textile	20273	16336	10006
Cottonseed	4794	3840	2305
Cottonseed oil	8539	6839	4105
Cottonseed cake	5993	4800	2881

The products that are obtained directly from the crop are known as the primary products (Mekonnen & Hoekstra, 2011). In the case of cotton, cotton lint and cottonseed are the primary products, whereas the products obtained on further processing are known as the secondary and tertiary products.

The VWC of the primary products cotton lint and cottonseed are based on the VWC of seed cotton. As described in the methodology, the VWC of seed cotton has to be proportionally distributed between cotton lint and cottonseed based on their product fractions and value fractions. The PF and VF are mentioned in the annexure along with the product trees.

The average VWC of cotton lint for the period 1980-1990 is 18038 m^3/ton. In the subsequent periods, it falls to 14446 m^3/ton for 1991-2001 and 8671 m^3/ton for 2002-2013. Since the VWC of cotton derived products is based on the VWC of seed cotton, any changes in the VWC of cotton lint are attributed to change in the VWC of seed cotton. Thus, we see that the VWC of cotton lint follows the same pattern as that of seed cotton. With CWR assumed to be constant and only yield affecting the VWC of seed cotton, a declining trend in the VWC of seed cotton is reflected in the trend for the VWC of cotton lint as well. Moreover, since ginning is a rather dry process, the process water requirement to obtain cotton lint is assumed to be zero. Thus, VWC of cotton lint is entirely dependent on the VWC of seed cotton and observed to decline over the years.

The average VWC of cotton seed also falls from 4794 m^3/ton in 1980-1990 to 3840 m^3/ton in 1991-2001 and finally to 2305 m^3/ton in 2002-2013. The reduction in the VWC of cotton seed follows the same argument as that for cotton lint.

From the cotton lint, we obtain cotton, which is not carded or combed. The VWC of this cotton is the same as that of cotton lint since it has a PF and VF value of 1. On carding or spinning this cotton, we obtained the carded or combed cotton, and a by-product- garnetted stock, which is waste. When the combed cotton is knitted or weaved, we obtain the grey fabric and some yarn waste.

The VWC of grey fabric is shown in table 2 above. The grey fabric undergoes wet processing to obtain the fabric. The wet processing involves bleaching, dyeing, and printing. Since these processes consume a huge amount of water, while calculating the VWC of fabric, we add the process water requirements. 30 m^3/ton is added for bleaching, 140 m^3/ton for dyeing and 190 m^3/ton for printing. The exact water requirements depend on the techniques and technology used and are bound to vary from region to region. Thus, these are rough averages that have been taken from Chapagain et al., (2006a). The next step is to obtain the final textile from the fabric. This process involves finishing and thus, another 140 m^3/ton is added as process water required for finishing (Chapagain et al.,2006a). The values for VWC of fabric and the final textile are reported in Table 2. Following a similar argument as that for cotton lint, these secondary and tertiary products are obtained from the primary products and hence their VWC is based on the VWC of those primary products. Thus, a similar pattern is observed in the fall in the volume of water consumed or virtual water contained in these products over the years. However, two cautionary observations are in line here. First, we have assumed technology to be constant over the years, since we practically cannot observe the change in technology. Thus, our estimates are solely based on the VWC of the input product and the water requirement of the particular process in which we obtain the product for which we are calculating the VWC. Any change in water-saving technology is not accounted for. Secondly, we know that a primary product like cotton lint or a secondary product like combed cotton or grey fabric in most likelihood will be processed and produced within the country. However, there is a chance that the combed cotton or the grey fabric might be exported to another country and be further processed into the fabric and final textile at some other place, and then be imported back into the country for consumption or for re-exporting it. Thus, our estimates for the VWC of secondary and tertiary products like fabric and finished textile must be taken with caution, or under the assumption that the entire production chain was completed within the country. The results for the products obtained for cottonseed, which are cottonseed cake and cottonseed oil are also shown in the table above. The VWC for these is comparatively lesser than that for cotton lint and its associated products since the product fraction for cottonseed is lesser than that for cotton lint and also since the processing of cotton seed into cakes and oil is expected to be less water-intensive as compared to that of obtaining a cotton textile.

Sugarcane

The primary products obtained from sugarcane are cane molasses and raw sugar. Raw sugar is further processed to obtain refined sugar in solid form. From refined sugar, maple sugar & maple syrup, glucose & glucose syrup, fructose & fructose syrup, etc. are obtained. In our study, we focus predominantly on VWC of raw sugar and refined sugar.

Table 3. National averages for VWC of sugarcane derived products for different periods

Product	VWC (1980-1990) (m^3/ton)	VWC (1991-2001) (m^3/ton)	VWC(2002-2013) (m^3/ton)
Raw sugar	1605	1363	1400
Refined sugar, in solid form	1509	1281	1316

Since the VWC of raw sugar is based on VWC of sugarcane, we see that VWC of raw sugar follows the same pattern as that of sugarcane. The average VWC for both raw sugar and refined sugar falls during 1991-2001 as compared to 1980-1990 but increases again slightly during 2002-2013.

Virtual Water Trade of Cash Crops and Products Derived From Them

This section contains the results for the water traded virtually from India, in the form of trade in cash crops and products derived from them. The results are divided into three time periods as earlier, the 1980s, 1990s, and the 2000s up till 2013. Results for each crop and crop product are discussed individually.

Cotton

We discuss the VWT pattern for cottonseed, cottonseed cake, cottonseed oil, cotton lint and carded or combed cotton. India has been a net virtual water exporter of cottonseed. The average net virtual water import (NVWI) for the period 1980-1990 was -76,228 m^3/year, meaning there was net export of virtual water. This value increased for the post-liberalization period to -2,455,676 m^3/year in the period 1991-2001, and further to -4,925,923 m^3/year during 2002-2013. However, there were inter-annual variations. India was a net VW importer in the early 1980s and in the late 1980s, India was neither a VW importer nor a VW exporter since zero quantities of cotton was traded in these years. However, India has been a net VW exporter for all the years post-liberalization. Yet, there have been inter-annual variations. The net virtual water exports (NVWE) grew rapidly during 2002-2008, and fell for a couple of years, before regaining momentum again by 2011. The global recession could be held responsible for this. India has been an NVW exporter of cottonseed cake. However, the volume of VW exported shows a declining trend over the years, as can be seen in the table in the annexure. The reason for a net VW export is that India does not import much cottonseed cake. Zero quantities are imported for most of the years. A declining trend in the volume of NVW exported can also be accredited to the fact that VWC has fallen over the years.

Exports and imports for most of the years before liberalization have been reported as zero for cottonseed oil. Imports took place in only two years in the early 80s. During the period 1991-2001, India was an NVW importer of cottonseed oil. It exported virtual water in the form of cottonseed oil for a few years from 2002-2007, exporting on an average 0.5 million m^3/year VW, before becoming an NVW importer again from 2008 onwards. The rise in exports during 2002-2007 could be accredited to the boom in the Indian economy witnessed during this period.

Large inter-annual variation can also be witnessed for the VWT of cotton lint. However, for the case of cotton lint, India was an NVW exporter for the pre-liberalization period, but an NVW importer for the post-liberalization period, since India imported greater quantities of cotton lint than it exported, during some years in the 90s and early 2000s. However, it started exporting virtual water again after 2005. The average values of NVWI are depicted in the table.

India imported zero amounts of carded or combed cotton during the pre-liberalization period, and up till 1993. Even after this period, India was a net exporter of virtual water, and an increasing trend is seen over the years.

Sugarcane

Sugar cane is a perishable commodity and hence it is not traded much internationally since it is expected to perish in transit itself. Due to this, trade values for sugar cane are very small, and hence beyond the scope of this study. We study the VWT pattern for refined sugar, a product derived from sugar cane. For most of the years before liberalization, India has been an NVW importer of refined sugar. For the period 1991-2001, it is an NVW exporter in some years and NVW importer in the others. For the period 2002-2013, India has been an NVW exporter for refined sugar for all the years except in 2009, where imports exceeded exports, which could be possible due to the global recession. The annual NVWI values are given in the table in the annexure.

Tea

India has consistently been an NVW exporter of tea for the entire period 1980-2013. There hasn't been much inter-annual variability in the values too. The average NVWI ranges between -1200 million m^3/year to -1700 million m^3/year.

Coffee

India has been an NVW exporter of green coffee for the entire period 1980-2013. Import quantities equal to zero for 1980-1990. The average NVW exports have seen a rising trend over the years, with the maximum rise during the late 1990s and the early 2000s. The exports witnessed a slight fall during 2009 but regained momentum after that. The average NVWE was about 1500 million m^3/year. For roasted coffee, data on imports is not available for the period 1980-1995. So, we consider the period 1996-2013. India exported an average NVW of 7 million m^3/year during this period in the form of roasted coffee. We see that trade in green coffee is much larger than the trade-in roasted coffee.

Jute

Jute is the only commodity in which India has majorly been an NVW importer. The average NVWI amounted to 29 million m^3/year during 1980-1990. This amount rose to 149 million m^3/year in the post-liberalization period and further to 175 million m^3/year during 2002-2013. Imports fell during the 2008 global crisis and the year after, but gradually improved by 2011.

Tobacco

India has been an NVW exporter of tobacco for the entire period. The average NVWE for the period 1980-1990 was 241 million m^3/year. It fell slightly to 238 million m^3/year for the period 1991-2001 but shot up remarkably to 433 million m^3/year during 2002-2013.

Table 4. Average NVWI for crop derived products for different periods.

Product [Average NVWI (million m^3/year)]	1980-1990	1991-2001	2002-2013
Cotton lint	-1,537	423	-6,322
Carded or combed cotton	-4	-21	-28
Cottonseed	-.0076	-2.4	-4.9
Cottonseed cake	-612	-52	-27
Cottonseed oil	70	117	1.4
Refined sugar	352	70	-1,377
Green coffee	-1,322	-1,788	-1,882
Roasted coffee	NA	-7	-6
Tea	-1,796	-1,322	-1,414
Jute	29	149	175
Tobacco	-241	-238	-433

CONCLUSION

The current study analyzed the trend and pattern of WF and VWT of cash crops and their derived products. Over the years, the VWC of these cash crops is observed to have been reduced. This means a lesser volume of water is required to produce per ton of crop now, than it was during the 1980s. Since we assume the crop water requirements to be constant over the period of the study, we say that the reduction in VWC of crops is due to improvement in yield over the years. This could be true for primary crops since the crop water requirements depend on climatic conditions and crop parameters. However, for secondary and tertiary crop derived products, it could be possible that over the years, with better technology, water use efficiency has improved and led to reduction in the VWC of those products. This is supported by literature, an example of which is given by Leenes & Hoesktra (2009) where they assume process water requirements in the sugar cane mill to be zero since modern industries recycle their water.

Evidence from literature (Hoekstra & Hung, 2002) and our study establish the fact that virtual water is majorly traded in the form of agricultural commodities. In the case of cash crops, we saw that India has majorly been a net virtual water exporter for almost all the crops, except jute. Large volumes of agricultural commodities are exported annually from India to other parts of the world, and generally exceed the imports for the same. With free trade policies and opening up of the economy, export quantities increased during the 1990s and the period thereafter, leading to larger virtual water exports. India ranks among the top 15 cotton-producing countries and is also one of the largest exporters of sugar (Chapagain & Hoekstra, 2006a; Leenes & Hoekstra, 2009).

Although WF and VWT are seen across the literature as a viable instrument to mitigate water scarcity, certain contentions are in order. It is not enough to look at the volume of virtual water consumed to produce a product. Rather, it is important to trace the type of water used. The opportunity cost of using blue water is higher than that of using green water. Sugarcane has a higher blue water footprint, which puts stress on the water resources, rather than tea or coffee plants which are mainly rain-fed. It has been seen that sugarcane is grown in river basins such as the Indus and the Ganges, which are water-scarce (Leenes & Hoekstra, 2009).

It has been widely observed that VWT does not take place from water abundant regions to water-scarce ones. This can be seen from the fact that wealthy countries like Germany and Japan import virtual water, despite being water abundant. Developing countries like India, on the other hand, are virtual water exporters, despite facing growing water scarcity (Chapagain et al., 2006b).

Studies have shown that water endowments are not sufficient to explain the virtual water flows (De Fraiture et al., 2004). Arable land availability, infrastructure, land reforms and income of a country also determine the flows of virtual water. Virtual water flows are impacted by the income of the country. Poor countries cannot afford to import commodities. Sufficient foreign exchange is required to import goods, which would have been produced domestically otherwise. Therefore, the VWT is unable to justify the Hecksher-Ohlin Model of trade. Water scarcity cannot be depicted through water pricing, causing the H-O model to fail in the case of virtual water trade (Verma *et al.* 2007).

Other than this, countries importing agricultural goods must face the risk of unemployment in the agricultural sector of their country (Chapagain et al., 2006b).

Finally, the countries that export virtual water must bear the brunt of environmental damage. VWT may generate global water savings, but for these savings to be sustainable, the price of these exported goods must reflect the opportunity costs and the negative impact on the environment in these countries. Otherwise, only the importing countries benefit from these water savings (Chapagain et al., 2006b).

Talking about developing countries like India, they must improve their management and auditing system to prevent such large virtual water exports. Moreover, water productivity should be improved. India has a growing population pressure, rapid urbanization, and unfavorable weather conditions due to climate change. In this scenario, it must act on countering its water issues.

To reduce the pressure on freshwater resources, countries should aim to reduce their agricultural WF. WF benchmarks established by a study over the period 1996-2005 show that if all countries reduce the green and blue WF of crops to the best 25th percentile, 39% global water savings could be achieved, and with a reduction to the best 10th percentile of global production, 52% water savings are achievable (Mekonnen & Hoekstra, 2013).

WF of crops can be reduced by improving the yield, managing the soil nutrients by following crop rotation, lesser tillage, judicious application of manure, and proper irrigation and use of better irrigation techniques, using the rainfall effectively, etc. (Mekonnen & Hoekstra, 2013).

Studies have suggested better cotton farming practices for India, to reduce its cotton WF. Cotton in India is mostly grown using conventional methods of farming. Organic farming is seen as a solution to reducing the grey water footprint. However, this reduces the yield in the initial years. Hybrid farming is proposed as an alternative, as it has a lesser negative impact on the environment than conventional farming, and does not impact the livelihoods of farmers also.

Other than this, proper land leveling and reduced tillage can reduce water use. Moreover, it is important to choose appropriate planting dates, correct seed selection, practices like crop rotation and intercropping which help in better yield, thus reducing the WF (Chapagain et al., 2017).

Likewise, sustainable agricultural practices for all crops, and in all countries, can help in reducing the WF of these crops and help in controlling the water scarcity solution. Freshwater is the most basic necessity of life and must be conserved for the future generation to lead an equally content livelihood.

Limitations

This study was based on certain assumptions. To begin with, to calculate the VWC of crops, we assume crop water requirement to be constant over the years. However, with a change in climate over the past three decades, the CWR are expected to change too. Because of this assumption, we expect the VWC of crop derived products too to be rough estimates. However, it must be noted that the climatic data taken for the calculation of CWR is usually a thirty-year average, which means that we might not after all be that wrong in taking constant CWR values.

Because of the above assumption, any changes in the VWC of crops is completely due to changes in the yield of those crops. However, yield depends on land productivity as well. Thus, more studies need to be reviewed to study water productivity patterns.

Next, for the VWC of primary crop derived products, we assume the process water requirements to be zero, because most of the water that is consumed is in the agricultural stage.

For secondary and tertiary products, we do consider the process water requirements for the products, such as for fabric and finished textile of cotton. However, these values must be considered as rough estimates, taken from the literature, since the actual values vary, depending on technology, which cannot be measured.

Also, for a supply chain as complex as that of cotton, it is quite possible that combed cotton or grey fabric, or cotton at any stage of the production process, is exported, processed elsewhere and then re-imported into the country as finished textile. Thus, in that case, the values for the VWC of fabric or finished textile must be taken with a pinch of salt.

There were some data limitations as well. For example, data for roasted coffee was available only after 1996. Also, due to limited coverage of crops, we could not depict a broader pattern of VWT for India.

Lastly, our study does not distinguish between blue, green and grey WF, since the motive was to analyze the total VWC trend and VWT patterns.

Scope for future study involves analyzing which countries does India export VW in the form of cash crops, and from which countries does it import VW through cash crops. Also, the study could be done at a sub-national level to see if the VWT of cash crops is sustainable at that level.

REFERENCES

Allan, J. (1993). Fortunately, there are substitutes for water otherwise our hydro-political futures would be impossible. In Priorities for water resources allocation and management (pp. 13-26). London: Academic Press.

Allen, R. G., Pereira, L. S., Raes, D., & Smith, M. (1998). *Crop evapotranspiration—guidelines for computing crop water requirements—FAO irrigation and drainage paper.* FAO.

Chapagain, A., Mathews, R., & Zhang, G. (2017). *A guide to reducing the water footprint of cotton cultivation in India*. C&A Foundation. WFN.

Chapagain, A. K., & Hoekstra, A. Y. (2003a). *The water needed to have the Dutch drink coffee*. Value of Water Research Report Series No. 14. UNESCO-IHE.

Chapagain, A. K., & Hoekstra, A. Y. (2003b). *The water needed to have the Dutch drink tea*. Value of Water Research Report Series No. 15, UNESCO-IHE. www.waterfootprint.org/Reports/Report15.pdf

Chapagain, A. K., & Hoekstra, A. Y. (2004). *Water footprints of nations*. Value of Water Research Report Series No. 16, UNESCO-IHE. www.waterfootprint.org/Reports/Report16Vol1.pdf

Chapagain, A. K., & Hoekstra, A. Y. (2004). *Water footprints of nations*. Value of Water Research Report Series No. 16, UNESCO-IHE.

Chapagain, A. K., & Hoekstra, A. Y. (2007). The water footprint of coffee and tea consumption in the Netherlands. *Ecological Economics*, *64*(1), 109–118. doi:10.1016/j.ecolecon.2007.02.022

Chapagain, A. K., Hoekstra, A. Y., & Savenije, H. H. G. (2006b). Water-saving through international trade of agricultural products. *Hydrology and Earth System Sciences Discussions*, *10*(3), 455–468. doi:10.5194/hess-10-455-2006

Chapagain, A. K., Hoekstra, A. Y., Savenije, H. H. G., & Gautam, R. (2006a). *The water footprint of cotton consumption*. Value of Water Research Report Series No. 18, UNESCO-IHE.

De Fraiture, C. (2004). *Does international cereal trade save water?: the impact of virtual water trade on global water use* (Vol. 4). IWMI.

FAO (Food and Agriculture Organization). (2003). *Technical conversion factors for agricultural commodities*. FAO. www.fao.org/fileadmin/templates/ess/documents/methodology/tcf.pdf www.fao.org/faostat/en/

Gerbens-Leenes, W., & Hoekstra, A. Y. (2009). *The water footprint of sweeteners and bio-ethanol from sugar cane, sugar beet, and maize*. Value of Water Research Report Series No. 38, UNESCO-IHE.

Hoekstra, A. Y. (2003). Virtual water trade: A quantification of virtual water flows between nations in relation to international crop trade. In *Proceedings of the International Expert Meeting on Virtual Water Trade* (pp. 25-47). Academic Press.

Hoekstra, A. Y. (2003, February). Virtual water: An introduction. In *Virtual water trade: Proceedings of the international expert meeting on virtual water trade* (pp. 13-23). The IHE Delft Institute for Water Education.

Hoekstra, A. Y. (Ed.). (2003). *Virtual water trade: Proceedings of the International Expert Meeting on Virtual Water Trade*. UNESCO-IHE. www.waterfootprint.org/Reports/Report12.pdf

Hoekstra, A. Y., Chapagain, A. K., Aldaya, M. M., & Mekonnen, M. M. (2011). *Water footprint manual: State of the art 2009*. Water Footprint Network. www.waterfootprint.org/downloads/WaterFootprint-Manual2009.pdf

Jain, S. K., Agarwal, P. K., & Singh, V. P. (2007). *Hydrology and Water Resources of India*. Springer.

Kampman, D. A. (2007). *The water footprint of India* (Master's thesis). University of Twente.

Katyaini, S. (2016). *Science-Policy interface to mitigate water scarcity in India: An assessment of virtual water flows* (Doctoral dissertation). Indian Institute of Technology Guwahati, Guwahati, India.

Katyaini, S., & Barua, A. (2017). *Assessment of interstate virtual water flows embedded in agriculture to mitigate water scarcity in India (1996–2014).* Water Resources Research.

Kumar, M. D., & Singh, O. P. (2005). Virtual water in global food and water policy making: Is there a need for rethinking? *Water Resources Management, 19*(6), 759–789. doi:10.100711269-005-3278-0

Kumar, V., & Jain, S. K. (2007). Status of virtual water trade from India. *Current Science*, 1093–1099.

Kumar, V., & Jain, S. K. (2011). Export and import of virtual water from different states of India through food grain trade. *Hydrology Research, 42*(2-3), 229–238. doi:10.2166/nh.2011.089

Mekonnen, M. M., & Hoekstra, A. Y. (2010). *The Green, Blue and Greywater footprint of crop and derived crop products*. Value of Water Research Report Series No. 47. Enschede: University of Twente.

Mekonnen, M. M., & Hoekstra, A. Y. (2011). The Green, Blue and Greywater footprint of crop and derived crop products. *Hydrology and Earth System Sciences, 15*(5), 1577–1600. doi:10.5194/hess-15-1577-2011

Mekonnen, M. M., & Hoekstra, A. Y. (2013). *Water footprint benchmarks for crop production.* Value of Water Research Report Series No. 64, UNESCO-IHE.

Singh, O. P., Sharma, A., Singh, R., & Shah, T. (2004). Virtual water trade in the dairy economy: Irrigation water productivity in Gujarat. *Economic and Political Weekly*, 3492–3497.

Verma, S., Kampman, D. A., van der Zaag, P., & Hoekstra, A. Y. (2009). Going against the flow: A critical analysis of inter-state virtual water trade in the context of India's National River Linking Program. *Physics and Chemistry of the Earth Parts A/B/C, 34*(4-5), 261–269. doi:10.1016/j.pce.2008.05.002

APPENDIX

Table 5. Crop Water requirements for various cash crops (Source: Chapagain & Hoekstra, 2004)

Name of crop	Crop Water requirement (m^3/ha)
Seed cotton	5290
Coffee	11020
Tea	13370
Sugarcane	11010
Jute	5640
Tobacco	3770

Table 6. VWC of crops for 1980-2013 (in m3/ton) (Source: Authors' calculations)

Year	Seed cotton	Tea	Green Coffee	Sugarcane	Jute	Tobacco
1980	1015.74	8964.73	13606.62	223.07	4529.39	3657.35
1981	1016.253	9180.80	17654.60	190.34	3811.58	3540.24
1982	1016.766	9418.15	14056.12	188.66	3869.37	3217.00
1983	1017.279	9107.01	17037.72	195.07	3764.01	3258.43
1984	1017.792	8325.55	21731.41	196.68	3996.32	3365.77
1985	1018.305	8148.96	11827.84	190.90	3297.86	3387.55
1986	1018.818	8866.05	19309.62	183.54	3420.67	3392.42
1987	1019.331	8866.64	12362.58	182.15	3771.06	3177.41
1988	1019.844	8212.53	19580.67	183.48	3226.18	3263.22
1989	1020.357	7900.49	11343.28	180.51	3001.44	2884.03
1990	1020.87	8063.45	20621.26	167.86	3077.59	2823.34
1991	1021.383	7814.60	14488.56	168.36	3069.55	2785.99
1992	1021.896	7871.19	13682.64	166.45	3037.16	2754.64
1993	1022.409	8509.42	15204.19	172.37	2957.52	2645.06
1994	1022.922	7563.93	12000.44	163.95	2894.24	2577.25
1995	1023.435	7590.55	13990.10	154.64	3008.80	2534.62
1996	1023.948	7551.54	11958.76	162.55	2821.55	2775.32
1997	1024.461	7387.96	13508.21	165.57	2849.92	2610.98
1998	1024.974	7163.52	13806.06	154.78	3008.00	2707.94
1999	1025.487	7250.94	12568.43	143.86	2816.90	2601.97
2000	1026	7931.42	11640.44	155.21	2784.22	3142.19
2001	1026.513	7955.49	11493.53	160.55	2584.78	2882.92
2002	1027.026	7984.47	11742.14	163.43	2630.11	2399.13
2003	1027.539	8154.93	12834.85	173.18	2595.37	2539.06
2004	1028.052	7909.37	13245.19	185.42	2579.70	2534.62
2005	1028.565	7679.94	13333.33	170.03	2387.30	2516.35
2006	1029.078	7827.87	13728.67	164.50	2402.35	2545.23
2007	1029.591	7791.38	13125.30	159.49	2501.22	2682.51
2008	1030.104	7835.67	14490.47	159.85	2555.27	2692.86
2009	1030.617	7958.33	14724.75	170.56	2263.24	2364.82
2010	1031.13	7810.04	13528.11	157.24	2406.45	2427.40
2011	1031.643	7322.82	13153.50	159.00	2301.57	2225.63
2012	1032.156	7126.49	12938.83	155.22	2359.83	2114.89
2013	1032.669	6238.04	13032.17	163.28	2320.99	2190.33

Table 7. Product and value fraction of sugarcane derived products (Source: Chapagain and Hoekstra, 2004; Mekonnen and Hoekstra, 2010)

Product	Product Fraction	Value Fraction
Cane molasses	.05	.13
Raw sugar, cane	.11	.87
Refined sugar	.94	1.00

Figure 2. Commodity tree and product & value fractions of cotton and its derived products (Source: Chapagain and Hoekstra, 2004; Chapagain et al., 2006a; Mekonnen and Hoekstra, 2010)

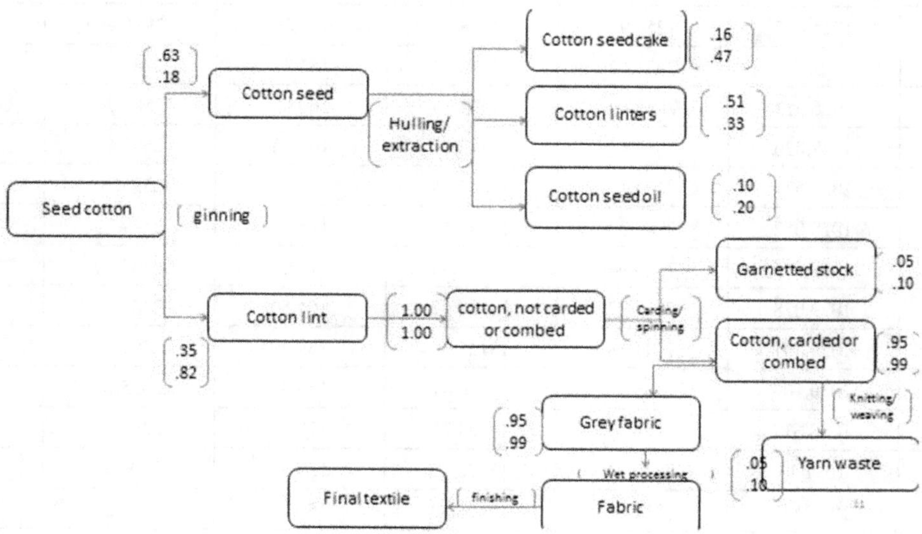

Table 8. VWC of cotton derived products for 1980-2013 (in m3/ton)

Year	Cotton seed	Cotton seed oil	Cotton seed cake	Cotton lint	Cotton, carded or combed	Grey fabric	Fabric	Final textile
1980	5255.17	9359.46	6568.96	19770.91	20700.15	21673.05	22033.05	22173.05
1981	5223.81	9303.61	6529.76	19652.94	20576.62	21543.72	21903.72	22043.72
1982	5339.96	9510.48	6674.96	20089.93	21034.15	22022.76	22382.76	22522.76
1983	6174.68	10997.10	7718.34	23230.26	24322.08	25465.22	25825.22	25965.22
1984	4432.82	7894.85	5541.02	16677.07	17460.89	18281.55	18641.55	18781.55
1985	4409.77	7853.79	5512.21	16590.35	17370.09	18186.49	18546.49	18686.49
1986	5140.69	9155.57	6425.86	19340.22	20249.21	21200.92	21560.92	21700.92
1987	5171.06	9209.65	6463.82	19454.46	20368.82	21326.15	21686.15	21826.15
1988	4289.87	7640.25	5362.33	16139.27	16897.81	17692.01	18052.01	18192.01
1989	3441.69	6129.64	4302.11	12948.26	13556.82	14193.99	14553.99	14693.99
1990	3861.92	6878.08	4827.40	14529.24	15212.12	15927.09	16287.09	16427.09
1991	4028.76	7175.21	5035.94	15156.92	15869.29	16615.15	16975.15	17115.15
1992	3378.70	6017.46	4223.37	12711.28	13308.71	13934.22	14294.22	14434.22
1993	3481.87	6201.21	4352.34	13099.44	13715.11	14359.72	14719.72	14859.72
1994	3382.07	6023.46	4227.58	12723.95	13321.98	13948.11	14308.11	14448.11
1995	3588.69	6391.46	4485.87	13501.32	14135.88	14800.27	15160.27	15300.27
1996	3273.94	5830.89	4092.43	12317.17	12896.07	13502.19	13862.19	14002.19
1997	4174.39	7434.59	5217.99	15704.81	16442.94	17215.76	17575.76	17715.76
1998	3884.03	6917.45	4855.03	14612.42	15299.21	16018.27	16378.27	16518.27
1999	3859.17	6873.19	4823.97	14518.91	15201.30	15915.76	16275.76	16415.76
2000	4538.84	8083.67	5673.54	17075.93	17878.50	18718.79	19078.79	19218.79
2001	4650.05	8281.74	5812.56	17494.35	18316.58	19177.46	19537.46	19677.46
2002	4542.63	8090.43	5678.29	17090.22	17893.46	18734.46	19094.46	19234.46
2003	2826.84	5034.61	3533.55	10635.10	11134.95	11658.30	12018.30	12158.30
2004	2732.07	4865.83	3415.09	10278.57	10761.66	11267.46	11627.46	11767.46
2005	2396.05	4267.37	2995.07	9014.39	9438.07	9881.66	10241.66	10381.66
2006	2063.55	3675.18	2579.43	7763.44	8128.32	8510.35	8870.35	9010.35
2007	1857.09	3307.48	2321.37	6986.72	7315.10	7658.91	8018.91	8158.91
2008	2157.90	3843.21	2697.37	8118.40	8499.96	8899.46	9259.46	9399.46
2009	2192.59	3905.00	2740.74	8248.93	8636.63	9042.55	9402.55	9542.55
2010	1702.49	3032.14	2128.11	6405.08	6706.12	7021.31	7381.31	7521.31
2011	1723.25	3069.10	2154.06	6483.17	6787.88	7106.91	7466.91	7606.91
2012	1788.43	3185.20	2235.54	6728.42	7044.65	7375.75	7735.75	7875.75
2013	1677.34	2987.34	2096.68	6310.46	6607.06	6917.59	7277.59	7417.59

Table 9. VWC of products derived from green coffee and sugarcane for 1980-2013 (in m3/ton)

Year	Roasted coffee	Refined sugar
1980	16198.35	1778.48
1981	21017.38	1517.55
1982	16733.48	1504.17
1983	20283.00	1555.29
1984	25870.73	1568.13
1985	14080.76	1522.06
1986	22987.64	1463.36
1987	22987.64	1452.27
1988	22987.64	1462.87
1989	22987.64	1439.23
1990	22987.64	1338.31
1991	22987.64	1342.33
1992	22987.64	1327.09
1993	22987.64	1374.29
1994	22987.64	1307.15
1995	22987.64	1232.90
1996	22987.64	1295.96
1997	22987.64	1320.11
1998	22987.64	1234.03
1999	22987.64	1146.98
2000	22987.64	1237.49
2001	22987.64	1280.05
2002	22987.64	1302.98
2003	22987.64	1380.73
2004	22987.64	1478.30
2005	22987.64	1355.66
2006	22987.64	1311.58
2007	22987.64	1271.59
2008	22987.64	1274.46
2009	22987.64	1359.83
2010	22987.64	1253.68
2011	22987.64	1267.67
2012	22987.64	1237.57
2013	22987.64	1301.80

Chapter 16
Water Systems in a Circular Economy:
Extracting Value Through Integration

Arvind Deshmukh
Deshmukh Global Management Solutions, India

ABSTRACT

The circular economy is based on three fundamental principles as defined by the Ellen MacArthur Foundation: design out waste and pollution, keep products and materials in use, and regenerate natural systems. This chapter explores the relationship between the circular economy principles and the water management systems to identify the integration points where the water systems can be aligned with the circular economy. The chapter also ascertains the impediments which hinder this transition and identifies the opportunities that will present themselves in this endeavor. This chapter aims to help the readers understand the social, economic, and environmental impacts that will be created when water systems get integrated into the circular economy framework.

INTRODUCTION

Water is an essential resource of human beings that can neither be replaced not discarded. It is the very essence of sustaining life on earth. Water is used for several purposes that can be either consumptive or non-consumptive. Around 71% of our planet's surface area is covered with water with oceans holding close to 96.5% of the water on earth (USGS). Water also exists in the atmosphere as water vapor and is also present in rivers, lakes, swamps, and glaciers. A large quantity of water is held by the soil and underground layers of permeable rocks called the aquifers. The water that is extracted from the ground is known as groundwater. Even the bodies of living beings are not devoid of water. 60% of an adult human body is made up of water (School, Water Science).

Water is constantly changing forms and moving from place to the other. This movement of water above and below the surface of the earth is called the 'Water Cycle' or the 'Hydrological Cycle'. The

DOI: 10.4018/978-1-7998-4990-2.ch016

consistent natural supply of water on earth is attributed to this Water Cycle. (The Water Cycle for Adults and Advanced Students)

Despite the abundance of water on earth, the shortage of water is felt by the world very often because over 97% of Earth's surface water is saline leaving less than 3% of all water as 'Freshwater' (Earthdata). More than two-thirds of the available freshwater is frozen in the form of snow and ice, and a big chunk of the remaining is groundwater. A mere 0.3% of freshwater on the earth is stored in rivers, lakes, and swamps and is easily accessible to us to fulfill the need of the people around the world (P. H. Gleick, 1996). Low availability, poor accessibility, and uneven distribution of freshwater resources have resulted in an extreme 'Water Stress'. One-quarter of the world's population spread across 17 countries faces an 'Extremely High' level of baseline water stress (Rutger Willem Hofste, 2019).

Unlike oil and other resources, water cannot be substituted with other products. Neither it is economically viable and sustainable to transport water from 'water-rich' to the 'water-stressed' areas. It is projected that in the next three decades the growing population and economy will push the water stress to its limits and freshwater availability may become the world's biggest impediment for growth. Southern California is already experiencing such a situation (Veolia Water).

Water Stress has created a huge water crisis in several developing and developed countries of the world. The highest number of water-stressed countries (12 out of 17) are in the MENA (the Middle East and North Africa) region. The World Bank estimates an economic loss amounting to 6-14% of the GDP because of the acute water crisis (Rutger Willem Hofste, 2019). The water situation in India is no better. In 2018, the apex think tank of India, the National Institution for Transforming India (NITI Aayog) announced that the country is suffering from its worst water crisis with 600 million people facing high to extreme water stress-causing 200,000 deaths every year. It is projected that by 2030 severe water scarcity will result in a ~6% loss in the country's GDP (NITI Aayog, 2018). A subsequent report released the following year declared that if corrective actions are not taken then 70% of the country's thermal power plants will face high water stress by 2030 that will result in higher power cuts to industrial units and which in turn will slow down the economic growth. Besides the economy, the ecology and biodiversity of the country may be compromised because of increased efforts to find new water sources (NITI Aayog, 2019). Even the countries that face low overall water stress may contain territories that experience extreme water stress. The Water Research Institute (WRI) has pointed out that places like New Mexico in the United States face extreme water stress despite the US being ranked 71 on WRI's list of water-stressed countries.

The current water crisis can be attributed to poor water system management. Water management is the activity of planning, sourcing, treating, distributing, and managing water resources under a defined set of regulations. Water management is a sub-set of water cycle management (OMICS International).

In the present system, water, like other materials is managed linearly. A linear system is a step by step plan to collect, create, and dispose off the products as waste. Therefore, the common cliché, Take-Make-Dispose associated with the linear economy can be inferred as Take-Use-Discharge strategy in water-based systems. The key takeaway from a linear system is 'Waste'. More than 80% of wastewater worldwide is drained away without being treated. The release of untreated water in the environment not only limits water re-use but also contaminates the rivers and the oceans and destroys the marine ecosystems. Over 800,000 people died from drinking contaminated water in 2012 (UNESCO World Water Assessment Programme], UNESCO. Director-General, (Bokova, I.G.), 2017).

Wastewater is an untapped resource that offers tremendous potential to benefit the economy and the environment. It is already playing a substantial role in several resource cycles. The reuse of properly treated water in agriculture and electricity generation can ensure food and energy security. Water reuse can also create new opportunities and avenues for businesses and livelihood generation.

However, to reap the colossal benefits from wastewater reuse, it becomes imminent to integrate water management in alternate enterprise models. One such enterprise model is the 'Circular Economy Model' that is an economic system of closed loops as opposed to open linear models. Circular Economy is designed to eliminate waste and reuse the existing resources. Water Management is a perfect example that can get well positioned in the Circular Economy. In this chapter, we will explore how water management can wholly or partially be integrated into the circular economy, the alignment of opportunities, and the economic value that will be generated when the two ideas will intersect with one another.

The Circular Economy

According to the Ellen MacArthur Foundation, the circular economy is based on three fundamental principles:

1.) Design out waste and pollution
2.) Keep products and materials in use
3.) Regenerate natural systems

The first principle necessitates the optimal use of energy, minerals, and other substances in operating the water systems. The principal calls for preventing excessive use of water and finding alternate means to water resources.

The second principle calls for optimization of resource yields and their continuous reuse in a closed-loop fashion and third principle seeks to reduce water consumption to restore and regenerate the natural water bodies.

To determine the points of intersection of the circular economy principles with water management, we would need to view various aspects of water management through principles of the circular economy.

Dimensions of Water Use

Water offers us value in different ways and is used in several dimensions. Water can be a service, a source of energy and a carrier (Water and Circular Economy, 2018)

Water is used as a service such as sanitation in our homes and workplaces, the coolant in air conditioners, and as a production utility in factories.

The physical attributes of water include energy that is used for electricity generation in thermal and hydro plants.

Water is used as a carrier in our body to transport nutrients. It also acts as a carrier in the ecosystem to carry the minerals and sediments from one place to another.

Governing of Water Cycle

We need to understand the governance of the present-day water cycle if we were to realize that the magnitude of impact that will be made by applying the principles of the circular economy in this context. According to USGS, water is used in five broad categories - public supply, domestic, irrigation, industrial, and thermoelectric power. These categories represented 97% of water use in 1995 in the United States (Estimated Use of Water in the United States, 2000). There are other sub-categories such as livestock, aquaculture, and mining, however, so the sake of discussion, we will restrict ourselves for the 5 main categories.

Industries use water majorly for manufacturing, refineries, and metallurgy. Products such as steel, chemicals, metals, and petroleum need a significant amount of water for their processing. The use of water in the industry is dominated by large industries. Thermoelectric power uses water for electricity generation from fossil fuel, biomass, radioactive materials, solid water, and geothermal plants. The power plants themselves are the largest consumers of water in this category. The maximum use of water is done in irrigation to cultivate crops and plants. Water is provided to the households for their daily water needs through the public supply. The public supply of water is managed by the municipalities. Irrigation and public supply are the two largest user categories of water and they source water both from the surface and the ground. The domestic water is used for drinking and cooking. In this category, the water can be sourced from in house water sources or public water supply. Domestic water needs to be provided in its safest form because it is being used for consumptive purposes (Water Use Data and Their Application, 2002).

Water Systems

The water system can be both *nature-managed* and *human-managed.*

Figure 1.
Image Courtesy: US Geological Survey

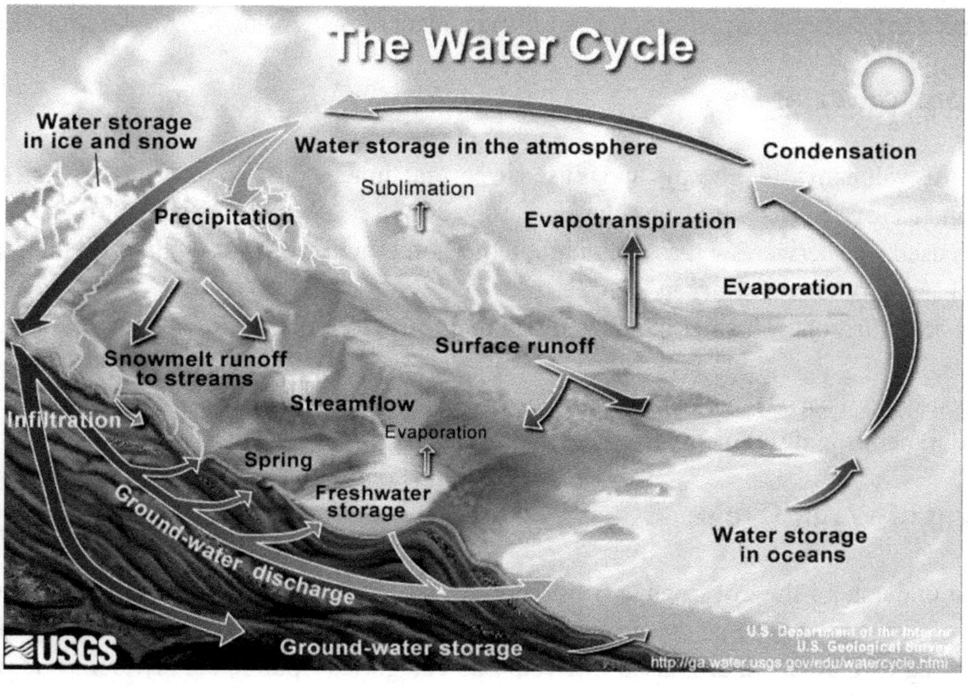

Nature Managed Water System

Nature managed water system is a perfect representation of a circular system. In a natural system, there is a continuous flow of water between the surface, ground, and the atmosphere. The natural system of water movement is represented by the 'water cycle'.

Since the movement of the water is circular, there is no beginning or an endpoint. The movement of water is a continuous process across several natural reservoirs such as seas, oceans, rivers, ice, and atmosphere by a series of processes. The natural water cycle consists of seven processes that facilitate water movements such as Evaporation, Sublimation, Evapotranspiration, precipitation, runoff, and substance flow.

During the circular water cycle, water is transported from one water source to using energy from the environment and eventually returned to a similar source in one way or the other. Water changes form as solid (ice), liquid, and vapor. The total mass of the water on earth and atmosphere remains fairly constant in a natural water cycle. The basin needs a consistent supply of water to endure the climatic variables. The water cycle is the nature's way of treating, storing and supply water to maintain the 'watershed balance'[1]

The circularity of a natural water system is managed in three steps – Re-optimize, Reuse, and Replenish (Water and Circular Economy, 2018).

Re-optimize: Our ecosystem is an intricate and biologically diverse system that needs a continuous supply of water to sustain itself. The quantity of water varies according to the climatic variables and ecological complexity of the environmental system. The water cycle ensures uninterrupted supply to the ecosystem by re-optimizing the water resources to support the flora and the fauna that exists in this natural ecosystem.

Reuse: Nature treats the water as it moves below and above the ground. The processes of the evaporation, upward and downward movement of water purifies water and makes it available for reuse.

Replenish: The final phase of the water cycle is replenished where the naturally treated water is returned to the surface of the basin through Eva transportation and surface water flows.

Human Managed Water Cycle

The human managed water system works on the same principles as that of nature managed system – re-optimize, reuse, and replenish. However, the circularity of the system is disrupted by human actions. The interference breaks the water cycle and as a result, the water basins do not get replenished leading to an unprecedented water crisis.

The water systems that work on linear principles face challenges similar to other sectors operating in a linear economy and if we don't change the water management systems and processes radically, the world might have a difficult situation in hand. To ensure water sustainability new enterprise models are needed to address the growing global demands. (Water and Circular Economy, 2018).

The three pillars of wise freshwater allocation are Environmental Sustainability, Social Equity, and Resource Efficiency (Hoekstra, 2013).

Sources of Waste Water in a Linear Economy

In a linear economy model, there are 3 interventions where water is used and wasted (not reused or recycled) in a circular economy. These interventions are:

1.) Municipal and Urban Wastewater
2.) Industry
3.) Agriculture

Let us take a look into each of these interventions to determine the type and the extent of water wasted in each one of them.

Municipal Wastewater

The municipal wastewater is generated from the domestic, intuitional, and commercial sources within a human settlement or a community. The urban wastewater comprises of both municipal wastewater and urban runoff (WWDR, 2017). The wastewater production depends heavily on the form and function of the urban municipal systems and city design. A lack of due consideration in urban planning to account for water wastage leads to a poor and inefficient urban infrastructure.

The Impact of Urbanization on Wastewater Production

Urban areas across the globe face colossal challenges. The expansion of cities and urban conglomerations, changes in the family structures, and uncontrolled migration from the villages to the cities have created a constant challenge to provide adequate services to an ever-growing population. This impact gets compounded because of unforeseen events, climate change, and diminishing natural resources. These changes in urban bodies have created more inequity and conflict in society, specifically for the urban poor both in developing and developed regions of the world. According to an UN-Habitat report, the global demand for water and energy may spike up 40% and 50% by 2030 respectively. A bulk of this growth will be in the cities and urban townships. These changes call for new approaches to be adopted in wastewater management and also in the styles and functioning of the municipal bodies.

In the urban areas, the water resources remain significantly stressed because of an ever-increasing demand for water. The situation becomes even worse when these demands are not met in the urban agglomerations. Almost 80 percent of the water supply to municipalities flows back into the ecosystem as untreated wastewater, which poses a critical environmental and ecological hazard (WRG, 2016)

Most of the wastewater treatment plants do not function at maximum capacity nor conform to regulatory standards prescribed to discharge water in the streams and other water bodies. Both in smaller and larger urban settlements the municipal sewage and industrial effluents are not separated from each other. Several political, technological, social, and political challenges impair the smooth management of wastewater in the urban sector.

The demarcation of urban vs. rural territories is most commonly done by country-specific definitions based on geographic boundaries ignoring the larger considerations such as size, population, and other defining features. To understand, wastewater production it is critical to understand the different urban forms because they determine not just the production of wastewater but also its collection, treatment, and use.

1.) **Large Urban Centers:** These centers have a well-defined infrastructure, a proper central business district (CLB), expertly laid sewerage systems and networks. These centers comprise of megacities with varying degrees of expansion into smaller satellite towns. Another characteristic of these centers are growing cities and uniformly spreading population densities.
2.) **Large urban centers resulting from conurbations:** In this category, two urban centers grow individually in terms of the city area and population and finally merge into a single metropolitan area. These sewage networks are extensive but developed variedly with a few places unsewered as well.
3.) **Smaller Urban Centers:** These centers have smaller CLBs and limited sewerage networks and mostly rely on on-site sanitation.
4.) **Large villages and smaller towns:** These are compact townships with either well defined or limited sewage architectures. These could also be settlements developed around businesses or industries such as schools, college campuses, etc.
5.) **Rural areas:** These spaces entirely fall in the rural spectrum and have very little to no sewer networks. These places depend almost exclusively on on-site systems.

Sources of Water Wastage in Municipal and Urban Systems

The amount of wastewater generated in the municipal and urban systems depend upon how wastewater is collected and treated. In several lesser developed countries, only a small portion of wastewater is collected by the municipality. A large amount of the wastewater is discharged in the drained informally.

The heavily industrialized economies where the environmental laws are weak, large volumes of water are discharged without treatment. Water is also used to dilute the biological, industrial, and municipal wastes before being flushed out in the environment. Broken pipes and leakage in water networks add up to the woes of wastewater management.

In urban slum-dwellings, a high amount of fecal matter and solid wastes are discharged into the water draining canals and ditches. The solid wastes block the sewer pipes and result in flooding. The uncollected water and urban runoffs are also equally toxic as the wastewater from the sewers.

Composition of Waste Water

The exact composition of wastewater is difficult to determine, however, several factors contribute to contamination of water including domestic water use and the level of industrialization. Some of the common pollutants in wastewater are suspended solids, biodegradable organic matter, pathogens, nutrients, metals, and inorganic dissolved solids. To toxicity levels of these pollutants vary from each other.

Wastewater resulting from domestic use usually does not contain very hazardous contaminants, however, the increasing dilution of medications in domestic water waste has given rise to several health concerns. The industries that use 'Red List' materials are strictly advised to follow proper discharge norms. However, because of the lack of proper regulatory laws and enforcements, industries particularly the informal enterprises release these substances into the environment.

Small hospitals discharge medical waste through their wastewater. The waste generated because of intense farming practices is also released in the environment through water waste.

Wastewater Produced by Industries

Wastewater discharged from Industrial activities has been a challenge since the dawn of the Industrial revolution. In the earlier days, dilution was considered as the solution to pollution. With the increasing number of industrial units specifically the SMEs discharging the wastewater in the environment, the ramifications started becoming visible leading to a global calling to reduce wastewater by starting to treat it.

One of the biggest challenges with this intervention is the lack of the data available about the volumes of wastewater released in the environment and the real extent of this resource is unknown. Some limited data is available from European countries that have brought some important trends in our notice. The data shows that manufacturing is the largest producer of wastewater. Estimates also show that Industry is regarded as a single major polluter because the wastewater is seldom treated before being discharged. One estimate also suggests that the industrial wastewater will double by 2025 (WWDR, 2017). According to some biennial industrial water surveys in Canada, paper industries account for 40% of the volume of production discharges. Thermal-electric power was the largest user and discharger of water with 58% going untreated in the water bodies.

The dairy industry produces a large amount of wastewater. In the US, to produce 1 liter of milk, 1.5 – 3 liters of water are needed. Other industries such as Iron and Steel, Mining, Food, and Textiles also produce large amounts of wastewater.

Wastewater by Agriculture

Agriculture both uses and produces wastewater. The intensification of agriculture in recent years has contributed to high volumes of food production and also higher waterborne pollution loads giving rise to significant health hazards and affecting the environment at the same time.

In the past few years, agricultural practices have amplified to accommodate the growing food needs of a rapidly growing population. The area equipped under irrigation has doubled and the livestock has gone up by 3 times, from 7.3 billion in 1970 to 24.2 billion in 2011. Aquaculture has grown by 20 folds over the past 30 years.

However, the intensification of agriculture has increased soil erosion and sediment loads in water. The overuse of chemicals in agriculture (pesticides and fertilizers) have also contributed to the increased pollution loads in the environment. Excessive use of irrigation has resulted in contaminated water flowing back to the water bodies and deposited in acquirers. The pathways to pollution include percolation to groundwater, surface water run-offs, water drainage, and water flowing back to the water bodies and sediment absorption by soil erosion. The contaminated wastewater travels to the environment through these pathways. Excess nitrogen and phosphates percolate to the ground whereas water-soluble ammonia travels to the streams and rivers through soil erosion. The plant organic matter and livestock droppings also get dissolved in water to pollute it further. Other water contaminants through agriculture include salts, metals, pathogens, and drug residues.

Intersections with the Circular Economy

We are living in an age where we are witnessing a global shift from a linear economy to a circular economy. Concerns about climate change and the role of wastewater have been raised in several important forums including the UN and other global summits. An integrated approach to re-optimize, reuse, and replenish our water basins is necessary and is possible in the water sector. The use of innovative technologies to facilitate revenue generation holds very true in the wastewater intervention especially with the increasing water scarcity and rising water prices. Therefore, instead of disposing of used water as waste, it should be considered as a resource to recycle and reuse over and over again, just like the natural water cycle. A paradigm change from 'Use and Dispose' to 'use, treat and reuse' in a closed loop is needed to yield a positive impact on the environment and the economies.

To find the opportunity areas where we can extract value by the intersection of wastewater management with the circular economy, it is necessary to first understand the factors that are important to determine the feasibility of a successful water intervention for wastewater management with the circular economy. A study conducted by the 2030 water resources group in India revealed a series of factors that were important in this regard. These factors are listed below:

1.) **Drivers for initiating wastewater management:** Water Scarcity is the most important factor to push for wastewater reuse. The water reclaimed through the treatment of wastewater can be an important input for the industry. Dependence of imported water can also be a driver for wastewater management. For example, Singapore imports water from Malaysia to meet its water requirements. In this wake of this situation, the island nation deployed many water treatment wastewater reuse initiatives.
2.) **Government Policies and Regulations:** The intersection of wastewater management with the circular economy is only possible if the national and local governments demonstrate a political will to implement the change through regulations on wastewater discharges and favorable policies to develop wastewater management.
3.) **Access to technology and finance:** The initial cost of implementing wastewater treatment and management systems is high. Therefore, if a city or an urban agglomeration has the land and finances to develop wastewater management systems, then the entry of private entities operating in this space will become easier. Access to water treatment technology is also necessary for profitable implementation.
4.) **The scale of Intervention:** Even though centralized systems work better to meet the demands on a large scale, however, they are not always easy to deploy and operate. The decentralized systems present an interim but effective solution to the problem. The decentralized treatment systems can be established at entrepreneurial/community levels and can appropriately perform wastewater management at the local level. The decentralized models also present opportunities for self-employment and women empowerment.
5.) **Strategy and Partnerships:** The intervention may require a range of stakeholders to work together to implement wastewater management solutions. This is needed to bring expertise and institutional power to the project. The government is the key stakeholder that needs to partner with water implementers, community leaders, NGOs, and CSR units of donor corporations. Industry collaboration should be encouraged to bring a strong economic perspective to the intervention.

6.) **Public Perception:** Community awareness and consumer sentiment are critical if the project needs to scale commercially. The government and other stakeholders should keep aside some funds to create awareness and community mobilization.

Opportunity Areas for Extracting Value

According to the current projections, the world population will become 9.1 billion by 2050 with over 60% of the population living in the cities. To accommodate the growing needs of the population, it will become critical to improve the water circularity to make sure that the stability of the environment is not lost. Some areas of intervention are energy systems, food production, Industry, and Agriculture.

Water is the key component in electricity generation from thermal and hydropower plants. Globally 15% of freshwater withdrawals and made to generate power. There are opportunities to reduce water in energy and also generate energy from wastewater. Water use can also be cut down in food production and industrial processes.

Water can be reused both for potable and non-potable applications. Some businesses can directly use the wastewater if it of the appropriate quality. Some noteworthy non-potable purposes of recycled water are:

- Irrigation of public parks and recreation centers, sports complexes, golf courses, schoolyards, highways, public places, etc
- Irrigation of landscaped areas surrounding residential complexes
- Irrigation of landscaped areas surrounding commercial and industrial complexes
- Commercial uses such as laundry and cars washing
- Ornamental surroundings such as fountains, artificial waterfalls, and pools

In industries, wastewater can be recycled several times over. This reduces the cost of sourcing freshwater from water bodies and lessens the toxic discharges in the environment. Industrial symbiosis can be attained if the by-products of one industry become the feedstocks of the others. For example, steam or hot wastewater can be reused for industrial purposes and easily recoverable solvents can bring economic value. The best application of industrial symbiosis can be seen in the Eco-Industrial parks where the industries are strategically located near one another so that the industries can take benefits of the proximity of each other. The eco-industrial parks provide the benefits of in house water recycling in a closed-loop, however, they require long term commitments to justify the initial CAPEX.

The Industries can reclaim the water from municipalities for industrial uses. In a few countries, the municipalities custom treat water for Industry requirements.

Symbiosis can be achieved in the agricultural sector as well. Integrated aquaculture-agriculture where crops, vegetables, livestock, trees, and fish are managed at the same place, leads to better optimization of resources, increased efficiency, and water re-use in closed loops. Similarly, integrated farming could lead to better resource utilization.

Wastewater can be used both directly and indirectly in agriculture. Using water directly means using water for some directly beneficial purpose irrigation or livestock maintenance. Indirect water usage means refilling groundwater, aquifers, lakes, and ponds with treated and semi-treated water. This water remains with nature as a safe deposit for later use. The uses of wastewater can also be realized in irrigation, aquaculture, and livestock.

Assessments and Frameworks

There are several assessment tools available to establish a framework that links water to a circular economy. One of the important frameworks is ReSOLVE that has been developed by Mckinsey and Ellen Mac Arthur Foundation. The framework consists of six action areas for businesses and countries that want to gravitate towards a circular economy. The six action areas are:

- Regenerate
- Share
- Optimize
- Loop
- Virtualize and
- Exchange

Some other similar assessment tools are 'Water Utility Pathways in Circular Economy' developed by the International Water Association and the 7s Model and AWS standard developed by Arup.

CONCLUSION

The circular economy is an apt alternative to currently operational linear systems to ensure sustainable consumption and growth. The water sector is one of the most underrated areas in terms of economic potential and social impact. It is also an area that can be integrated into the circular economy more easily than other sectors. Most importantly, there is a critical need for the water sector to transition towards a circular economy model. A positive step in this direction will bring a huge paradigm shift in our lives and work systems.

REFERENCES

Aayog, N. I. T. I. (2018). *Composite Water Management Index*. NITI Aayog.

Aayog, N. I. T. I. (2019). *Composite Water Management Index 2.0*. NITI Aayog.

Earthdata. (n.d.). *Freshwater Availability*. Retrieved from https://earthdata.nasa.gov/: https://earthdata.nasa.gov/learn/toolkits/freshwater-availability

Estimated Use of Water in the United States. (2000). Retrieved from https://water.usgs.gov/: https://water.usgs.gov/watuse/data/2000/

Gleick, P. H. S. H. (1996). Water resources. In *Encyclopedia of Climate and Weather* (pp. 817-823). New York: Oxford University Press. Retrieved from Freshwater Watch: https://freshwaterwatch.thewaterhub.org/content/water-limited-resource

Hoekstra, A. Y. (2013). Sustainable, efficient, and equitable water use: The three pillars under wise freshwater allocation. *WIREs. Water*.

OMICS International. (n.d.). *Water Management Importance.* Retrieved from https://www.omicsonline.org/water-management-importance.php

Rutger Willem Hofste, P. R. (2019, August 6). *17 Countries, Home to One-Quarter of the World's Population, Face Extremely High Water Stress.* Retrieved from https://www.wri.org/: https://www.wri.org/blog/2019/08/17-countries-home-one-quarter-world-population-face-extremely-high-water-stress

School, Water Science. (n.d.). *The Water in You: Water and the Human Body.* Retrieved from https://www.usgs.gov/special-topic/water-science-school/science/water-you-water-and-human-body?qt-science_center_objects=0#qt-science_center_objects

The Water Cycle for Adults and Advanced Students. (n.d.). Retrieved from https://www.usgs.gov/: https://www.usgs.gov/special-topic/water-science-school/science/water-cycle-adults-and-advanced-students?qt-science_center_objects=0#qt-science_center_objects

UNESCO World Water Assessment Programme. (2017). *The United Nations world water development report, 2017: Wastewater: The untapped resource.* UNESCO.

USGS. (n.d.). *How Much Water is There on Earth?* Retrieved from https://www.usgs.gov/: https://www.usgs.gov/special-topic/water-science-school/science/how-much-water-there-earth

Veolia Water. (n.d.). *The Water Impact Index and the First Carbon-Water Analysis of a Major Metropolitan Water Cycle.* Water and Circular Economy. (Original work published 2018)

Water Use Data and Their Application. (2002). In Estimating Water Use in the United States: A New Paradigm (pp. 36-67). The National Academies Press.

WRG. (2016). *Circular Economy Pathways for Municipal Wastewater Management in India: A Practitioner's Guide.* WRG.

WWDR. (2017). *Wastewater the untapped resource.* United Nations Educational, Scientific and Cultural Organization.

ENDNOTE

1 *Watershed Balance:* The total volume of water present at a given time in the water basin.

Chapter 17
Protection of Intangible Heritage:
Need to Reassess the Framework

Vinayak Jhamb
University School of Law and Legal Studies, Guru Gobind Singh Indraprastha University, India

Konpal Kaur
University of Oxford, UK

ABSTRACT

The convention concerning the protection of cultural and natural heritage only emphasizes the protection of tangible cultural heritage. However, the present convention completely turned a blind eye and a deaf ear to the intangible cultural heritage. "Cultural heritage" as a term and its content are largely taken from other fields like anthropology and archaeology. The legal aspect of cultural heritage is most complex and difficult to understand. There also exist elements of intangible culture which would include songs or folklore musical traditions, ceremonial or ritual traditions, aspects of the life of ancient societies, and any special relationship between the people and the land that they inhabited. With the term property also comes the idea of assigning the artifact a market value whereas they are historically priceless. Cultural heritage has been made global and a part of universal heritage or "common heritage of mankind."

INTRODUCTION

Every country is endowed with a specific cultural frame which is not only unique but is genetically embedded in each and every person living in that country. There are certain practices and usages which predominantly guide one's behaviour. Every country has a plethora of activities which are crucial for the very existence of that country. It is time and again quoted that people living in a specific cultural set up should never forget their roots. But, in this post-modern world, all these tradition principles and practices have taken a backseat. The values which have been cherished since time immemorial have hid

DOI: 10.4018/978-1-7998-4990-2.ch017

themselves under the veil of so-called modernity. Also, the international community at large is promoting "pluralism" at the forefront which directly intersects "cultural relativist" tendencies of the world.

Everyone wishes to get attached with their own set of ideas governed by the culture they are brought up in. However, in the post-modern world, these traditional cultural nuances have taken preceded by new set of ideologies emanating out of the new world order. There has always been a persistent debate among the academicians about the definition of the term "cultural heritage". It is a comprehensive term which is difficult to define with utmost precision. Even, the legal aspect of cultural heritage is highly difficult to comprehend and thus, it's over arching connotations are inextricably interwoven with law.

"Cultural heritage" as a term and its content are difficult to maneuver. The legal aspect of cultural heritage is most complex and difficult to understand (Prott and O'Keefe, 1989 pp.8). The term cultural heritage in legal sense as per UNESCO regulations of 1973 encompasses several main categories of heritage namely:

1. Tangible cultural heritage
2. Intangible cultural heritage
3. Natural heritage
4. Heritage affected in cases of armed conflict

The intangible heritage is intangible as stated above is not in strict terms but due to their evolvement process. The process of intangibility in heritage goes far beyond aesthetic contemplation and has some practical usage to it (Bortolotto 2007, p21).

Let us understand this by an example. When we talk about performers of intangible heritage like Kutiyattam dance form of Kerala we are talking not just about the performance but also the space it theoretically takes up along with the notion that what is being performed belongs to the public, created by them or their forbears and also performed for them. Tangible heritage is easy to identify but intangible heritage can only be discovered by practical observation (Wittgenstein 1958 p 43).

GLOSSARY

Before going any further, basic terms which shall appear in the chapter have been defined hereunder:

A. **Common Heritage of Mankind**: This principle of international law states that some cultural and natural resources are prevalent irrespective of the territorial boundaries. Everyone has an inherent right over these resources.
B. **Cultural relativism**: It refers to those practices which form the core of a cultural group or a nation. They do not get subdued by the universal practices which are being adopted by the post-modern world.
C. **Folklore tradition:** The activities which have been an intrinsic part of the cultural practices of a nation. These include songs, dance forms and other skills.
D. **Heritage in the event of armed conflict:** These includes monuments, complex of buildings of archaeological and historic significance, ancient works of art which have been abandoned as the off-shoot of any armed conflict.
E. **Intangible cultural heritage:** oral traditions, performing arts, rituals of a particular cultural group.

F. **Natural heritage:** natural sites with cultural aspects such as cultural landscapes, physical, biological or geological formations of a nation.

G. **Performer's rights:** any person who practices music, art or any other activity which can be recorded and put to further use should have rights. It includes economic as well as moral rights.

H. **Tangible cultural heritage**: movable cultural heritage (paintings, sculptures, coins, manuscripts, immovable cultural heritage (monuments, archaeological sites, and so on) and underwater cultural heritage (shipwrecks, underwater ruins and cities).

BACKGROUND

UNESCO conventions deal with mainly tangible cultural heritage. Also "cultural property" in legal sense restricts to tangible objects. Property is the basic premise around which some significant theories have come up (Prott and O'Keefe 1989, p 307). With the term property, comes the concept of allocating the artifact a market value whereas they are historically priceless. This leads to a question on ethics of trading the artifact. Therefore, the category of intangible heritage cannot be covered under the term "cultural property" for some of them are only expressed in terms of idea or knowledge and they are part of IPR and copyright rules (Gerntsblith, 2007).

Definition and understanding of cultural heritage were generally promoted by western world. These definitions were too narrow and considered only tangible heritage for eg say "Taj Mahal" and did not consider any idea or expression of our weavers say "Sambalpuri" or "Ikkat" weaving. The understanding needs to be broadened specially in developing countries to completely understand and protect it (Prott 1998, pp.222-236). When the idea of inheritance is added further to cultural heritage it gains some more meaning. Inheritance of intangible heritage has an implicit connotation of being passed from present generation to future. Cultural Heritage has been made global and a part of universal heritage or "Common Heritage of Mankind" (Lowenthal 2014).

Out of all the categories of the cultural heritage explained above, the focal point of the present research shall be Intangible cultural heritage. But, before delving into the intricacies of the topic, it is better to explore various connotations which can be attached to the term, "intangible cultural heritage". As the name suggests, it highlights all those oral traditions, usages and customary rituals which have been practiced in a country since time immemorial. The contours of this term are wide and expanding. It shall entail all those dance forms and localised songs which have remained an eternal part of one's culture. The Kutiyattam dance form of Kerala is a clear exemplification of "intangible cultural heritage". Whenever there is a discussion pertaining to performers of intangible heritage like Kutiyattam dance form of Kerala, it is not just about the performance but also the space it theoretically takes up along with the notion that what is being performed belongs to the public, created by them or their forbears and also performed for them (K Ranganathan, 2009). But, the present research paradigm revolves around one particular question, "How can these traditionalized dance forms or songs be protected under the realms of the law of the land?' Therefore, protection of rights of these performers is the fundamental objective of this study. But, this protection has been provided by the performer's right given in Section 38 in the Copyright Act, 1957 in India which was added by the Copyright Amendment Act, 2012. Not only in India, but there are specific international conventions and treaties which have governed the performers rights since a long time. These are as follows:

1. Rome Convention of 1961

The first international convention governing the "neighbouring rights" of the artists was the Rome Convention of 1961. This convention gave audio-visual rights of the performance to the artists. However, the scope of this convention was restricted in terms of sound-only recordings which did not enjoy the benefits emanating out of this convention. So, this convention was not sufficient to address the issues relating to the rights of performers and therefore, two different set of conventions came up at the forefront.

2. The WIPO Copyright Treaty 1996 and The WIPO Performances and Phonograms Treaty 1996

These conventions deal with the rights of two kinds: (i) performers rights (ii) producers of phonograms rights

These holistically provided the legal framework for the rights of performers at an international level. So, with this set of international framework in mind, the researchers shall go ahead emphasising the need and the sanctity of the rights of these local performers who have been ignored since a long time.

1. MAIN FOCUS OF THE CHAPTER

1.1 *Issues Involved in the Chapter*

It is difficult to comprehend the right of possessor over the cultural heritage. There are flourishing IP laws but Cultural autonomy and preservation are at the heart of the right to culture and a society needs to balance the competing right of private ownership against collective use of protected intellectual property. The rights of possessor need to be restricted and there should be separation of access and control from ownership.

There are three main issues:

- First, it is difficult to identify the exact connotation of intangible heritage to be protected and more difficult to formulate common framework for its identification.
- Secondly, the characterization of something as intangible heritage such as folklore as part of "common heritage of mankind" has its inherent contradiction. The character of heritage is intimately linked with specific community and the idea of it being heritage of mankind holds lesser ground (Lowenthal 2014, p. 227).
- Lastly, ensuring the dignity of labour of the performers have been a herculean task as they are highly unorganized and the governmental agencies have always turned a blind eye and a deaf ear to the pleas of these localized performers. The unorganized sector has always been vehemently criticized for ill-treatment and drudgery for the workers. So, in the light of such exploitation, this step can illuminate the lives of those marginalized people who solely rely on their locale skills for their living.

The Convention on Biological Diversity was adopted at the Earth Summit in Rio de Janeiro in 1992. It is an international treaty for the conservation of biodiversity, the sustainable use of the same thereby establishing sovereignty of States over the natural and genetic resources geographically located in the

State. However, there needs to be a careful balance between international interest in conservation and the sovereignty of the state over the resources.

1.2 *Connotations of the Term Cultural Heritage vis-à-vis Cultural Property*

Before analyzing the law pertaining to the cultural heritage, it is essential to attribute definite connotations to the term, "cultural heritage". The definition provided by the Convention concerning the Protection of Cultural and Natural Heritage under Article 1 includes and entails:

1. All the monuments, architectural works, scriptures, paintings which are of exceptional value from the point of view of history, science and art.
2. Buildings or group of buildings which are of exceptional value from the point of view of history, science and art.
3. Sites, whether natural or artificial which are also of exceptional value from the point of view of history, science and art.

The definition has restricted amplitude as only three categorical classifications are included under the realms of the Convention. Therefore the researchers look to establish that not only above items but others like various art forms, dances, songs of a particular cultural set up that have been accepted and inherited by people of that nation /community for a long time should also be part of cultural heritage. Those peculiar usages should also find a due place under the Convention. However, this particular convention turns a blind eye and a deaf ear to these intangible songs or dance forms which have been performed in various nations. Even the Statute of International Court of Justice under Article 38(c) (ICJ Statute) discusses general legal principles around the world as a source of international law. They are considered as a source of international law because of their stature, eminence and usage across the globe uniformly irrespective of the different legal systems prevailing around the Earth. Similarly, there are many examples of cultural nuances which are inherently imbedded in the minds of people in that nation, continent. So, these intangible cultural items like folk songs, localized dance performances etc. should also come under the purview of the Convention (William, 1986).

At present, this is not the case as the convention under Article 1 defines it as any monument, sites or group of buildings etc. Thus, the definition of the term, "cultural heritage" is restricted to physical or tangible cultural heritage only and completely excludes the intangible part of the cultural heritage. Also, the term "cultural property" under Article 11 of the Convention is restricted to tangible objects only. Whenever the idea of property is talked about, it always comes with the idea of assigning the artifact a market value whereas they are historically priceless. This leads us to a more important question on the ethics of trading that artifact in the market. Therefore, the category of intangible heritage cannot be covered under the term "cultural property" for some of them are only expressed in terms of idea or knowledge and they are part of IPR and copyright rules. Not only this, but the prospective chapter shall also revolve around the plight of these local performers whose art and skills have not been acknowledged by the civil society. So, all those monuments which are visible on the face of it, not only become an intrinsic part of the "cultural heritage" but even the intangible art forms and skills have to be included under the definition of "cultural heritage". So, all the localized dance forms or any plays, anecdotes shall be preserved as they provide the trajectory of enhancing the culture of that particular nation.

2. PROBLEMS IDENTIFIED BY THE AUTHORS UNDER THIS CHAPTER

The authors have identified the following problems around which the entire chapter revolves:

- Lack of cognizance of intangible cultural heritage

Intangible cultural heritage is a new area which needs to be explored fully so that framework can be framed for the same. The existing international convention, as discussed above does not acknowledge the intangible form of cultural heritage. So, the international community needs to reconsider the existing framework pertaining to protection and preservation of cultural heritage by expanding the contours of the definition of cultural heritage.

- Lack of clarity on performer's rights

The international regime does not completely address the rights of the localized performers under the IPR framework. This leads to the ill-treatment of the localized performers. So, the need for a specific convention on the performer's economic and morals rights has to be worked upon. The scope of the existing international conventions on this issue is restricted and limited and thus, do not fully cover the rights of the performers.

3. RESEARCH QUESTIONS OF THE CHAPTER

The authors shall be covering these set of research questions within the framework of this Chapter:

- Analysis of existing laws on the issue

The authors intend to analyze the existing laws pertaining to performer's rights in India and their sanctity thereof. The purpose of this study is to have a deep understanding of the present legal paraphernalia on the issue and analyze the detailed nuances of the same.

- Exploring the concept of intangible cultural heritage

The researchers shall also discuss the paradigm of intangible cultural heritage in the international as well as national context. It is a novel concept and not much work has been done under its realms. Therefore, the authors shall deeply explore the various paradigms and contours of this new concept on the bloc and examine its sanctity thereof.

- Examining the contours of cultural rights in India and abroad

The researchers shall analyze the international legal framework relating to cultural rights and their application in India territory as well. It is a herculean task to define the term cultural rights with utmost clarity and precision. Therefore, the authors shall discuss the concept in detail and find out the present definition and connotations of the same in the present scenario.

- Suggestions for a broader and better framework

Lastly, the authors shall give adequate suggestions for the enhancement and advancement of law over the issues stated above. The suggestions given shall essentially talk about creation of a broader framework wherein old paradigms are wiping off and new shifts are being witnessed. So, the new law has to pave way for the changes happening around it.

4. HERITAGE CONSERVATION FRAMEWORK - ANALYSIS OF THE INTERNATIONAL LAW AT PRESENT

Need of reservation of artifacts has been felt since ancient times (Trigger 2006, pp 29-36). However, it was only in 1907 that Cultural Heritage first found a place for discussion in international arena where the total number of countries involved in discussion was just 65. UNESCO came with The Convention for the Protection of Cultural Property of Armed Conflict in 1954 (Convention, 1907) which is treated as one of the earliest international heritage protection texts. It dealt only with movable and immovable property and was primarily aimed at response to destruction (Blake 2000). It had an element of reconciliation with only 76 states becoming a part of it and only 6 of them were from South East Asia. It is under Hague convention that for first time it was decided that "Cultural Property" could not be sold without reflection of heritage. The idea was mooted that artifacts need protection and their illicit movement needs to be controlled.

In 1956 UNESCO adopted a Recommendation on the Conduct of Archaeological excavation. This was very limited in its approach but subsequently became fundamental to UNESCO's approach to heritage protection. It lays down that the protection of cultural heritage is the need of the hour in the international as well as national regime. Further recommendations of UNESCO followed on specific issues like Accessibility of Museums (1960) Safeguarding the beauty of landscapes rights (1962)' and Preserving cultural property endangered by public or private works (1968). Two UNESCO Conventions were adopted in the early 1970s, and they related to Prohibition and Prevention of trafficking in Cultural Property (1970), Protection of World Cultural and Natural Heritage (1972).

It is post 1972 that trend developed towards the concept of defining and understanding "Common heritage of Mankind". Intangible heritage more often than not is presented by nations as emblems of their identity for tourism. This leads us to "Cultural identity" which is closely related to "Cultural Rights". The commitment of UNESCO in the specific field of non-material cultural expression has a long history. However, there was a pivotal shift during 1990s in western academic perspective and method, to a process-oriented approach based largely on Japanese paradigm which was shifting towards intangible heritage or the idea of a "living cultural property". The recent intangible cultural heritage programs of UNESCO include, The living Human Treasures programme (1993), and Proclamation of the Masterpieces of oral and intangible heritage (1997).

The final adoption of Convention of Safeguarding of Intangible Cultural Heritage (Paris, 17 October 2003) was a landmark in the movement of protection of intangible heritage. This is very helpful for countries like India for they give a voice to previously excluded grassroots communities and seeks to safeguard living processes which are under threat from capitalism. The developing member states like India face vast under-elaboration in the field of traditional culture. Japanese took lead and reiterated that their culture was living process-oriented culture and not monument based. To explain they believe that

Mt Fuji is Fuji san i.e. living-mountain. This coincided with the growth of a wider discontent concerning to provincial approach to heritage as defined in 1972 convention (Ogino 1995). This has found many allies amongst African and South Asian countries for their history and culture very much like India where issues of national culture and multiple ethnicity comes into frequent conflict. In the course of recent years, internationally legal efforts have been made to safeguard cultural heritage.

Then the Convention on Protection and Promotion of Diversity of Cultural Expression 2005 came at the international forefront. UNESCO has faced increasing criticism from members, civil society and academicians. Current legal regime also faces challenges in these areas. There is a question whether heritage is matter of international law at all. It is general consensus that cultural heritage needs to be preserved. The method to protect needs introspection and change in assumptions.

Certain universality is given to cultural heritage law by UNESCO and legal instruments. Legal scholars view these instruments as the destruction of heritage as loss to the international community, or of 'great importance to mankind'. The heritage laws express universal value but overlook the concept of living heritage and Human Rights. However, there are certain situations in which international involvement becomes important so that cultural heritage can be protected. Security Council recognized it in Resolution no 2347 in 2017 and thus came UN council Declaration on the Rights of Indigenous people in September 2017.

It talks about the rights of the indigenous people over their cultural traditions and customs. The contours of these rights include a plethora of rights under its domain namely: right to maintain, protect and develop the manifestations of their cultures ranging from archaeological and historical sites, artifacts, designs, ceremonies, technologies and visual and performing arts and literature.

States need to work towards effective mechanisms with communities and their own customs. In case of heritage of indigenous people it can be safely said that the language of international law should to ensure the protection of the heritage of minorities within a given State.

This requires a need for a comprehensive definition of "Cultural" for the purpose of any attempt at identifying "Cultural Rights". In a quest to define "Cultural Rights" the same difficulties exist of identifying the nature of the "Culture" to which these rights are to be related as when identifying the nature of the "Culture" of which the "Heritage" is to be protected and passed on to future generations. When we try to assimilate and understand "Culture" in relation to "Rights" it is only then we can gain better understanding of the nature of "Cultural Heritage" itself for "Cultural Rights" especially intangible may include a set of rights of people (Kamenka 1982). This new understanding of "Cultural Rights" thus extends a right to protection of heritage. Intangible heritage involves an element of construction of "Cultural identity" which needs to be preserved (Kamenka 1982 pp. 134). However, the consideration of the existence and nature of cultural rights associated with cultural heritage involves complex issues of identity that can lead to widely conflicting interest. It is not far-fetched that Human Rights have an element of "Cultural Heritage" which Universal Declaration of Human Rights in 1948 refers to as "Cultural Rights" in its preamble. (LAW of this is UNGA Res.127A(III); UN Doc. A/811). This is generally seen in the sense of religious freedom and expression. Its connection with historical heritage is something very recent. Prott sees this as a very natural transition and understanding for the purpose of protection and preservation (Prott and O'Keefe 1989, p 95). It also seems appropriate that rather than creating new right to "Cultural Heritage" it is better to enforce of existing cultural heritage instruments and the develop the laws already in place. There is need to take conscious effort in UNESCO to focus away from its founding western museological principals in favour of a more anthropological and global vision of cultural properties (Bortolotto 2007).

There is an urgent threat off erosion and exploitation of traditional cultural expression and popular "ethnic" culture specially under emerging right-wing politics (Kreps 2003). We need to acknowledge that rhetoric of nation building has changed in India partly in answer to transformation in global order and partly, because of political trend in the country. It is in these times that we need heritage protection and preservation especially in relation to ethnic minorities. India is going through the process of Neoliberal nationalism where privatization is influencing not only national ideology but even the state sentiment in form of personal responsibility. Here state is playing two roles where it simultaneously supports a private industry along with trying to promote the public culture on which the very industry is founded on. We are seeing a trend of commodification of not only cultural forms but also performers which is a blow to small scale craftsmen. The nationalist ideology is governed by growing hegemony of the economic order of globalization. Also, UNESCO Conventions are not enforceable and have advisory value which further reduces protection. There is lack of global consensus and negotiating skills of developing and undeveloped world where one can find most of cultural heritage.

Following the culmination of Uruguay Round of Multilateral Trade Negotiation, The Parliament came up with the 1994 amendment so that the Copyright law should become synchronized with the TRIPS Agreement. The TRIPS Agreement which was constituted in 1994 talked about "performer's rights" in brief. Thus, the Indian Parliament decided to come up with a law that caters to the needs of the performer's who have never got their due in terms of economic and moral rights.

The definition of performance was revamped and it meant as well as included, "any visual or acoustic presentation made live by one or more performers". Further, the amendment encompasses the definition of a performer which shall include an actor, singer, musician, dancer, acrobat, juggler, conjurer, snake charmer, a person delivering the lecture or any other person who makes a performance. Thus, a dancer comes under the definition of the performer. So, all those localized dancers and singers and other artisans relying on their traditional skills as the only source of their livelihood. But, they have never been equated with the other performers who perform at a massive scale. Even though they also perform live in front of the audience, the particular provision does not explicitly talk about the rights of those localized performers whose voices have been subjugated because of economic disparities.

5. CASE STUDY OF BELLY DANCE AS INTANGIBLE CULTURAL HERITAGE

The definition of cultural heritage is being widely interpreted, particularly after coming up of the Convention in the year 2003. The definition itself states that Intangible heritage is decided by individuals and groups in nations. However, the critics have always argued that cultural activities like dance cannot be country-specific and therefore, opinion of the individuals or groups should not be taken into consideration. There are some dance forms which have been adequately accepted in various parts of the world and therefore international recognition should be provided to them.

Ballet Dance heritage originated in the Middle East has spread around the world as a renowned form of dance style. It has taken up different forms and shapes in different jurisdictions. The international community has acknowledged its global prevalence. However, inclusion of the belly dance in the intangible cultural heritage is still questionable. This dance form is being practiced in various parts of the world: Chinese Ballet Swan, Grupo Corpo, Oriental Style Belly dancing etc. The world legal order needs to understand the sanctity of such cultural artefacts and include them under the domain of Intangible Cultural heritage as expounded under the Convention of 2003.

6. A CASE STUDY OF INTANGIBLE CULTURE HERITAGE-ANALYSIS OF PERFORMER'S RIGHTS IN INDIA

6.1 Introduction

The rights of the performers, record producers as well as the rights of broadcasting organizations are collectively known as neighboring rights. They are called likewise as they do not form an intrinsic part of the Copyright Act, 1957 but operate in absolute parallel with the Copyright law.

The performers also constitute an essential element of the Copyright law. Even though they are well-versed with their skill but still they do not get the due recognition for their art. There are many traditional skills like weaving and plethora of songs and dance forms which are sacrosanct to the roots of a country's culture have not been adequately recognized. So, these local artisans and dancers are not able to secure protection or any benefits from the Copyright Act, 1957. Prior to the Copyright Amendment Act, 1994 there was no mention of the "performer's rights" under the statute as well. Copyright subsisted in translation or abridgement but the performance rights were never granted to the performers. Therefore, this Amendment Act brought a ray of hope for these localized performers in getting the due recognition. The performance of these performers did not fit into any of the categories mentioned under section 13 of the Copyright Act, 1957.

The question whether performance rights can be covered by Copyright Act came up before Bombay High Court in the case of *Fortune International Film v. Dev Anand* wherein the actor was approached for a movie named, "Darling Darling" and para 7 of the agreement stated that all the rights pertaining to the performance shall be vested in the producers and the performers (actors) in this case. The respondent filed a case against the producers for claiming the rights over his own performance and the lower court accepted his proposition in totality. However, the producers were not happy with the decision of the lower court and appealed against the said decision in the Appellate court. This Court categorically stated that the actor's performance does not become a part of the 'artistic work'. Therefore, the Court did not acknowledge the performer's rights of the actor in the film. It can be clearly understood that prior to the 1994 amendment, the Copyright Act, 1957 was absolutely silent on the issue in question.

The present Chapter revolves around a different question which discusses the lacuna of the Act full-fledgedly. The entire research circles around the need of having a legislative cover for the traditional performers who solely rely on their parochial skills as a source of livelihood. But, the Copyright Act, 1957 does not explicitly talk about any specific provision for the issue in question. Even though they give broad provisions in the form of section 38A and section 38B to boost up the performer's rights in the country but still they did not cover the targeted population under the present research.

The local artisans, dancers, singers still suffer even after the amendment. So, to bridge the gap between the present Copyright law and the problem in question, the legislators should try to come up with certain rules as well as regulations so that these parochial performers should also get the benefit of the Copyright law. However, it has to be stated that the law does not categorically distinguish between any performer and it uses a holistic term, "performer". The term performer entails all types or kinds of performers including those traditional performers who have been relying on their parochial skills for earning a livelihood. But, owing to these reasons, these traditional performers are not able to derive the benefit of the Copyright law in India:

1. Emanation from a village setup- These traditional performers generally hail from small villages and are usually indifferent to the legal system which is operating on a macro-level.
2. Unawareness about law- These people do not know much about the prevailing law and neither do they intend to know it.
3. Financial circumstances- The traditional performers usually suffer from abject poverty and do not possess the requisite interest to carry-forward their claim.

So, these are some of the plausible reasons because of which the traditional performers have not been able to get the benefit of the Copyright law in India. Thus, these localized performers have always been facing the brunt of these nuances of Copyright law in India.

The Court has also taken varied stance on the issue of performers rights under the Copyright Act, 1957. There have been instances where the Court has taken up a particular stand but eventually changed that stand in a subsequent case. There is plethora of cases wherein the Court has taken a different standpoint owing to the same issues which arose in those cases. Like in a recent case, which has been termed as a setback to composers and lyricists of music in India wherein a Division Bench of the Delhi High Court in the case of *IPRS v. Aditya Pandey & CRI Events*, which dismissed IPRS's appeal against the order of a Single Judge who had held that radio stations etc., who were broadcasting/communicating 'sound recordings' were required to pay royalty to only the owner of the sound recording and not the owner of the lyrics or the musical works which had been incorporated into the sound recordings. The judgment which can be accessed over here is the latest in series of similar judgments from a Single Judge at the Bombay High Court and a Division Bench at the High Court of Kerala. So, this judgment clearly indicates the performer's rights at time are compromised as well.

6.2 Economic Rights of Performer's

However, still the Copyright law in India lays down the rights of the performers under section 38A of the Copyright Act, 1957. This provision was added by the Copyright (Amendment) Act, 2012. The provision reads as under:

"The exclusive rights of the performers are without prejudice to the rights conferred on author, and subject to the provisions of the Act. The performers have exclusive rights to do or authorize the doing of any of the following acts in respect of the performance or any substantial part thereof, namely:

1. To make a sound recording or a visual recording of the performance, including:
    a. Reproduction of it in any material form including the sorting of it in any medium by electronic or any other means;
    b. Issuance of copies of it to the public not being copies already in circulation;
    c. Communication of it to the public;
    d. Selling or giving it on commercial rental or offer for sale or for commercial rental any copy of the recording.
2. To broadcast or communicate the performance to the public except where the performance is already broadcast".

These economic rights of the performers were laid down for the first time in the Copyright (Amendment) Act, 2012. These economic rights were available for all the activities which were provided under section 13 of the Copyright Act, 1957. But, post 2012 amendment the economic rights were also bestowed upon the performers as well. However, the only exception with respect to these rights is whenever a performer has expressed his consent to the incorporation of his performance in a cinematographic film by written agreement, he shall not be allowed to question the producer's claim over the economic rights which were earlier bestowed upon the performer himself. So, in this scenario, the performer cannot claim his rights back once he enters into such an agreement.

6.3 Moral Rights of The Performers

Not only the economic rights, but even the moral rights have been provided to the performers who have been deprived of such rights before the Copyright (Amendment) Act, 2012. This amendment inserted a new provision in the Copyright Act, 1957 which talks about the moral rights of the performers. Section 38B of the Act is similar to section 57 of the same Act which explicitly deals with moral rights of a Copyright holder. This was done to bring the present Copyright law in India in absolute conformity with the provisions of WIPO Performances and Phonograms Treaty, 1996.

Section 38B talks about two set of moral rights to the performer. These are available to them even after their economic rights have been exhausted partly or completely. These are as follows:

1. Right of identification- First moral right discusses the right of identification of the performer. This right essentially delves into the process of identifying the original performer so as to give the performer his/her due recognition. The only exception to this rule is that the nature of performance does not indicate the true and original performer.
2. Right to claim damages- The performer, once identified has the right to claim damages or compensation for any destruction, mutilation or modification/alteration of his performance which becomes detrimental for the performer's reputation. However, any modification or alteration for the purpose of recording or for purely technical reasons shall not amount to mutilation/destruction.

These two moral rights have been provided by the Copyright (Amendment) Act, 2012 which not only ensure financial stability but also adequate recognition to the original performers.

But, the applicability of the performer's rights is not universal in nature. There are striking exceptions to the above norm. These are as follows:

1. Making of any sound or video recording for the private use or solely for the purposes of bona fide teaching or research.
2. Using the excerpts of a performance or its broadcast solely for the purpose of bona fide teaching or research.
3. Such other acts which do not cause infringement under section 52 of the Copyright Act, 1957.

6.4 Law Relating to Term for Performer's Rights

The Copyright (Amendment) Act of 1994 discussed the duration of performer's rights for the first time under the realms of Copyright law in India. It fixed the duration of 25 years from the date of the performance. But, it did not completely comply with the TRIPS Agreement as Article 14 of the Agreement laid down the term of copyright for a performer as 50 years. Thus, the provisions came in direct conflict with each other.This anamoly was overcome by introducing adequate amendment in the year 2012 in Copyright law in India which increased the duration from 25 to 50 years.

6.5 An Analysis of Traditional Knowledge law and Localized Performers

The present chapter revolved around linking the problem of localized performers with existing laws of the country. The interpretation clause of The Protection of Traditional knowledge, Genetic Resources and Expressions of Folklore Act, 2016 talks about the definition of "expressions of folklore" which is defined as *"any form, whether tangible or intangible, in which traditional culture and knowledge is expressed, appears or manifests, and includes the following forms of expressions or combinations:*

a. verbal expressions, including stories, epics, legends, poetry, riddles and other narratives, words, signs, names and symbols;
b. musical expressions, including songs and instrumental music;
c. expressions by movement or incorporating movement, including dances, plays, artistic forms, rituals and other performances, whether or not reduced to a material form;
d. tangible expressions, including productions of art, drawings, designs, paintings, body painting, carvings, sculptures, pottery, terracotta, mosaic, woodwork, metal ware, jewelry, baskets, needlework, textiles, glassware, carpets, costumes, handicrafts, musical instruments and architectural forms;
e. any other output of creative and cumulative intellectual activity characteristic of a traditional community's distinctive cultural identity and traditional heritage developed and maintained by that traditional community, individuals or groups who have the right or responsibility to do so in accordance with customary laws and practices."

Thus, this definition of folklore expression entails all the localized dance forms and songs and all the traditional skills and traits which are an essential part of the folklore should be provided the due legal sanctity. Thus, the rights of the localized performers should not only come under the domain of Copyright law in India but this law as well.

CONCLUSION AND SUGGESTIONS

Cultural heritage is an integral part of cultural identity which justifies the requirement to protect and preserve cultural heritage. Intangible heritage needs to be viewed as being a vehicle of expression of identity of nation or social group (Keitumetse 2006). This is where there arises a need for professionals from mixed fields specially lawyers representing India in the legal arena to come together to tackle the problem better, for lack of coherent definitions leaves a lot to interpretation which in turn is done with political status bias amongst the members states. There is need to assess the term "Cultural Heritage" for the term itself has been imported without taking in account its theoretical background and conceptual framework. While this is not a criticism of the treaties but it does hope to reassess the purpose of International law for the "Cultural Heritage". Decisions concerning "Cultural Heritage" often have important political consequences but more fundamental point is that the identification of "Cultural Heritage" is in itself a political act given its symbolic relationship to culture and society in general (Blake 2000). Difficulties arise when narrowly targeted responses are formulated to specific problems (collapse of a heritage monuments, dying of a specific art form etc), for they do not provide a single, generally agreed definition of cultural heritage and fails to recognize the deeper implications of the concepts applied. While International law has uncertainty because of jurisdiction, this can be cleared up at national level to create better understanding internationally.

Very much like our freedom struggle we need break free our culture from persistence traditional and "elist" vision of heritage in international discourse for it reduces our heritage to "great" monuments subservient to its aesthetic character. This is very important for behind the monument are multiple processes which led to its fruition such as knowledge, values and social relationships. There is need and demand for UNESCO and its recognition for it can help document the heritage, identify its element, analyze its mode of transmission, and safeguard (Hafstein 2015). This can be very necessary for developing countries which might not have sufficient fund. However, it has to be kept in mind that while we cultivate a meta-cultural relationship it should not come at the cost of pre- existing relation to the practice that heritage already has. We need not depart from one fundamental premise: that the protection of cultural heritage requires global effort phenomenon There needs to be meaningful participation and support from those whose heritage the international community seeks to Keeping these inferences in mind, the following suggestion scan help revamp the entire system extensively:

- **Revamping the existing definition of cultural heritage**

The scope of the definition of the term, "cultural heritage" is extremely myopic and limited. The international Convention only talks about monuments, buildings etc. and completely turn a blind eye towards the intangible form of cultural heritage like various localized dance form, songs and other forms. This definition needs to undergo change and should be inclusive of all these genres which have not been taken into consideration while framing the definition of the term, "cultural heritage".

- **Exploring the contours of Intangible cultural heritage**

It has been time and again asserted by the authors that the definition of cultural heritage completely ignores the intangible aspect of the cultural heritage. But, the legal scholars have always been inconsistent in defining the term, "intangible cultural heritage" with any settled definition. Therefore, it becomes the first and foremost responsibility of the international community to frame a specific definition of the same covering all of its contours and genres. The term intangible cultural heritage should include and entail:

a. Dance forms prevailing across the globe
b. Different forms of songs and local folklore rhymes.
c. Any other form of skill like weaving etc. shall also be covered under this category.
  - **Need for a comprehensive code for performer's rights of localized people**

There is a dire need for a developing country like India to come up with a stringent code which can ensure the performer's rights of these localized people who rely on their parochial skills for their living. The Code would specifically target these traditional performers who, at times are not able to claim the benefits of the Copyright Act, 1957.

- **Inter-connected effort of nations**

The world community is like a big family which should work in close coordination. So, the entire world needs to re-think about the issue in question and work in this direction so that the definition of intangible cultural heritage can be revamped and altered.

- **Empowerment of Economic and Social Council (ECOSOC)**

One of the suggestions to improve the present framework could be the empowerment of ECOSOC. It delves into uplifting of culture at the international culture therefore it should be first and foremost duty of ECOSOC to define "cultural heritage" and "intangible cultural heritage". The institution should lay down rules in its regular meetings and should try to emphasize more on the issue in question.

FUTURE DIRECTION OF THE RESEARCH

- Reassessment of international framework on cultural heritage
  The international community needs to rethink about the "cultural heritage" framework by including intangible cultural heritage under its domain.
- Subsequent amendments in Indian law
  India should also work in this direction by coming up with a law especially focused on intangible cultural heritage which does not get due recognition.
- Creation of international institutions
  The international community with the concurrence of ECOSOC should help in creating more international institutions for the betterment of the intangible cultural heritage.

REFERENCES_

Blake, . (2000). On Defining the Cultural Heritage. *The International and Comparative Law Quarterly*, *49*(1), 61–85. doi:10.1017/S002058930006396X

Bortolotto, C. (2007). From objects to processes: UNESCO's 'intangible cultural heritage.' *Journal of Museum Ethnography*, (19), 21–33.

Gernsblith, P. (2007). Cultural Heritage legal Summary. *Journal of Field Archeology,* 83-90.

Hafstein, V., & Valdimar, T. (2015). Intangible Heritage as Diagnosis, Safeguarding as Treatment. *Journal of Folklore Research*, *52*(2–3), 281–298. doi:10.2979/jfolkrese.52.2-3.281

Kamenka, E. (1982). *Community as a Social Ideal. Ideas and Ideologies*. London: EArnold.

Keitumetse, S. (2006). UNESCO 2003 Convention on Intangible Heritage: Practical Implications for Heritage Management Approaches in Africa. *South African Archaeological Bulletin*, *61*(184), 166–171. doi:10.2307/20474924

Kreps, C. F. (2003). *Liberating Culture: Cross-Cultural Perspectives on Museums, Curation, and Heritage Preservation*. Psychology Press.

Lawyer's Comm. (n.d.). *Cultural Heritage Preservation.* http://www.culturalheritagelaw.org/Default.aspx?pageID=595025

Lowenthal, D. (2014). *The Heritage Crusade and the Spoils of History.* Cambridge University Press.

Ludwig. (1958). *Philosophical Investigations* (2nd ed.). Oxford: Basil Blackwell.

Ogino, M. (1995). La Logique d'actualisation. Le Patrimoine et Le Japon. *Ethnologie Francaise, 25*(1), 57–64.

Prott, . (1998). *International Standards for Cultural Heritage. In UNESCO World Culture Report.* Unesco Publishing.

Prott, L. V., & O'Keefe, P. J. (1989). Law and the Cultural Heritage: Movement. Butterworths.

Prott, L. V. (1984). Law and the Cultural Heritage. Volume 1, Discovery and Excavation. Abingdon: Professional Books.

Rome Convention of 1961

Scher, & Philip, W. (2010). UNESCO Conventions and Culture as a Resource. *Journal of Folklore Research, 47*(1–2), 197–202. doi:10.2979/jfr.2010.47.1-2.197

The Protection of Traditional knowledge. (2016). Genetic Resources and Expressions of Folklore Act.

Trigger, & Bruce, G. (2006). *A History of Archaeological Thought* (2nd ed.). Cambridge: University Press. https://ezproxy-prd.bodleian.ox.ac.uk/login?url=http://dx.doi.org/10.1017/CBO9780511813016

TRIPS Agreement, 1994.

Williams, R. (1986). A vocabulary of culture and society (Rev. ed.). Oxford University Press.

Chapter 18
Prospects of Artificial Intelligence (AI) Towards the Circular Economy

K. Pallavi
Independent Researcher, India

Hergovind Singh
Maulana Azad National Institute of Technology, India

ABSTRACT

Artificial intelligence has become a large part of everyday life. The world is heading towards new heights of adaption of various decision support technologies. In the present era, the rate at which we are consuming natural finite resources and depleting them, through producing chemicals, soil pollution, water pollution, air pollution, etc., is destroying our ecosystem. We have tried several recycling methods to minimize wastage, but it is insignificant. Now there is a need to think about state-of-the-art technological support like artificial intelligence (AI). This chapter explores the prospects of artificial intelligence in the circular economy.

1.BASICS OF ECONOMY

Circular economy (CE), popularly known as circularity aims at eliminations waste and continual utilization of scarce resources. It follows a life cycle of make, use, reuse, remake, recycle and again use. It creates a closed loop system, minimizing the wastage of residual amount of resources. It basically follows the principle of "utilizing the maximum of a resource" (Ellen MacArthur Foundation, 2012). Let us take a basic example of food cycle, we as vegetarians depends on plants to eat, so we cook the food, eat, and throw off the residual amount of food. But instead of throwing it off, if we put it in soil, it becomes compost and supplies maximum nutrients to plants. We again use plants to eat. This is a regenerative process which is totally in contrast to traditional linear economy. Thus, CE also support the idea of sustainability (Heshmati A. 2017).

DOI: 10.4018/978-1-7998-4990-2.ch018

Scope

CE has a broad scope. The circular economy includes products, infrastructure, equipment and services, and applies to every industry sector. It includes 'technical' resources (metals, minerals, fossil resources) and 'biological' resources (food, fibres, timber, etc.). A shift from fossil fuels towards renewable sources of energy is such an example of moving towards CE.

Background

In 1960s, Kenneth Boulding raised idea of "open economy" shifting from "closed economy". Open economy supports an idea of unlimited input resources and output sinks. Closed economy, on the contrast, supports idea of limited input resources and output sinks.

CE basically defines the idea of non-linear economy, which enhances the concept of closed loop systems. Some of the relevant theoretical influences are cradle to cradle, laws of ecology (e.g., Barry Commoner's The Closing Circle), looped and performance economy (Stahel,W. 2016), regenerative design, industrial ecology, biomimicry and blue economy.

British renowned economists David W. Pearce and R. Kerry Turner in 1989, further developed the meaning of CE. As per their opinion, traditional open-ended economy has no tendency to recycle, it follows make-use-throw concept.

In 1990s, Tim Jackson began to enrich the concept of this circular economy. Going years by, this idea of CE began to be adopted by the people at large. In 2006, China started working towards implementing CE in its governmental policy.

Linear Economy and Circular Economy

Evolution changed the economy to a big extent. It helped evolve us from stones to metals, electrical vehicles to ICE. Thus, moving from traditional economy to new economy is a must. The concept of circular economy was devised by David Pearce and Kerry Turner, two British environmental economists. They said, "Human lifestyle based on a linear model is unsustainable due to high rates of consumption and disposal, far exceeding the regenerative capacity of natural ecosystems to sustain human lifestyles."(Pearce, D.et.al. 1989). Of course, we, as a world, need to rethink the use of traditional economy and think of stepping in into a new and much more effective economy, i.e., circular economy, that is regenerative, resourceful and recyclable.

Basics of CE

As agreed, a simple equation created is Circularity = Competitiveness.

This clearly indicates that circularity is directly proportional to competitiveness. Whereas, competitiveness mainly depends upon economics of resources or capital. It can further be glorified in four areas such as, costs, material security, innovation and design and reduced externalities.

Costs includes true costs, having materials and regulatory compliance

Material security includes foreseen and unforeseen shortages Innovation and design includes materials, products and business models. Reduced externalities include true costs of products.

Circular Economy (CE) helps in competitiveness by making a difference to materials use – type, quantity, procurement, logistics, processing, and post-use. As regulatory regimes upgrade to include Extended Producer Responsibility, the costs in post-use phases of products can be managed by moving up-stream in appropriately designing products in parts or in full. When true-cost accounting begins to seep into calculating price of products or costs of procurement, more ecologically compatible alternates will become economically compelling.

Circular Economy in an Emerging Market

A known fact that Indian markets have high input costs in comparison to all other emerging markets. This affects their cost competitiveness not only in international markets but also in domestic markets. This creates a hunger to move into circular economy. Another big reason to move towards circularity is material security. A country like India is the third largest economy in PPP terms which in turn needs financing at increasing levels. Thus, finally, CE can help India mange costs and moving from sustenance to sustainability.

Moving Away From the Linear Model

We are well known that our present global economy is largely dependent upon material resources which uses a traditional concept of 'make-take-dispose'. This concept is no longer sustainable. Thus, we need to shift to newer kind of economy such as "Circular Economy".

A necessary Transition to Circular Economy

During the Paris 2015 United Nations summit6 (COP21), countries agreed to limit any further temperature rise below 2°C by 2030. So, we need to rethink overall economic model, certain emissions linked to industrial production processes and waste must be decreased to a large extent.

As per Ellen MacArthur Foundation, a leading think tank on Circular Economy, CE is an"industrial system that is restorative or regenerative by intention and design"(Ellen MacArthur Foundation, 2019). It focuses more on reutilizing the resources simultaneously reducing waste production (Jacobsen, 2006; Park et al., 2010; Yuan et al.,2006).

In the above diagram, the linear economy has a life cycle like, raw materials are input, production is done, then the materials are used and non recyclable waste is thrown off. The amount of wastage is too high. In the recycling economy, raw material are processed via production, materials are used and a part of waste generated(which can be recycled) is put in into recycling so that it can be again used. Here, the amount of wastage is pretty less. In the circular economy, raw materials are put to production, materials used and the total waste generated is put into recycling. Thus, it creates zero amount of wastage.

1.4.2 Circular Transformation Driven by Innovative Business Models

Of course, till now we must have understood that the shift from linear to circular economy is desirable and a must.

Typically, the majority of Circular Economic opportunities can be linked to these five business models (Han. J. et.al., 2020):

Figure 1. Diagram representing linear economy, recycling economy and circular economy

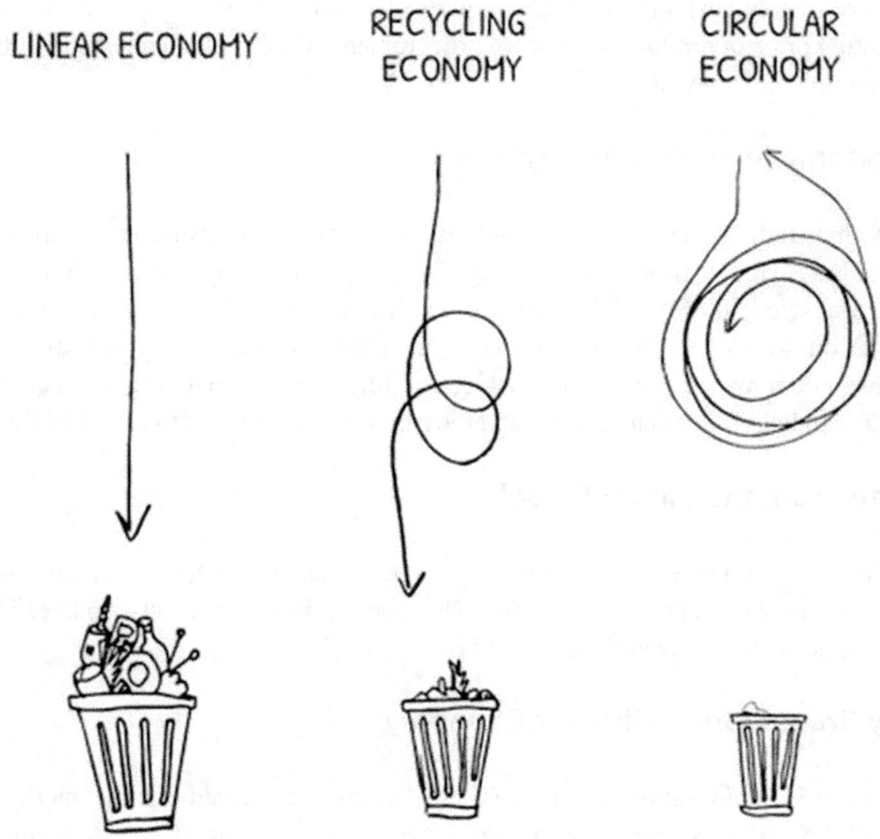

Circular supplies:- Replacing scarce resources like wind and solar energies with renewable ones. This is accompanied with using smart meters to make efficient use of the resources.

Resource recovery:- Encouraging organizations to innovate and increase resource efficiency through reuse and re/up-cycling of existing materials.

Product life extension:- Innovative design, eliminating material waste and enabling repair helps in extending product lifecycle manifold.

Sharing platforms:- Sharing platforms means more efficient use of the existing products and services which promote collaboration in the ecosystem.

Product as a service:- Products offered as a service through lease, or pay-for-use gives an alternative to "buy and own" while ownership remaining with the existing owner.

1.4.3 Governments are Setting Ambitious CE Targets

Many countries are setting up ambitious targets to own and adopt CE. One like, European Commision adopted new set of measures in January 2018. They said:

By 2030, all plastics packaging should be recyclable;

Published a directive on the inter-relationship between chemical, product and waste legislation that assesses how these factors co-synergise;

Set up a monitoring Framework on progress towards a circular economy at EU and national level. It is composed of a set of ten key indicators which cover each phase – i.e. production, consumption, waste management and secondary raw materials – as well as economic aspects – investments and jobs - and innovation;

A report on critical raw materials and the CE that highlights the potential to make the use of such materials within in our practices to be more circular.

While Finland was the first country to adopt this CE concept in 2016, to publish a roadmap to make its' economy circular by 2025. They planned this through offering good services and long-lasting recyclable products to its citizens.

1.4.4 Funding is Available to drive Circular Economy Businesses

The targets and goals set to achieve being circular by the countries may not be fulfilled without financial aid. Thus, countries have been allocating surplus funds in order to sustain this goal. The Dutch government has announced an additional contribution of 80 million EUR9 to promote CE in 2019 and 2020. Across the EU, new types of loans are being set up to address the specific financing needs of circular businesses, incorporating a lower interest rate and risk sharing. For that matter, the European Commission has allocated funds of over 650 million EUR under 'Horizon 2020' to support circular initiatives and 5.5 billion EUR under their structural funds. In the investment framework for 2014-2020, there is significant funding for waste management, with funds in total reaching 150 billion EUR. The European Commission has also been working on a new financing package beyond 2020; the European Investment Bank (EIB) can also play the role of a partner for circular investments and has provided 2.1 billion EUR in co-financing for circular projects over the last five years. In October 2019, the world's largest asset management firm BlackRock has launched together with Ellen MacArthur Foundation a new circular economy fund, starting with 20 million USD.

2. UNDERSTANDING ARTIFICIAL INTELLIGENCE (AI)

World progressing day-by-day is going hand-in-hand with technology. Thus, mentioning about Artificial Intelligence is a must. But as we all know, everything has its pros and cons. So is AI. Even great physicist like Stephen Hawking and a successful CEO of SpaceX Corp., Elon Musk have warned of AI's threats.

2.1 Concept of AI

According to the father of Artificial Intelligence, John McCarthy, Articial Intelligence is the "The science and engineering of making intelligent machines, especially intelligent computer programs" (McCarthy et al., 2010).

The English Oxford Living Dictionary gives this definition: "The theory and development of computer systems able to perform tasks normally requiring human intelligence, such as visual perception, speech recognition, decision-making, and translation between languages."

Merriam-Webster defines artificial intelligence this way: A branch of computer science dealing with the simulation of intelligent behavior in computers or the capability of a machine to imitate intelligent human behavior.

The Encyclopedia Britannica states, "artificial intelligence (AI), the ability of a digital computer or computer-controlled robot to perform tasks commonly associated with intelligent beings." Intelligent beings are those that can adapt to changing circumstances.

The proposal for the conference said, "The study is to proceed on the basis of the conjecture that every aspect of learning or any other feature of intelligence can in principle be so precisely described that a machine can be made to simulate it."

The digital platform giant Amazon defines AI as "the field of computer science dedicated to solving cognitive problems commonly associated with human intelligence, such as learning, problem solving, and pattern recognition."

2.1.1 About AI

Artificial Intelligence (AI) also popularly known as, Machine intelligence, is intelligence demonstrated by machines, unlike natural intelligence attributed by humans and animals. It is also been named as study of intelligent agents. Those agents/devices that imitate functions that humans associate like learning, problem solving etc.

AI has developed its importance and relevance in years and was also recognized as academic discipline in 1955. Furthur, AI was divided in sub fields based on technical considerations, use of particular tools, or deep philosophical differences, social factors etc.

2.1.2 History of AI

AI is not new now in this present era. AI has progressed and even progressing to newer heights. Let us understand the history of AI. It all started with study of mathematical logic. Alan Turing's theory of computation suggested that by mere shuffling symbols as 0 and 1 mathematical deduction can be simulated by the help of digital computers. This insight is known as the Church–Turing thesis. All this grew a curiosity in researchers for a possibility to develop an electronic brain.

This field of AI was first invented at a workshop at Dartmouth College in 1956 and the term "Artificial Intelligence" was coined by John McCarthy. He named it so to distinguish the field from that of cybernatics. By the year, 1959, the AI has developed itself much that it started solving word problems, proving logical theorems and also speaking English. By 1960s, with the help of Dept. of Defense, U.S., various laboratories for AI also established. Even, Herbert Simon said "machines will be capable, within twenty years, of doing any work a man can do".Marvin Minsky wrote, "within a generation ... the problem of creating 'artificial intelligence' will substantially be solved"(Minsky, M.1961).

Unfortunately, due to lack of funding and support form the then Congress Govt. in U.S., the research field slowed down. This downfall continued for say, two decades. But in 1980s. research on AI was revived. Researchers gradually started understanding the importance of AI. In 1985, the market of AI peaked some billion dollars. Same time, Japan's fifth generation computer emerged to realize the US govt and world at large to encourage AI. But of course, market has ups and downs. With the collapse of Lisp Machine market in 1987, AI once again faced failure.

But with the development of metal–oxide–semiconductor (MOS) very-large-scale integration (VLSI), artificial nueral networks (ANN) developed in 1980s. In 1990-200s, AI began to be used for logistics, data mining, medical diagnosis and many other areas. AI then also started to develop tie ups with other fields like, statistics, economics and mathematics. From then AI drastically improved its importance. AI started to be useful in renowned social media platforms like, Skype, Facebook. And, now, country like China is funding its AI labs exuberantly and striving to become the "AI superpower.

2.2 Types of AI

There are basically 2 types of AI:

Weak/Narrow AI- It signifies "not too intelligent" machines nad focuses on one narrow task, in which the instructions are to be manually entered into the machine system and thus it can work. For example: a poker game installed in computer system plays with human and beats him, but all the rules, moves and the commands are previously installed into the machine.

Strong AI- These are "intelligent" and of course smart machines that think and act on their own. They, when put into complex situations think and act just like a human brain. Robots, now a days can be taken as example of this kind.

Basically, AI is furthur divided based on there functionality, say,

Reactive machines- It is one of the basic forms of AI. It does not have past memory and cannot retrieve past information to make future decisions or actions.

Limited memory- It has past storage memory, but it can implement it for a limited period of time.

Theory of mind- It is a "social" machine that is built so to understand human emotions, belief, thoughts, expectations and act accordingly.

Self awareness- It is a "complete human" machine that has its own conscious, is super intelligence, has sentiments to understand and judge decisions.

Applications of AI

Of course, by now, we have understood relevance of AI in our everyday lives. Let us now understand the relevance of AI in various prominent fields,

Healthcare- AI has vast usage in healthcare, for CT scan, ECG or identifying high risk patients. AI assists doctors in treatments of complex health problems like cancer. It helps in decision making, performing surgeries, and developing medicines. It performs minor and major surgeries with precision.

Automative- Manual operated cars are to almost disappear in current scenario as self driving cars are to occupy the industry totally. Technology giants like Tesla, Google and Apple are working on adopting this technology.

Finance and economics- AI has applications in banking like, book keeping, organize operations, invest in stocks and many more. It also has helped reduce frauds and financial crimes. It helps in decision making in stocks and online trading.

Cybersecurity- It signifies privacy of one's data by ensuring security of data and preventing fraudulent activities. For this, apart from AI, Natural Language Processing(NLP) is also been used to automatically sort the data networks into high risk and low-risk information to prevent cyber attacks.

Government- AI in governance is used in mass surveillance. It is used to put on traffic signals to manage traffic system. Using facial recognition system it helps using recognize faces and make system and security more stronger.

Law-related profession- It helps in doing entry level job for lawyers which was a tedious work previously for them.

Video games- AI used in video games in generating dynamic purposeful behavior in non-player characters (NPCs). Play stations are one such examples.

Military- AI has so far been used in enhancing C2, Communications, Sensors, Integration and Interoperability. It helps in monitoring borders to mark entry of enemy.

Hospitality- It helps in reducing staff load and increase efficiency by cutting repetitive tasks frequency, trends analysis, guest interaction, and customer needs prediction. Hotel services backed by Artificial Intelligence are represented in the form of a chatbot, application, virtual voice assistant and service robots.

Audit- It helps in easy auditing and increasing level of assurance and duration of audit be reduced.

Advertising- As per the choice of customers, they can be given better suggestions based on their previous choices. AI can be used in advertising products and thus can further reduce cost of advertising campaigns.

Art- AI can help architects to build houses. It helps desing good and feasible designs for houses. A virtual platform is used to predict how a design will look and mix match the colour coding. It optimizing the cost effectiveness in designing houses and help predict what amount of material to be used.

3. DIGITAL, AI AND CIRCULAR JOINING FORCES

3.1 Digital Technologies Accelerating Circular Economy

One of the most critical drivers of CE is digitization, that strengthen digital information to enhance business processes. Still, companies are striving to achieve this fit. Governments and businesses are setting defined targets on achieving CE goals, say, for example, Netherlands is working towards achieving 100% CE by year 2050.

Artificial Intelligence (AI) is an essential element to dive in into Fourth Industrial Revolution. It basically can replicate human behavior that includes learning, reasoning, problem solving, knowledge representation, perception, motion, social intelligence and creativity. It has a combination of algorithms that fetch useful information from data at large and draw patterns to understand and replicate this human behavior. This is done using an approach named Machine Learning. Machine Learning methods are dynamic and so flexible thus they are capable of adjusting to the input data and so can be applied to many domains.

The algorithms that are used by this Machine learning is broadly grouped into 3 types.

Supervised learning
Unsupervised learning
Reinforcement learning

Supervised learning follows a input-output pairing fashion, which means each input dataset provided gives a defined known output. Unsupervised learning, unlike supervised learning, follows cluster pattern, that is, the data set provided as input is without any labeled responses and finds for new and undetected patterns.

Fig. shows the diagrammatic representation of supervised learning and unsupervised learning.

Figure 2. Showing patterns for supervised and unsupervised learning. In supervised learning, red particles are segregated from blue ones giving a specific pattern whereas in unsupervised learning there is no definite pattern of particles.

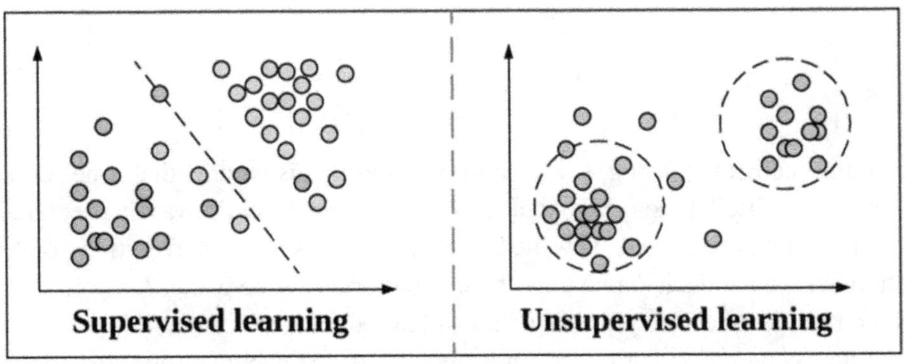

Let us understand this better with a general example. A teacher teaching a kid that 2+2=4. There is no other output to this input. Universally proven that, adding 2 and 2 will only give 4 and not 5 or any other number. This is an example of supervised learning.

On the other hand, a fruit vendor bringing fruits to sell may give him all fruits sold one day at an exuberant price and may give him loss on the other day. The input(the vendor bringing good quality fruits) is constant here, but the output(profit) is not defined here. This is an example of unsupervised learning. Plus, there is no supervisor allotted to the vendor telling him to bring the amount of fruits or to sell at what price. This is example of unsupervised learning.

Alongside supervised and unsupervised learning, Reinforcement learning is a method in which the agent(typically a machine), learns to make best of a reward oriented decision in a complex situation, based on trial and error strategy.

Figure 3. shows reinforcement learning where an agent takes an action towards environment and gets its reward from environment.

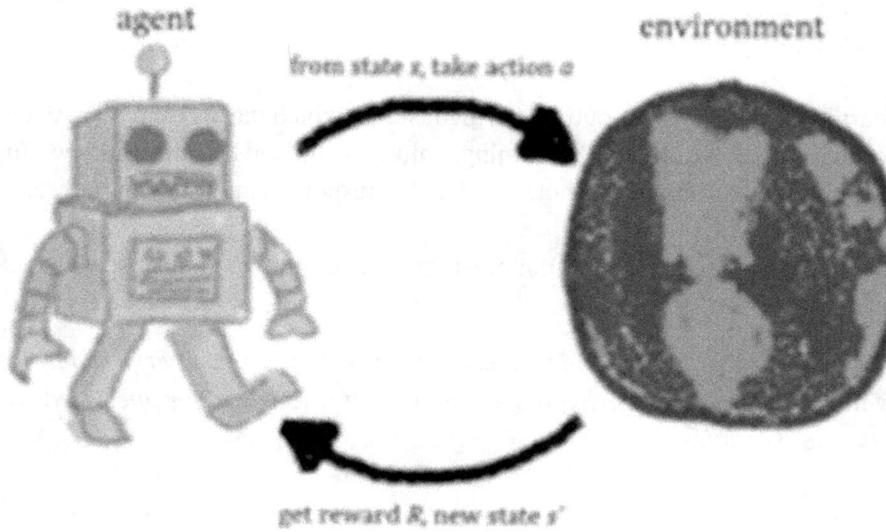

Example of reinforcement learning, say, a child was told by his parents that if he scores 95% in his board exams he will be gifted a motorbike, but the catch here is the child wasn't attentive in the whole year so he missed learning the course. Now, he has only 3 months to learn everything on his own. It's a complex situation here, what decision he takes here is important, if he panics he won't be able to reach his goal. Thus, he has to make a proper study plan and execute it.

A shift from linear economy towards circular economy can be the biggest opportunities for the global economy as a whole which can be achieved with AI as a tool. This paradigm shift in various companies iterating digital transformation moving towards CE goals is essential. Say, products developed with both technological and circular principles has much an innovation angle and economic opportunities.

3.1.1 Benefits of Digital Transformation in Circular Economy

A circular economy is a substitute to traditional/linear economy. The traditional economy has just taught us to make-use-dispose which creates more wastage of the material. Circular economy, on the other hand, is a restorative kind of economy where the maximum value is extracted from a resource, then, at the end it is recovered and regenerated. This digital transformation has its implications in Circular economy in various fields say, information services, logistics services, delivery capabilities, and shared logistics capabilities.

One of the main ideas behind the digital transformation process is the concept of economising; an idea which refers, not only to economising on time, but also to economising on the use of any resources which could have a negative impact on the environment when used in excess.

A good example of this is Katty Fashion; Katty Fashion is a fashion company that has replaced standard prototypes with 3D models in order to ensure that no materials are wasted. By implementing this 3D model system, the company is not only able to save money and make a positive impact, but it is also able to create value through innovation and sustainability.

3.1.2 Role of Big Data in CE

Big data is basically large sets of data which can be analysed computationally to reveal patterns to understand or analyse something. This big data basically, provise smart cities with information on the flows (energy, waste, pollution), to better manage them and recover these flows. In recent years, a device like smart grid is viral. These grids basically use big data for efficient electricity distribution. This is possible by use of connected sensors. For example, In France, the GreenLys project successfully tested the smart grids principle with 1,000 customers and forty companies in Lyon and Grenoble for four years. The experiment was based on the use of Linky, a smart meter that will be deployed throughout the entire French electricity network by 2021.

Not only this but also, Big data has its uses in water management. In partnership with Veolia and IBM, the city of Lille launched "Vig'ileo", a smart water service, in 2016. Sensors, installed along the 4,300 kilometers of water network, allow various incidents (peak consumption, leaks, pollution, etc.) to be detected and responded to in real time.

This real time sensors can be used in optimizing waste collection by placing these sensors in waste bins in better, smart and efficient waste collection. A few applications in relation to the same have also been developed like, "Urban Pulse", "Too Good To Go".

Last but not the least, Big data has its applications in reducing pollution as well. Logistic chains are increasingly greener thanks to digital data. Companies will soon have all the information about their stocks and deliveries to be made at their fingertips: customer availabilities, routes, weather conditions, road traffic, etc. This data will allow them to adjust their flows in real time and organize their deliveries so that they are more efficient and pollute the city less. Eco Mobility solutions are also developing allowing people to travel with minimum possible greenhouse gas emissions, such as BlaBlacar, the famous pooling service, Drivy, which allows individuals to rent their vehicles to each other, and ZenPark, the application dedicated to shared car parks.

3.2. AI Modules Applicable in Circular Innovation

Of course, through a brief discussion yet, we have come to get a fair idea of how AI is useful in CE. Not necessarily a strict step-by-step process need to be followed but also, a 'mix-and-match' approach can be also be applied as per potential needs.

3.2.1 Clustering

While a single data entry set can be described using many quantifiable attributes, say, for example, phones can be described based on their attributes like, android, keypad etc. This method of clustering alike data together can help simplify the processes. The relation of clustering with this CE is that it can help create clusters of those that own specialised equipment and those that want to use it can be quantified in this manner and bring stakeholders together.

3.2.2 Timeseries Analysis

Timeseries analysis describe how a variable progress over a time. It includes methods that predict future event through detecting a defined pattern created earlier. The methods include Fourier transforms, spectrograms, lines of best fit and extrapolation and even deep learning models like Long Short-Term Memory (LSTM). Applications can be found in the preventative maintenance of electronic equipment by monitoring device health, urban resource monitoring such as water and even efficient food production where consumption can be monitored to predict future demand.

3.2.3 Outlier Detection

A normal body temperature for a human being is at 98.6°F, if the thermometer raises above it signifies fever, Thus, 98.6°F is the "normal". Similarly, Outlier detection technique basically works on the principle of "normal operating conditions" where the data is being read and define normality conditions by looking at statistical measures such as mean, standard deviation, kurtosis (the sharpness of the peak of a frequency-distribution curve) etc. This method generally detects the deviation from normality. Applicability in practicality is in product maintenance, urban resource monitoring (e.g. average water consumption of a given household), healthcare and many more.

3.2.4 Computer Vision, Object Detection (and Classification)

When a particular object is found within an image, the algorithms find such pattern and predict the output, this technique is also known as Image analysis or object detection. A few such object detection algorithms include logistic regression, Support Vector Machines (SVMs) and (deep) Neural Networks (NN). Computer vision can be applied in many purposes such as, waste management (detecting when waste bins are full), healthcare (detecting bone fractures in X-rays), recycling (sorting objects into those that can be recycled or reused and those that cannot) and food production (detecting the colour and size of mature crop).

3.2.5 Chat Bots

Conversational agents, popularly known as Chat bots is used to engage with humans. Chat bots actually understands human query raised and reply back accordingly with appropriate information. Natural Language Processing (NLP) is one such algorithm that extract meaning from the text. Chat bots uses many such algorithms like NLP.

Chats bots are used in education, healthcare. Another prominent service of chat bots is in client contact, account management etc.

3.2.6 Entity Recognition

Entity recognition (ER), an NLU (natural Language understanding) algorithm takes digital text as input and produces structured data as output in the form of annotated entities. For example, in the sentence "John has been diagnosed with mild headache and was prescribed paracetamol".

A possible output is "Person: John, Name: John, diagnosis: headache, medicine: paracetamol". Various applications of ER are in healthcare to review patients and quickly revive their medical history. ER has also its uses in industry dealing with parsing texts such as the regulatory or financial services industries.

3.2.7 Summarization

As the name depicts, Summarization is also an NLU based algorithm that takes huge amount of data as input and extracts a summary of it. The creation of summary involves weighing each word by its frequency in the text given. This method is useful in healthcare, education (converting large data of educational material in summaries).

3.2.8 Text Classification with NLU

Converting words into quantifiable objects is done by NLU (Natural Language Understanding) algorithm. This technique is useful in healthcare to easily index existing and new documents by processing their contents. Another use of this text classification is that, it is used to access customer's risk in financial and regulatory industry by gathering the data containing information about their activities like, money-laundering, imprisonment etc. It depicts high risk or low risk profile of customers.

3.3 The Cross-industry Application of AI to Release Circular Economy Benefits

As we have already understood the various uses of AI in Circular economy, we are now heading towards understanding the uses of AI in a few sectors (Ghoreishi. M. 2020):

Demand and Supply management of goods and resources:- Naturally, we know the need of resources in our daily lives. But the only issue raises here is we are unable to utilize our resources to the full extent, we rather utilize 60% of it. The biggets example is textiles. People use clothes for a lesser time and throw them, they are then either burnt or ends up in landfill sites. This further increases level of pollution in environment. Here, AI has a big role to play. AI can do this digitally by applying the ability to track product or material usage and create reports.

Production, maintenance & analytics:- Product designing is a crucial part in developing product lifestyle so that the parts be easily replaced, upgraded or adjusted, which will in turn extend the life time of a product. AL algorithms can here learn patterns that are able to inform if a device is healthy or needs maintenance.

Resource & waste monitoring:- In an overpopulated city like Mumbai, the distribution of people per area is more than average, thus people living in this much proximity will need monitoring of basic resources like water, waste and non-recyclable goods. Here, AI can be used to ensure proper distribution.

Agriculture & food production:- AI can help include monitoring the crop growth process, from nutrient supply all the way to harvest having a good use in agriculture and food production sector as well. AI can also help in water management, by enabling proper water reuse and its discharge.

E-healthcare:- Of course, AI is no new in healthcare industry as of now. AI can assist in patients visiting doctors by alerting patients and doctor-in-charge well in advance to an appointment booked. Routine diagnosis can be done using AI, it can also detectparts of body where the fracture exists. AI can be used to support digital text analysis, summarizing lengthy patient report history. One future possibility in this context is the creation of sharing platforms and using specialized equipment with a Product-as-a-Service (PaaS) model.

Regulation, Reporting and Risk Management:- AI can help in KYC(know your customer) process, AI-based algorithms present opportunities to improve risk management and decision making processes by discovering such trends, optimising risk models, scenario analysis, formulating climate and environmental adaptation strategies and improve risk reporting.

Education & engagement tools:- AI 'chatbots' can be purposefully built to engage with customers and employees of a company. They can be used for query resolution process.

CONCLUSION

So far, we have got a fair idea that how our economy is in need of transforming into CE. Also the, role of AI in CE. The various business strategies which help in implementing CE into our economy. Of course, governments have also been understanding the need for this strategic shift and are been investing surplus funds in order to achieve and sustain it. They have set up a definite time goal to do so. Many big foundations and companies are also stepping towards achieving this. Thus, a shift towards circular economy is a necessity in today's world and simultaneously understanding the prospects of AI in it.

REFERENCES

Bennett, J. W. (1991). Pearce, D. W., and R. K. Turner. Economics of Natural Resources and the Environment. Baltimore MD: Johns Hopkins University Press, 1990, 378 pp. *American Journal of Agricultural Economics, 73*(1), 227–228. doi:10.2307/1242904

Ellen MacArthur Foundation. (2012). *Towards the circular economy: Economic and business rationale for an accelerated transition*. Author.

Ellen MacArthur Foundation. (2019). *Artificial intelligence and the circular economy - AI as a tool to accelerate the transition*. Artificial Intelligence and the Circular Economy Ellen MacArthur Foundation. http://www.ellenmacarthurfoundation.org/publications

Ghoreishi, M., & Happonen, A. (2020). New promises AI brings into circular economy accelerated product design: a review on supporting literature. *E3S Web of Conferences, 158*. https://doi.org/ doi:10.1051/e3sconf/202015806002

Han, J., & Heshmati, A., & Rashidghalam, M. (2020). Circular Economy Business Models with a Focus on Servitization. *Sustainability*, *12*(21), 8799. doi:10.3390u12218799

Heshmati, A. (2017). A review of the circular economy and its implementation. *International Journal of Green Economics*, *11*(3/4), 251. doi:10.1504/ijge.2017.089856

Jacobsen, N. B. (2006). Industrial symbiosis in Kalundborg, Denmark: A quantitative assessment of economic and environmental aspects. *Journal of Industrial Ecology*, *10*, 239–255.

McCarthy, J., & Minsky, M. (2010). *Artificial Intelligence*. Academic Press.

Minsky, M. (1961). Steps toward Artificial Intelligence. *Proceedings of the IRE*, *49*(1), 8–30. doi:10.1109/jrproc.1961.287775

Park, J., Sarkis, J., & Wu, Z. (2010). Creating integrated business and environmental value within the context of China's circular economy and ecological modernization. *Journal of Cleaner Production*, *18*, 1494–1501.

Stahel, W. R. (2016). The circular economy. *Nature*, *531*(7595), 435–438. doi:10.1038/531435a

Yuan, Z. W., Jun, B., & Moriguichi, Y. C. (2006). The circular ecology: A new development strategy in China. *Journal of Industrial Ecology*, *10*, 4–8.

Compilation of References

United States Environmental Protection Agency. (n.d.a). *Managing and Reducing Wastes: A Guide for Commercial Buildings*. Retrieved February 15, 2020, from https://www.epa.gov/smm/managing-and-reducing-wastes-guide-commercial-buildings

United States Environmental Protection Agency. (n.d.b). *National Overview: Facts and Figures on Materials, Wastes and Recycling*. Retrieved February 15, 2020, from https://www.epa.gov/facts-and-figures-about-materials-waste-and-recycling/national-overview-facts-and-figures-materials

Food's Carbon Footprint. (n.d.). Retrieved February 16, 2020, from https://www.greeneatz.com/foods-carbon-footprint.html

United States Environmental Protection Agency. (2014). *Municipal Solid Waste Generation, Recycling, and Disposal in the United States: Facts and Figures for 2012*. Retrieved from https://www.epa.gov/sites/production/files/2015-09/documents/2012_msw_fs.pdf

Sheila, S. (n.d.). *How Minimalism Can Help You Live A Sustainable Lifestyle*. Retrieved February 17, 2020, from https://www.practigalblog.com/minimalism-sustainable-lifestyle/

UNIQLO Sustainability. (n.d.). Retrieved February 18, 2020, from https://www.uniqlo.com/en/sustainability/recycle/

Ornes, S. O. (2018, August 14). *Core Concept: How does climate change influence extreme weather? Impact attribution research seeks answers*. Retrieved January 25, 2020, from https://www.pnas.org/content/115/33/8232

BBC News. (2020, January 31). *Australia fires: A visual guide to the bushfire crisis*. Retrieved February 5, 2020, from https://www.bbc.com/news/world-australia-50951043

What is the difference between global warming and climate change? (n.d.). Retrieved February 10, 2020, from https://www.usgs.gov/faqs/what-difference-between-global-warming-and-climate-change-1?qt-news_science_products=0#qt-news_science_products

Kennedy, L. (2015, May 17). *What's the difference between global warming and climate change?* Retrieved February 10, 2020, from https://www.climate.gov/news-features/climate-qa/whats-difference-between-global-warming-and-climate-change

What are the long-term effects of climate change? (2002, May 29). Retrieved February 11, 2020, from https://www.usgs.gov/faqs/what-are-long-term-effects-climate-change-1?logstash-usgs-pw%3Apalladium_root_topics=&logstash-usgs-pw%3Apalladium_root_publication_year_date=&sort=&qt-news_science_products=4#qt-news_science_products

Climate Change. (n.d.). Retrieved February 11, 2020, from https://www.un.org/en/sections/issues-depth/climate-change/

United Nations. (n.d.). *Cities and Local Action to Combat Climate Change*. Retrieved February 12, 2020, from https://unfccc.int/topics/education-youth/youth-engagement/global-youth-video-competition/global-youth-video-competition-2019/cities-and-local-action-to-combat-climate-change

FCC Environment CEE. (n.d.). *From Linear to Circular Economy – closing the loop*. Retrieved February 14, 2020, from https://www.fcc-group.eu/en/fcc-cee-group/news-and-media/stories-of-waste/from-linear-to-circular-economy-closing-the-loop.html

Circular Economy. School of Thought. (n.d.). Retrieved February 15, 2020, from https://www.ellenmacarthurfoundation.org/circular-economy/concept/schools-of-thought

Aayog, N. I. T. I. (2018). *Composite Water Management Index*. NITI Aayog.

Aayog, N. I. T. I. (2019). *Composite Water Management Index 2.0*. NITI Aayog.

Abdullah, A., & Ramay, I. (2012). Antecedents of organizational commitment of banking sector employees in Pakistan. *Serbian Journal of Management*, *7*(1), 89–102. doi:10.5937jm1201089A

Abernathy, W. J., & Wayne, K. (1982). Limits of the Learning Curve. In Management of Innovation. Pitman.

Adhana, D. (2020). E-waste management in India: A study of current scenario. International *Journal of Management. Technology And Engineering*, *9*(1), 1–13.

Agrawal, S., Singh, R. K., & Murtaza, Q. (2014). Forecasting product returns for recycling in Indian electronics industry. *Journal of Advances in Management Research*, *11*(1), 102–114. doi:10.1108/JAMR-02-2013-0013

Ahmed, M. E., Khan, M. M., & Samad, N. (2016). Income, Social Class and Consumer Behaviour: A Focus on Developing Nations. *Journal of Applied Business and Economic Research*, *14*(10), 6679–6702.

Akenji, L. (2014). Consumer scapegoatism and limits to green consumerism. *Journal of Cleaner Production*, *63*, 13–23.

Al Shaikh, F. N. (1995). Organization Commitment in the banking sector in Jordan: An Empirical Investigation. *Journal of Administrative Science & Economics, 6*.

Allan, J. (1993). Fortunately, there are substitutes for water otherwise our hydro-political futures would be impossible. In Priorities for water resources allocation and management (pp. 13-26). London: Academic Press.

Allen, N. J., & Meyer, J. P. (1990). The measurement and antecedents of affective, continuance and normative commitment to the organization. *Journal of Occupational Psychology*, *63*(1), 1–18. doi:10.1111/j.2044-8325.1990.tb00506.x

Allen, R. G., Pereira, L. S., Raes, D., & Smith, M. (1998). *Crop evapotranspiration—guidelines for computing crop water requirements—FAO irrigation and drainage paper.* FAO.

Altman, B. W., & Vidaver-Cohen, D. (2000). A framework for under-standing corporate citizenship: Introduction to the special edition of Business and Society Review 'corporate citizenship for the new millennium'. Business and Society Review, 105(1), 1–7.

Alvial Muñoz, A. (2015). *Economía Azul: Una revisión en el marco de nuevas tendencias en Economía.* Obtenido de Bioeconomía Argentina: http://www.bioeconomia.mincyt.gob.ar/wp-content/uploads/2014/12/1.-Econom%C3%ADa-azul-A.-Alvial.pdf

Amara, N., Halilem, N., & Traoré, N. (2016). Adding value to companies' value chain: Role of business schools scholars. *Journal of Business Research*, *69*(5), 1661–1668. doi:10.1016/j.jbusres.2015.10.035

Ambec, S., & Lanoie, P. (2008). Does it pay to be green? A systematic overview. *The Academy of Management Perspectives*.

Antoine, R. (2000, Nov. 14). Entrepreneuriat, qualité de la vie, citoyenneté: trois tartes à la crème du recrutement. *Le Monde.*

Arya, S., & Kumar, S. (2020). E-waste in India at a glance: Current trends, regulations, challenges and management strategies. *Journal of Cleaner Production, 271*, 122707. doi:10.1016/j.jclepro.2020.122707

Ayog. (n.d.). *Strategy for Secondary Materials Management for promoting Resource Efficiency (RE) and Circular Economy (CE) in Electrical and Electronic Equipment Sector.* Ministry of Communication & Information Technology.

Bagnoli, M., & Watts, S. (2003). Selling to socially responsible consumers: Competition and the private provision of public goods. *Journal of Economics & Management Strategy, 12*(3), 419–445. doi:10.1162/105864003322309536

Balboa, C. H., & Domínguez Somonte, M. (2014). *Economía circular como marco para el ecodiseño: el modelo ECO-3.* Obtenido de Universidad Nacional de Educación a Distancia: https://www2.uned.es/egi/publicaciones/articulos/Economia_circular_como_marco_para_el_ecodiseno_el_modelo_ECO-3.pdf

Bank of Baroda. (2013-14). Annual Report-Bank of Baroda. Vadodara.

Bank of India. (2013-14). *Annual Report.* Bank of India Mumbai.

Bashford, S. (2008). *Brownie points for green workers.* Human Resources.

Beardwell, I., & Holden, L. (1997). *Human Resources Management. A Contemporary Perspective.* Pitman Publishing.

Bechtel, R., Marans, R., & Michelson, W. (2013). *Methods in environmental and behavioral research.* Academic Press.

Becker, T. E., Randall, D. M., & Riegel, C. D. (1995). The multidimensional view of commitment and the theory of reasoned action: A comparative evaluation. *Journal of Management, 21*(4), 617–638. doi:10.1177/014920639502100402

Bennett, J. W. (1991). Pearce, D. W., and R. K. Turner. Economics of Natural Resources and the Environment. Baltimore MD: Johns Hopkins University Press, 1990, 378 pp. *American Journal of Agricultural Economics, 73*(1), 227–228. doi:10.2307/1242904

Berg, A., & Hukkinen, J. (2011). The paradox of growth critique: Narrative analysis of the Finnish sustainable consumption and production debate. *Ecological Economics, 72*, 151–160. doi:10.1016/j.ecolecon.2011.09.024

Bhaskar, K., & Kumar, B. (2019). Electronic waste management and sustainable development goals: Is there a business case for linking the two? *Journal of Indian Business Research, 11*(2), 120–137. doi:10.1108/JIBR-01-2018-0051

Bhaskar, K., & Turaga, R. M. R. (2018). India's e-waste rules and their impact on e-waste management practices: A case study. *Journal of Industrial Ecology, 22*(4), 930–942. doi:10.1111/jiec.12619

Bhattacharya, K. K. (2002). A Model of Integration of Information Technology in Agriculture Extension for Improving Crop Production. *2nd Global Conference on Flexible System Management.*

Bihari, S. C. (2010). Green banking-towards socially resonsible banking in india. *International Journal of Business Insights & Transformation, 4*(1).

Binswanger, H. C. (2013). *Die Wachstumsspirale: Geld, Energie und Imagination in der Dynamik des Marktprozesses.* Metropolis-Verlag.

Biswas, A., & Roy, M. (2015). Green products: An exploratory study on the consumer behaviour in emerging economies of the East. *Journal of Cleaner Production, 87*, 463–468. doi:10.1016/j.jclepro.2014.09.075

Bjorn, A., & Strandesen, M. (2011). Absolute versus Relative Environmental Sustainability: What can the Cradle-to-cradle and Eco –efficiency Concepts Learn from Each Other? *Journal of Industrial Ecology.*

Blake, . (2000). On Defining the Cultural Heritage. *The International and Comparative Law Quarterly*, *49*(1), 61–85. doi:10.1017/S002058930006396X

Blanco, T. M. (2014). The meaning of employability in the new labour relationships between company-employee: A model of training in companies. *Procedia: Social and Behavioral Sciences*, *139*, 448–455. doi:10.1016/j.sbspro.2014.08.039

Blomsma, F., & Brennan, G. (2017). The emergence of circular economy: A new framing around prolonging resource productivity. *Journal of Industrial Ecology*, *21*(3), 603–614. doi:10.1111/jiec.12603

Boiral, O. (2009). *Greening the corporation through organizational citizenship behaviors*. Journal. doi:10.100710551-008-9881-2

Borthakur, A., & Govind, M. (2019). Computer and mobile phone waste in urban India: An analysis from the perspectives of public perception, consumption and disposal behaviour. *Journal of Environmental Planning and Management*, *62*(4), 717–740. doi:10.1080/09640568.2018.1429254

Bortolotto, C. (2007). From objects to processes: UNESCO's 'intangible cultural heritage.' *Journal of Museum Ethnography*, (19), 21–33.

Bouma, J. J., Jeucken, M., & Klinkers, L. (Eds.). (2017). *Sustainable banking: The greening of finance*. Routledge. doi:10.4324/9781351282406

Bowers, T. (2010). From image to economic value: A genre analysis of sustainability reporting. *Corporate Communications*, *15*(3), 249–262. doi:10.1108/13563281011068113

Brand, U. (2012). Green economy – the next oxymoron? No lessons learned from failures of implementing sustainable development. *GAIA - Ecological Perspectives for Science and Society, 21*, 28–32.

Brundtland, G. H. (1987). *Our Common Future*. Obtenido de UN: http://www.un-documents.net/our-common-future.pdf

Brundtland, G. H. (1987). *Our common future: report of the 1987 world commission on environment and development*. United Nations.

Brundtland, G. H. (1987). Our common future—Call for action. *Environmental Conservation*, *14*(4), 291–294. https://doi.org/10.1017/s0376892900016805

Bukhari, S. S. (2011). Green Marketing and its impact on consumer behavior. *European Journal of Business and Management*, 375–383.

Bureau of Energy Efficiency. (2015). *Perform, Achieve and Trade*. Retrieved from https://www.beeindia.gov.in/content/pat-3

Bureau of Energy Efficiency. (2017). *About Standards & Labelling Program*. Retrieved from https://www.beeindia.gov.in/content/pat-

Bureau of Indian Standards. (2016). *Operation of ECO Mark Scheme*. Retrieved from http://www.bis.org.in/cert/echo_mark_scheme.htm

Button, K. (2009). Social change and demand for mobility. *Transportation Engineering and Planning*, *II*, 13–35.

Caceido García, C. L. (2017). *Economía circular y su papel en el diseño e innovación sustentable*. Obtenido de Libros Editorial UNIMAR: http://ojseditorialumariana.com/index.php/libroseditorialunimar/article/view/1154

Camacho & Salazar-Concha. (2020). Article. *Journal of Economics Studies and Research*. Doi:10.5171/2020.472317

Carroll, A. B. (1979). A three-dimensional conceptual model of corporate social performance. *Academy of Management Review*, *4*(4), 497–505. doi:10.5465/amr.1979.4498296

Carroll, A. B. (1991). The pyramid of corporate social responsibility: Toward the moral management of organizational stakeholders. *Business Horizons, 34*(4), 39–48. doi:10.1016/0007-6813(91)90005-G

Chadichal, S. S., & Misra, S. (2012). Exploring the online service quality dimensions in service sectors impact on developing e-CRM in Indian banking sector. *Global Journal For Research Analysis, 2*(1), 115-117. doi:10.15373/22778160/january2013/8

Chapagain, A. K., & Hoekstra, A. Y. (2003a). *The water needed to have the Dutch drink coffee.* Value of Water Research Report Series No. 14. UNESCO-IHE.

Chapagain, A. K., & Hoekstra, A. Y. (2003b). *The water needed to have the Dutch drink tea.* Value of Water Research Report Series No. 15, UNESCO-IHE. www.waterfootprint.org/Reports/Report15.pdf

Chapagain, A. K., & Hoekstra, A. Y. (2004). *Water footprints of nations.* Value of Water Research Report Series No. 16, UNESCO-IHE.

Chapagain, A. K., & Hoekstra, A. Y. (2004). *Water footprints of nations.* Value of Water Research Report Series No. 16, UNESCO-IHE. www.waterfootprint.org/Reports/Report16Vol1.pdf

Chapagain, A. K., Hoekstra, A. Y., Savenije, H. H. G., & Gautam, R. (2006a). *The water footprint of cotton consumption.* Value of Water Research Report Series No. 18, UNESCO-IHE.

Chapagain, A. K., & Hoekstra, A. Y. (2007). The water footprint of coffee and tea consumption in the Netherlands. *Ecological Economics, 64*(1), 109–118. doi:10.1016/j.ecolecon.2007.02.022

Chapagain, A. K., Hoekstra, A. Y., & Savenije, H. H. G. (2006b). Water-saving through international trade of agricultural products. *Hydrology and Earth System Sciences Discussions, 10*(3), 455–468. doi:10.5194/hess-10-455-2006

Chapagain, A., Mathews, R., & Zhang, G. (2017). *A guide to reducing the water footprint of cotton cultivation in India.* C&A Foundation. WFN.

Chen, M.-L., & Lin, C.-P. (2014). Modelling perceived corporate citizenship and psychological contracts: A mediating mechanism of perceived job efficacy. *European Journal of Work and Organizational Psychology, 23*(2), 231–247. doi:10.1080/1359432X.2012.734455

Chen, Z. X., & Francesco, A. M. (2000). Employee Demography, Organizational Commitment, and Turnover Intentions in China: Do Cultural Differences Matter? *Human Relations, 53*(6), 869–887. doi:10.1177/0018726700536005

Circle Economy (2019). *The Circularity Gap Report: Closing the Circularity Gap in a 9% World.* The Platform for Accelerating the Circular Economy (PACE).

Circular economy and electronic waste. (2019). Retrieved from: https://www.nature.com/articles/s41928-019-0225-2

Circular Economy. (2017). *Business Imperative for India.* Retrieved from https://www.teriin.org/sites/default/files/2018-03/TERI-YES_BANK_Circular_Economy_Report.pdf

Coderoni, S., & Perito, M. A. (2020). Sustainable consumption in the circular economy. An analysis of consumers' purchase intentions for waste-to-value food. *Journal of Cleaner Production, 252*, 119870. doi:10.1016/j.jclepro.2019.119870

Commonwealth Scientific and Industrial Research Organisation (CSIRO). (2013). *Recent trends in material flows and resource productivity in Asia and the Pacific, UNEP.* Retrieved from http://hdl.handle.net/20.500.11822/9318

Confederation of Indian Industry. (2014). *Innovation Ecosystem in India.* Retrieved from https://www2.deloitte.com/content/dam/Deloitte/in/Documents/technology-media-telecommunications/in-tmt-innovation-ecosystem-of-india-noexp.pdf

Costa, M. A., Torres, N. H., Vilca, F. Z., Nazato, C., & Tornisielo, V. L. (2012). Residue of 14C paclobutrazol in mango. *IOSR J. Eng*, *2*(05), 1165–1167. doi:10.9790/3021-020511651167

Coyle-Shapiro, J. A., Morrow, P. C., & Kessler, I. (2006). Serving two organizations: Exploring the employment relationship of contracted employees. *Human Resource Management*, *45*(4), 561–583. https://doi.org/10.1002/hrm.20132

Current Affairs Review. (2020). *The scenario of e-waste management in India*. Retrieved from: https://currentaffairsreview.com/the-scenario-of-e-waste-management-in-india/

D'souza, G., & Ikerd, J. (1996). Small farms and sustainable development: Is small more sustainable? *Journal of Agricultural and Applied Economics*, *28*(1), 73–83. doi:10.1017/S1074070800009470

Daily, B. F., Bishop, J. W., & Govindarajulu, N. (2009). *A conceptual model for organizational*. Academic Press.

Daily, B. F., Bishop, J. W., & Govindarajulu, N. (2009, June). citizenship behavior directed toward the environment. *Business & Society*, *48*(2), 243–256. doi:10.1177/0007650308315439

Davies, A., Fidler, D., & Gorbis, M. (2020). *Future Work Skills*. University of Phoenix Research Institute.

De Fraiture, C. (2004). *Does international cereal trade save water?: the impact of virtual water trade on global water use* (Vol. 4). IWMI.

de Wit, M., Verstraeten-Jochemsen, J., Hoogzaad, J., & Kubbinga, B. (2019). The Circularity Gap Report 2019. *Circle Economy*. Available at https://www.circularity-gap.world/

Deniz, O., & Kirmizi, A. (2009). The organisational commitment of IT professionals in private banks. In *European and Mediterranean Conference on Information Systems* (pp. 13-14). Academic Press.

Department of Heavy Industry. (2012). *National Electric Mobility Mission Plan 2020*. Retrieved from https://www.dhi.nic.in/UserView/index?mid=1347

Department of Industrial Policy and Promotion. (2017). *National Policy Design*. Retrieved from https://dipp.gov.in/sites/default/files/CFPC_2017_FINAL_RELEASED_28.8.17.pdf

Department of Science and Technology. (2013). *Science, Technology and Innovation Policy, 2013*. Retrieved from http://dst.gov.in/sites/default/files/STI%20Policy%202013-English.pdf

Di Maio, F., & Rem, P. C. (2015). A robust indicator for promoting circular economy through recycling. *Journal of Environmental Protection*, *6*(10), 1095–1104. doi:10.4236/jep.2015.610096

Dixit, S. &. (2013). Sustaining environment and organisation through e-waste management: a study of post consumption behaviour for mobile industry in India. *International Journal of Logistics Systems and Management*, 1-15.

Drucker, P. F. (1964). The Concept of the Corporation. The New American Library.

Earthdata. (n.d.). *Freshwater Availability*. Retrieved from https://earthdata.nasa.gov/: https://earthdata.nasa.gov/learn/toolkits/freshwater-availability

Easterlin, R. A. (2005). Feeding the illusion of growth and happiness: A reply to Hagerty and Veenhoven. *Social Indicators Research*, *74*(3), 429–443. doi:10.100711205-004-6170-z

Eccles, R. G., & Serafeim, G. (2013). The performance frontier: Innovating for a sustainable strategy. *Harvard Business Review*.

Ecointeligencia. (2017). *¿En qué consiste la Economía del Rendimiento?* Recuperado el Mayo de 2019, de Ecointeligencia: https://www.ecointeligencia.com/2017/01/economia-rendimiento/

Ecología, U. N. A. M. (2015). *Fundación UNAM*. Obtenido de UNAM: https://www.fundacionunam.org.mx/ecologia/sostenibilidad-vs-sustentabilidad/

Egri, C. P., & Herman, S. (2000). Leadership in the North American environmental sector: Values, leadership styles, and contexts of environmental leaders and their organizations. *Academy of Management Journal*.

Ehnert, I. (2009). *Sustainable Human Resource Management*. Springer.

Ellen Mac Arthur Foundation. (2016). *Circular Economy in India: Rethinking growth for long term prosperity*. Retrieved from https://www.ellenmacarthurfoundation.org/assets/downloads/Summary_Circular-economy-in-India_5-Dec_2016.pdf

Ellen Mac Arthur Foundation. (2016). *Money makes the world go round*. Retrieved from https://www.ellenmacarthurfoundation.org/assets/downloads/ce100/FinanCE.pdf

Ellen MacArthur Foundation & GRANTA. (2015). *Project Overview: An Approach to Measuring Circularity*. Ellen Mac Arthur Foundation.

Ellen MacArthur Foundation. (2012). Economic and business rationale for an accelerated transition. *Towards the Circular Economy*, I.

Ellen MacArthur Foundation. (2012). *Towards the circular economy: Economic and business rationale for an accelerated transition*. Author.

Ellen Macarthur Foundation. (2013). *Towards the circular economy, economic and business rationale for accelerated transition*. Retrieved from https://www.ellenmacarthurfoundation.org/assets/downloads/publications/Ellen-MacArthur-Foundation-Towards-the-Circular-Economy-vol.1.pdf

Ellen MacArthur Foundation. (2016). *Circular Economy in India: Rethinking growth for long-term prosperity*. Retrieved from https://www.ellenmacarthurfoundation.org/publications/

Ellen MacArthur Foundation. (2019). *Artificial intelligence and the circular economy - AI as a tool to accelerate the transition*. Artificial Intelligence and the Circular Economy Ellen MacArthur Foundation. http://www.ellenmacarthurfoundation.org/publications

Ellen MacArthur Foundation. (2019). *Completing the Picture: How the Circular Economy Tackles Climate. Material Economics*. III.

Ellen MacArthur Foundation. (2019a). *Economía Circular: Escuelas de pensamiento*. Recuperado el 16 de Mayo de 2019, de Ellen MacArthur Foundation: https://www.ellenmacarthurfoundation.org/es/economia-circular/escuelas-de-pensamiento

Ellen MacArthur Foundation. (2019b). *Economía Circular: Concepto*. Recuperado el 10 de Mayo de 2019, de Ellen MacArthur Foundation: https://www.ellenmacarthurfoundation.org/es/economia-circular/concepto

Emerson, R. W. (1996). Achieving competitive advantage through strategic innovation. *The Essence of Corporate Strategy*, 1-36.

Environmental Information System CPCB. (n.d.) *National Air Quality Monitoring Programme*. Ministry of Environment, Forests & Climate Change. Retrieved from http://cpcbenvis.nic.in/airpollution/finding.htm

Estimated Use of Water in the United States. (2000). Retrieved from https://water.usgs.gov/: https://water.usgs.gov/watuse/data/2000/

European Commission. (2019). *Closing the loop: Commission delivers on Circular Economy Action Plan, Press Release 4th March 2019*. Retrieved from https://ec.europa.eu/commission/presscorner/detail/en/IP_19_1480

European Environment Agency. (2019). *Plastic waste trade in circular economy*. Available at: https://www.eea.europa.eu/themes/waste/resource-efficiency/the-plastic-waste-trade-in

Evans, W. R., Goodman, J. M., & Davis, W. D. (2010). The impact of perceived corporate citizenship on organizational cynicism, OCB, and employee deviance. *Human Performance*, *24*(1), 79–97. doi:10.1080/08959285.2010.530632

FAO (Food and Agriculture Organization). (2003). *Technical conversion factors for agricultural commodities*. FAO. www.fao.org/fileadmin/templates/ess/documents/methodology/tcf.pdf www.fao.org/faostat/en/

Ferguson, P. (2014). The green economy agenda: Business as usual or transformational discourse? *Environmental Politics*, *24*(1), 17–37. doi:10.1080/09644016.2014.919748

Fernandez, E., Junquera, B., & Ordiz, M. (2003). Organizational culture and human resources in the environmental issue. *International Journal of Human Resource Management*.

Fiksel, J., Sanjay, P., & Raman, K. (2020). *Steps toward a resilient circular economy in India*. Clean Technologeis and Environmental Policy. doi:10.100710098-020-01982-0

Fioramonti, L. (2014). The world's most powerful number: An assessment of 80 years of GDP ideology. *Anthropology Today*, *30*(2), 16–19. doi:10.1111/1467-8322.12098

Fiorita, J. A., Bozeman, D. P., Young, A., & Meurs, J. A. (2007). Organization Commitment, Human Resource Practices, and Organization Characteristic. *Journal of Managerial Issues*, *19*(2), 186–207.

Fryxell, G. E., & Lo, C. W. H. (2003). The influence of environmental knowledge and values on managerial behaviours on behalf of the environment: An empirical examination of managers in China. *Journal of Business Ethics*.

Gaidajis, G., Angelakoglou, K., & Aktsoglou, D. (2010). E-waste: Environmental Problems and Current Management. *Journal of Engineering Science and Technology Review*, *3*(1), 193–199. Advance online publication. doi:10.25103/jestr.031.32

Garlapati, V. K. (2016). E-waste in India and developed countries: Management, recycling, Business and biotechnological initiatives. *Renewable & Sustainable Energy Reviews*, *54*, 874–881. doi:10.1016/j.rser.2015.10.106

Geels, F., McMeekin, A., Mylan, J., & Southerton, D. (2015). A critical appraisal of Sustainable Consumption and Production Research: The reformist, revolutionary and reconfiguration positions. *Global Environmental Change*, *34*, 1–12.

Geissdoerfer, M., Savaget, P., Bocken, N. M. P., & Hultink, E. J. (2017). The circular economy: A new sustainability paradigm? *Journal of Cleaner Production*, *143*, 757–768. doi:10.1016/j.jclepro.2016.12.048

Gelder, J. W. V. (2006). The do's and don'ts of Sustainable Banking: A BankTrack Manual. *BankTrack*. Available from: https://www.banktrack.org/download/the_dos_and_donts_of_sustainable_banking/061129_the_dos_and_donts_of_sustainable_banking_bt_manual.pdf

Gerbens-Leenes, W., & Hoekstra, A. Y. (2009). *The water footprint of sweeteners and bio-ethanol from sugar cane, sugar beet, and maize*. Value of Water Research Report Series No. 38, UNESCO-IHE.

Gernsblith, P. (2007). Cultural Heritage legal Summary. *Journal of Field Archeology,* 83-90.

Ghoreishi, M., & Happonen, A. (2020). New promises AI brings into circular economy accelerated product design: a review on supporting literature. *E3S Web of Conferences, 158*. https://doi.org/ doi:10.1051/e3sconf/202015806002

Girardet, H. (2014). *Creating regenerative cities*. Routledge. doi:10.4324/9781315764375

Gleick, P. H. S. H. (1996). Water resources. In *Encyclopedia of Climate and Weather* (pp. 817-823). New York: Oxford University Press. Retrieved from Freshwater Watch: https://freshwaterwatch.thewaterhub.org/content/water-limited-resource

Global Alliance for Banking on Values (GABV). (2012). *Strong, Straightforward and Sustainable Banking: Financial Capital and Impact Metrics of Values Based Banking*. Available from: https://www.gabv.org/wp-content/uploads/GABV-Summary-final.pdfi

Govindan, K., Shankar, K. M., & Kannan, D. (2016). Application of fuzzy analytic network process for barrier evaluation in automotive parts remanufacturing towards cleaner production–a study in an Indian scenario. *Journal of Cleaner Production, 114*, 199–213. doi:10.1016/j.jclepro.2015.06.092

Green Human Resource Management: A Review and Research Agenda. (2012). *International Journal of Management Reviews.*

Gregson, N., & Crang, M. (2015). From waste to resource: The trade in wastes and global recycling economies. *Annual Review of Environment and Resources*, *40*(1), 151–176. doi:10.1146/annurev-environ-102014-021105

Grit, K. (2004). Corporate citizenship: How to strengthen the social responsibility of managers? *Journal of Business Ethics*, *53*(1/2), 97–106. doi:10.1023/B:BUSI.0000039402.72867.1a

Gro Harlem Brundtland. (1987). *Our Common Future.* Obtenido de UN Documents: http://www.un-documents.net/our-common-future.pdf

Grown, H. (n.d.). *Diseño Regenerativo.* Recuperado el Mayo de 2019, de Heaven Grown: http://heavengrown.com/arquitectura-regenerativa/

Gupta, B. (2011). *A comparative study of organizational strategy and culture across industry. Benchmark Int. J.*

Gupta, D. S. (2015). Key Determinants ofSustainable Product Design and Manufacturing. Procedia CIRP, 26. doi:10.1016/j.procir.2014.07.166

Habisch, A., Meister, H.-P., & Schmidpeter, R. (Eds.). (2001). *Corporate citizenship as investing in social capital.* Logos.

Hafstein, V., & Valdimar, T. (2015). Intangible Heritage as Diagnosis, Safeguarding as Treatment. *Journal of Folklore Research*, *52*(2–3), 281–298. doi:10.2979/jfolkrese.52.2-3.281

Han, J., & Heshmati, A., & Rashidghalam, M. (2020). Circular Economy Business Models with a Focus on Servitization. *Sustainability*, *12*(21), 8799. doi:10.3390u12218799

Hawken, P. (2013). *The Guide to Sustainable Banking 2013. Blue and Green Tomorrow*. Available from: http://blueandgreentomorrow.com/wp-content/uploads/2013/10/guide-to-banking-2013-10MB.pdf

Hawken, P., Lovins, A., & Lovins, L. (2000). *Natural Capitalism: Creating the Next Industrial Revolution.* Obtenido de Research Gate: https://www.researchgate.net/publication/265074221_Natural_Capitalism

HDFC Bank. (2014). *Sustainability Report 2013-14.* HDFC Bank Mumbai.

Healey, P. (1998). Building institutional capacity through collaborative approaches to urban planning. *Environment & Planning A*, *30*(9), 1531–1546. doi:10.1068/a301531

Heinberg, R. (2011). *The end of growth: Adapting to our new economic reality.* Clairview.

Herod, A., Pickren, G., Rainnie, A., & McGrath-Champ, S. (2013). *'Waste, commodity fetishism and the ongoingness of economic life'*. *Area*, *45*(3), 376–382. doi:10.1111/area.12022

Heshmati, A. (2017). A review of the circular economy and its implementation. *International Journal of Green Economics, 11*(3/4), 251. doi:10.1504/ijge.2017.089856

Hobson, K., & Lynch, N. (2016). *Diversifying and de-growing the circular economy: Radical social transformation in a resource-scarce world.* Academic Press.

Hobson, K. (2015). Closing the loop or squaring the circle? Locating generative spaces for the circular economy. *Progress in Human Geography.*

Hoekstra, A. Y. (2003). Virtual water trade: A quantification of virtual water flows between nations in relation to international crop trade. In *Proceedings of the International Expert Meeting on Virtual Water Trade* (pp. 25-47). Academic Press.

Hoekstra, A. Y. (2003, February). Virtual water: An introduction. In *Virtual water trade: Proceedings of the international expert meeting on virtual water trade* (pp. 13-23). The IHE Delft Institute for Water Education.

Hoekstra, A. Y., Chapagain, A. K., Aldaya, M. M., & Mekonnen, M. M. (2011). *Water footprint manual: State of the art 2009.* Water Footprint Network. www.waterfootprint.org/downloads/WaterFootprintManual2009.pdf

Hoekstra, A. Y. (2013). Sustainable, efficient, and equitable water use: The three pillars under wise freshwater allocation. *WIREs. Water.*

Hoekstra, A. Y. (Ed.). (2003). *Virtual water trade: Proceedings of the International Expert Meeting on Virtual Water Trade.* UNESCO-IHE. www.waterfootprint.org/Reports/Report12.pdf

Hofman, P., & Newman, A. (2014). *The impact of perceived corporate social responsibility.* Academic Press.

Hofman, P. S., & Newman, A. (2014, March 09). on organizational commitment and the moderating role of collectivism and masculinity: Evidence from China. *International Journal of Human Resource Management, 25*(5), 631–652. doi:10.1080/09585192.2013.792861

Horrigan, L., Lawrence, R. S., & Walker, P. (2002). How sustainable agriculture can address the environmental and human health harms of industrial agriculture. *Environmental Health Perspectives, 110*(5), 445–456. doi:10.1289/ehp.02110445 PMID:12003747

Human resources development as an element of sustainable HRM – with the focus on production engineers. (2021). *Elseiver- J Clean Prod.*

Humphrey, C. (2018). *Channeling private investment to infrastructure: What can multilateral development banks realistically do?* ODI Working paper 534, London: Overseas Development Institute Available at https://www.odi.org/sites/odi.org.uk/files/resource-documents/12176.pdf

Imeson, M., & Sim, A. (2010). *Sustainable Banking: Why Helping Communities and Saving the Planet is Good for Business?* SAS White Paper Issued by SAS Institute Inc. World Headquarters.

ING. (2015). *Rethinking finance in a Circular Economy.* Retrieved from https://think.ing.com/uploads/reports/Financing_the_Circular_Economy.pdf

Innovation and growth: how business contributes to society. (2010). *Acad. Manag. Perspect.*

International Cooperation Division. (2019). *Office Memorandum F.No. 3(4)/5/2019-IC-II(pt.1).* Delhi: Ministry of Environment, Forest & Climate Change.

Jackson, T. (2005). *Motivating Sustainable Consumption: A Review of Evidence on Consumer Behaviour and Behavioural Change: a Report to the Sustainable Development Research Network.* Centre for Environmental Strategy, University of Surrey.

Jacobsen, N. B. (2006). Industrial symbiosis in Kalundborg, Denmark: A quantitative assessment of economic and environmental aspects. *Journal of Industrial Ecology*, *10*, 239–255.

Jain, A., & Sareen, R. (2006). E-waste assessment methodology and validation in India. *Journal of Material Cycles and Waste Management*, *8*(1), 40–45. doi:10.100710163-005-0145-2

Jain, S. K., Agarwal, P. K., & Singh, V. P. (2007). *Hydrology and Water Resources of India*. Springer.

Jänicke, M. (2012). Green growth: From a growing eco-industry to economic sustainability. *Energy Policy*, *48*, 13–21. doi:10.1016/j.enpol.2012.04.045

Jawaid, M. F., Pipralia, S., & Kumar, A. (2018). Review of environment responsiveness of building regulations in Jaipur. *Journal of Urban Management*, *7*(2), 111–120. doi:10.1016/j.jum.2018.06.001

Jessica, K. (2018). *Individual Sustainable Consumption and the Circular Economy: Research challenges and Opportunities.* Retrieved from https://www.schumacherinstitute.org.uk/download/pubs/res/201810-Individual-Sustainable-Consumption-and-the-Circular-Economy-Research-Gaps-and-Opportunities-Jessica-Klaver.pdf

Jeucken, M. (2010). *Sustainable finance and banking: The financial sector and the future of the planet*. Earthscan.

Juana, O. C., Casper, B., & Ida, P. N. (2018). Consumption in the Circular Economy: A Literature Review. *Sustainability*, *10*, 2758.

Kamenka, E. (1982). *Community as a Social Ideal. Ideas and Ideologies*. London: EArnold.

Kampman, D. A. (2007). *The water footprint of India* (Master's thesis). University of Twente.

Kamp-Roelands, N. (2013). *Private sector initiatives on measuring and reporting on green growth*. OECD Publishing.

Katyaini, S. (2016). *Science-Policy interface to mitigate water scarcity in India: An assessment of virtual water flows* (Doctoral dissertation). Indian Institute of Technology Guwahati, Guwahati, India.

Katyaini, S., & Barua, A. (2017). *Assessment of interstate virtual water flows embedded in agriculture to mitigate water scarcity in India (1996–2014).* Water Resources Research.

Kavinski, H., De Souza-Lima, J. E., Maciel-Lima, S. M., & Floriani, D. (2010). La apropiación del discurso de la sustentabilidad por las organizaciones empresariales brasileñas. *Cultura y Representaciones Sociales*, *4*(8), 34–69.

Keitumetse, S. (2006). UNESCO 2003 Convention on Intangible Heritage: Practical Implications for Heritage Management Approaches in Africa. *South African Archaeological Bulletin*, *61*(184), 166–171. doi:10.2307/20474924

Kell, G. (2005). The global compact selected experiences and reflections. *Journal of Business Ethics*, *59*(1/2), 69–79. doi:10.100710551-005-3413-0

Khatri, Garg, & Dangayach. (n.d.). Critical Success Factors of Sustainable Manufacturing and Procurement: An Empirical Study. *International Journal of Social Ecology and Sustainable Development*, *10*(3).

Khetriwal, D. S., Kraeuchi, P., & Widmer, R. (2009). Producer responsibility for e-waste management: Key issues for consideration–learning from the Swiss experience. *Journal of Environmental Management*, *90*(1), 153–165. doi:10.1016/j.jenvman.2007.08.019 PMID:18162284

Kilian, T., & Hennigs, N. (2014). Corporate social responsibility and environmental reporting in controversial industries. *European Business Review*, *26*(1), 79–101. doi:10.1108/EBR-04-2013-0080

Kirsten, J., & Sartorius, K. (2002). Linking agribusiness and small-scale farmers in developing countries: Is there a new role for contract farming? *Development Southern Africa*, *19*(4), 503–529. doi:10.1080/0376835022000019428

Kramar, R. (2014). Beyond strategic human resource management: Is sustainable human resource management the next approach? *International Journal of Human Resource Management.*

Kreps, C. F. (2003). *Liberating Culture: Cross-Cultural Perspectives on Museums, Curation, and Heritage Preservation.* Psychology Press.

Kumar, A., Wasan, P., Luthra, S., & Dixit, G. (2020). Development of a framework for selecting a sustainable location of waste electrical and electronic equipment recycling plant in emerging economies. *Journal of Cleaner Production, 277*, 122645.

Kumar, M. D., & Singh, O. P. (2005). Virtual water in global food and water policy making: Is there a need for rethinking? *Water Resources Management, 19*(6), 759–789. doi:10.100711269-005-3278-0

Kumar, V., & Jain, S. K. (2007). Status of virtual water trade from India. *Current Science*, 1093–1099.

Kumar, V., & Jain, S. K. (2011). Export and import of virtual water from different states of India through food grain trade. *Hydrology Research, 42*(2-3), 229–238. doi:10.2166/nh.2011.089

Lacy, P., Spindler, W., & Dutton, J. (2021). *The circular economy can help save the planet –if we start innovating now.* World Economic Forum. Retrieved from https://www.weforum.org/agenda/2021/02/the-circulars-accelerator-circular-economy-zero-waste/

Lalon, R. M. (2015). Green banking: Going green. *International Journal of Economics, Finance and Management Sciences, 3*(1), 34-42.

Lam, M. L. L. (2009). Beyond credibility of doing business in China: Strategies for improving corporate citizenship of foreign multinational enterprises in China. *Journal of Business Ethics, 87*(1), 137–146. doi:10.100710551-008-9803-3

Lamm, E., Tosti-Kharas, J., & Williams, E. G. (2013). Read this article, but don't print it: Organizational citizenship behavior toward the environment. *Group & Organization Management, 38*(2), 163–197. doi:10.1177/1059601112475210

Lane, M. B., & Robinson, C. J. (2009). Institutional complexity and environmental management: The challenge of integration and the promise of large-scale collaboration. *Australasian Journal of Environmental Management, 16*(1), 16–24. doi:10.1080/14486563.2009.9725213

Lawyer's Comm. (n.d.). *Cultural Heritage Preservation.* http://www.culturalheritagelaw.org/Default.aspx?pageID=595025

Lin, C. (2010). Modeling Corporate Citizenship, Organizational Trust, and Work Engagement Based on Attachment Theory. *Journal of Business Ethics, 94*(4), 517–531. doi:10.100710551-009-0279-6

Lin, C., Lyau, N., Tsai, Y., Chen, W.-Y., & Chiu, C.-K. (2010). Modeling Corporate Citizenship and Its Relationship with Organizational Citizenship Behaviors. *Journal of Business Ethics, 95*(3), 357–372. doi:10.100710551-010-0364-x

Lindhqvist, T. (2000). *Extended Producer Responsibility in Cleaner Production. The International Institute for Industrial Environmental Economics.* Lund University.

Lin, L. W. (2010). Corporate Social Responsibility in China: Window Dressing or Structural Change. *Berkeley Journal of International Law, 28*(1), 64–100.

Linley, P. A., Maltby, J., Wood, A. M., Osborne, G., & Hurling, R. (2009). Measuring happiness: The higher order factor structure of subjective and psychological well-being measures. *Personality and Individual Differences, 47*(8), 878–884. doi:10.1016/j.paid.2009.07.010

Logsdon, J. M., & Wood, D. J. (2005). Global business citizenship and voluntary codes of ethical conduct. *Journal of Business Ethics, 59*(1-2), 55–67. doi:10.100710551-005-3411-2

Lowenthal, D. (2014). *The Heritage Crusade and the Spoils of History*. Cambridge University Press.

Ludwig. (1958). *Philosophical Investigations* (2nd ed.). Oxford: Basil Blackwell.

Lülfs, R., & Hahn, R. (2013). Corporate greening beyond formal programs, initiatives, and systems: A conceptual model for voluntary pro-environmental behavior of employees. *European Management Review*, *10*(2), 83–98. doi:10.1111/emre.12008

Lumley, E. J. (2009). *Exploring the relationship between career anchors, job satisfaction and organisational commitment* (Doctoral dissertation). University of South Africa.

MacArthur, E. (2013). Towards the circular economy. *Journal of Industrial Ecology*, *2*, 23–44.

Mael, F., & Ashforth, B.E. (1992). Alumni and their alma mater: a partial test of the reformulated model of organizational identification. *Journal of Organizational Behaviour.*

Maheshwari, S. P. (2014). *Awareness of green marketing and its influence on buying behavior of consumers: Special reference to Madhya Pradesh. AIMA Journal of Management & Research.*

Maignan, I., & Ferrell, O. C. (2000). Measuring corporate citizenship in two countries: The case of the United States and France. *Journal of Business Ethics*, *23*(3), 283–297. doi:10.1023/A:1006262325211

Maignan, I., & Ferrell, O. C. (2004). Corporate social responsibility and marketing: An integrative framework. *Journal of the Academy of Marketing Science*, *32*(1), 3–19. doi:10.1177/0092070303258971

Maignan, I., Ferrell, O. C., & Hult, G. T. M. (1999). Corporate citizenship: Cultural antecedents and business benefits. *Journal of the Academy of Marketing Science*, *27*(4), 455–469. doi:10.1177/0092070399274005

Manohar, B., & Kumar, C. V. (2012). Green Banking: Bye-bye cheques, hello electronic payments. *Asia Pacific Journal of Management & Entrepreneurship Research*, *1*(3), 60.

Marcus, A., & Fremeth, A. (2009). Green management matters regardless. *The Academy of Management Perspectives*.

Marsden, C., & Andriof, J. (1998). Towards an Understanding of Corporate Citizenship and How to Influence It. *Citizenship Studies*, *2*(2), 329–352. doi:10.1080/13621029808420686

Martín, G. (2015). Knowledge management and innovation in knowledge-based and high-tech industrial markets: The role of openness and absorptive capacity. *Industrial Marketing Management*, *47*(May), 143–146. doi:10.1016/j.indmarman.2015.02.032

Martin, V. Y., Weiler, B., Reis, A., Dimmock, K., & Scherrer, P. (2017). 'Doing the right thing': How social science can help foster pro-environmental behaviour change in marine protected areas. *Marine Policy*, *81*, 236–246. doi:10.1016/j.marpol.2017.04.001

Maxfield, S. (2008). Reconciling corporate citizenship and competitive strategy: Insights from economic theory. *Journal of Business Ethics*, *80*(2), 367–377. doi:10.100710551-007-9425-1

McCarthy, J., & Minsky, M. (2010). *Artificial Intelligence*. Academic Press.

McDonald, S., Oates, C. J., Alevizou, P. J., Young, C. W., & Hwang, K. (2012). Individual strategies for sustainable consumption. *Journal of Marketing Management*, *28*, 3–4, 445–468.

McDonough, W., Braungart, M., & Bollinger, A. (2007). *Cradle-to-cradle design: creating healthy emissions – a strategy for eco-effective product and system design.* Obtenido de Science Direct: https://www.sciencedirect.com/science/article/pii/S0959652606002587

McIntyre, M., & Nast, H. (2011). Bio(necro)polis: Marx, surplus populations, and the spatial dialectics of reproduction and "race". *Antipode, 43*(5), 1465–1488. doi:10.1111/j.1467-8330.2011.00906.x

Meadows, D. H. (1972). *The Limits to growth; a report for the Club of Rome's project on the predicament of mankind.* Universe Books.

Meadows, D. H., Meadows, D. L., Randers, J., & Behrens, W. W. (1972). *The limits to growth.* Universe Books.

Mejía Dugand, S. (2010). *La Ecología Industrial.* Obtenido de El Colombiano: https://www.elcolombiano.com/historico/la_ecologia_industrial-HEEC_101107

Mekonnen, M. M., & Hoekstra, A. Y. (2010). *The Green, Blue and Greywater footprint of crop and derived crop products*. Value of Water Research Report Series No. 47. Enschede: University of Twente.

Mekonnen, M. M., & Hoekstra, A. Y. (2013). *Water footprint benchmarks for crop production.* Value of Water Research Report Series No. 64, UNESCO-IHE.

Mekonnen, M. M., & Hoekstra, A. Y. (2011). The Green, Blue and Greywater footprint of crop and derived crop products. *Hydrology and Earth System Sciences, 15*(5), 1577–1600. doi:10.5194/hess-15-1577-2011

Merli, R. (2018). How do scholars approach the circular economy? A systematic literature review. *Journal of Cleaner Production, 178*, 703-722.

Meyer, J. P., Stanley, D. J., Herscovitch, L., & Topolnytsky, L. (2002). Affective, continuance, and normative commitment to the organization: A meta-analysis of antecedents, correlates, and consequences. *Journal of Vocational Behavior, 61*(1), 20–52.

Milliman, J., & Clair, J. (1996). Best environmental HRM practices in the U.S. Academic Press.

Ministry of Electronics & Information Technology. (2019a). *National Policy for 2019.* Retrieved from "https://meity.gov.in/writereaddata/files/Notification_NPE2019_dated25.02.2019.pdf

Ministry of Electronics & Information Technology. (2019b). *National Policy for 2012.* Retrieved from https://meity.gov.in/writereaddata/files/NPE_Notification.pdf

Ministry of Environment and Forest & Climate Change. (1999). *The Fly Ash Notification, 1999.* Retrieved from http://envfor.nic.in/legis/hsm/flyash.html

Ministry of Environment and Forest & Climate Change. (2006). *National Environment Policy 2006.* Retrieved from http://www.moef.gov.in/sites/default/files/introduction-nep2006e.pdf

Ministry of Environment and Forest & Climate Change. (2010). *Batteries Management and Handling) Amendment Rules 2010.* Retrieved from http://enfor.nic.in/legis/hsm/SO1002.pdf

Ministry of Environment and Forest & Climate Change. (2016). *Waste Management Rules.* Retrieved from http://envfor.nic.in/sites/default/files/waste%20Management%20Rukes%202016pdf

Ministry of Environment and Forest & Climate Change. (2016). *Waster management Rules.* Retrieved from http://www.mppcb.nic.in/proc/Batteries%20(Management%20and%20Handling)%20Rules,%202001.pdf

Ministry of Environment and Forest & Climate Change. (n.d.). Retrieved from http://moef.gov.in/environment/waste-management/

Ministry of Environment and Forest. (2003). *Corporate Responsibility for Environmental Protection (CREP).* https://hspcb.gov.in/Charter%20on%20corporate%20responsibility%20for%20Env.%20Protection.pdf

Ministry of Environment Forest and Climate Change (MOEFCC). (2015). Retrieved from http://www.ismenvis.nic.in/Database/Fly-Ash-Amendment_Draft-MoEF_3366.aspx

Ministry of Environment Forest and Climate Change. (2016). Retrieved from http://www.indiaenvironmentportal.org.in/files/file/BMW%20Rules,%202016.pdf

Ministry of Micro, Small and Medium Enterprises. (2017). *National Manufacturing Competitiveness Programme*. Retrieved from http://dcmsme.gov.in/schemes/nmcp.scm.htm

Ministry of Mines. (2017). *The Mines and Minerals (Development and Regulation) Amendment Act 2016*. Retrieved from https://prsindia.org/billtrack/the-mines-and-minerals-development-and-regulation-amendment-bill-2016-4228

Ministry of New and Renewable Energy. (2009). *National Policy on Biofuels*. Retrieved from http://mnre.gov.in/schemes/new-technologies/biofuels

Ministry of Petroleum and Natural Gas. (2019). *National Auto Vision Fuel Policy 2025*. Retrieved from http://petroleum.nic.in/sites/default/files/autopol.pdf

Ministry of Steel. (2019a). *National Steel Policy 2017*. Retrieved from https://steel.gov.in/sites/default/files/draft-national-steel-policy-2017.pdf

Ministry of Steel. (2019b). *National Mineral Policy, 2008*. Retrieved from https://www.nepa.gov.jm/documents/NATIONAL_MINERALS_POLICY_DRAFT_JULY_2008.pdf

Minsky, M. (1961). Steps toward Artificial Intelligence. *Proceedings of the IRE*, *49*(1), 8–30. doi:10.1109/jrproc.1961.287775

Mishra, J. L., Chiwenga, K. D., & Ali, K. (2019). Collaboration as an enabler for circular economy: A case study of a developing country. *Management Decision*, *ahead-of-print*(ahead-of-print). Advance online publication. doi:10.1108/MD-10-2018-1111

Missé, A., Moreno, J. A., Vázquez Oteo, O., Escorsa, P., & Casado Cañeque, F. (2015). *Responsabilidad Social de la Empresa: ¿RSE o RIP?* Obtenido de jstor: http://www.jstor.org/stable/26360524

Mohan, V. (2020). India third largest e-waste generator in the world, capacity. *The Times of India*. https://timesofindia.indiatimes.com/india/india-third-largest-e-waste-generator-in-the-world-capacity-limited-to-treat-only-one-fourth-of-its-waste/articleshow/76780611.cms

Moncada Niño, Á. F., & Oviedo Franco, M. L. (17 de Junio de 2013). Las TIC como fuente de ventaja competitiva en las PYMES. *Sotavento M.B.A.*, *21*, 126-134. Recuperado el Mayo de 2019, de Universidad Externado de Colombia: https://revistas.uexternado.edu.co/index.php/sotavento/article/view/3441/3128

Mowday, R. T., Steers, R. M., & Porter, L. W. (1979). The measurement of organizational commitment. *Journal of Vocational Behavior*, *14*(2), 224–247.

Mukherjee, K., & Mondal, S. (2009). Analysis of issues relating to remanufacturing technology–a case of an Indian company. *Technology Analysis and Strategic Management*, *21*(5), 639–652. doi:10.1080/09537320902969174

Narula, S. A., & Desore, A. (2016). Framing green consumer behaviour research: Opportunities and challenges. *Social Responsibility Journal*, *12*(1), 1–22. doi:10.1108/SRJ-08-2014-0112

Nason, R. S., & Wiklund, J. (2018). An assessment of resource-based theorizing on firm growth and suggestions for the future. *Journal of Management*, *44*(1), 32–60. doi:10.1177/0149206315610635

Niesten, E., Jolink, A., de Sousa Jabbour, A. B. L., Chappin, M., & Lozano, R. (2017). Sustainable collaboration: The impact of governance and institutions on sustainable performance. *Journal of Cleaner Production*, *155*, 1–6. doi:10.1016/j.jclepro.2016.12.085

Nitish, A., Souvik, B., Avishek, G., Pallavi, G., Chandan, B., Arnesh, S., & Himanshu, S. (2018) Report on *Circular Economy: A Business Imperative for India.* Retrieved from https://wsds.teriin.org/2018/files/teri-yesbank-circular-economy-report.pdf

OECD. (2001). *Extended Producer Responsibility: A Guidance Manual for Governments*. OECD.

OECD. (2011). Towards green growth: monitoring progress: OECD indicators Organisation for Economic Co-operation & Development. OECD Publishing.

OECD. (2018). *International Trade and the Transition to a Circular Economy*. Available at: https://www.oecd.org/environment/waste/policy-highlights-international-trade-and-the-transition-to-a-circular-economy.pdf

OECD. (2018a). *Improving Markets for Recycled Plastics: Trends, Prospects and Policy Responses*. OECD Publishing. Available at: https://www.oecd-ilibrary.org/environment/improving-markets-for-recycled-plastics_9789264301016-en

OECD. (2020). *Environment at a Glance Indicators – Circular economy, waste and materials*. Available at: https://www.oecd.org/environment/environment-at-a-glance/Circular-Economy-Waste-Materials-Archive-February-2020.pdf

Ogino, M. (1995). La Logique d'actualisation. Le Patrimoine et Le Japon. *Ethnologie Francaise*, *25*(1), 57–64.

Okoye, A. (2009). Theorising corporate social responsibility as an essentially contested concept: Is a definition necessary? *Journal of Business Ethics*, *89*(4), 613–628. doi:10.100710551-008-0021-9

Oliver, C. (1998). *Sustainable Competitive Advantage: Combining Institutional and Resource-Based Views*. Recuperado el Mayo de 2019, de Strategic Management Journal: http://www.jstor.org/stable/3088134

OMICS International. (n.d.). *Water Management Importance*. Retrieved from https://www.omicsonline.org/water-management-importance.php

Omkar, G., Arun. A.K. Vishal, M., & Arindam, D. (2002). Competitiveness of Indian Manufacturing –results from a firm level survey. CII Report.

On the Dynamic Mechanism of Developing Recycling Economy for Enterprises in China. (2010). *International Journal of Social Ecology and Sustainable Development*, 20–29. www.igi-global.com/article/dynamic-mechanism-developing-recyclingeconomy/41957?camid=4v1a

Organ, D. W. (1988). *Organizational Citizenship Behavior: The Good Soldier Syndrome*. Lexington Books.

Özçelik, F., Öztürk, B. A., & Gürsakal, S. (2015). Corporate Sustainability: A Research on Firms That Issue Sustainability Reports in Turkey. *Business and Economic Research Journal*, *6*(3), 33–49.

Pacini, H. (2018). *Circular Economy: The New Normal*. Policy Brief No. 61, United Nations Conference on Trade and Development (UNCTAD). Available at: https://unctad.org/en/PublicationsLibrary/presspb2017d10_en.pdf

Park, H., & Kim, J. D. (2020). Transition towards green banking: Role of financial regulators and financial institutions. *Asian Journal of Sustainability and Social Responsibility*, *5*(1), 1–25.

Park, J., Sarkis, J., & Wu, Z. (2010). Creating integrated business and environmental value within the context of China's circular economy and ecological modernization. *Journal of Cleaner Production*, *18*, 1494–1501.

Pelling, M., & Manuel-Navarrete, D. (2011). From resilience to transformation: The adaptive cycle in two Mexican urban centers. *Ecology and Society*, *16*(2), 1–11. doi:10.5751/ES-04038-160211

Pelling, M., O'Brien, K., & Matyas, D. (2014). Adaptation and transformation. *Climatic Change*, *133*(1), 113–127. doi:10.100710584-014-1303-0

Pfeffer, J. (2010). Building sustainable organizations: The human factor. *The Academy of Management Perspectives*.

Philpott, J., & Davies, G. (2007). *Labour Market Outlook*. CIPD/KPMG.

Porter, E. M. (1985). Competitive advantage. The Free Press.

Porter, M. (1996). *¿Qué es la estrategia?* Recuperado el Mayo de 2019, de Harvard Business Review: https://s3.amazonaws.com/academia.edu.documents/37851742/4_Que_es_Estrategia.pdf?AWSAccessKeyId=AKIAIWOWYYGZ2Y53UL3A&Expires=1558381861&Signature=132Q27yedrcb1MADZWvjsnckcC8%3D&response-content-disposition=inline%3B%20filename%3DQue_es_la_estrategia.pdf

Porter, M. (2015). *Ventaja Competitiva: Creación y sostenimiento de un desempeño superior*. Recuperado el Mayo de 2019, de Grupo Editorial Patria: https://books.google.com.mx/books?hl=es&lr=&id=wV4JDAAAQBAJ&oi=fnd&pg=PT3&dq=que+es+ventaja+competitiva&ots=mwvClbT58A&sig=O2eioD4ADfMxwU5PBfOy20qH-SA#v=onepage&q=que%20es%20ventaja%20competitiva&f=false

Prakash, G., & Pathak, P. (2017). Intention to buy eco-friendly packaged products among young consumers of India: A study on developing nation. *Journal of Cleaner Production*, *141*, 385–393. doi:10.1016/j.jclepro.2016.09.116

Press Information Bureau. (2011). *National Manufacturing Policy*. Retrieved from https://dipp.gov.in/policies-rules-and-acts/policies/national-manufacturing-policy

Pretty, J. N. (1994). Alternative systems of inquiry for a sustainable agriculture. *IDS Bulletin*, *25*(2), 37–49. doi:10.1111/j.1759-5436.1994.mp25002004.x

Prott, L. V. (1984). Law and the Cultural Heritage. Volume 1, Discovery and Excavation. Abingdon: Professional Books.

Prott, L. V., & O'Keefe, P. J. (1989). Law and the Cultural Heritage: Movement. Butterworths.

Prott, . (1998). *International Standards for Cultural Heritage. In UNESCO World Culture Report*. Unesco Publishing.

Puentes-Poyatos, R., Yebra-Rodríguez, Á., & Guerrero, F. (2016). *Responsabilidad Social Corporativa: El compromiso de la Universidad con los ciudadanos*. Obtenido de Revista de Antropología Experimental: https://revistaselectronicas.ujaen.es/index.php/rae

RAE. (2017). *Real Academia Española*. Obtenido de DLE: http://dle.rae.es/?w=diccionario

Raghupathy, L., & Chaturvedi, A. (2013). Secondary Resources and Recycling in developing Economies. *The Science of the Total Environment*, *461*, 830–834. doi:10.1016/j.scitotenv.2013.05.041 PMID:23768896

Rahim, A. A. O. S., Elamin, O. M., & Bangerth, F. K. (2011). Effects of paclobutrazol (PBZ) on floral induction and associated hormonal and metabolic changes of biennially bearing mango (Mangifera indica L.) cultivars during off year. *Journal of Agricultural and Biological Science*, *6*, 55–67.

Rajput, N., Kaura, R., & Khanna, A. (2013). Indian banking sector towards a sustainable growth: A paradigm shift. *International Journal of Academic Research in Business and Social Sciences*, *3*(1), 290.

Raju, P. M., & Srivastava, R. C. (1994). Factors contributing to commitment to the teaching profession. *International Journal of Educational Management*.

Ramnarain, T. D., & Pillay, M. T. (2016). Designing Sustainable Banking Services: The Case of Mauritian Banks. *Procedia - Social and Behavioral Sciences, 224*, 483-490. doi:10.1016/j.sbspro.2016.05.424

Ramnarain, T. D., & Pillay, M. T. (2016). Designing sustainable banking services: The case of Mauritian banks. *Procedia: Social and Behavioral Sciences*, *224*, 483–490.

Ramus, C. A. (2002). *Encouraging innovative environmental actions: What companies and managers must do. Journal of World Business.*

Ramus, C. A., & Killmer, A. B. (2007). Corporate greening through prosocial extrarole behaviours—A conceptual framework for employee motivation. *Business Strategy and the Environment*, *16*(8), 554–570. doi:10.1002/bse.504

Rathi, S. (2006). Alternative approaches for better municipal solid waste management in Mumbai. *Waste Management*, 1192-1200. https://www.epw.in/engage/article/institutional-framework-implementing-solid-waste-management-india-macro-analysis

Reddy, Y. T. N., & Kurian, R. M. (2008). Cumulative and residual effects of paclobutrazol on growth, yield and fruit quality of'Alphonso'mango. *Journal of Horticultural Sciences*, *3*(2), 119–122.

Redman, T., & Snell, S. (Eds.), *The Sage Handbook of Human Resource Management*. Sage.

Reganold, J. P., Papendick, R. I., & Parr, J. F. (1990). Sustainable agriculture. *Scientific American*, *262*(6), 112–121. doi:10.1038cientificamerican0690-112

Rehber, E. (1998). *Vertical integration in agriculture and contract farming* (No. 1299-2016-102484). Academic Press.

Rehber, E. (1998). *Vertical integration in agriculture and contract farming*. Regional Research Project No. NE-165: Private strategies, public policies, and food system performance. Department of Resource Economics. Amherst, MA: University of Massachusetts.

Reike, D., Vermeulen, W. J. V., & Witjes, S. (2017). (in press). The circular economy: New or Refurbished as CE 3.0? *Resources, Conservation and Recycling.*

Reike, D., Vermeulen, W. J., & Witjes, S. (2018). The circular economy: New or refurbished as CE 3.0?—exploring controversies in the conceptualization of the circular economy through a focus on history and resource value retention options. *Resources, Conservation and Recycling*, *135*, 246–264. doi:10.1016/j.resconrec.2017.08.027

Renewable Energy Certificate Registry of India. (2010). *Renewable Energy Certification (RECs) 2010*. Retrieved from https://www.recregistryindia.nic.in/index.php/publics/AboutREC

Renn, O., Jager, A., Deuschle, J., & Weimer-Jehle, W. (2009). A normative-functional concept of sustainability and its indicators. *International Journal of Global Environmental Issues*, *9*(4), 291–317.

Rezaee, Z. (2016). Business sustainability research: A theoretical and integrated perspective. *Journal of Accounting Literature*, *36*, 48–64. doi:10.1016/j.acclit.2016.05.003

Richard, B. (2000). Building a Vision-Guided, Values-Driven Organization. *Triple Bottom Line Conference*, Rotterdam, The Netherlands.

Ricke, K. L. D. (2018). Country-level social cost of carbon. *Nature Climate Change*, *10*(8), 895–900. doi:10.103841558-018-0282-y

Robertson, G. P. (2015). A sustainable agriculture? *Daedalus*, *144*(4), 76–89. doi:10.1162/DAED_a_00355

Robinson, B. H. (2009). E-waste: An assessment of global production and environmental impacts. *The Science of the Total Environment*, *408*(2), 183–191. doi:10.1016/j.scitotenv.2009.09.044 PMID:19846207

Rome Convention of 1961

Russo, M., & Harrison, N. (2005). Organizational design and environmental performance: Clues from the electronics industry. *Academy of Management Journal.*

Rutger Willem Hofste, P. R. (2019, August 6). *17 Countries, Home to One-Quarter of the World's Population, Face Extremely High Water Stress.* Retrieved from https://www.wri.org/: https://www.wri.org/blog/2019/08/17-countries-home-one-quarter-world-population-face-extremely-high-water-stress

Saavedra García, M. L., & Saavedra García, M. E. (2014). La PYME como generadora de empleo en México. *Revista Clío América*, 153-172.

Sahaas. (n.d.). *Alag Karo, Har Din Teen Bin, 2020.* Retrieved from https://saahas.org/our-work/programs/sensitization-and-behavioral-change/alag-karo,-har-din-teen-bin

Salvatori, G., Holstein, F., Böhme, K., Wills, T., & Hans, S. (2019). *Circular economy strategies and roadmaps in Europe Identifying synergies and the potential for cooperation and alliance building*. The European Economic and Social Committee (EESC). Retrieved from https://mail.google.com/mail/u/0/#inbox/FMfcgxwGDNWQqjxBjKqBcspNKTnvvqjr?projector=1&messagePartId=0.1

Savarova, M., & Vrchota, J. (2014). Influence of competitive advantage on formulation business strategy. *Procedia Economics and Finance*, *12*, 687–69. doi:10.1016/S2212-5671(14)00394-3

Savini, F., & Dembski, S. (2016). Manufacturing the creative city: Symbols and politics of Amsterdam North. *Cities (London, England)*, *55*, 139–147. doi:10.1016/j.cities.2016.02.013

Scher, & Philip, W. (2010). UNESCO Conventions and Culture as a Resource. *Journal of Folklore Research*, *47*(1–2), 197–202. doi:10.2979/jfr.2010.47.1-2.197

School, Water Science. (n.d.). *The Water in You: Water and the Human Body.* Retrieved from https://www.usgs.gov/special-topic/water-science-school/science/water-you-water-and-human-body?qt-science_center_objects=0#qt-science_center_objects

Schor, J. (2005). Prices and quantities: Unsustainable consumption and the global economy. *Ecological Economics*, *55*, 309–320.

Secretaria Internacional de la Carta de la Tierra. (2019). *La Carta de la Tierra.* Obtenido de https://cartadelatierra.org/descubra/la-carta-de-la-tierra/

Sell, M., & Pajunen, N. (2018). *The circular economy – What's trade got to do with it?* International Centre for Trade and Sustainable Development. Available at: https://www.ictsd.org/opinion/the-circular-economy-

Sennett, R. (1999). Growth and failure: The new political economy and its culture. In M. Featherstone & S. Lash (Eds.), *Theory, culture and society: Spaces of culture: City, nation, world.* SAGE publications. doi:10.4135/9781446218723.n1

Sharma, V., Garg, S. K., & Sharma, P. B. (2016). Identification of major drivers and roadblocks for remanufacturing in India. *Journal of Cleaner Production*, *112*, 1882–1892. doi:10.1016/j.jclepro.2014.11.082

Singh, S.K., & Singh, A.P. (2019). Interplay of organizational justice, psychological empowerment, organizational citizenship behavior, and job satisfaction in the context of circular economy. *Manag. Decis.*

Singh, B., Singh, S., & Sandhu, S. (2012). Effect of growth retardants on vegetative growth, flowering and fruiting of litchi cv. Calcuttia. *HortFlora Research Spectrum*, *1*(1), 29–33.

Singh, O. P., Sharma, A., Singh, R., & Shah, T. (2004). Virtual water trade in the dairy economy: Irrigation water productivity in Gujarat. *Economic and Political Weekly*, 3492–3497.

Soundarrajan, P., & Vivek, N. (2016). Green finance for sustainable green economic growth in India. *Agricultural Economics*, *62*(1), 35–44.

Stahel, W. R. (2010). *The Performance Economy* (2nd ed.). Palgrave Macmillan.

Stahel, W. R. (2016). The circular economy. *Nature*, *531*(7595), 435–438. doi:10.1038/531435a

Stahel, W. R., & Reday-Mulvey, G. (1981). *Jobs for Tomorrow, the potential for substituting manpower for energy*. Vantage Press.

Steg, L., & Vlek, C. (2009). Encouraging pro-environmental behaviour: An integrative review and research agenda. *Journal of Environmental Sciences (China)*, *29*, 309–317.

Stiglitz, J. E., Sen, A., & Fitoussi, J.-P. (2009). *Report by the Commission on the Measurement of Economic Performance and Social Progress*. Commission on the Measurement of Economic Performance and Social Progress.

Sustainable banking: The Greening of finance. (2001). Greenleaf Publishing.

The Commission to the European Parliament, The Council, The European Economic And Social Committee And The Committee Of The Regions. (2019). *Report on the implementation of the Circular Economy Action Plan*. European Commission.

The Gallup Organization. (2010). Employers' Perception of Graduate Employability. Author.

The greening of Euro-pean management education. (n.d.). InWehrmeyer, W. (Ed.), *Greening People: Human Resources and EnvironmentalManagement* (pp. 289–300). Greenleaf Publishing.

The Indo-German Environment Partnership programme. (2013). *India's Future Needs for Resources*. Retrieved from http://www.hrdpnetwork.com/live/hrdpmp/hrdpmaster/igep/content/e48745/e50194/e58089/ResourceEfficiency_Report_Final.pdf

The Protection of Traditional knowledge. (2016). Genetic Resources and Expressions of Folklore Act.

The Water Cycle for Adults and Advanced Students. (n.d.). Retrieved from https://www.usgs.gov/: https://www.usgs.gov/special-topic/water-science-school/science/water-cycle-adults-and-advanced-students?qt-science_center_objects=0#qt-science_center_objects

Thelen, D., Van Acoleyen, M., Huurman, W., Tom, T., van Brunschot, C., Edgerton, B., & Ben, K. (2018). *Scaling the Circular Built Environment: Pathways for Business and Government*. World Business Council for Sustainable Development & Circle Economy.

Torres-Baumgarten, G., & Yucetepe, V. (2009). Multinational firms' leadership role in corporate social responsibility in Latin America. *Journal of Business Ethics*, *85*(1), 217–224. doi:10.100710551-008-9940-8

Trigger, & Bruce, G. (2006). *A History of Archaeological Thought* (2nd ed.). Cambridge: University Press. https://ezproxy-prd.bodleian.ox.ac.uk/login?url=http://dx.doi.org/10.1017/CBO9780511813016

TRIPS Agreement, 1994.

Tse, Esposito, & Soufani. (2015). Why the circular economy matters. *European Business Review*.

Turban, D. B., & Greening, D. W. (1997). Corporate social performance and organizational attractiveness to prospective employees. *Academy of Management Journal*, *40*(3), 658–672.

Türkeli, S., Kemp, R., Huang, B., Bleischwitz, R., & McDowall, W. (2018). Circular economy scientific knowledge in the European Union and China: A bibliometric, network and survey analysis (2006–2016). *Journal of Cleaner Production*, *197*, 1244–1261. doi:10.1016/j.jclepro.2018.06.118

UANL. (2013). *El desarrollo sustentable en México*. Obtenido de Sustentabilidad: http://sds.uanl.mx/el-desarrollo-sustentable-en-mexico-3/

UNAM. (2015). *Ecología UNAM*. Obtenido de Fundación UNAM: https://www.fundacionunam.org.mx/ecologia/sostenibilidad-vs-sustentabilidad/

UNCSD. (2012). *The Future we want, outcome of the United Nations Conference on Sustainable Development (Rio+20)*. UNCSD.

UNDESA. (2010). Progress to date and remaining gaps in the implementation of the outcoms of the major summits in the area of sustainable development, as well as an analysis of the themes of the Conference. Preparatory Committee for the UNCSD.

UNEP. (2012a). *Indicators: a UNEP green economy briefing paper*. United Nations Environment Programme.

UNEP. (2012b) *Measuring progress towards a green economy: draft working paper*. United Nations Environment Programme.

UNEP. (2014). International Declaration on Cleaner Production: Implementation Guidelines for Facilitating Organizations. UNEP.

UNEP. (2014). *Using indicators for green economy policymaking United Nations Environment Programme*.

UNESCO World Water Assessment Programme. (2017). *The United Nations world water development report, 2017: Wastewater: The untapped resource*. UNESCO.

USGS. (n.d.). *How Much Water is There on Earth?* Retrieved from https://www.usgs.gov/: https://www.usgs.gov/special-topic/water-science-school/science/how-much-water-there-earth

Valenzuela, F., & Böhm, S. (2017). Against wasted politics: A critique of the circular economy. *Ephemera*, *17*(1), 23–60.

Valle-Cabrera, R. (2005). Organizational learning capability: A proposal of measurement. *Journal of Business Research*, *58*(6), 715–725. doi:10.1016/j.jbusres.2003.11.002

Valles, G. (2016). *The circular economy in international trade*. UNCTAD. Available at: https://unctad.org/fr/pages/newsdetails.aspx?OriginalVersionID=1400

Veolia Water. (n.d.). *The Water Impact Index and the First Carbon-Water Analysis of a Major Metropolitan Water Cycle*. Water and Circular Economy. (Original work published 2018)

Verma, S., Kampman, D. A., van der Zaag, P., & Hoekstra, A. Y. (2009). Going against the flow: A critical analysis of inter-state virtual water trade in the context of India's National River Linking Program. *Physics and Chemistry of the Earth Parts A/B/C*, *34*(4-5), 261–269. doi:10.1016/j.pce.2008.05.002

Waddock, S. A. (2004). Parallel universes: Companies, academics, and the progress of corporate citizenship. *Business and Society Review*, *109*(1), 303–319. doi:10.1111/j.0045-3609.2004.00002.x

Wagner, M. (2004). Sustainable reporting? The link of environmental reports and environmental performance. *Corporate Environmental Strategy.*

Warde, A. (2005). Consumption and Theories of Practice. *Journal of Consumer Culture*, *5*(2), 131–153.

Waste and Resources Action Programme (WRAP). (n.d.). Available at: https://www.wrap.org.uk/about-us/about/wrap-and-circular-economy

Water Use Data and Their Application. (2002). In Estimating Water Use in the United States: A New Paradigm (pp. 36-67). The National Academies Press.

Wath, S. B., Vaidya, A. N., Dutt, P. S., & Chakrabarti, T. (2010). A roadmap for development of sustainable E-waste management system in India. *The Science of the Total Environment*, *409*(1), 19–32. doi:10.1016/j.scitotenv.2010.09.030 PMID:20951410

WBCSD & IEA. (2013). *Technology Roadmap: Low-Carbon Technology for the Indian Cement Industry*. World Business Council on Sustainable Development and International Energy Agency.

Weber, O., & Feltmate, B. (2016). *Sustainable banking: Managing the social and environmental impact of financial institutions*. University of Toronto Press.

Wezel, A., Casagrande, M., Celette, F., Vian, J. F., Ferrer, A., & Peigné, J. (2014). Agroecological practices for sustainable agriculture. A review. *Agronomy for Sustainable Development*, *34*(1), 1–20. doi:10.100713593-013-0180-7

Widmera, R., Krapf, O. H., Khetriwal, S. D., Schnellmann, M., & Boni, H. (2005). Global Perspectives on E-Waste. *Environmental Impact Assessment Review*, *25*(5), 436–458. doi:10.1016/j.eiar.2005.04.001

Wilkinson, A., Hill, M., & Gollan, P. (2001). The sustain-ability debate. *International Journal of Operations and Production Management, 21*, 1492–1502.

Williams, R. (1986). A vocabulary of culture and society (Rev. ed.). Oxford University Press.

Williams, J. (2019). Circular cities. *Urban Studies (Edinburgh, Scotland)*, *56*(13), 2746–2762. doi:10.1177/0042098018806133

Winans, K., Kendall, A., & Deng, H. (2017). The history and current applications of the circular economy concept. *Renewable & Sustainable Energy Reviews*, *68*, 825–833. doi:10.1016/j.rser.2016.09.123

Wolz, A., & Kirsch, O.C. (1999). *Equitization of agribusiness in Vietnam: options for small-scale farmers with special emphasis on coffee production in Daklak Province*. Discussion Paper No. 69. Heidelberg, Germany: Research Centre for International Agrarian and Economic Development.

Wood, D. J. (1991). Corporate social performance revisited. *Academy of Management Review*, *16*(4), 691–718. doi:10.5465/amr.1991.4279616

World Bank. (2013). *Turn Down the Heat: Climate Extremes, Regional Impacts, and the Case for Resilience, A report for the World Bank by Potsdam Institute for Climate Impact Research and Climate Analytics*. World Bank.

World Economic Forum. (2014). *Reorganize and streamline pure materials flows.* Retrieved http://reports.weforum.org/toward-the-circular-economy- accelerating-the-scale-up-across-global-supply-chains/reorganize-and-streamline-pure-materials-flows

World Economic Forum. (2018). *Circular Economy in Cities Evolving the model for a sustainable urban future*. Retrieved from http://www3.weforum.org/docs/White_paper_Circular_Economy_in_Cities_report_2018.pdf

WRG. (2016). *Circular Economy Pathways for Municipal Wastewater Management in India: A Practitioner's Guide*. WRG.

WWDR. (2017). *Wastewater the untapped resource*. United Nations Educational, Scientific and Cultural Organization.

Yeshitela, T. B. (2006). *Effect of cultural practices and selected chemicals on flowering and fruit production in some mango (Mangifera indica L.) cultivars* (Doctoral dissertation). University of Pretoria.

Yeshitela, T., Robbertse, P. J., & Stassen, P. J. C. (2004). Paclobutrazol suppressed vegetative growth and improved yield as well as fruit quality of 'Tommy Atkins' mango (Mangifera indica) in Ethiopia. *New Zealand Journal of Crop and Horticultural Science*, *32*(3), 281–293. doi:10.1080/01140671.2004.9514307

Yip, A. W., & Bocken, N. M. (2018). Sustainable business model archetypes for the banking industry. *Journal of Cleaner Production*, *174*, 150–169.

Yuan, Z. W., Jun, B., & Moriguichi, Y. C. (2006). The circular ecology: A new development strategy in China. *Journal of Industrial Ecology*, *10*, 4–8.

Yu, F., Han, F., & Cui, Z. (2015). Evolution of industrial symbiosis in an eco-industrial park in China. *Journal of Cleaner Production*, *87*, 339–347. doi:10.1016/j.jclepro.2014.10.058

About the Contributors

Taranjeet Duggal is a Professor at Amity Business School with 22 years of teaching and research experience in the area of HRM, Organizational Behaviour, and behavioral science. As a facilitator & Coach, she had conducted Faculty Development Programmes, corporate trainings and workshops in topics related to emotional intelligence, positive attitude, motivation, team building, transaction analysis, psychometric profiling, etc.

* * *

Richa Agarwal is an Associate Professor at the Institute of Management Studies, Ghaziabad. Her research interests are organizational behaviour, human resource, ethics, sustainability, and strategy. She has published extensively in international journals.

Sunakshi Budhiraja is an alumnus of TERI School of Advanced Studies, where she pursued her Masters' of Science in Economics, with a specialisation in environment and natural resources. She is currently working as a quantitative researcher with one of the leading market research firms, handling projects for clients in the online and digital space.

Varun Chotia is presently working as Assistant Professor, Economics at Jaipuria Institute of Management, Jaipur campus, Rajasthan, India. Prior to this, he has worked at LM Thapar School of Management, Thapar Institute of Engineering and Technology (Deemed to be a University). He has completed his PhD in Economics from Department of Economics and Finance, Birla Institute of Technology and Science, Pilani (BITS Pilani). Before coming into academics, he has around two years of industry experience in corporate firms like IMS Health and Accenture Management Consulting. He has authored number of research papers in international and national journals of high repute.

Sweety Gupta has more than 5 years of teaching experience in Rukmini Devi Institute of Advanced Studies, Guru Gobind Singh Indrapratha University. She is UGC-NET qualified and has completed her MBA from Maharaja Agrasen Institute of Technology, GGSIPU and B.Com(H) from Sri Guru Gobind Singh College of Commerce, Delhi University. She has published numerous research papers and Case Studies in national and International Journals.

Vranda Jain is presently working as Assistant Professor (Economics), Jaipuria Institute of Management, Noida, India. She is at present the Area Chair, Department of Economics and International Business. She has more than a decade of teaching experience to post graduate students of Management. Her Ph.D is in the area of International Economics. She has participated in various Conferences and has to her credit several publications in journals of repute. Her research interest includes International Trade, Sustainable development and Socio Economic Policy Analysis.

Konpal Kaur completed BA (History Hons) from LSR college for women (University of Delhi) in 2014 and Mphil from Kellogg College, University of Oxford in 2017. She is the youngest ever candidate invited to the M.Phil program at Institute of Archaeology, University of Oxford. She has interned with Institute of Maritime History (in relation with Maryland Historical Trust, USA from April-July 16 and helped in Database creation for Naval History and Heritage command in US. She has keen interest in studying the relationship and interface between law, history and society. She has also organized capacity building workshop for gender sensitisation of police and judiciary– conducted by National Commission for Women, India and Amity Law School, GGSIPU, India. She has many times volunteered for Legal Awareness camps conducted and sponsored by National Commission for Women, India. She has five research publications to her credit in interdisciplinary journals. The researcher is currently based in Toronto working as a freelancer.

Santosh Kumar has been an active researcher and has published papers in domestic and international journals. He has also presented his contributions to various national and international conferences (IFC, AICIBS Oxford, LAIBSRC, and IBFR). He is also the coordinator for Research Cell and Centre for Small Micro Enterprises and Capacity Building at CIMP. He is also the reviewer of the Journal of Asset Management and Macroeconomics and Finance in Emerging Market Economies. His research interest lies in behavioural finance, asset pricing, market microstructures, Government regulations in financial markets etc.

Aakriti Mathur is an alumnus of the University School of Law and Legal Studies, Guru Gobind Singh Indraprastha University, where she pursued her doctorate in Law. In her doctoral thesis, she has proposed a Carbon Consumption Tax for India. She is practicing as an Advocate in the Supreme Court of India and the Delhi High Court specializing in socio-economic offences and customs and trade laws. She is also actively involved in teaching International Trade Law as a visiting lecturer at various universities in New Delhi. Her areas of interest include Climate Change Law and Policy, International Environmental Law, International Trade Law and Laws relating to Socio-Economic Offences.

K. Pallavi is an MBA (Finance & HR) Graduate from MANIT, Bhopal. She worked in ICICI Bank served at Bhopal (Central India) location managing retail banking and business loans operations. She is taking up some voluntary research works under the able guidance of Dr. Hergovind Singh (prof. MANIT).

Hergovind Singh competed his Bachelor of engineering (Electrical engineering) from Jiwaji University, Gwalior, India, and MBA from Indian Institute of Information Technology and Management, Gwalior, India, than PhD from Indian Institute of Information Technology and Management, Gwalior, India. Presently working as "Asst. Professor" in the Department of Management Studies, Maulana Azad National Institute of Technology, Bhopal India. Work experience is about 14 years which includes Industry, Academia and research. Area of interest, Includes, Technology & Innovation Management (Strategic Management), Information Management (e-governance).

Kanwal D. P. Singh is part of academics since the year 1999 in the public funded university in New Delhi, India. She Joined University School of Law and Legal studies , Guru Gobind Singh Indrprastha University(GGSIPU) in the May 2013 as Professor and served as the Dean of Law School from 2016-19. She is currently also heading the Legal Aid Centre of GGSIPU supported by Delhi State Legal Service authority. Prof Kanwal has been involved in projects and workshops conducted by National Commission for Women , and Ministry of Law and Justice, Government of India . Prof Singh has also been convener of National moot in her university for almost two decades. She has been working in areas of Poverty and Human rights on research schemes funded by the university. She is Vice President of Asian Association of Law Professors(AALP) and Life Member of several legal institutions like Indian Law Institute, New Delhi; Indian Society of International Law, New Delhi; Institute of Constitutional and Parliamentary studies and Indian Institute of Public Administration(IIPA) . She has presented numerous research papers in international Conferences in India and abroad. Prof Kanwal has been principal investigator in action taken projects funded by Department of Justice, Government of India.

José G. Vargas-Hernández, M.B.A., Ph.D., Member of the National System of Researchers of Mexico and a research professor at University Center for Economic and Managerial Sciences, University of Guadalajara. Professor Vargas-Hernández has a Ph. D. in Public Administration and a Ph.D. in Organizational Economics. He has undertaken studies in Organisational Behaviour and has a Master of Business Administration, published four books and more than 200 papers in international journals and reviews (some translated to English, French, German, Portuguese, Farsi, Chinese, etc.) and more than 300 essays in national journals and reviews. He has obtained several international Awards and recognition.

Shinu Vig is an Assistant Professor at the Institute of Management Studies, Ghaziabad. She is a qualified Company Secretary and a law graduate, having an experience of more than ten years in corporate and academics. Her teaching and research interests include corporate governance, corporate social responsibility, business ethics and sustainability. She has presented research papers at international and national conferences and has several publications to her credit.

Anshu Yadav is Assistant Professor at Amity Business School, Noida. She did her MBA for Banasthali Vidhyapith Jaipur and Ph.D. form Jai Narain Vyas University, Jodhpur. She is UGC NET qualified and has total of 12+ years of teaching experience. In these years she has published several research papers and cases in the many indexed journals from the field of Human Resource and Organisational Behaviour. She has also conducted soft skill training programs.

Index

V

W

www.ingramcontent.com/pod-product-compliance
Lightning Source LLC
LaVergne TN
LVHW080527300926
849162LV00007B/1557